Sixth
Edition

PUBLIC RELATIONS PRACTICES

Managerial Case Studies and Problems

Allen H. Center, Fellow PRSA

Distinguished Resident Lecturer
San Diego State University
Retired Vice President, Public Relations, Motorola Inc.

Patrick Jackson, Fellow PRSA

Editor, pr reporter
Senior Counsel, Jackson Jackson & Wagner
Former Adjunct Faculty, Boston University

Prentice
Hall

UPPER SADDLE RIVER, NEW JERSEY 07458

Library of Congress Cataloging-in-Publication Data

Center, Allen H.
  Public relations practices: managerial case studies and problems/Allen H. Center, Patrick Jackson.--6th ed.
    p. cm.
  Rev. ed. of: Public relations practices/Patrick Jackson, Allen H.Center.5th ed. c1995.
  Includes bibliographical references and index.
  ISBN 0-13-613803-9
  1. Public relations--Case studies.   I. Jackson, Patrick, 1932- II. Jackson, Patrick, 1932- Public relations practices.   III. Title.

  HM263 C332 2002
  659.2--dc21

                                                            2002021128

Senior Editor: Bruce Kaplan
Editor-in-Chief: Jeff Shelstad
Assistant Editor: Melissa Pellerano
Editorial Assistant: Danielle Serra
Senior Marketing Manager: Michelle O'Brien
Marketing Assistant: Christine Genneken
Managing Editor (Production): John Roberts
Permissions Coordinator: Suzanne Grappi
Associate Director, Manufacturing: Vincent Scelta
Production Manager: Arnold Vila
Manufacturing Buyer: Michelle Klein
Cover Design: Kiwi Design
Cover Illustration: Cutis Parker/Scott Hull Associates
Full-Service Project Management and Composition: BookMasters, Inc.
Printer/Binder: Hamilton

Credits and acknowledgments borrowed from other sources and reproduced, with permission, in this textbook appear on appropriate page within text.

Pearson Education LTD.
Pearson Education Australia PTY, Limited
Pearson Education Singapore, Pte. Ltd
Pearson Education North Asia Ltd
Pearson Education, Canada, Ltd
Pearson Educación de Mexico, S.A. de C.V.
Pearson Education–Japan
Pearson Education Malaysia, Pte. Ltd

10 9 8 7 6 5 4 3 2
ISBN: 0-13-613803-9

To the teachers of public relations who are
giving us a new generation of true professionals.
P. J.

To all my former colleagues and students: May their careers
each make a difference in the advancement of the calling.
A. H. C.

Brief Contents

Contents

Problems

CHAPTER 5   Investor Relations   118

Cases

Problems

CHAPTER 6   Consumer Relations   163

Cases

Problems

CHAPTER 7   Media Relations   206

Cases

Problems

Preface

Fifteen new cases have been added to this edition, reflecting the many major and rapid changes occurring in relationships, communications, and behavior.

On a grand scale, huge enterprises and wings of government are seeking to adjust to the global village of disparate cultures, values, and standards of behavior. At the local community level, life is strained as jobs fall victim to technology or are moved to an area of lower wages and costs, resulting in the tax base and public services such as education suffering. The function of public relations must be to mediate in these changing circumstances, as they have in the past. Textbooks and courses must keep pace.

The practical purpose of this text remains the same. We seek, with case studies and problems, to help future practitioners develop agility in the principles and the application of effective two-way communications in a wide variety of situations likely to confront them and their employers.

- We retained several timeless cases that involved turning-point issues or broke new ground in the maturing of the public relations function. These are identified as classics.
- Several cases with evolving subjects were updated.
- Cases that have lost timely significance were dropped.

New cases are of such a nature that entry-level practitioners can readily identify with the topics. They deal with broad matters of public concern such as treating employees by the Golden Rule, closing a hospital in a win-win way, selling stock directly to customers, and a company's efforts in working with a town on PCB cleanup and avoiding Superfund status.

HOW THE BOOK IS ORGANIZED

1. *The first two chapters* describe the purposes of public relations and the manner in which the function deals with problems and opportunities.
2. The bulk of the book contains *real-life case studies* in eight chapters organized according to primary publics such as employees and media or major problems such as public issues, crisis management, and standards or ethics.
3. Each chapter has a *definitive introduction* providing insights that come to life in the cases that follow. Introductions vary in size and substance, tailored to the assumed knowledge of students. Employee relations, for instance, reflects that

most students have had work experience of some kind, whereas crisis management contains elements most students will not yet have encountered.

4. Each chapter closes with a *case problem* or two for class discussion closely
related to the thrust of the chapter.

5. The last chapter deals candidly with *career preparation.*

We believe that there is enough variety to permit selectivity by educators, fitting
the size of the class and the structure of the course—and enough provocation for lively
classroom participation.

THE AUTHORS AND THEIR APPROACH

Patrick Jackson taught at several institutions, was senior counsel at the public relations
firm Jackson Jackson & Wagner, and in 1986, received The Gold Anvil, the highest
honor in public relations for "lifetime achievement and contribution to the profession." However, Jackson was best known as editor of the public relations newsletter
pr reporter. He was a highly sought speaker and presenter of workshops, and a practitioner who instigated several new strategies. His thinking is reflected throughout the
book. Every new case and updated chapter reflects his ideas and the models he left for
those who follow—his legacy to the public relations profession. Definitive passages
were amended and updated to reflect the changes in the nature and emphasis of the
calling and the roles and responsibilities of practitioners. Allen Center originated the
book and remains its guiding spirit.

The author purposely chose to use a narrative description and avoided a set format
for presenting each case. The real world does not come neatly packaged. The many
teachers who regularly share their experiences with the text tell us they want students
to gain experience in picking out the problem situation, delineating an environmental
scan, and having to decide whether the solutions chosen were wise or flawed. Outlining
the cases according to a formula denies them this most important learning from case
studies.

Putting together a text of real-life case *studies*, contrasted with a collection of successful case *histories,* requires objective cooperation by the organizations represented,
particularly when the subject, the scenario, or the conclusion is not laudatory. We are
grateful for the information and illustrations supplied. We hope the cooperation pays
off and this text enables instruction to be better attuned to the pressing needs of
employers and the profession.

And finally, we would like to stress the importance and necessity of combining all
public relations actions with both personal and professional ethics in behavior. PRSA's
Member Code of Ethics (see the following and Chapter 10 for further discussion) deals
with this combination. As the Code purports: "The foundation of our value to our companies, clients and those we serve is their ability to rely on our ethical and morally
acceptable behavior.

THE PRSA CODE OF MEMBER ETHICS

The Code has three parts:

1. Its **Values** are designed to inspire and motivate each member every day to the highest levels of ethical practice. These Values include: advocacy, honesty, expertise, independence, loyalty, fairness.

2. Its **Code Provisions** are designed to help each member clearly understand the limits and specific performance required to be an ethical practitioner. The Provisions cover: free flow of information, disclosure of information, safeguarding confidences, conflicts of interest, enhancing the profession. Each Provision includes discussion of the core principle, its intent, and guidelines on what a member is to do and not do. These will be continuously expanded by precedent-setting cases and experience in applying the Code.

3. Its **Commitment** mechanism ensures that every member understands the obligations of membership and the expectation of ethical behavior. It is a pledge that each must sign.

ACKNOWLEDGMENTS

Thank you to Frank Stansberry, APR, Fellow PRSA, for his devoted attention to the multitude of updates, changes and additions to the sixth edition of this textbook. He spent his summer vacation from University of Central Florida, where he teaches public relations, tirelessly reading and guiding the work that is reflected in this edition. His belief in the value of this textbook and in Pat's vision for the profession is reflected in his dedication to seeing this book completed.

Thank you also to colleagues Isobel Parke, Gail Winslow-Pine, Robin Schell, Stacey Smith, and Roger Stephenson for their professional guidance, and to Chris deZarn-O'Hare and June Barber for their diligence in researching and preparing the updated material for the sixth edition. Thanks additionally go out to Jackson Jackson & Wagner's student interns who contributed to the book in many ways: Rachel Allen, Megan Schinkel, Stacy Stacks, and Meredith Topalanchik. And for everyone's attention to aligning the additions and changes with the models and insights Pat Jackson developed during his lively career and left for those who follow to steer the growth of the public relations profession.

DEDICATED TO PAT JACKSON

Patrick Jackson was one of the most widely known and respected practitioners in the field of pr—referred to as "the public relations counselor's counsel." He recently had marked his fiftieth year of public relations counseling advising clients and colleagues alike on almost every national issue over the past five decades. His death in March 2001 was an enormous loss to those who knew him and to the profession, which looked to him for trailblazing leadership. Pat will be remembered for his passion for the profession and his desire to inspire, encourage, even push students and peers alike to see his vision and make it their own.

A Colleague Remembers

Pat inspired and encouraged us to think outside the box. He served as a beacon in a sea of professionals. Pat Jackson provided vision.

At a 1984 Schranz Lectureship at Ball State University, Pat challenged students and attending professionals to "lift their eyes above process and to concentrate on behavioral outcomes." The lecture is as fresh today as it was then. When the lecture was handed out in a recent conference where Patrick was speaking, he said, "Mel, have I been speaking on this need that long?" Of course, he had, and he kept challenging professionals to think about behavioral outcomes and to apply behavioral knowledge to performance until his death.

So how do we pay tribute to a man who influenced a profession, influenced public relations education, influenced recognition of the importance of high ethical values, and who stood as a leader in the profession and education in every sense of the word?

The answer is simple.

It is the only answer we can have. We simply must not allow the torch that Pat carried as the result of his love and belief in the public relations profession to go out or to touch the ground. Pick it up. A thousand hands. Carry it forward. When we do so, we will adequately honor him and what he stood for in our profession. Pat built vision and that is what we must have.

We treasure his memory and the values for which he stood.

—Melvin L. Sharpe, APR, Fellow PRSA,
Professor & Coordinator PR,
Department of Journalism,
Ball State University
Muncie, Indiana

1

THE PURPOSES OF PUBLIC RELATIONS

PUBLIC RELATIONS IS AN APPLIED SCIENCE

However firm our grasp of the principles, the history, and the theories of any field, we must be able to apply them to actual cases. This statement is true for the entry-level recent graduate and for the seasoned professional. The proof of capability is in handling cases successfully for employers or clients.

- The bottom line of public relations practice is in the results that come from putting theories and principles to work—in a way that benefits the organization issuing the paycheck *and* the society of which that organization is a part.

For this reason, the case study method of learning about public relations is an essential part of a practitioner's education. Case studies accurately model situations that organizations, managers, and public relations practitioners routinely face.

Though this book came into being primarily for use in the classroom—and includes practical exercises in each chapter suitable for students—it is also the major collection of carefully analyzed case studies for the field. Students can feel confident that they are using these cases right alongside seasoned veterans.

PUBLIC RELATIONS IS A RESPONSIBILITY OF MANAGEMENT

Although everyone in the organization affects the organization's relationships with various publics, establishing public relations policies, goals, and activities is a managerial function. Public relations staffers are part of management.

The term *public relations* is often confusing because it is frequently used inaccurately. Used correctly, *public relations* describes the *processes* of practice—the techniques, strategies, structures, and tactics of the field. As such, the term is analogous to *law, medicine, nursing,* and so on. Too often, *public relations* is also used to describe the *outcomes* of effective practice—so we hear of "good public relations." The proper term for the desired outcomes of public relations practice is public *relationships*. An organization with effective public relations will attain positive public relationships.

In approaching the cases and problems presented in this book, an understanding of the meaning of management is essential. Here is a basic definition.

- *Management is getting things done with people.*

This statement means that managers work with and through others to carry out their assignments. Their job is not to do the work themselves but to guide and assist others in doing it. But there is another implication here that is related directly to public relations:

- *Management must be able to get the cooperation of people both inside and outside the organization in order to achieve the organization's objectives.*

Thus, *public relations* managers must build capabilities in both the internal and external aspects of management. For this reason, they are usually selected as much for their managerial abilities in leading a staff and counseling others in the organization as for their public relations skills. The cases and problems in this book will help you practice both aspects.

THE FOCUS OF PUBLIC RELATIONS IS ON BEHAVIOR

When an organization invests resources in public relations, it expects that something will be different than before or than it would have been had the investment not been made. Examples of change might be:

- Improved purchases by, and relationships with, customers
- Better community relationships
- Active support on issues from opinion leaders
- Reduced tension with watchdog agencies
- Greater employee loyalty or productivity
- More confidence in the value of a company's stock
- For a nonprofit agency, increased donations

If all public relations does is maintain the status quo, it is being used ineffectually. In addition, if it changes only the way people feel or think about the organization—and vice versa—it has not realized its full potential. Effective public relations elicits mutually favorable *behavior* from both the organization and its publics.

Behavior May Be of Three Types

Getting people to *do* something	Getting them *not* to do something	Winning their consent to *let the organization* do something

Looked at from another perspective, the type of change sought may be to:

1. *Motivate* new behavior,
2. *Reinforce* existing positive behavior, or
3. *Modify* negative behavior.

In studying the cases we present, ask yourself what is different about behaviors after the public relations activities have been carried out. If the answer is nothing, you must consider whether public relations has failed.

ELEMENTS THAT MAKE UP THE FUNCTION

In general, public relations is what public relations *does* (which is true of every field). The employer or client, by formulating objectives, and practitioners, by accepting those objectives, define the function for that organization at that time. Historically, the function has evolved from *one-way information transfer,* to a *two-way concept* of sending messages and listening to feedback, to the present idea of an organization's *adjusting harmoniously* with the publics on which it depends.[1] Underpinning this perspective, however, are at least six activities that are basic and endemic to practice:

Research. The first step in any project is to gather intelligence, in order to understand the variables in the case. What are key publics' opinions and attitudes? Who are the opinion leaders that matter? Which groups or persons are concerned enough to act?

Strategic planning. The situation and the data need to be formed into a strategy. Where are we now? How did we get here? Where do we want to be? How do we get there?

Counseling. Fellow managers must understand the plan and agree it should be implemented. They may have a role in implementation and, at least, will need to explain it to their staffs.

Internal education. People in the organization need to be informed about the plan and their roles in it. Public relationships are not formed only by the executives or the public relations professionals, but far more by *everyone who interacts* with customers, employees, the community, stockholders, and all other publics.

Communication/action. The plan must be carried out. Messages or appeals are sent to the various publics involved; activities or actions are staged; feedback must be interpreted; and everyone must be kept informed as the project unfolds.

Evaluation. Another type of research—evaluation—charts effectiveness, or lack of it, and very likely will result in a new plan.

Chapter 2 reviews how this sequence is applied with a four-step model.

---

[1]For thoughtful analysis of the evolving definition, see Scott M. Cutlip, Allen H. Center, and Glen M. Broom, *Effective Public Relations,* 8th ed. Upper Saddle River, NJ: Prentice Hall, 1999, Chapter 1.

PLANNING: MANAGEMENT BY OBJECTIVES

Effective organizations have a business plan made up of *long-range goals* for the future and *short-term objectives* attainable soon. The name commonly given to this type of plan is *management by objectives,* or *MBO.*[2]

Within the statement of goals and objectives, the role expected of public relations is usually stated in general terms. Public relations activities are tied to overall objectives, creating what is called the **management concept** or **public relations strategy**.

The public relations staff then draws up a set of specific departmental goals and objectives. The staff members devise programs or campaigns, hire any needed outside talent, plan budgets, establish timetables, implement activities and communications, and evaluate results—all tied to the organization's overall business plan. This working process is called the **functional concept**, or **public relations tactics**.

One key to success in planning—observable in several cases in this book—is to anticipate problems and opportunities. This proactive, or preventive, approach is preferable to the reactive, after-the-fact, approach because it lets you take the lead, rather than being forced to respond to others. Increasingly, this **issue anticipation** approach is becoming one of the major values public relations is expected to provide.

WHAT COMES ACROSS IS VALUES

More than anything, what public relations activities communicate are the values and vision of the organization—for better or worse. These may be socially positive, acceptable values or questionable ones. But whatever the explicit message sent forth, with it goes an implicit message of whether the organization really cares about people, the community, and the future; or instead is self-centered and concerned only with its immediate profits or success—or possibly even antisocial.

The primary value public relations professionals promote inside organizations is the *open system.* An open system fosters the willingness to adjust and adapt to change, with management sensitive to all interactions in the environment. Such managers are available, listen well, and communicate forthrightly both within the organization and with external stakeholders.

In contrast is the *closed system* organization, where change is difficult. Managers cling to the status quo, and seek to change the environment that is unfavorable to the old ways. Usually they try to limit or tightly control the flow of information. In such organizations, public relations is often on the defensive, forced to put forth the view, "If only you knew us better, you'd agree with us."

Private enterprise, as a system, is often accused of being closed. Often it seems to insist its ways are inviolate. "Everything, everybody else, must change to our ways" is the value that sometimes comes across. Needless to say, this attitude limits effectiveness.

---

[2]Courses in marketing and business methods are recommended for all students planning a career in public relations whether in profit or nonprofit enterprises. Readers who want a detailed understanding of management by objectives (MBO) should see Norman Nager and T. Harrell Allen, *Public Relations Management by Objectives,* Lanham, MD: University Press of America, September 1, 1991.

For public relations practitioners, the conflict between open and closed systems of management poses a major issue:

- Must an organization always go along with public opinion?
- When is it acceptable to advocate change in public opinion?

Many cases discussed here illuminate this conundrum.

THE COMMON DENOMINATORS

In almost all programs or campaigns, seven common characteristics prevail:

1. Concern about social norms, group attitudes, and individual behavior
2. A strategy embodying specific objectives, selected audiences, careful timing, and cost controls
3. Actions that are consistent with the policies, standards, and personality of the organization represented
4. Emphasis on the use of **communications and participative activities to persuade**, rather than the use of coercion
5. Consideration of the ethical and legal implications and consequences
6. A method of assessing the outcome in terms of benefits and costs
7. Translation of this assessment into decisions for continuation, alteration, or termination of the program

PROVEN MAXIMS THAT EVERY PRACTITIONER MUST KNOW

As the library of case studies and the experience of scholars and practitioners have grown, the practice has accumulated an inventory of maxims with a high degree of reliability. Many of them derive from timeworn adages applied to persuasion and the formation of public opinion. Here are some examples of these maxims.[3]

1. An appeal to audience **self-interest** is most likely to be effective.
2. A **source of information** regarded as trustworthy, expert, or authoritative is most likely to be believed.
3. **Personal, face-to-face contact** is the most effective means of communication.
4. **Understanding a subject** is the first requisite for a communicator wishing to explain the subject to others.
5. **A suggested action or appeal**, as part of a message or coupled to it, is more likely to be accepted than a message by itself.
6. **Participation in, or awareness of, the decision process** increases the likelihood of acceptance.

---

[3]The "maxims" offered here are, for the most part, simple restatements of tenets advanced as "laws" of public opinion by Hadley Cantril, "barriers to communication" described by Walter Lippmann, Roper's "hypothesis," and Gallup's "regulators of the absorption rate of new ideas." Students can develop some of their own "maxims" or "precedential guidelines" by relating such concepts as the diffusion process, the concentric circle theory, and the two-step flow of information to situations with public relations overtones in their lives or in the news.

7. **Personality needs and drives as well as peer group identity** affect the acceptance of messages and positions on issues.
8. **Degree of clarity, simplicity, and symbolism** has a direct and measurable effect on message acceptance.
9. **Explicitly stated messages** and appeals tend to produce more behavior or opinion change than explanations of concepts or theories.
10. **Major issues and events** cause wide swings in public opinion for brief periods. The degree of lasting change tends to diminish with the passage of time.
11. **Self-imposed censorship by the audience** in not paying attention or not feeling involved can vary the degree of opinion or behavior change substantially.
12. **Subsequent events that reinforce the original stimulus** for opinion or behavior change will tend to increase the degree and durability of the change.
13. **Messages related to goals** are more readily acceptable than messages related to the steps and methods of attaining the goals.
14. **When a public is friendly in a controversial situation**, presenting only one side of the issue tends to be effective. If the audience is not friendly, or is likely to be receptive to both sides, presenting both sides tends to be more effective.
15. In controversy, **opposing views seeking major change of opinion** tend to strengthen the positions held. Similarly, a strong threat to those positions tends to be less effective than a mild threat. A reliable assumption is that **people tend to resist change.**
16. When there is little to choose from between opposing views, a determining factor tends to be **the argument heard last.**
17. In a confusing situation involving opposing messages, people tend to **believe what they want to and hope for**, rather than messages that strike discord.
18. **Sensitivity to public leadership** is heightened in times of crisis or controversy. At such times, people affirm or disapprove more forcefully and openly.

GUIDELINES FROM BEHAVIORAL SCIENCE

While there are few strict rules in psychology, sociology, or anthropology, following are four well-proven guidelines from these disciplines as they apply to public relations.

FOUR RULES FROM THE BEHAVIORAL SCIENCES
1. **The rule of ABUSE from Sociology**
   - People who *perceive* they have been, or *might* be, abused by an organization, its policies, or actions cannot hear what it is trying to say to them until the abuse is eliminated or at least acknowledged.
2. **The rule of PARTICIPATION from Psychology**
   - People will fully support only those ideas or programs they perceive they have had a voice in creating.
3. **The rule of REWARDS from Psychology**
   - People will ultimately do only those things for which they feel rewarded.
4. **The rule of CHEERLEADING from Anthropology**
   - Every successful organization of any type has at its core someone or several persons we would today call cheerleaders, urging the members on to success.

PROFESSIONALISM

Edward L. Bernays described a **profession** as "an art applied to a science in a manner that puts public interest ahead of personal gain."[4] The practice of public relations lays claim to professionalism on seven counts:

1. A codified body of knowledge[5] and a growing bank of theoretical literature, precedents, and case studies
2. Insight into human behavior and the formation and movement of public opinion
3. Skill in the use of communications tools, social science technology, and persuasion to affect opinions, attitudes, and behavior
4. Academic training including the Ph.D., offered in colleges throughout the world, and professional development available through a multiplicity of professional societies
5. A formal code of ethics[6]
6. A service that is essential in contemporary society
7. Nobility of purpose in harmonizing private and public interests—thus enabling individual self-determination and democratic societies to function

In the cases presented in this book, observe whether the practitioners involved are meeting these tests of professionalism—and whether application of or failure to observe these guidelines has an impact on their effectiveness.

SUCCESS
must be **CONFERRED** on us
by **OUTSIDERS** like
customers
opinion leaders
neighbors
elected officials
vendors
voters
prospective employees
coalitions
stakeholders
shareowners
Therefore, the bottom line for every organization is
to **BUILD RELATIONSHIPS**
that **EARN TRUST**
and **MOTIVATE SUPPORTIVE BEHAVIORS**

---

[4]Bernays, Edward L. *The Later Years: Public Relations Insights* 1956–1986, Rhinebeck, NY: H&M Publishers, 1986, p. 138.
[5]See *The Public Relations Body of Knowledge,* updated periodically by The Public Relations Society of America (PRSA) (available in computer disk and book form).
[6]See PRSA's *Member Code of Ethics,* Chapter 10, p. 365-366.

References and Additional Readings

Awad, Joseph. *The Power of Public Relations.* New York: Praeger, 1985.

Baskin, Otis, Craig Aronoff, and Dan Lattimore. *Public Relations: The Profession and the Practice,* 4th ed. New York: McGraw-Hill Higher Education, 1996.

Bernays, Edward L. *Crystallizing Public Opinion.* New York: Liveright, 1961. The first book on the field when it appeared in 1923 — and still a good overview. *Public Relations.* Norman, OK: University of Oklahoma Press, 1952. *Engineering of Consent.* Norman, OK: University of Oklahoma Press, 1955.

Budd, John, Jr. "When Less Is More: Public Relations' Paradox of Growth," *Public Relations Quarterly* 35 (Spring 1990): 5–11.

Burson, Harold. "Beyond PR: Redefining the Role of Public Relations." Presented to the 29th Annual Distinguished Lecture of the Institute for Public Relations Research and Education, Inc., the Union League Club, New York, October 2, 1990.

Cutlip, Scott, Allen Center, and Glen Broom. *Effective Public Relations,* 8th ed. Upper Saddle River, NJ: Prentice Hall, 1999. Chapters 1–4.

Grunig, James, et al., *Excellence in Public Relations and Communications Management.* Mahwah, NJ: Lawrence Erlbaum Associates, 1992.

Grunig, James, David Dozier, and Larissa Grunig, *Manager's Guide to Excellence in Public Relations and Communications Management.* Mahwah, NJ: Lawrence Erlbaum Associates, 1995.

Haynes, Colin. *A Guide to Successful Public Relations.* Glenview, IL: Scott-Foresman, 1989.

Hiebert, Ray Eldon. *Precision Public Relations.* New York: Addison-Wesley, 1988. Compendium of essays by public relations notables.

Jackson, Patrick. "Tomorrow's Public Relations." *Public Relations Journal* 41 (March 1985).

Lesly, Philip. *Lesly's Handbook of Public Relations and Communications,* 5th ed. Chicago, IL: NTC Business Books, 1998.

pr reporter Vol. 31 No. 38 (September 26, 1988). Deals editorially with acceptance yet insecurity of function, urges re-energizing through social compact and professionwide management awareness program.

The Public Relations Body of Knowledge compiled by The Public Relations Society of America (PRSA). This resource provides abstracts of articles, lectures, books, and book chapters relating to relevant areas of public relations. Available from PRSA, 33 Irving Place, New York, NY 10003.

Wilcox, Dennis, et al. *Public Relations Strategies and Tactics,* 6th ed. New York: Longman, 2000.

Problem 1-A Breaking in an Employer

Although you have graduated with a major in public relations from Northern Illinois University, you have had no luck during the summer finding a job that will keep you in the Chicago area where your fiancee works. It seems as if the big firms and companies are downsizing and you have lost out to experienced people changing jobs.

You haven't given up. You have listed with a well-known employment agency specializing in communications and marketing jobs. You're living at home on the north side of Chicago, and you're making ends meet as a waiter in a large restaurant.

In mid-August the employment agency calls you. There's a growing catering service, Kitchens On Wheels, Inc., headquartered in West Allis, Wisconsin, a suburb of Milwaukee on the interstate highway. They're looking for a young public relations person with some experience and interest in food services.

The fifteen-year-old business is run by its founder, George Workard. As a child, he was a helper in his father's small restaurant. He then worked in the kitchen at a large, busy highway truck stop, and by age twenty-one he was a cook in a company that supplied airline meals. Two years later, he bought one of their damaged food trucks, fixed it up, rented a vacant building, borrowed money to equip it, and went into the catering business for himself. Today, he has a fleet of 40 shiny, specially fitted kitchens on wheels with the slogan "We Bring Your Lunch Pail" painted on the side. It's another Horatio Alger, Jr., success story . . . only in America. Naturally, you want to look into it.

The employment agency sets up an appointment for you to be interviewed. The personnel manager in West Allis has you fill out an application, then says that anybody new in the office has to be approved by Mr. Workard. While you wait, the personnel manager shows you around. The office is small, but the work area for cooking, sorting, packaging, and loading is huge and has some mechanization. Everybody handling food wears white and gloves. A few spotless trucks are in a separate building. You notice a few uniformed men and women who must be drivers or handle service at kitchen stops.

Finally, you go to Mr. Workard's office. It's a shambles of sample food cartons, utensils, cups, glasses, vending apparatus, menu lists, and other paraphernalia that suppliers have left behind. Mr. Workard, a small, rotund, continuous-talking and fast-acting bundle of energy and nerves, darts in. He waves the personnel man away and sits you down.

He tells you the business is getting too big for him to do everything. He wants a public relations person who will put out a newsletter "telling everybody what they should know" in order to get a better job done faster, work up an instruction manual to "help my people riding the trucks," "get our services written up in the local trade papers," and "get to know some of the important people around the area so they will appreciate how we do our part for the community."

After describing what he wants done, Mr. Workard adds what he doesn't want. He doesn't want to be bothered by reporters "aiming to write up how he came from nowhere and didn't get through grade school." He doesn't have time to waste sitting around on community committees that are "mostly talk." He'd rather give a little money after they've made up their minds. He also makes it clear that he will "sell the trucks and close the business" before he will sign a contract with a union. He doesn't say why he has such a deep grudge. He does say that he has a good personnel manager who hires only the "right kind of drivers and salespeople." As for Wisconsin politics, he's "got a guy over in Madison who talks turkey to the politicians when they're off base." In running the business, he puts in his time "wherever the problem is, and that's not often in this room." Finally, in his staccato fashion, he tells you the PR job is a "one-year trial at $24,000. You get a secretary and an allowance of $20,000 for the newsletter and other expenses. Beyond that, ask for what you need." Finally, Mr. Workard says, "If the job sounds right to you, say so. If not, let's you and me not waste each other's time."

You ask him how long you have to think it over; there are the move from Chicago and other things to consider.

"What's to think over?" he says. "Either you want it, and can do it, or you don't and you can't. If you take it, and you do it right, you won't see or hear much from me. If you don't hear anything, or see me, that's good news. You're doing all right." Mr. Workard thinks that is really funny. He laughs heartily.

On the spur of the moment you decide to take the job, gambling that once you settle in, you'll be able to straighten Mr. Workard out as to what public relations is and isn't, what Kitchens On Wheels should or should not do in the name of public relations, and what his personal part in it should be.

Preparing to show up for work, you think about the purposes of public relations; the functional elements; the roles, tools, and media; the axioms or guidelines relevant to opinion formation and movement that you studied in school; and how to apply them here and now on the job. Specifically, in order for effective relationships to be a plus factor in the long-term growth and aspirations of Kitchens On Wheels, what modifications will you have to bring about in George Workard's notions about the function, his attitudes toward various public constituents and opposition groups, and, perhaps, his personal style? Put another way, what aspects of the situation do you see as problems requiring change or correction, and what do you see as opportunities to be seized, protected, and exploited?

Try converting the problems and opportunities on paper into a set of four or five personal and private goals that might take two or three years, and for each goal put down a specific objective to attain by six months and another to reach by the end of your trial year.

Looking at the objectives and the goals, write a proposal to Mr. Workard seeking his approval of a project or two that would get you started (consider, of course, whether it is a good or bad strategy at this point to reveal how your goals are related to him personally).

Problem 1-B Setting Professional Goals

As a recent college graduate, you are offered a job in the Midwest focusing on farming and the agricultural industry. Although you know nothing about this area of the country or the industry, you decide to take the job because corporations are downsizing and the chance of getting a job right now is slim. You would also like to explore a new area of the country.

The process for getting hired was interesting. It gave you many insights on how this small public relations firm handles situations. After going through a series of interviews you learn that the firm is looking for an innovative, young individual to bring new vision and energy to the firm. You also learn that the firm is interested in hiring someone with a strong communications background to write and produce a newsletter. This newsletter will be sent to clients, farmers, and others within the agricultural industry. You will also be responsible for drafting press releases concerning any governmental issues facing the industry as well as updates for farmers and others involved in agriculture. There are currently many hot topics in government that might affect the industry and you will be responsible for disseminating this information at the appropriate time to the appropriate people. You are intrigued by this opportunity because many of your personal and professional goals can be met by the challenges of moving to a new area of the country and learning about the problems and issues that face this industry.

As part of your job, you will also need to do research on the economic situation of farming and agriculture in the Midwest, as well as the effects environmental changes have on the industry's growth. For example, if the Mississippi River floods and crops are ruined, what happens to the industry and how will it survive? Through your limited knowledge of the area, you are aware that there have been floods, frosts, and arid heat that have greatly affected production. You also are aware that these situations affect the nation by reducing food sources, eliminating jobs, and depressing the economy. Your job will require you to do the research behind such situations and to help create crisis management plans in the event any of these or other scenarios occur.

You think this would be a great opportunity to expand your knowledge and use the skills you learned in college. At the same time, you noticed a few things within the firm that might need improvement. The firm's internal organization is not what you expected. Having worked with other firms while interning, you can tell this firm needs a little organizational help, as well as improvement with internal relationships. Your supervisor has many years of experience, yet hesitates to share it with the rest of the employees. There is little collaboration among employees; each person works individually and not collectively to obtain the goals of the firm. Based on this information, how would you go about building positive relationships and with whom in order to improve conditions internally?

In order to help others, you need to help yourself become acclimated and organized within the firm. Understanding that you are new to the area and to farming and agriculture, set five professional and private goals with a specific example for each that you would like to obtain. A few of the goals should be attainable within the first six months to a year of employment. By anticipating problems and opportunities that you might encounter, write your strategy or tactical plan for improving the current situation.

2

HOW PUBLIC RELATIONS DEALS WITH PROBLEMS AND OPPORTUNITIES

WHAT IS PUBLIC RELATIONS?

Here is a formal three-part definition of **public relations**:

1. Public relations is a condition common to every individual and organization in the human environment—whether or not they recognize or act upon the fact— that refers to their reputation and relationship with all other members of the environment.
2. Public relations is the systematized function that evaluates public attitudes and behaviors; harmonizes the goals, policies, and procedures of an individual or organization with the public interest; and executes a program of action to earn public understanding, acceptance, and supportive behavior.
3. Public relations is the full flowering of the democratic principle, in which every member of society is valued for himself or herself, and has both a right and a duty to express an opinion on public issues, and in which policies are made on the basis of free exchange of those opinions that result in public consent.

In other words:

- Public relations is something everyone has.
- Public relations fosters the improvement of public relationships through specific activities and policies.
- Public relations is the cornerstone of a democratic society.

PROACTIVE AND REACTIVE APPROACHES

An organization or corporation is a group of people working together for a specific purpose. That purpose invariably involves gaining the confidence of other people who will buy the product or use the service, invest in the organization's stock (or donate funds to nonprofit entities), and support its positions on issues. In short, every organization exists in a societal or people-orientated environment, first and foremost. Counselor Philip Lesly called this the *human climate*.

Because people form impressions and opinions of one another almost without thinking about it, every organization has a reputation, be it good or bad. Most likely, it will be good with some people and bad with others, depending on the perspective of those people and their particular interactions with the organization. As it does between persons, this reputation influences the ability of the organization to win friends, persuade others to do business with it, or be trusted in public matters.

- *The managerial challenge is whether something is consciously done to face the fact of reputation and relationships.*

When something is consciously done, the result is a public relations policy: recognition by management that positive relationships with key publics are essential to success. This management concept (See Chapter 1) is usually carried out by forming a public relations department and assigning it the responsibility for building and maintaining positive working relationships inside and outside the organization.

The approach the public relations department takes, however, is another challenge. Many companies—too many, some observers say—operate in a *reactive* mode. They wait for public criticism, emergencies, or bad publicity before they act. They are usually likened to firefighters who don't get going until there's a fire.

Because reputations are formed and re-formed in people's minds continuously, and because public issue debates are constantly taking shape, a more strategic approach is to be *proactive*. This approach is like fire prevention. It constantly looks for potential opportunities and problems. Proactive public relations practitioners will be ready to take advantage of opportunities when they arise and to prevent potential problems from flaring up.

STRATEGY AND PLANNING MAKE THE DIFFERENCE

Given the unpredictable nature of our world, there will always be unexpected situations that require reactive responses. But, just as promotions come to those who have worked hard for it, successful reactive responses are made by those who are prepared. The best preparation involves:

1. Understanding your organization's or client's business, operations, culture, and goals thoroughly
2. Learning as much as possible about the publics on which it depends for success
3. Putting that understanding and knowledge together in a formal strategic plan

With preparation, reactive responses are most likely to fit into the overall pattern of the public relations effort. Trouble comes when they do not fit—when what is put forward in response to customer complaints now contradicts what the company has been saying in publicity, publications, or advertising. The company is not speaking with One Clear Voice, and this "double talk" raises questions of its accuracy and trustworthiness.

In analyzing the cases in this book, you will not know as much about the subjects or organizations as you would want to were you actually involved in the case. Nevertheless, it should be apparent in most cases whether the public relations response was based on a strategic plan or just a hunch or gut feeling. More than anything else, planning makes the difference between success and failure.

PRELIMINARIES TO PLANNING

Many misunderstandings and poor public relationships occur because a legitimate inquiry is not promptly and properly answered by deed or word. Many others occur because responses are ill-timed, inaccurate, or altered by the interpretation given by a critic, or they are blown out of proportion by news media seeking sensational headlines.

Naturally, given a choice between spot reaction and time for a thoroughly considered response, public relations practitioners would opt for the latter. Sometimes there is no choice; microphones are being thrust in your face or a political figure is waiting impatiently in the reception area.

The substitute for a thoroughly considered response is a **strategic plan** that anticipates at least broad topics that are likely to arise. Specific problems that affect public opinion and relationships rarely exist in isolation. Each one is connected to larger matters of public concern. By considering these problems in a plan, in advance, one often can deal with a problem before it arises. Mastering the planning process is an essential and basic skill of public relations. Such plans must take place within the context of the goals and culture of the organization, of course (See Case 6-3).

THE PUBLIC RELATIONS PROCESS

In devising a program or campaign, practitioners follow a series of logical steps that overlap so that they constitute a continuous **four-step process**. Here is the sequence:

1. **Fact-finding and data-gathering**, often including formal research, to define clearly the specific problem or opportunity
2. **Planning and programming**, to devise and package a strategy
3. **Action, relationship-building, and communication**, to implement the strategy
4. **Evaluation**, to determine results and to decide what, if anything, to do next or to do differently

Contrast the preceding plan with one developed by well-known researcher Jim Grunig, professor of communications at the University of Maryland. His is a valuable planning tool that demonstrates where public relations fits into organizational planning and operations—where it adds the most value. An application of his theory is the ability to focus on a stakeholder group known to be skittish about a particular decision/policy and be able to predict the group's response (See Chapter 8).

Grunig's Paradigm

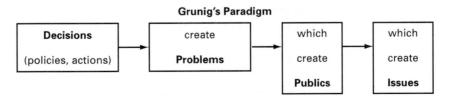

Decisions	create	which	which
(policies, actions)	**Problems**	create	create
		Publics	**Issues**

Organizations have two choices: They can call in public relations at the end of the process to put out the fire, or they can involve public relations at the beginning and avoid the fire.

A BEHAVIORAL STRATEGIC PLANNING MODEL CAN BE USEFUL

Major elements include:

1. What *behaviors* must be motivated, reinforced, or modified to achieve the goals?
2. Precisely *which stakeholder group* or *segments* must give these behaviors, or could keep you from achieving the goals by withholding the behaviors or by overt opposition?
3. Since people don't often go straight to the ultimate desired behaviors, what intermediate behaviors might you have to lead them through as way stations? If the intermediate activity puts the organization in direct contact with people—at, for example, a celebration, meeting or event—this is prime time to build relationships with stakeholders face-to-face.
4. Since groups/publics don't usually act spontaneously, who are the *opinion leaders* in these groups and what special behaviors must be sought from them to stimulate group behavior?

A RUNNING EXAMPLE: THE PROBLEM OF A RADIOACTIVE LEAK

A faulty valve at a nuclear reactor permits radioactive steam to escape. This defect raises questions about the functioning of the equipment, the danger to employees and neighbors, the qualifications of the utility to operate the plant, and more.[1] That such an incident occurs is related to the larger questions of nuclear power safety, protection of public health, regulatory safeguards, the adequacy of various energy sources, and the appropriateness of the design and construction of present-day nuclear facilities. At still another level of public interest, such an incident brings into question the quality of the environment, the politics of energy, the economics of turning to alternative energy sources, and the influence of even peaceful nuclear use on world affairs.

Audience Segmentation

On any public issue, and in any program to win allies or deal with opposition, the *variables* must be taken into account. Our example illustrates three major variables:

1. **The proximity of the audiences involved**, geographically and emotionally. In the radioactive emission at the nuclear plant
   - **employees** on the job would be vitally involved,
   - so would the **neighbors**;
   - the next circle of proximity could be the **executives and engineers** of the utility,
   - the **inspectors** who had approved the equipment, including the leaking valve,
   - and the **supplier** of the valve

---

[1]The example used is simulated. The risk of errors, mishaps, and accidents are inherent in the handling of flammable, toxic, and explosive substances. Our technological society routinely faces such problems and public relations practitioners must deal with them.

2. The extent to which an audience can be helped or hurt, rewarded, or penalized
3. Timeliness

There may be several important publics, but which ones need attention now, which a month from now, which next year? Because of proximity, but also because of *timeliness,* the employees and immediate neighbors of the nuclear plant are important publics for immediate communication. Once the emergency has passed, public relations efforts can target regulators and other government officials. Consumers of the nuclear-produced power may receive some information early regarding the availability of power, but a more extensive campaign may have to wait.

Both proximity and timeliness are examples of why *all publics are not created equal.* The importance of publics shifts with a change of events or because the campaign with one public has been completed. One of the important functions of the public relations professional is to counsel management about which publics should receive priority status. This counsel is based on the principle that public relations efforts generally are aimed at specific audiences or publics rather than at the general public or mass audiences. This principle raises the question of how to break the general public into smaller audiences that have particular importance for the organization. There are, however, even earlier questions to be answered.

FACT FINDING AND DATA GATHERING: THE FIRST STEP OF THE PROCESS

Much of what goes on in the name of public relations and persuasive communications is just plain busywork. Much more is wasted effort. Much is actually counterproductive, because it is unnecessary or because it is tactless, abrasive, immoral, or even unethical. Most of these problems can be avoided by making three preliminary determinations.

1. Do we really have a public relations problem?
2. If we do, is it a problem that can be
   a. alleviated,
   b. turned around in our favor, or
   c. countered by some sort of adjusting action or a planned program of communication?
3. If it can be resolved, is action on our part indicated now or later?

Let us apply these questions to the problem of the radioactive steam emission at the nuclear plant. Suppose the backup valve had worked as it was supposed to. Suppose the contaminating steam had been promptly brought under control. Would we have had a problem of immediate public concern? What purpose would then have been served by announcing anything to anyone outside the plant?[2] Such an announcement might have forced a regulatory agency to shut down the plant, putting employees out of work. If that happened, how would the economics of the whole community be affected? Would news about the mechanical problem, and an averted emergency, actu-

---

[2]The rules for routine reports to the Nuclear Regulatory Commission would of course apply, raising the possibility that the news would get out from that source.

ally be counterproductive if news media sensationalized it or if politicians, opposed to nuclear power or to the party in power, seized on it to make trouble for the administration and to further their own interests?

There is never a guarantee that practitioners can control any information that news media or Web site activists consider of public interest and within their prerogatives under the First Amendment. Nor is there any guarantee that one organization will not seize upon a competitor's problem to gain an advantage in the marketplace. There is often something to be gained and little to be risked, however, in refraining from the knee-jerk reaction to release information that helps one special interest at the expense of another—unless the greater interest of the whole public is at stake.

A great many isolated and insignificant situations are ballooned into problems of public proportion by management's lack of real strategic thinking, by the miscalculation of overzealous communicators, and by the competitive efforts of news media. In the ongoing practice of public relations, remember the old adages, "Look before you leap," and "Don't go off half-cocked."[3]

PLANNING AND PROGRAMMING: THE SECOND STEP OF THE PROCESS

The process of handling public relations problems is so dynamic, with all four phases sometimes compressed into minutes, that hard lines dividing one phase from another cannot always be drawn. The lack of a clear separation between research and planning is a good example.

The drawing up of a plan of action implies that such matters as identifying target stakeholders, setting specific objectives, figuring out a budget, and deciding on a timetable are all fixed in place like the numbered stops on an elevator. But they are not. All depend on an underlying strategy. Thus, there is a bridging that takes place in which the fact-finding and analysis of fact in the light of organizational goals and policies allow for choices to be made among the available alternatives.

RETURNING TO THE EXAMPLE

Continuing with the leaking valve problem at the nuclear plant and the concept of concentric circles of audience involvement, assume that (1) there is a public relations problem; (2) the problem can be alleviated by appropriate action or communication; and (3) the circles of involved publics are employees and neighbors, executives of the utility and of certain government agencies, the utility's shareholders, and the general public, in that sequence.[4]

Given these facts, what is the overriding *objective*? What are the desirable limits of responsive action? What form of response best attains the objective within the

---

[3]A remarkable number of homely old adages applicable to public relations reappear in new words, sometimes as principles or maxims. Here are a few: "One false step can ruin the reputation of a lifetime," "One picture is worth a thousand words," "A stitch in time saves nine," "Me thinks the lady doth protest too much," "Everybody loves a winner," "Once burned, twice shy."

[4]The concentric circle concept derives from Elmo Roper's hypothesis that ideas penetrate to the whole public very slowly, moving from great thinkers to disciples, then to disseminators, next to the politically active, and finally to the politically inert.

desired limits? What should be the content of the message and who the carrier? Or what should be the action and who the initiator? Are there allies we can call on for assistance?

Practitioners answer these questions by considering the pros and cons for each available alternative. For example, at the nuclear plant, assuming that news media will inquire, there are at least four available responses in the short term:

1. Deny that anything out of the ordinary has happened.
2. Admit a mechanical problem, but deny that there is any danger.
3. Admit a mechanical problem and indicate that it is being brought under control.
4. Admit a mechanical problem and indicate that it will be corrected as soon as possible.

Strategic thinking might conclude that the first response is deceitful or misleading. Lying to or misleading the public may be illegal and is certainly unethical. Even if this action were not illegal, getting caught would pose a threat to the future of local relationships, to the integrity of the utility, and to public acceptance of nuclear power. Obviously, that alternative would be rejected. Responses 2 and 3 run the same risks where credibility and public safety are concerned, if all does not turn out well. The fourth alternative is the truth *as the truth is known at the moment.* Thus, this response is acceptable, no matter what the outcome. (See Chapter 9 for details on effective programming in a crisis.)

Strategic thinking on a matter as grave as a nuclear accident, or the threat of one, would of course go to much greater depths than outlined in this example. It would involve top-level people in the utility, the energy industry, the government, the community, and probably the employees, as a bare minimum. The point to remember is that strategic thinking encompasses research, analysis and a plan of action. This relationship is shown in Figure 2-1.

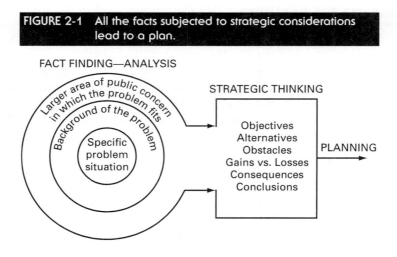

FIGURE 2-1   All the facts subjected to strategic considerations lead to a plan.

FACT FINDING—ANALYSIS

Larger area of public concern in which the problem fits

Background of the problem

Specific problem situation

STRATEGIC THINKING

Objectives
Alternatives
Obstacles
Gains vs. Losses
Consequences
Conclusions

PLANNING

PLANNING

In much the same manner that fact-finding leads to and merges into **planning**, plans lead to and merge into **programs of action**. When a plan is written, it usually takes the form of a proposal. It may propose a public statement, a position paper, a detailed special event, opinion leader contacts, a campaign, or an extended program to stimulate favorable reaction. It may propose as well that the organization take certain steps in its operations, or perhaps adopt or change a policy.

The actual submission or presentation of a plan of action must deal with more than long-term goals. It is expected to cover practical matters such as theme and appeal, budget, media, tools and vehicles, personnel and special talent, logistics, audience profiles, and the timetable. Above all, public relations plans must support an organization's particular objectives.

The specific response or message to be sent is sometimes determined by the situation confronted. If not, then it usually develops in the situation analysis or the strategic thinking. Decisions regarding the targeting of publics and the selection of message-carrying media may emerge as an aspect of strategic thinking. More often, they are determined as an aspect of the planning phase. We separate them here for emphasis.

SELECTION OF AUDIENCES: PRIMARY, INTERVENING, SPECIAL

One way to select priority audiences is to divide the whole public into primary, intervening, and special publics, and then to select a priority public from these groupings.

- A **primary public** comprises those who can do or not do what you need or want done. They should be the target of any actions, activities, or communication.
- An **intervening public** is a specific group that carries a message to the primary public. For example, if parents are a primary audience, an intervening public can be their children. Such publics are often referred to as *gatekeepers*. Historically, the three principal gatekeepers are news media, politicians, and activists. Opinion leaders, finally, are being considered part of this group.
- A **special public** is an organized group generally with a set of bylaws and with regular meetings. There are two kinds of special publics:
  1. An *inward special public* is organized for the primary objective of serving its own members rather than nonmembers. Examples include a neighborhood association or a trade association.
  2. An *outward special public* is organized for the primary reason of serving people other than its own members. Examples include public interest or cause-related organizations and charities.

If we apply these definitions to the nuclear plant example, employees, neighbors, and consumers of the electricity produced at the plant will be directly affected by the actions at the plant; they are the primary publics. They can each give us the behavior we want. Intervening publics include the media, politicians, and some technical groups—each of whom may affect the primary audiences. Outward special publics for this example include environmentalists as well as the many groups that are organized to oppose nuclear energy publicly. Inward special publics include national or regional associations representing electrical producers or manufacturers of electrical appliances, and unions representing employees.

Once such a listing of publics is made, the next step is to select those that warrant immediate attention and others that, although important, can wait. In this example, employees and neighbors, because of the safety factor, rate a high priority. Also very high, because of their long-range impact on the company, are consumers of the plant's nuclear-generated electricity and regulatory government officials. Media also rate a high ranking. Once the safety problem has lessened, the special publics opposing nuclear power would rank high. Electrical consumers in other areas, stockholders, and associations would rank further down the list.

The example of the nuclear plant accident explains why problem solving in public relations places great emphasis on the selection of target audiences preparatory to a planned public response.

SELECTION OF MESSENGERS

Information tools, the *messengers,* fall into several categories. The main criterion for choosing one over another is its credibility and thus its ability to motivate a receiving audience into an attitude or a behavioral action.

> The term *media* is too often used to mean *news* media. For public relations practitioners, it means *any* medium of communication or feedback.

In the example of the incident at the nuclear plant, the audience motivation sought by the utility would be an attitude of calm confidence that all is well, or will turn out to be so. Contributing factors in media selection for each situation, crisis or not, can be (1) the importance and thus the priority of each audience, (2) the time allowed or required to get information to the audience, (3) the level of authority required for credibility, (4) the accuracy of a medium in hitting a target audience, and (5) the medium's ability to influence behavior efficiently in terms of cost and effort. For simplicity, we touch on seven basic categories: individuals, personalized message tools, publications, mass media, advertising, special events, and the Internet.

Individuals

People are the most effective messengers. When a qualified person communicates, there can be emphasis, credibility, body language reinforcement, and the all-important opportunity for instant feedback. If the message is misunderstood, or only partially understood, questions can be asked. More details can be given until understanding is achieved. Action, too, can be as immediate as getting a donation, signatures on a petition, or volunteer workers.

Individuals can carry the message in the following ways, from most effective to least effective:

- **One-to-one**, ideally between peers, whether neighbors or corporate vice presidents
- **One-to-a-small group**, retaining the personalized aspect and offering opportunity for clarification, as in a meeting or open house
- **One-to-a-large group**, providing the presence and credibility of a good speaker—there may be some sacrifice in the clarification process, however, because of the reluctance of some people to ask questions in this setting

Personalized Message Tools

When face-to-face delivery by a person is not possible, there are media that allow personalization without serious sacrifice of credibility or control. Examples include:

- **Telephone calls** are approximately the one-on-one ideal, providing opportunity for clarification, emphasis, and immediate reaction, losing only the face-to-face visual impression that gives notification by the attention span, facial expressions, and body language whether there is understanding and perhaps acceptance. Voice mail is personalized, and campaigns using group voice mail are now common.
- **Letters or cards** run the gamut of good, bad, and indifferent, depending on whether personally written, addressed, and signed, or the computer letter perceived as junk mail and consigned to the nearest wastebasket. There persists in our culture, however, a special psychological attachment to personal mail. It is controllable by the sender. Handled with skill and empathy, it can be credible and productive. Enclosures such as brochures or reproductions of media articles can impart important information.
- **New computer, television, and other visual technology** is opening the way to new approximations of "personalized" media. These include the picture phone, interactive computer dialoguing, teleconferencing, two-way television, and others. (But one-way messaging, like e-mail, is impersonal unless it is sent by people who have established relationships with the addressees.)

Publications

Publications that are specialized and focused narrowly on a particular audience interest have appeal and utility for their readers, and therefore for public relations practitioners. This category does not embrace publications of a mass market or mass media nature and circulation. Specialized publications with a high efficiency ratio include:

- **Organizational or group newsletters** that go to individuals as members or as a special-interest group—assuring knowledge of and interest in the organization's doings and well-being. Examples are legion, such as dog lovers, conservationists, and chamber of commerce or church members.
- **Business or professional publications**, some of which have paid subscriptions and advertising, and others that are free. Receivers of paid subscriptions tend to

expect more than receivers of free publications. In public relations practice alone, there are several professional publications. *Communications World* is one of the monthly magazines; *pr reporter* and *The Ragan Report* are among the weekly newsletters.

- **Employee publications** express a commonalty of membership and self-interest and provide specific significant information.

The weakness of *all* print matter today is getting people to actually *read* it.

Mass Media

Newspapers, magazines, radio, and television offer larger, though shrinking, audiences and have the most demanding standards for usable messages. In these media, the sender forfeits control over the use of the information as to timing, emphasis, amount, or phraseology. Once material has been released, the media's editorial values and judgment take over. As a rule, the closer a news item is to the competitive self-interests of a medium, the greater will be its value to the audience covered by that medium; the more professionally the information is prepared and documented, the better are the chances it will be used. Awareness of demographics, each medium's set of priorities, and the philosophy and stance of media owners and editors all have a bearing on whether an item will be accepted and on how it will be presented. Media selection is not an arena for amateurs.

Advertising

Advertising has long been a tool of public relations. It is used to control the message, the timing, and the position in relation to other information carried by an outlet and to develop either continuity or a complex message. However, the public's growing skepticism about advertising must be taken into account.

Special Events

Special events can combine the personalized touch of one-to-one or one-to-a-group encounters with the excitement of a rally, march, or convention. They can also be used to distribute publications, from leaflets to books. Question-and-answer forums are usual features. Exhibits, displays, films, or audiovisuals can be used. There are several types of special events, ranging from a simple meeting or open house to an attempt to attract attention to an issue or cause by picketing. A basic question in using events is whether the target audience is the attendees or those not attending—or both.

The Internet

This rapidly evolving medium is basically impersonal, yet interactive features make it more personal than a brochure or catalogue. Yet a Web site is only a catalogue on the screen, at base. Web sites are "mass" media in that anyone can access them, and some sites get millions of hits. But they are "pull" media in that, unless a person takes the trouble to visit a site, it is doing nothing for the sponsoring organization.

PLANNING INVOLVES A TEAM

A public relations plan of action normally involves the participation of several groups in the organization. Usually the human resources, financial, legal counsel, and marketing or sales departments, and operating or field staff, are involved. Obviously, advance agreement on cooperation or collaboration is required. Finally, implementation of a plan of action requires the approval and commitment of top management. The current jargon for this aspect is "getting buy-in."

A classic example of commitment exists in the public posture of the oil industry. When the price of a gallon of gasoline began to rise rapidly in the 1970s, an official of one company made the statement publicly that the price would have to go to $1.50 a gallon, and then it would be practical to go out and explore for new oil resources. This statement set policy in the company. Consequently, it gave direction and management commitment to its communicators whether in news, advertising, or other forms of public contact. Another oil company's management committed itself to aggressive advocacy of the industry, the profit motive, and the private enterprise system. The communications programming to implement this stance proceeded with complete assurance.

When elaborate or bold public relations campaigns falter or are withdrawn midstream, it is usually because they run into adverse reaction or opposition within the organization, and the original conviction and commitment of top management was so marginal that it refused to follow through. When the winds of public opinion shift, organizations tend to react like a sensitive person. *Approvals based on conviction, and supported by management participation and adequate budget, are essential to effective public relations programming.*

The manner in which the planning phase of the problem-solving process moves into the action phase is shown in Figure 2-2.

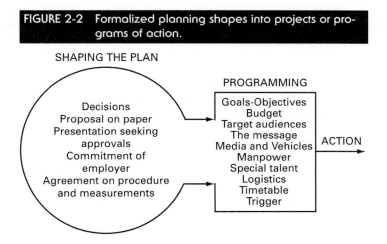

FIGURE 2-2 Formalized planning shapes into projects or programs of action.

ACTION, RELATIONSHIP-BUILDING, AND COMMUNICATION: THE THIRD STEP OF THE PROCESS

When the problem is defined, audiences prioritized, and the strategic plan approved, action commences.

- It may take the form of a policy change, launching an internal or public campaign, redesigning a product, or countless other forms. This is most effective when key stakeholders have been consulted or participate.
- Although the action is the *substance* of the plan, little benefit can be expected unless affected publics *know about it.* Therefore, communication with the hope of persuading and affecting behavior is built into almost all public relations activity. Even when the objective is to censor, to inhibit, to neutralize, or to ignore, some sort of communicative action can be required.

A bulletin at the nuclear plant warning employees that gossip, speculation, or exaggeration about the leaky valve problem could endanger their jobs would constitute communication, although designed in its own self-interest to inhibit it. Similarly, a telephone call to the inquiring reporter saying "off the record" that repair was imminent and asking whether release of the information could be delayed or the news value minimized to avoid risk of panic in the community would constitute a communicative action designed to edit or censor needlessly harmful public communication.

In practice, decisions on media, vehicles, talent, and budget concerning the implementation of a program usually are made during the planning phase rather than the action phase. These aspects of the process are shown in Figure 2-2 as independent activities simply for convenience. Usually, approvals granted by top managers allow latitude for alterations in media selection, timing or timetable, frequency of message, and other accommodations of changing circumstances.

There are a host of variables and unpredictables making this flexibility advisable. Among them are internal publication frequency; availability of news media contacts; competition for newsprint space or airtime; the differing level of public attention on a weekday versus a weekend; delays in copy composition, graphic art, filming, or printing of materials; delays caused by the illness or resignation of staff members; or interruptions caused by other tasks with higher priority or a greater immediacy.

EVALUATION: THE FOURTH STEP OF THE PROCESS

Almost as important as the origination and activation of a program, and the running changes that may need to be made, is the follow-up (See Figure 2-3). Too many well-conceived and successful projects and programs are launched without any thought or commitment to continuity or encores.

As we have seen, public relations programs, like those in marketing, finance, or public administration, are subject to running changes to improve them. They are also subject to questions about their future: Should they continue? The tools for answering such questions are *monitoring* and *measurement.*

ACTION

Launching
Follow-up
Evaluation of
feedback
Decisions on what to
do next

FIGURE 2-3 Action involves two-way communication, outbound and incoming.

Monitoring

There are many ways to attain the benefits of monitoring. Clipping and broadcast services will monitor news media for their clients. They cut out newspaper and magazine articles mentioning the client's products, services, and viewpoints. They tabulate airtime mentions. But they do not see, hear, or clip all the news on any subject. Ten to fifteen percent of an organization's total publicity is a good estimate of what these services do deliver.

Similar services exist for Web site hits. Staff can evaluate attendance and questions asked at speeches or special events. Opinion leader interest and behavior is often tracked in a database.

Other methods of monitoring include research among employees, community, or special-interest audiences, whether members, donors, students, or investors. Advisory boards, test panels, and focus groups are used. Special events are gauged by feedback from participants or by exit interviews. There are specialized firms that monitor activities concerned with legislative or financial affairs and with fundraising or membership campaigns.

Perhaps the largest share of the vehicles set up to monitor the impact and progress of programs is tailor-made to an organization's particular needs. As hypothetical examples, a computer company wanting to be known as definitive in its field might monitor new books dealing with cybernetics. A food company might retain a prominent university nutritionist. The oil industry might lean heavily and regularly on its lobbyists for input. A local retailer might put coupons in advertisements or run a contest among customers to see if its messages are getting through.

Measurement

There is a tendency in public relations practice to point at the size of an audience, at the linage or minutes of publicity, at the prestige of news outlets carrying material, and at the number of "friendly" media personnel or opinion leaders as meaningful indicators of a program's value or progress. There is the tendency to use these quantitative and qualitative features to predict success. To avoid such fallacious thinking, remember:

- Public appearance alone (circulation of a message) does not equal public reception (readership, listenership, viewership), nor does a third-party opinion leader or news medium's impartiality (credibility) indicate or guarantee public acceptance (agreement or behavior)

Efforts to quantify results are often reported by practitioners as circulation attained per dollar of cost or as program cost as a percentage of gain in sales, funds raised, or members attracted. Or they might be reported in terms of coupons returned or inquiries per dollar of expenditure or as behaviors observed in key publics or individuals. Increasingly, the emphasis is on *behavioral measurement* because it doesn't really matter whether a public received your message or attended your event *unless they did something about it.*

In the more sophisticated public relations operations, the degree of involvement of public relations with other organizational functions and the directness of the relationship of programs to organizational goals constitute the best measurements and the best indication of what lies ahead.

New methods of evaluating relationships, customer satisfaction and loyalty, and employee motivation to be ambassadors are quickly evolving. As the state of the art matures, computer technology is enabling measurement of the relative utility of the function, based on all the factors that go into programs and their impact individually and collectively on the behaviors of various audiences that make up an organization's constituency and opposition. The necessary information is accumulated and stored in computers for ultimate retrieval.[5] Measurement and evaluation are the major emerging steps in effective practice.

ASSESSMENT OPTIONS

From whatever feedback is obtained for evaluating a program, one of five conclusions can be drawn.

1. Continue the program as is.
2. Continue the program with some changes.
3. Terminate the program; it has served its purpose.
4. Gradually wind down the program.
5. Start a new program to succeed this one.

THE NUCLEAR PLANT EXAMPLE AGAIN

Consider once more the problem posed by the leaking valve and the radioactive steam at the nuclear reactor. Had the backup valve worked, the faulty one been replaced quickly, the employees undisturbed, and no harm been done, the third choice might have been the best: terminate the program. But if rumors had spread, making the community uneasy, then the fourth choice might have been made: gradually wind down the program, with provisions for a calm and reassuring recap of the situation to employees and the residents.

---

[5]For current research, see Glen Broom and David M. Dozier, *Using Research in Public Relations,* Upper Saddle River, NJ: Prentice Hall, 1989.

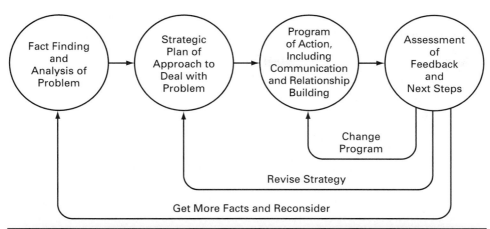

FIGURE 2-4 Problem solving portrayed as a continuous process.

If the situation at the nuclear plant had been such that communication could not be terminated or wound down, then public relations considerations would have had to be recycled into one or another of the earlier basic steps: fact finding research, planning and programming, or action and communication. For example, assume that the utility's top management has decided, as a means of avoiding any conceivable possibility of another scare, that the company is going to set an example of maximum preventive maintenance for the whole industry to copy. As part of this decision, management wants public relations programming that will give its constituent publics and its critics, from employees to investors, from government regulatory bodies to competitors, good reason to appreciate what it is doing. With this turn of events, the role of public relations becomes that of public educator. Such a role calls for extensive research of factual and scientific information; strategic thinking addressed to the long haul, not to crisis; and planned programming on several levels of technology adapted to the ability of diverse audiences to comprehend.

Problem solving is a continuing process of adapting to changing circumstances. This process is shown in Figure 2-4.

PUTTING IT ALL TOGETHER

A step-by-step approach to problem solving as outlined on the preceding pages is not a panacea. It is not a surefire way to get the wanted result. It is not the only way to structure a sequential approach. Knowing how to proceed within a structure, however, is vastly better than having to operate on impulse. The process of responding to a public relations problem is like any other decision-making process by professionally trained managers. There is rarely only one absolutely right or best answer to a public relations problem, or to one in marketing, fund-raising, or political campaigning.

This statement is easily put to a test. Gather together a few trained public relations consultants and present them with a communications problem, such as a rumor of a boycott, inevitably requiring some kind of reaction or response. The chances are that these experts, even though having a common training, will come up with different reactions and approaches. In each case, the reaction and approach will generally represent the honest conviction of the consultant, based on his or her experience and knowledge of the science of public relations. Effectiveness is enhanced by enthusiasm, personal conviction, and individual skills.

Suppose, however, that in the absence of a group of consultants, a resident practitioner was confronted with the fact that somebody had just thrown a brick through the window of the organization's headquarters. Assume that this action is a provocation calling for some kind of immediate response. The practitioner, in seconds or minutes, must decide whether to react by hurling the rock back at the attacker, ignoring the incident, or perhaps inviting the rock thrower to come in and talk things over and stay for dinner. Obviously, the circumstances here are extraordinary. Even though the decision process is compressed into seconds or minutes, the chances are that others in the organization—some junior to the practitioner, and some senior—would be involved. Whatever decision and response emerged would be the "right" one for that organization, at that moment, under the existing circumstances, and in consideration of whatever lay ahead.

Experience shows that a trained practitioner who knows how to apply a logical step-by-step analysis is always more able than an untrained person to deal with the unexpected. It is also in the nature of professional work that a practitioner is asked, on occasion, to follow a course of communication or action with which he or she does not fully agree, to assist a spokesperson or a cause for whom or which he or she has little enthusiasm, or to further a public interest that is felt to be at odds with his or her self-interest. The practitioner's acceptance or rejection of such requests is a personal matter.

BEHAVIORAL PUBLIC RELATIONS MODEL[6]

In public relations, behavior is the only evaluation that counts. This means motivating people to (1) do something, (2) not do something, or (3) let you do something. Yet too many practitioners think of themselves as communicators. They believe their objective is to move information, facts, data, or feelings. And they evaluate success by the number of clips, attendance, "reach," and similar measurements. To all of which knowledgeable employers or clients ask: So what? What has changed because of this? Never mind what our publics are thinking; the question is what are they *doing?*

The behavioral public relations model (See Figure 2-5) basically shifts the objective away from awareness to a behavioral response, and with it the focus of thinking, strategizing, and planning. Practitioners ask, "What behaviors am I trying to motivate?" rather than "What information am I trying to communicate?"

---

[6]Pat Jackson's behavioral pr model is an attempt at a unifying theory for public relations. One objective of the model is to identify pressure points where pr activities can be persuasive. "Though I have citations to support each segment, the science underpinning, at least the origin of the model, is Francis Bacon's original definition of science: observation followed by study, i.e. my 50 years of experience in the practice of public relations," explained Jackson.

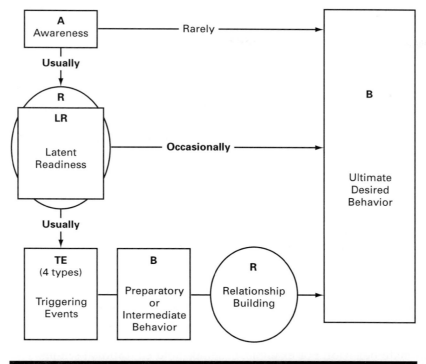

FIGURE 2-5   Behavioral Public Relations Model

A behavioral strategic planning model can be useful:

1. What **behaviors** must be motivated, reinforced, or modified to achieve the goals? Beginning every project by making a desired behaviors list gives you a specific guide for what you are trying to accomplish. This is the most important step toward engendering those behaviors—instead of thinking right away about messages, media, or activities.
2. Precisely which stakeholder group or segments must give these behaviors, or could keep you from achieving the goals by either withholding the behaviors or by overt opposition?
3. Since people don't often go straight to the ultimate desired behaviors, what intermediate behaviors might you have to lead them through as way stations?
4. Since groups/publics don't usually act spontaneously, who are the opinion leaders in these groups and what special behaviors must be sought from them to stimulate group behavior?

Understanding **triggering events** is key to this strategy. People are available to do, even ready to do, more than they actually do. Lack of time or money, other priorities, laziness, and a thousand other barriers inhibit them from undertaking the behavior spontaneously. Overcoming these barriers requires:

1. *Constructing a triggering event* that pushes the behavior into priority position. For example, retailers hold sales to lure shoppers to buy goods they previously felt they couldn't afford or that weren't a high priority.
2. *Usurping naturally occurring triggering events* in the lives of your stakeholders. For example, 40th birthdays start us thinking about our health future.
3. *Capitalizing on those triggering events that randomly come along* in the social environment. For example, *Sesame Street* tipped a revolution in early childhood education.
4. *Defensively being able to fend off triggering events launched by competitors and opponents,* or occurring in the environment.

Appealing to people to go straight to the ultimate behavior is usually futile. There are intermediate behaviors most of us work through, on most decisions, before proceeding to the ultimate behavior. The focus for pr efforts should be leading people to the intermediate behavior by concentrating our appeals there. Asking right off for the ultimate behavior is usually resisted.

If the intermediate activity puts the organization in direct contact with people—perhaps a celebration, meeting, or event is held—this is prime time to build relationships with stakeholders face-to-face. The combination of attracting them to an intermediate event, then building a relationship, provides entrée for them to act the ultimate behavior. For example, hospitals hold educational seminars—building relationships between staff and attendees during the events—as a means of stimulating attendees to make the hospital their healthcare center.

5-STEP PUBLIC RELATIONS STRATEGY FOR THE 21ST CENTURY

1. **Go Direct:**
   Go around the critics and gatekeepers directly to the important people whose support you need.
2. **To Key Stakeholders:**
   Those who are interested can give supportive behaviors now, or could stop needed action by their opposition.
3. **Via Opinion Leaders:**
   Publics don't just spontaneously act; they are stimulated by the movers and shakers we call opinion leaders.
4. **Using Members of the Organizational Family:**
   Involve employees at all levels in customer relations activities, ambassador programs, and community relations outreach teams; put them in charge of building *local* relationships that earn *supportive behaviors.*
5. **On a Local Basis:**
   People relate to their local environments, and all issues are local.

WHAT TO LOOK FOR IN THE CASES

In the case studies and the problems that make up the balance of this textbook, it is not expected that all students or practitioners will agree on the controversial issues posed, such as gun control, birth control, smoking, product recalls, standards of ethics, or nuclear power. Disagreement does not mean that one is right and the other wrong. It means that different people are reacting to the same data according to differing perceptions and value judgments. It is expected that individuals will differ in analysis of the campaigns and programs offered. They will favor a variety of solutions to the cases and to the job-related problems derived from actual situations. This is all as it should be for a learning experience. It is hoped that differing views will hone professionalism.

Three tenets bear mention for their significance and relevance.

1. When there is a choice, a carefully considered and **structured approach** to public communication increases the odds of audience acceptance.
2. The measure of true professionalism can often be taken in terms of **objectivity**, as expressed in **empathy** toward the views of others and in the ability to set aside personal bias.
3. When the philosophy, convictions, and public posture of a practitioner and an employer are in **harmony**, the chances of **credibility** and **persuasion** are measurably enhanced.

Cases are presented in narrative form, rather than outline, because that most closely approximates the way information comes to practitioners working on a case. This presentation gives the reader responsibility for sorting the critical information from mere static—as in real life.

In making judgments about how well organizations and practitioners handled the situations outlined in the cases, perhaps the best guide is whether they demonstrated an awareness of the process of public relations—as shown in the illustrations in this chapter. Good, bad, or somewhere in between, the reader must judge.

References and Additional Readings

Allen, T. Harrell, and Norman Nager. *Management by Objectives.* Lanham, MD: University Press of America, 2000. See Chapter 3.

Baskin, Otis, Craig Aronoff, and Dan Lattimore. *Public Relations: The Profession and the Practice.* 4th ed. New York: McGraw-Hill Higher Education, 1996.

Baus, Herbert, and Philip Lesly. "Preparation for Communicating." Chapter 20 in *Lesly's Handbook of Public Relations and Communications.* 5th ed. Chicago, IL: NTC Business Books, 1998.

Bennis, Warren. *Organizational Development: Its Nature, Origins, and Prospects.* Reading, MA: Addison-Wesley Publishing Company, 1969.

Brody, E. W. *Communication Tomorrow: New Audiences, New Technologies, New Media.* New York: Praeger, 1990.

Brody, E. W. *Public Relations Programming and Production.* New York: Praeger, 1988.

Broom, Glen, and David Dozier. *Using Research in Public Relations: Applications to Program Management.* Upper Saddle River, NJ: Prentice Hall, 1989.

Caywood, Clarke, editor. *The Handbook of Strategic Public Relations & Integrated Communications.* New York: McGraw-Hill, 1997.

Cutlip, Scott, Allen Center, and Glen Broom. *Effective Public Relations.* 8th ed. Upper Saddle River, NJ: Prentice Hall, 1999. See the four-step process. Chapters 10–13.

Goldhaber, Gerald. *Organizational Communication.* 6th ed. New York: McGraw-Hill Higher Education, 1993.

Grunig, James, and Todd Hunt. *Managing Public Relations.* New York: CBS College Publishing, 1984. See Chapters 6 and 7.

Haberman, David, and Harry Dolphin. *Public Relations: The Necessary Art.* Ames, IA: Iowa State University Press, 1988.

Hendrix, Jerry. *Public Relations Cases.* 3rd ed. Belmont, CA: Wadsworth, 1994. Case histories drawn from PRSA Silver Anvil Winner summaries.

Klein, Gerhart. *PR Law: The Basics.* Mt. Laurel, NJ: Anne Klein & Associates, 1990.

Lerbinger, Otto, and Nathaniel Sperber. "Contingency Plans." Chapter 2, Checklists 4 & 5 in *Manager's Public Relations Handbook.* Reading, MA: Addison-Wesley, 1982.

Lesly, Philip. "Analysis, Planning and Programming." Chapter 17 in *Lesly's Handbook of Public Relations and Communications.* 5th ed. Chicago, IL: NTC Business Books, 1998.

Londgren, Richard. *Communication by Objectives.* Upper Saddle River, NJ: Prentice Hall, 1983. An application of MBO to communications.

Marston, John. "A Formula for Successful Public Relations Practices." Chapter 9 in *Modern Public Relations.* New York: McGraw-Hill, 1979. Describes the RACE formula, a variation of the four-step process.

Newsom, Doug, Judy Van Slyke Turk, and Dean Kruckeberg. *This Is PR: The Realities of Public Relations.* 6th ed. Belmont, CA: Wadsworth, 1996.

Ott, Richard. *Creating Demand.* Homewood, IL: Business One Irwin, 1991.

Pavlik, John. *Public Relations: What Research Tells Us.* Thousand Oaks, CA: Sage Commtext Series, Vol. 16, 1987.

pr reporter Vol. 43 No. 47 (November 27, 2000). "Rationalizing Hi-Tech Tools: Necessary but Tough," and "To Measure PR, We Must Understand Its Precepts."

pr reporter Vol. 39 No. 44 (November 4, 1996). "A Process for Practicing Behavioral Public Relations."

pr reporter Vol. 36 No. 38 & 41 (September 27 and October 18, 1993). Two-part report on twenty-ninth annual survey of significant trends in the structure, stature, and functional activities as seen by practitioners.

pr reporter Vol. 36 No. 11 (March 15, 1993). "Twelve Trends That Are Steering Public Relations Practice."

pr reporter Vol. 33 No. 30 & 32 (July 30 and August 13, 1990). "Behavioral Model Replacing Communication Model as Basic Theoretical Underpinning of PR Practice," and "More on Behavioral Public Relations . . ."

The Public Relations Body of Knowledge. New York: PRSA. See abstracts dealing with the "Public Relations Process."

Shockley-Zalabak, Pamela. *Fundamentals of Organizational Communication.* 4th ed. Needham Heights, MA: Allyn & Bacon, 1999.

Walsh, Frank. *Public Relations and the Law.* Gainesville, FL: Institute for Public Relations, 1991.

Problem 2-A Putting the PR Process to Work

You're two years out of Bell College, with a major in journalism and an emphasis in public relations. You're working for State Capital Public Relations, Inc. Your main account, so far, is Mothers Against Drunk Driving (MADD) statewide. It's been a breeze. There is not much money to spend, but the people are nice to work with.

There's a lot of talk, some publicity, and some publications for mailers, but not much action.

One day, your contact, the director at MADD, calls up and says that their project — "tie a red ribbon on your car door or antenna" — during the Christmas holiday period didn't go over very well for their relatively new chapter in Munsea. The director is mystified. There was generous local media publicity; plenty of ribbons, posters, and bumper stickers were made available in stores, banks, and public buildings. There was a timely mailing to thousands of homes, with a ribbon and a plea for donation. "Our people down there say the project just didn't catch on," your MADD contact tells you. Then she says, "Please go down to Munsea, find out what you can, and make recommendations as to where we should go from here."

You don't mind the assignment. Munsea is a bustling city of 80,000 including Bell College, with an enrollment of 7,000 students and nationally ranked year after year in basketball. No doubt some of your Bell teachers are still at the school and some local alumni you went to school with are still in town. You already know some things about the town and the school that might be relevant. It will be interesting to pay a visit on official business.

You remember well how a basketball game at Munsea always packed the splendid field house with fans from as far away as 100 miles and that many stayed overnight to celebrate or drown their sorrow. You recall that Munsea couldn't fully control the celebrating or the drinking. In fact, when you were in school at Bell, the city council passed an ordinance prohibiting any more bars or discos within the city limits. No more than a year later, a dozen or more roadhouses and motels had sprung up on the border of town. You also recall that there was a move to impose a curfew on the nights when Bell played a home game at the field house. The owners of hotels and restaurants, several unions, and most members of the chamber of commerce were successful in getting it voted down.

The Current Situation

Before you leave the office for the Munsea trip, your boss fills you in about the Munsea MADD chapter. It is headed by Ima Determined, a grade school principal. She initiated a MADD chapter in Munsea after experiencing a personal tragedy at the beginning of the basketball season just six weeks ago. A male Bell student, the son of a state highway commissioner, and Ima's daughter, also a Bell student, were involved in a head-on collision with an out-of-town driver visiting for the game. It was 1:00 A.M. The commissioner's son and the driver of the other car were killed. They both had been drinking heavily. Ima's daughter survived, disfigured and crippled for life. That incident, unknown to you when it happened, made rumbles in the state legislature about curbing liquor sales during sports events and about stricter accountability for vendors of alcohol. Nothing happened. The pendulum of public attention that had swung widely toward drastic action gradually came back to normal.

In the meantime, Ima had gone into action getting a MADD chapter charter, assembling a board including such influential persons as the mayor, superintendent of schools, Mercy Hospital administrator, United Way executive director, the spouses of the Bell College and Munsea National Bank presidents, and a dozen or more other people at the top of the civic pyramid. The disappointing result of the red-ribbon project over the Christmas holidays was a second blow for Ima to endure.

Your boss at the firm alerts you to expect Ima to be very subjective, even bitter, about public attitudes and behavior when it comes to drinking and driving. He expects that she will be not only subjective but demanding about corrective measures devised by State Capital Public Relations, and you as its representative. Reassure her as best you can, he says, but don't promise more than can be delivered.

Ima is demanding in a constructive way. She tells you that an anonymous donor has come up with $15,000 for you and your firm to spend figuring out why the red-ribbon campaign flopped in Munsea—despite success elsewhere—and what can be done in the two-month period between now and the Regional Basketball Tournament when Munsea will be overrun by basketball fans.

You call your home office. Your boss says to tell Ima that you've got some investigating to do, and that within two weeks you'll be back with a proposal for her and for her board, if she wants such a meeting. In the meantime, he says, you should nose around Munsea for a couple of days to find out as much as you can that might be helpful in deciding what can be done to help Munsea, Bell, and MADD officials get reasonable control of the basketball-drinking-driving problem. Time is short, so if you want any opinion soundings done in Munsea, arrange for that while you're there. He suggests that you organize your findings into a situation analysis that can be the basis for a strategic planning session directly as soon as you return. He'll set up that meeting and another one with the MADD home-office public relations director a day or two later.

Try putting on paper exactly how you will proceed, step by step. Be as specific as you can. After all, you went to school and lived in Munsea for four years. From that experience, you could have more and better insight than outsiders into contacts, methods, and improvisations with high potential for success. After you've done that and thought it through, make a situational outline of what you'll say at the firm's meeting to lead off discussion—your initial contribution to the decision process.

Problem 2-B Raising Awareness and Achieving Goals

You are a new junior account executive with a public relations firm in South Florida. One of your clients is a nonprofit organization that supports the preservation of the Everglades National Park. So far, your work for this client has been promoting awareness of the group and getting publicity. Occasionally, you set up interviews with reporters to cover developments in the Everglades. Now a local referendum is up for a vote in the next election that, if passed, will greatly increase funding for the Park.

Before you took this job, the Everglades National Park had a campaign focusing on local elementary, middle, and high schools and inviting them to see firsthand how they can help preserve this environment. In the beginning, the campaign was widely enjoyed, with many schools taking trips to the Everglades to witness what needed to be done and learning how they could help preserve the wildlife in South Florida. By targeting school children, the message of the Park's needs also reached parents.

Recently, however, the effectiveness of the campaign has worn off and reports projecting the success of the project look poor. Your supervisor calls you in to discuss the current situation and explains that you will need to (1) reorganize and revitalize the campaign and (2) build support for the local referendum that is approaching. You are given the following background about the campaign:

- It started over a year ago with the intention of raising the awareness of the Everglades for students between the ages of 6 to 18—and through them their parents.
- Park rangers spoke to science classes during school days and made presentations with photographs and wildlife animals.
- A series of posters and banners were placed on local highways to support donations to help preserve the area.
- Articles ran in local and community newspapers featuring the Everglades National Park and its battle with funding for preservation.

As you think about the campaign, consider who are your targeted audiences. Can your program reach beyond the schools? What message do you want each group to receive? Is there an action you would like them to do? How will you reach each of the various groups?

Go through the public relations process. Then write your plan of action as to how you intend to raise awareness and achieve the desired goals.

3 | EMPLOYEE RELATIONS

The first public of any organization is its employees—the people who make it what it is. As management guru Peter Drucker reminds us, an organization is "a human community" that needs the contributions of everyone to function and be successful. Many times it appears that management does not recognize this fact. Sometimes managers act as if *they* are the organization and the others just an impediment. An interchange at the annual meeting of an auto company illuminates the truth of the matter. A shareholder asked the CEO why funds were being allocated to improve employee benefits instead of increasing dividends. "Because," he responded, "you and I don't know how to build cars, and they do!"

The situation is complicated by the fact that, in the overwhelming majority of business organizations today, managers and administrators are employees. They do not own the company but merely manage it for the stockholders. Senior managers may own stock—but so may production workers, secretaries, and janitors. Executives can be hired and fired like everyone else. The true employer is the board of directors elected by the stockholders to oversee the business. In community hospitals, school districts, public interest organizations, government agencies, or membership associations, of course, there is no question of management ownership.

A DANGEROUS ATTITUDE

It is easy, and perhaps all too common, to view employees as a cost in a line-item budget determining the price of a product or service. This attitude fosters the idea that the less an organization has to pay its employees, the lower the price of the product or service and, therefore, the more competitive the product or service can be in the marketplace.

This one-dimensional view of the labor force provided fertile soil for the tremendous growth of unions, which fought to have labor seen in a multidimensional view. Throughout the decades, unions forced their way into the smallest and largest companies. They won concessions on wages, safety, medical benefits, vacation, and retirement benefits, to mention just a few. Unions became as big as big business. Their influences are reflected in national and state laws as well as in volumes of judicial and regulatory decisions.

The 1980s, however, saw a tapering off of union influence. Union membership dropped; part of this drop is attributed to the significant population move from the unionized Northeast and Midwest to the Sunbelt, which has significantly fewer unions. The impact of foreign competition—foreign cars, for example—as well as the exporting of jobs to countries where labor is cheaper are two other trends that have an impact on the labor market.

Another major change in the employer-employee relationship is automation. The computer radically changes the role of the individual in many workplaces. The individual now competes with the robot for a place in the assembly line; in most instances the individual will lose the contest. If the computer and the robot take on most of the heavy work in the steel mill, most of the positions on the assembly line, and much of the information gathering and dissemination usually associated with general office work, what is left for the current and future individuals who would fill those jobs?

The trend is to a downsizing of the work force and to a service-oriented economy. This movement creates major reshuffling of jobs and people, with all the emotional stress attendant on such upheaval and readjustment. Layoffs and restructuring of organizations also weaken the loyalty of workers, which can affect morale and productivity. So can mergers and acquisitions.

During this significant time of transition, employer-employee relations change, but they are no less critical than in the past. Indeed, most people would argue that they are now more important than ever.

In a very real sense, frontline workers *are* the organization. They produce the product, provide the service, operate support systems, count the money, deal with customers, work with vendors—in short, the activities that make the organization function.

BENEFITS OF EMPLOYEE PARTICIPATION

Because they are accountable to the board—the real and legal seat of power in most organizations—executives have responsibility as "the employer." Others needed to carry out the operations become "the employees." Yet if there is one significant trend in successful organizations worldwide, it is the melding of interests and heightened cooperation between management and employees. Recognition of several benefits from a united effort has brought this "workplace democracy" about:

1. As the founder of Honda Motors puts it, just as cars are gauged by horsepower, so organizations can be gauged by mindpower. If only the CEO thinks about possible improvements, there is one mindpower. If only management, maybe 100–500 mindpower. But if everyone is encouraged to think about the company and his or her work in it, and then make suggestions, an organization can have 20,000 or more mindpower.

2. In a highly competitive economy, successful organizations are those that deliver customer delight. But customer delight depends on employee satisfaction; that is, dissatisfied employees are unlikely to delight customers, because their own irritations or feelings of abuse will get in the way. (The next time a retail clerk

fails to give you delightful service, remember that he or she is probably the lowest paid, least valued, least trained worker in the store—and most likely part-time to boot. Yet the retail industry expects such employees to conduct *the* most important job, serving customers.) Success involves *everyone*—those who make the policies, those who design and produce the product or service, the sales personnel, janitors who keep the premises attractive, secretaries who answer the phone, and so on.

3. To build trusting relationships with customers, shareholders, communities, government, and other stakeholder publics, organizations need to speak with One Clear Voice. Management cannot say one thing in official pronouncements from the ivory tower and then have employees telling another story to the people with whom they interact. Achieving one voice requires shared values, which arise when employees are encouraged to participate in organizational decision making.

The benefits of mutually satisfactory employee-employer relations are significant. There are fewer work stoppages, less absenteeism, higher productivity, and fewer errors. Sometimes the benefits are symbolized, as when the employees of Delta Air Lines gave the airline an airplane during tough economic times. In a similar case, the 480 employees of Piggly Wiggly Carolina, a Charleston, South Carolina, grocery store and distributing business, conceived and organized the $40,000 "Rig for the Pig" campaign. Ninety-eight percent of the employees participated, voluntarily contributing two days' pay. In the end, they raised $7,000 more than was needed to buy the tractor-trailer truck they gave to the company.

PUBLIC RELATIONS' ROLE

The public relations function, providing the communications channel between employers and employee groups, is important on both sides of the relationship. Practitioners are called on to participate more or less continuously in four phases of an employee's work experience:

- **The start.** For example, recruiting programs or help-wanted advertising, orientation sessions, tours, or kits of information.
- **On-the-job working conditions.** For example, employee publications, bulletin boards, feedback systems, training meetings, morale boosters, surveys of attitudes, complaint sessions, and teleconferencing.
- **Rewards and recognition.** For example, award programs, implementation of employee participation in civic affairs, staging of political science or economic education events, old-timers' parties, open houses, wage increases or bonuses, promotions, annual reports to employees, and so on.
- **Work stoppage or termination.** For example, communications in a strike, layoff, or boycott problem, news about benefits for retirees, a retiree publication, projects to help laid-off employees relocate, or exit interviews.

In carrying out duties related to these four phases, the public relations people are usually teamed up with the human resources department in a large organization. In small organizations, all the duties related to employee relations and communication may be vested in one functionary, public relations or personnel.

No matter who is assigned the duties, the responsibility is as communicator, interpreter, and persuader for the employer. The duties include feedback of employee opinion and ideas as a guide to management. So public relations practices are the fulcrum of a two-way relationship-building and communication system, and therefore must earn the trust of the employees.

RULES OF EFFECTIVE EMPLOYEE RELATIONS

Although there are a variety of tools available to accomplish employee-employer communications, five basic principles prevail as guidelines for the practitioner.

1. **Employees must be told first.** Employees should be the first to be told information affecting them and their jobs; they should be told directly by the employer. The relationship is adversely affected when employees learn from outside sources about matters that affect them. If this happens, two-way trust is jeopardized. As a practical matter, external sources cannot do as complete a job of informing employees as the employer can. The grapevine is one of the worst possible sources in the eyes of employees, even though it ranks as high as No. 2 in actuality, according to a recent survey. News media as a source are just as bad.

2. **Tell the bad news along with the good.** All too often, organizations exploit internal news channels to report only "good" news, usually complimentary to the employer. That practice wears thin. The tools and the messages lose credibility. Motives become suspect. Employees look to other sources, such as unions and the grapevine, for a more balanced, objective perspective. Revealing good and bad news, openly and candidly, builds trust, common purpose, and productivity.

3. **Ensure timeliness.** Information important to employees has the same obsolescence as news of other kinds. Getting it out fast and accurately builds dialogue and trust. Delay opens the door to sources with half-truths, distortions, and bias unfavorable to the employer. Delay is the cause of most rumors, and, once started, rumors are difficult to dislodge. The employer's task is to be the first and most reliable source for employees. To do or be otherwise puts, and keeps, an employer on the defensive with those on whom the organization depends most for its success.

4. **Employees must be informed on subjects they consider important.** Years of studying employees' views of communication within their organizations reveals specific items they want to know about—often quite different from what management thinks they want to know about (or *ought* to be told). The list has changed very little during the 30 years such research has been conducted. The chart in Table 3-1 summarizes biennial studies conducted in the 1980s (and updated in the 1990s) by the International Association of Business Communicators and Towers, Perrin, Forster & Crosby, a consulting firm specializing in internal relations (also known as the IABC-TPFC studies). Respondents were asked to rank subjects they want to read about on a scale of 1 to 10, with 1 being highest.

TABLE 3-1 Subjects of Interest to Employees Change Little	
Rank	*Subject*
1	Organizational plans for the future
2	Job advancement opportunities
3	Job-related "how-to" information
4	Productivity improvement
5	Personnel policies and practices
6	How we're doing vs. the competition
7	How my job fits into the organization
8	How external events affect my job
9	How profits are used
10	Financial results
11	Advertising and promotional plans
12	Operations outside of my department or division
13	Organizational stand on current issues
14	Personnel changes and promotions
15	Organizational community involvement
16	Human interest stories about other employees
17	Personal news (birthdays, anniversaries, and so on)

5. **Use the media that employees trust.** The IABC-TPFC Studies also replicate others in telling the sources from which workers want to receive information. In order, they are:
   1. Immediate supervisor
   2. Small group meetings
   3. Top executives
   4. Large group meetings
   5. Employee handbook or other booklets
   6. Orientation program
   7. Regular local employee publication
   8. Bulletin boards
   9. Annual report to employees
   10. Regular general employee publication
   11. Upward communication programs
   12. Audiovisual programs
   13. Union
   14. Mass media
   15. Grapevine

Employees were asked in the above study which were their *actual* information sources, as opposed to this listing of *preferred* sources. Two were far out of line: *grapevine,* last on the preferred source list, was ranked second as an actual source; *bulletin boards,* number eight in preference, in actuality ranked third.

Participants in a 1999 communications study by IABC and Watson Wyatt cite e-mail as the most frequently used communications tool now (90 percent). But it is not a magic communications pill, according to the study. It received a low (55 percent) effectiveness rating. Clutter is a factor in its ineffectiveness. Employees receive a significant number of e-mails each day, both business and personal. An organization cannot be sure its employees are really taking the time to process and understand their electronic messages.

Using a focused communication strategy that combines a mix of methods and tools brings the most success, finds the study. This mix includes in-person meetings, printed newsletters, intranets, open-door policies, and e-mail.

- Key strategy is face-to-face interchanges, with managers and supervisors seen as communication links first and foremost—not only from the top down and the bottom up but also laterally (between departments and work groups). Consequently public relations departments often must coach and train supervisors and managers in interpersonal communication skills.

FRONTLINE SUPERVISORS AS THE KEY COMMUNICATORS

The source employees most want to receive information from is their immediate or frontline supervisor—the most effective vehicle for communicating with employees, according to the previous list. Frontline supervisors are trusted and therefore more believable.

The communication process that passes information from top management down to employees through their immediate supervisors is sometimes called cascading meetings. It involves:

- Providing resources and training for frontline supervisors to relay information to their direct reports
- Giving supervisors advance notice and in-depth and meaningful information to share with employees
- Making subject matter experts available to immediately answer questions

This process helps relationship building within the management team. Supervisors get information in a timelier manner and feel more plugged into what's going on. And messages are delivered face-to-face to all employees in 24 hours using this process—which beats both the news media and the grapevine.

TRUST IS ESSENTIAL

Trust directly impacts an organization's success and profits.[1] It contributes to job satisfaction, which leads to effectiveness, financial strength, competitiveness, and productivity. Trust must start with initiatives from the top.

---

[1]According to a study by the International Association of Business Communicators, "Measuring Organizational Trust: A Diagnostic Survey & International Indicator." More information from 800/776-4222 or e-mail at service_center@iabc.com.

If we look at organizations realistically, it is apparent that the most important people are those at the bottom—the frontliners. They make the product, deliver the service, sell the goods, and provide essential support mechanisms. In short, they more than anyone *are* the organization.

If, as shown in the diagram, you draw a line above the frontline supervisors (whether called team leaders, managers, or whatever), everyone above the line is overhead. The top of the pyramid is cost, not income generating. Those positions exist to support what the frontliners do.

Therefore, if management wants to earn trust, it must acknowledge this, and then formulate policies and processes that prove and continually symbolize it to the frontliners.

There are six components of trust:

1. **Openness.** Good news and bad must be shared with employees or they may suspect secrecy and conspiracy. Divulge plans in a timely fashion explaining the "whys."
2. **Shared values.** Management must share its vision with all employees and encourage employees to offer theirs.
3. **Consistency of words and actions.** Consistent treatment of all employees as well as consistency between management's words and actions is needed.
4. **Appreciation.** Management must show appreciation for employees' commitment to the organization.
5. **Feedback.** Employees' input must be solicited and considered, allowing them to speak out with impunity. Often, trouble stems from executives believing theirs is the only workable way.
6. **Autonomy.** Management must give employees respect, allowing them to work independently and monitor their own performance without breathing down their necks.

COMMUNICATING THROUGH TECHNOLOGY: PROS AND CONS

The convenience and speed of technology make it an alluring communication medium, but it needs to be used wisely. Once awareness has been created—preferably by face-to-face communication where possible—technology (e-mail, Internet, and intranet sites) is useful for reinforcing the message.

TRUSTWORTHINESS NOW MEANS HOLDING BACK NOTHING

Public relations counselor Bruce Harrison advises in dealing with key publics such as employees, it's not enough to just communicate honestly. Organizations are finding that in order to foster trust, they must be entirely open and show all evidence, a method called "transparent communication." Organizations need to let constituents know,

- Here's how we're making the decision. Here are the facts that led us to make this decision.

- Here are the options. Let's look at them together so you can help us make the decision.

- We believe we're being forthright and candid but you judge for yourself. Here are the data. What do you think?

Intranets are one way to implement this strategy with employees. Minutes of meetings, policies, plans and strategies, financial results, and other data are posted there for any interested employee.

This type of policy is the key for any organization to be considered trustworthy today.

pr reporter Vol. 35 No. 36, September 21, 1992, p. 3.

The advantages of technology include a quick way to give and get feedback which shortens the communication cycle time, convenient information storage and retrieval, reduces communication costs, flattens corporate hierarchy when an employee with an idea or concern can share it directly with an individual (from a senior manager to an immediate supervisor) without having the message reviewed and filtered by others, and the ability to collaborate with others. It allows people on different floors, different time zones, and different continents to have immediate access to working documents and data.

On the negative side it's impersonal and increases the risk of dehumanizing relationships; it's generally done quickly, even impulsively, and thus increases the likelihood for misunderstanding; it's a pull medium which means the receiver must want it and seek it; information security is still a big concern for many; and often it is not *information mapped* (a visual layout that makes text easy to read and understand, reduces long paragraphic text to bite-sized chunks bulleted for easy scanning, and offers a source for more details).

The main impact of technology, as one pr firm CEO put it, is "speed without analysis, data without wise interpretation."[2]

---

[2]*pr reporter's* 30th Annual Survey of the Profession, Vol. 41 No. 38, September 28, 1998.

References and Additional Readings

Bailey, John, and Richard Bevan. "Employee Communication." Chapter 12 in *Lesly's Handbook of Public Relations and Communications.* 5th ed. Chicago, IL: NTC Business Books, 1998.

Barr, Stephen. "Smile! You're on Corporate TV." *Communication World* 8 (September 1991): 28–31.

Beer, Michael, Russell Eisenstat, and Bert Spector. "Why Change Programs Don't Produce Change." *Harvard Business Review* (November/December 1990): 158–166.

Brody, E. W. *Communicating for Survival.* New York: Praeger, 1987.

Casarez, Nicole B. "Electronic Mail and Employee Relations: Why Privacy Must Be Considered." *Public Relations Quarterly* 37 (Summer 1992): 37–40.

Cutlip, Scott, Allen Center, and Glen Broom. "Media for Internal Publics." Chapter 9 in *Effective Public Relations.* 8th ed. Upper Saddle River, NJ: Prentice Hall, 1999.

Davids, Meryl. "Labor Shortage Woes: How Practitioners Are Helping Companies Cope." *Public Relations Journal* 44 (November 1988).

Drucker, Peter. "The Responsible Worker." Chapter 21 in *Management: Tasks, Responsibilities, Practices.* New York: Harper and Row, 1974.

Herman, Roger, and Joyce Gioia. *How to Become an Employer of Choice.* Winchester, VA: Oakhill Press, 2000.

Holtz, Shel. *Public Relations on the Net.* New York: AMACOM, 1999.

Pfeffer, Jeffrey. *The Human Equation: Building Profits by Putting People First.* Boston, MA: Harvard Business School Press, January 1998.

pr reporter Special Report: A Probing Look at Employee Relations Today: How to Shape World-Class Internal Relationships and Communications. Exeter, NH: PR Publishing, 1998.

pr reporter Vol. 42 No. 29 (July 26, 1999). "'Are You Being Served?' Study Finds Employee Politeness Is Huge Determinant of Customer Loyalty, as PR Has Insisted."

pr reporter Vol. 42 No. 1 (January 4, 1999). "In an Era of Mistrust and Skepticism, Making Your Organization One People Can Trust Is the Ultimate Differentiator."

pr reporter Vol. 40 No. 15 (April 14, 1997). "The Psychology of Customer Delight: PR's Vital Role."

pr reporter Vol. 39 No. 34 (August 26, 1996). "Some Metrics on How Well Employee Participation Pays Off."

pr reporter Vol. 37 No. 21 (May 23, 1994). "Action Research Unites Staff and Management in Satisfying Customers."

pr reporter Vol. 36 No. 40 (October 11, 1993). "Communication, PR Ideas Drive Unique Re-Engineering Plan"—An outstanding case study that puts all the organizational trends together.

pr reporter Vol. 34 No. 49 (December 16, 1991). "PR's Role in Culture Change."

pr reporter Vol. 32 No. 34 (August 28, 1989). "Survey Finds Trust in Management Translates into Quality."

Skutski, Karl. "Conducting a Total Quality Communications Audit." *Public Relations Journal,* April 1992, 20–32.

Smith, Alvie. *Innovative Employee Communication: New Approaches to Improving Trust, Teamwork and Performance.* Upper Saddle River, NJ: Prentice Hall, 1991.

CASES

CASE 3-1 INVESTING IN EMPLOYEES PAYS OFF

Aaron Feuerstein, president of Malden Mills, celebrated his 70th birthday at a family party on the evening of December 11, 1995. At the same time, less than 30 miles away, his factory exploded into flames. By midnight, a company official summoned Feuerstein to the scene. At stake was the future of more than 3,000 employees and their families. What happened within the next 72 hours are the guts and the glory of this story.

Feuerstein and his management team needed effective crisis management and to tap into the company's reservoir of employee goodwill. In a business environment of layoffs, mergers, and downsizing, it was assumed that a fire of this magnitude would bring an end to an era for Malden Mills. But that was not the Feuerstein way of doing business, nor had it been in the 90 years since his grandfather began the business in the mill town of Lawrence, Massachusetts.

HISTORY OF THE MILL

Malden Mills is a family owned and operated mill situated on the riverbanks of Lawrence, Massachusetts. During the Industrial Revolution, the Merrimack River was home to many textile factories. Over the years, and as technology progressed, most of these mills were abandoned for areas with cheaper labor. Feuerstein, contrary to the trend of cutting labor costs to increase profits, moved into those empty mills. "It depends on your vision of business," was his comment.

FEUERSTEIN'S VISION OF BUSINESS: EMPLOYEES ARE ASSETS

Feuerstein is a devout Jew and his belief drives his decision making. A cornerstone of his thinking is a 2,000-year-old saying from the Jewish tradition: When everything is moral chaos, try your hardest to be a "mensch,"—a man of highest principles. Malden Mills has no board of directors or shareholders. Feuerstein answers to his own belief system, and its wisdom is apparent:

➤ In 1980, Malden Mills declared Chapter 11 bankruptcy and laid off workers. Research and development was aggressively pushed—making an investment in brand equity. Out of this came the discovery of the lightweight, resilient, wool-like fabrics under the brand names Polarfleece® and Polartec®. This put Malden Mills back in business. Feuerstein *hired back every worker* he had let go after the bankruptcy.

➤ Feuerstein knows the correlation between loyal employees and loyal customers. Customer retention at Malden Mills runs roughly 95 percent, which is world class.[1]

➤ Major retailers such as L.L. Bean, Eddie Bauer, Lands' End, Patagonia, and North Face carry the Malden Mills products not just as a picture in a catalog but with a history of the product and the company line itself.

➤ Malden Mills is a union shop and has long invested heavily in technology that eliminates jobs, but *has never had a strike.*

EMPLOYMENT AT THE MILL PRIOR TO DECEMBER 1995

Armed with new upscale product lines, Malden Mills flourished. Aaron Feuerstein, at the helm, geared up for plant expansion. Employees were happy with their wage and benefit package. An average employee received about $3 per hour more than at similar plants—with full benefits.[2] Employees were given annual bonuses in addition to other benefits. From 1982 to 1995, revenues in constant dollars more than tripled while workforces barely doubled.[3]

DECEMBER 11, 1995—THE NIGHT OF THE FIRE

Prior to the fire, the Malden Mills complex had nine functioning buildings. While the mills were poised to receive new and updated machinery, none of the current workforce was to be displaced. In a matter of hours, the fire leveled three of the nine buildings within the Malden Mills complex. A fourth was saved by the heroic efforts of employees and firefighters on the scene. No one was killed, however, 33 were injured. Some 1,800 of the 3,200 workers were temporarily displaced less than three weeks before Christmas.

DECEMBER 13, 1995—LESS THAN 48 HOURS LATER

In the local high school gymnasium, Feuerstein announced to his employees, and local and national media, that employee salaries and benefits, as well as holiday bonuses, would be paid. For 90 days the salaries of the displaced workers were paid; benefits continued for 6 months. He also assured them they would be called back to work. Plant reconstruction would begin immediately.

In repeated surveys, *the number 1 topic of interest to employees is organizational plans for the future.*[4] At Malden Mills, employees received this desired information. They knew where they stood and that they were a vital part of Feuerstein's decision to rebuild. He followed the four basic principles of employer-employee communications: (1) tell employees first, (2) tell the bad news along with the good, (3) ensure timeliness, and (4) inform employees on subjects they consider important.[5]

Media both lauded and mocked Feuerstein's decision. Was this man crazy? Or was he shrewd and calculating with a self-serving motive? In the days of massive

---

[1]Thomas Teal, "Not a Fool, Not a Saint," *Fortune,* November 11, 1996, Vol. 134 No. 9, pp. 201–203.
[2]Richard Jerome, "Holding the Line: After Fire Wrecked His Mill, Aaron Feuerstein Didn't Let His Workers Down," *People Weekly,* February 5, 1996, Vol. 45 No. 5.
[3]Teal, 201–203.
[4]See Chapter 3, page 41.
[5]See Chapter 3, page 40.

and cold-hearted downsizing—e.g., AT&T had experienced 44,000 layoffs and IBM had over 100,000 layoffs—why didn't this 70-year-old man take the money and run? Feuerstein's comment: "What kind of an ethic is it that a CEO is prepared to hurt 3,000 people who are his employees and an entire city of many more thousands . . . in order for him to have a short-term gain? It's unthinkable."

CORPORATE CONSCIENCE BRINGS FREE PUBLICITY

News of this event spread as quickly as the fire in the mills. Stories of his plans ran in many newspapers and magazines across the country. Feuerstein was invited to the 1996 Presidential State of the Union address. Post-fire publicity created an element of goodwill among consumers, increasing demand and building loyalty.

In 2001, aware of the goodwill generated by Feuerstein's actions, the Malden Mills story was presented in ads with Feuerstein as the spokesman surrounded by his employees.

THE PAYOFF

In the long run, Malden Mills' worldwide business grew 40 percent from pre-fire levels.[6] In less than two years, all but a handful of the original 1,800 displaced employees were back on the factory floor. "Customer and employee retention at Malden Mills runs roughly 95 percent."[7] The percentage of off-quality products went from 6 to 7 percent pre-fire to 2 percent post-fire.[8] Once the fourth plant, which wasn't completely destroyed in the fire, was up and running, Feuerstein walked among the employees. All present shared tears and thank yous. Employees promised to pay him back "tenfold." Before the fire, that plant produced 130,000 yards per week. After the fire, production increased to 200,000+ per week, clearly the result of employee goodwill. In the past decade, Malden Mills has grown 200 percent with sales over $300 million a year and customers in more than 50 countries.

To date, Malden Mills is a symbol of heroics. As one practitioner recently said, "I feel good wearing my Polartec jacket knowing how that man treats his employees." That kind of **customer loyalty is earned**, not sold.

The goodwill Malden Mills banked from the fire continued to pay dividends in late 2001 when the company sought bankruptcy protection. Lenders are not seeking to liquidate the company, which is an option available to creditors. Shaun Ambrose-Jones, chief executive of Dartex Coating, Inc., a supplier to Malden Mills, is optimistic and said, "They did the right thing by us at the time of the fire. I'm confident they'll use their best endeavors to support us again at this time." In December 2001, Aaron Feuerstein told the *Boston Globe,* "This chapter is merely one more hurdle on the road since the fire. That was a big hurdle and we got through it. This is a big hurdle, too, and we're going to overcome it. We're going to win." ■

---

[6]Julie K. Hall, "Malden Climbs Up From The Ashes," *Times Mirror Magazines, Inc.,* STN, Vol. 22, No. 2, p. 7.
[7]Teal, 201–203.
[8]Shelly Donald-Coolidge, "'Corporate Decency' Prevails at Malden Mills," *The Christian Science Monitor,* March 28, 1996.

QUESTIONS FOR DISCUSSION

1. Discuss the elements of an employee communications plan and how it impacted the decisions Feuerstein made.
2. What steps would have been taken had he decided not to re-build the factory?
3. How would the closing of the mills have impacted the branding that occurred after the fire?
4. If you were the public relations director, what would you have suggested be done differently?
5. What would you recommend be done to ensure continued high levels of employee satisfaction?

CASE 3-2   SOUTHWEST AIRLINES—WHERE FUN, LUV, AND PROFITS GO HAND-IN-HAND

Southwest Airlines is in business to make a profit, just as all the other airlines are, but its approach—making its customers happy—is what sets it apart. While this approach may not seem unusual in the highly competitive economy, its primary method of reaching it—through *employee* satisfaction—is innovative. By developing strong relationships with its employees, Southwest has pleased its customers and fueled its growth—from a three-destination, short-haul Texas airline to the fourth largest airline in the United States (in terms of passengers carried).

A TURBULENT BEGINNING

In 1966, Rollin King, a San Antonio entrepreneur who owned a small commuter service, and his banker, John Parker, noted how expensive and inconvenient it was to travel between Houston, Dallas, and San Antonio—all areas that were in the midst of strong economic and population growth. King approached Herb Kelleher, then one of his San Antonio lawyers, with an idea, and the three men researched the feasibility of the proposal.

By early 1967, Kelleher filed papers to incorporate Air Southwest Company. King and Kelleher raised the initial capital and political support for the venture. Kelleher was prepared for political and legal battles with established Texan Airlines, but he didn't realize the length to which they would have to go to get their planes in the air. Established airlines, contending that the market was saturated, filed lawsuits to stop Southwest, and a restraining order was granted. Southwest appealed the case to the Supreme Court of Texas and was granted a reprieve, only to be slapped with another suit. Four years later, after many restraining orders, appeals, and court cases, Southwest was finally able to take off. Unfortunately, most of its capital was gone, spent fighting for the chance to exist.

TIME TO FLY—WITH LIMITED RESOURCES

By the time it was ready to fly, Southwest had just four planes and fewer than 70 employees. The new airline was forced to set outrageously low rates—unheard of in the industry—to attract customers. Feeling threatened, the competition matched Southwest's fares, forcing the new airline to reduce prices even lower. At one point, Southwest management was unable to make payroll, and was forced to decide whether to lay employees off or sell a plane. In what was a turning point for the company that set a foundation for its future, management chose to put employees first. In return for not laying off a single employee, Southwest asked employees to master the "10-minute turn" so the airline could keep the same flight schedule it had planned with four airplanes. A plane would arrive at an airport, deliver passengers, refuel, and prepare the plane for departure of another flight—in 10 minutes.

> ➤ The faster the turnaround, the lower the operating costs, the more flights that can be achieved in one day, the lower the fare.
>
> ➤ This means employees must be exceptionally motivated.

An article in *Chief Executive Magazine*[1] points to this event as the foundation of Southwest's success. "The tradition of Southwest employees, from pilots to ramp agents, pitching in to do what's necessary to help the company, was born."

DISCOVERING THE KEY TO SUCCESS

From its earliest days the company has incorporated a focus on fun and love—for both passengers and employees—into its unique management style. Southwest flight attendants dress casually in khakis and polo shirts. Pilots wear WWII replica leather jackets. Comfortably dressed employees are happier and more relaxed which leads to happier and more relaxed passengers. Luv Nuts are served instead of meals on shorter flights, and have become a company symbol for fun in flight.

Passengers on a Southwest flight might hear flight safety instructions in the form of a song—sung by one of the flight attendants—if a particular employee feels like singing. One employee sang "Happy Birthday" to a passenger, Elvis style, over the public address system.[2] This relaxed and open working environment has encouraged customer service agents to hold holiest sock contests and encourage passengers to make faces at ground crews while waiting to board the plane.

This behavior may seem unprofessional to an employee of a traditional airline. But the employee who would look down on these antics is exactly the type of person Southwest does not want to hire. "We look for a sense of humor, a sense of service," says Colleen Barrett, president and chief operating officer and chairman Kelleher's right-hand woman. "We don't care if you're the best pilot in the USAF, but if you condescend to a secretary, you won't get hired."[3]

The positive corporate culture starts at the top at Southwest. Kelleher once heard that mechanics on the graveyard shift couldn't attend the company picnic, so he held a late-night barbecue, which featured him and pilots as chefs. Kelleher or Barrett personally send notes to employees for births, deaths, marriages, and promotions. And the generosity of management extends beyond employees to customers. Kelleher once read a letter from a teacher whose students had never been on a plane. He invited the entire class to fly to Austin for free for a tour of the capital.[4]

Southwest management firmly believes that employees who genuinely care about each other and the company take extra steps to ensure customer satisfaction. Along with the ideal of hard work, Southwest executives want employees to conduct business in a loving and understanding manner.

Southwest offers employees competitive wages and benefits, and was the first airline to offer a profit-sharing plan. Since the plan originated in 1974, employees now own 13 percent of the company's common

---

[1] *Chief Executive Magazine*, July 1, 1999.
[2] Patricia Kitchen, *Newsday*, March 7, 1999.
[3] *Chief Executive Magazine*, July 1, 1999.
[4] *Chief Executive Magazine*, July 1, 1999.

stock. The company contributes 16 percent of its pretax operating income to its profit-sharing plan.[5]

AN EDUCATED EMPLOYEE IS A VALUABLE TEAM MEMBER

The more employees know about their corporation, the better equipped they are to provide valuable input. To encourage a better understanding among employees of the various functions of the company, Southwest implemented the Walk a Mile program. Through the program, Southwest employees experience issues of other departments, which facilitates a company-wide understanding of the many airline functions, and what it takes to be profitable. This encourages effective communication and real teamwork, which is especially important among pilots and ground and flight operations.

Culture Committee, formed in 1990, aims to continually reinforce the "Southwest Spirit." With representatives from all areas of the company, from flight crews to executives, committee members promote the ideals of profitability, low cost, family, and fun.

BEHAVIOR AFFECTS THE BOTTOM LINE

All of these behaviors may satisfy employees and make great material for news articles. But when it comes to the bottom line, does this dynamic management style motivate employee behaviors that really pay off for Southwest? After all, the company is in business to make a profit.

> ➤ *Southwest posted seven consecutive years of record profits.*

In the early 1990s when most airlines suffered losses, Southwest was one of the only profitable airlines. The airline won the U.S. Department of Transportation's "Triple Crown" awards for best on-time performance, fewest customer complaints, and fewest mishandled bags. It has maintained the best cumulative baggage handling record among all major U.S. airlines since September 1987 when the Department of Transportation began tracking and reporting these statistics. In addition, Southwest:[6]

➤ Was profitable for 28 consecutive years, a period which included two major industry downturns

➤ Has the most enviable profit record in the industry, with the smallest number of employees per aircraft and the most customers served per employee

➤ Has been recognized by *Fortune* magazine in its annual "Best 100 Companies to Work For" list (1 in 1998; 4 in 1999; 2 in 2000; 4 in 2001)

➤ Received over 216,000 resumes in 2000; hired 5,134 new employees, bringing the total number of employees to over 30,000

➤ Planes have a turnaround of approximately 20 minutes, even with today's airline growth, carry-on luggage, and airport congestion

➤ Is ranked first in fewest customer complaints for the last nine consecutive years.

Southwest's focus on employee satisfaction has enabled it to deliver on customer satisfaction and, as a result, excel in an increasingly competitive industry. ■

---

[5]*Chief Executive Magazine*, July 1, 1999.
[6]Patricia Kitchen, *Newsday*, March 7, 1999.

THE MISSION OF SOUTHWEST AIRLINES

The mission of Southwest Airlines is dedication to the highest quality of Customer Service delivered with a sense of warmth, friendliness, individual pride, and Company Spirit.

TO OUR EMPLOYEES

We are committed to provide our Employees a stable work environment with equal opportunity for learning and personal growth. Creativity and innovation are encouraged for improving the effectiveness of Southwest Airlines. Above all, Employees will be provided the same concern, respect, and caring attitude within the organization that they are expected to share externally with every Southwest Customer.

QUESTIONS FOR DISCUSSION

1. In a tight labor market, it can be tough to find experienced employees—let alone ones that are willing to incorporate love and fun into their jobs. As manager of employee communications for Southwest, you are asked by the director of human resources to develop a recruiting plan using existing employees. What are some strategies you might suggest?
2. How would you handle this situation? You are working late one evening in Southwest's media relations office and receive a phone call from the police. It appears two Southwest employees were robbed on airport grounds. How will you respond to:

   ➤ Reporters questioning the company's ground security?
   ➤ Employees' concerns with safety?
   ➤ Calls for information from the victims' families?

CASE 3-3   A CLASSIC: MOTOROLA'S QUEST FOR QUALITY*

Whether it is called total quality management (TQM), continuous quality improvement, customer satisfaction, employee involvement/empowerment/engagement, or some other moniker, efforts to improve productivity and customer satisfaction are here to stay—key factors in global competitiveness.

➤ The basic premise is that when management pushes key decision making down to frontline workers, creates work teams, and tracks quality, employees gain pride in their work and customers get better products and services.

TQM and its spin-offs are based largely on basic public relations fundamentals such as customer satisfaction, employee participation, and maximum communication. It is critical that public relations practitioners understand the implications of the quality issue—and be able to speak the language of quality in order to serve their companies and clients more effectively.

This classic case discusses the efforts of Motorola's corporate public relations staff to support the company's introduction of a quality program, as well as its own internal department efforts to measure and enhance quality.

TQM'S BEGINNINGS AT MOTOROLA RESPOND TO COMPETITION

Motorola, a multinational manufacturer of everything from cellular telephones to semi-conductors for missile-guidance systems, had enjoyed robust sales, riding the explosive growth in high-tech electronics. But, like many other U.S. companies, Motorola woke up in the late 1970s to the inroads Japanese competition was making into world markets. Though Japanese brands were attracting increasing numbers of customers, Motorola didn't get serious about a response until the manager of the best-performing division in the company announced at an officers meeting, "Our quality levels really stink."

In looking for a solution, management toured factories of other companies around the world. They found Japanese plants where quality performance was a thousand times better than Motorola's. The Japanese, who had embraced the concept of total quality management (see *Primer of TQM Terms*, page 61), had structured their operations to achieve zero defects, on the basis of a do-it-right-the-first-time ethic. Motorola's chairman observed that "quality [is] like a religion over there . . . It's a whole different sense of urgency." It became clear that Motorola would have to make a quantum leap in quality if it was to compete successfully with Japan and other Pacific Rim countries.

At the same time, Motorola also saw that eventually Japan would have to open up its domestic market, previously closed to most U.S. goods, or suffer serious trade consequences. Identifying Japan's competitiveness

---

*We thank Chuck Sengstock, Fellow PRSA, former Director of Corporate Public Relations at Motorola Inc., for the wealth of information he provided for this case.

as an issue and showing that Motorola products could hold up to Japanese scrutiny became an aspect of the company's efforts to improve quality. By focusing on selling one specific product (pagers) to one company (Nippon Telephone & Telegraph), Motorola was able within a few years to open Japan's trade doors to become that company's only non-Japanese supplier. In fact, at one point Motorola was the leading supplier of pagers for Nippon Telephone & Telegraph among three competitors, all Japanese.

This success spawned additional successes. For example, the Japanese Space Agency was so impressed with the reliability of Motorola equipment used in NASA space shots that it specified Motorola equipment for use on many of its own space missions. Then, a Japanese national who was the first woman ever to climb Mt. Everest used a Motorola FM portable two-way radio to help guide her to the top—despite having plenty of Japanese radios to choose from. Markets in semiconductors and cellular telephones have also been opened through Motorola's efforts.

"MEETING JAPAN'S CHALLENGE"

Motorola believed that telling this story was important, not only to enhance its own reputation for quality, but also to sound a note of encouragement to other American companies whose self-confidence had been undermined by Japanese successes in consumer electronics, automobiles, steel, and a growing number of other industries. Further, by identifying the issue of opening up Japan to American manufacturers as an emerging issue, Motorola saw an opportunity to distinguish itself and ride an issue to its crest. (See Chapter 8 for a discussion of dealing with emerging issues.)

To explain its successful efforts to compete with Japan, Motorola invested in a major campaign called "Meeting Japan's Challenge." The campaign, which ran over four years, was designed to reach opinion leaders in business and government, particularly key executives in customer and prospect firms who might be actual purchasers or influence the purchase of Motorola products. As a collateral objective it also was designed to reach investors.

But first, employees had to be persuaded they could and should push themselves to deliver total quality.

The external strategy focused on dispelling the then-common American business notion of the Japanese as supermen—and showing how companies like Motorola were not only holding their own, but innovating and leading. The message was: America need not become a permanent weakling in foreign trade. It could compete effectively with Japan, if the rules were fair and U.S. companies had access to Japanese markets. Public opinion to the contrary, it could be a "win-win" situation. Instead of being trade enemies, Japan and the United States could become each other's customers, suppliers, and constructive competitors.

The campaign included efforts on five fronts: internal communications, advertising, media relations, government relations, and Japanese business development.

> ➤ A series of 22 advertisements ran in leading U.S. business magazines and newspapers (See Figure 3-1) with the key theme "Quality and productivity through employee participation in management."
>
> ➤ Editorial briefings and interviews were held with major media.
>
> ➤ Background papers called "Viewpoints" were developed on productivity, quality, and other topics.
>
> ➤ Talks given by Motorola executives at scores of forums with key

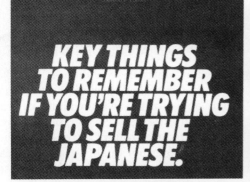

FIGURE 3-1 Sample advertisements from the "Meeting Japan's Challenge" series, which Motorola produced to reach opinion leaders in business and government.

(Courtesy of Motorola Inc.)

audiences were followed by merchandising of vest-pocket speech reprints.

➤ Weekly newspapers throughout the country received preprinted news fillers on relevant topics.

➤ Simultaneously, the program sought to place U.S.-Japan trade issues high on the agenda of policy makers through lobbying, testimony in Congress, personal visits to executives of other corporations, and direct lobbying in Japan.

➤ Internally, a film on "Meeting Japan's Challenge" was shown at all plants in the United States. A booklet with reprints of the ad series was distributed. Feature stories appeared in factory publications. Banners, buttons, T-shirts, and hats reading "Meet the Challenge" were distributed.

What were the results? Motorola moved from a major but self-effacing Midwestern manufacturer of technical products to a higher profile company identified as a major voice on the trade issue. Audience research showed that the campaign had been instrumental in triggering changes in the American public's attitude toward the Japanese industrial complex. Ninety-one percent of journalists queried felt that Motorola was associated with quality more than any other attribute. In 1994, Motorola was named the sixth most admired company in the United States according to a *Fortune* 500 report.

A more important result was that employees responded positively, developing pride and confidence in their employer as well as an understanding about what it takes to win in a tough marketplace.

WINNING THE MALCOLM BALDRIGE NATIONAL QUALITY AWARD

Motorola then decided to up the ante by going for zero defects. The company estimated that the cost of *not* having zero defects was at least $800 million a year. For the next several years, Motorola engaged in a campaign to achieve "Six Sigma," a total-quality term meaning achieving quality 99.9997 percent of the time—equivalent to just 3.4 defects per million opportunities! The goal was not to simply manufacture flawless products but to measure and eliminate defects throughout the organization, in everything from clerical output and delivery schedules to managerial decisions and production of the annual report.

To get employees excited about the concept, the company introduced another company-wide education campaign that included videotapes, Six Sigma posters in every office, and a course on "Understanding Six Sigma" that was required for every employee and tailored for each division. Executive perfor-

mance reviews and bonus incentives were tied to Six Sigma requirements. The result was that Motorola in 1988 won one of the first U.S. Commerce Department's Malcolm Baldrige National Quality Awards, named after the former Secretary of Commerce (See Figure 3-2).

The Corporate Public Relations staff played an important role in preparing the Baldrige Award application. They collected all the information, which was essentially in technical language or quality program jargon. They rewrote the entire application to give it continuity and punch. To prepare for the possibility of winning, they developed a contingency plan that included using an outside public relations firm to help implement internal and external communications.

QUALITY AS A CULTURE MEASURE

Soon after Motorola won, thousands of their suppliers were asked to pledge that they, too, would apply for the award within five years. Those refusing to sign the pledge were dropped from the rolls of qualified suppliers unless they did not qualify as an applicant because of size or other exclusions. Motorola's real intent was to make the Baldrige Award less a prize to be won than a *process* for inculcating *excellence in a corporate culture*. To help suppliers get started with quality, Motorola offers training at nominal fees in both basic and advanced quality techniques at Motorola University, the company's internal education and training center. Motorola also has a supplier certification program that ranks the supplier on the basis of total quality delivery.

"QUALITY DAY"

Though the Baldrige Award has become the country's most coveted and competitive prize, few knew about it when Motorola

MALCOLM BALDRIGE AWARD CRITERIA

Applicants are judged on seven criteria:

1. Leadership
2. Information and analysis
3. Strategic quality planning
4. Human resources utilization
5. Quality assurance of products and services
6. Quality results
7. Customer satisfaction

This constitutes a *systems approach* to managing for quality—an attempt to identify and work on all elements that impact it.

FIGURE 3-2   Thought by many to be the Super Bowl trophy of American business, awards in three categories of industry (manufacturing, service, and small business) are made annually out of a pool of thousands of applicants. Many companies spend vast amounts of time and money completing the complicated application and preparing for a grueling site visit. Pictured here is Motorola's award.

(Courtesy of Motorola, Inc.)

won. To publicize the achievement, Motorola held a "Quality Day" in 89 locations around the world, involving more than 100,000 employees. At each Quality Day event, a congressperson, senator, or governor attended, or an ambassador or foreign consul in overseas locations. Baldrige Award flags were distributed at every plant, along with brochures, videos, speeches for plant managers, pennants, and mugs (See Figure 3-3).

APPLYING TQM TO THE PRACTICE OF PR

Every department at Motorola was given the challenge of establishing some quantitative measures to demonstrate its achievements. Total quality methodologies work for many units but are not easily assimilated into the everyday tasks of creative, often reactive, departments such as public relations and communications. They tend to work best with more production-oriented tasks such as marketing communications or product publicity (data or catalog sheets, newsletters, and product news releases). For example, the zero defects method was used by the marketing department to measure just about anything that could be quantified—errors in photography or pricing, and grammar in brochures and press releases.

CYCLE TIME REDUCTION (CTR)

In cases where statistical techniques were too clumsy or required too much time and effort, or where the products or services

FIGURE 3-3   Motorola's "Quality Day" held at 89 locations around the globe helped to publicize the importance of winning one of the first Malcolm Baldrige Awards. Under the terms of the program, companies that win the award are required to promote it.

were nonstandard and nonrepetitive, cycle time reduction was used as a measure. This concept essentially means that the less time it takes to perform tasks, the more productivity is achieved. Although it is primarily a manufacturing term, *cycle time* can be applied to many tasks.

Motorola's Patent, Copyright, and Trademark Department, for example, has used the cycle time reduction process to analyze the patent applications function at Motorola and to identify ways it could be shortened. The result has been the elimination of bottlenecks and redundant approvals. Using CTR, the Law Department implemented a program for alternative dispute resolution as an option to costly litigation.

Cycle time reduction can also work in other administrative areas. For example, in 1989 it took Motorola six business days to close the books at the end of the year. A team of accountants from Corporate Finance began mapping the consolidation function and determining how to speed up the process. At the end of 1992, Motorola closed the books in four days, with less overtime than previously was used to close them in six days. The Finance Department has improved quality in its area—*and* reduced cost by $233,000 a year. This process has had an impact on accounting operations worldwide. By the end of 1992, Motorola estimated that throughout the entire company, it had saved up to $20 million a year by going from a six-day to a four-day close. The next goal was to achieve a three-day close.

THE "VALUE-ADDED YARDSTICK"

Another part of cycle time reduction is the elimination of activities that are redundant, nonessential, or do not add value. As an example, transmitting copy for a publication directly to a typesetter from a computer ter-

minal saves at least one whole keystroking operation, thereby saving time and money as well as eliminating potential errors. In 1993, Motorola reduced quarterly report production time from 10 days to 3 days by using the same copy for the printed report as was used in the news release. Though using the same copy for these two vehicles may seem inappropriate, this practice has been successful in addressing the two different audiences. Additionally, it saves one whole approval cycle.

Complex projects or processes such as product introductions, special events, and major publications may have to be mapped or diagrammed for analysis (See Figure 3-4). This process reveals that there are many smaller tasks within the larger task, many of which are unessential or do not add value (e.g. non-essential approvals and reviews, multiple proofreadings, waiting for phone calls to be returned, waiting for meetings, waiting for a document that's stuck in someone's in-basket).

MOTOROLA AND QUALITY TODAY

Though quality has become institutionalized at Motorola, one way it keeps enthusiasm and visibility high is through an annual competition among Total Customer Satisfaction teams. In 1990, the first year of the championships, nearly 2,000 teams from Motorola sites throughout the world competed. The challenge is to take a problem the team has been dealing with and try to solve it with the target of improving satisfaction for either internal or external customers. The final competition is judged by the company's most senior managers (CEO, president, and so on), who use specific criteria. The top 20–24 teams in the championship make presentations and compete for gold and silver medals.

Press Response Procedure

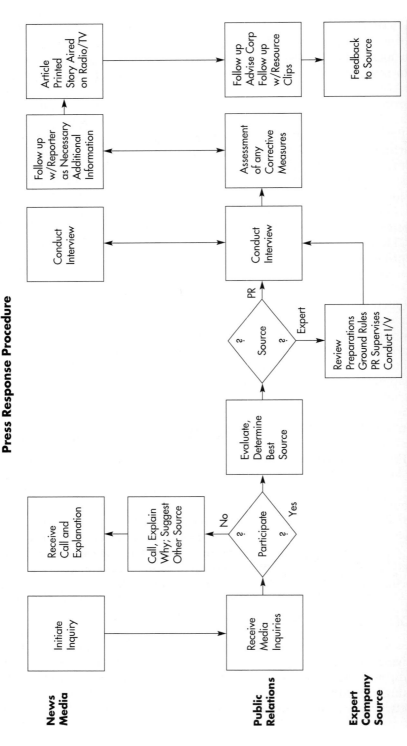

FIGURE 3-4 Sample mapping diagrams show how a process can be analyzed to modify or eliminate unnecessary steps. The procedure for producing and issuing a press release, for example, shows the pr director reviewing the release twice. If one review is eliminated, the process can be speeded up. A second area that can be accelerated is preparing the photo caption. Without any change, the photo caption writing and approval process can be run parallel to the news release process, ultimately saving time.

WHAT TQM HAS BORROWED FROM PR

As pointed out in the introduction to this case, many of TQM's premises are based on the same principles as public relations: customer satisfaction, participation, and communication. In fact, as many organizations began in the 1990s to question the value of TQM as an overly process-oriented management tool, public relations helped salvage the core values of TQM. Public relations still has a role in promoting the essential elements of TQM, such as facilitating continuous communication while leading employees through the typical four stages of quality programs: (1) enthusiasm, (2) frustration and discouragement, (3) exhilaration, and (4) satisfaction.

An Emst & Young report on Best Practices that affect performance regardless of the management program identified three factors that have a universally significant impact on worker performance: (1) process improvement methods, (2) supplier certification programs, and (3) deploying the strategic plan. Clearly, public relations has a role in building widespread understanding of and support for all three, both inside and outside the organization.

PRIMER OF TQM TERMS

This list should suggest why internal communications are vital. In our rapidly changing world, employees and managers are continually bombarded with new approaches and new language that they *must understand* to be effective in their jobs.

> **W. Edwards Deming.** American management consultant who in the 1950s worked in Japan; his fourteen points of management are considered largely responsible for Japanese industry's

post-World War II recovery and rise to dominance in world markets.

Statistical process control (SPC). A variety of techniques used to identify quality problems and root causes for them, such as pareto charts, histograms, and the like.

Cycle time reduction (CTR). Efforts to reduce time spent on tasks so that the process is completed in less time.

Benchmarking. Comparing one's own efforts against those of the best; usually done to identify best-in-class performance for a process (e.g., invoice processing, on-time delivery, manufacturing processes, supervisory communication, community relations activities).

Zero defects. Eliminating errors, a goal of many quality programs.

Customer delight. It is no longer enough to satisfy customers—they must be delighted.

WHY QUALITY AND OTHER IMPROVEMENT PROGRAMS FAIL

Since World War II, U.S. managers have latched onto over 50 programs like TQM, making them into fads that blossom and fade. PR departments are usually expected to get workers involved and excited.

Though some organizations continue on the quality bandwagon, growing doubt and uncertainty became apparent in the 1990s. Florida Power & Light, the first non-Japanese company to win the prestigious Deming Prize, dismantled its quality program, claiming the bureaucracy and paperwork were detracting attention from customer service. McKinsey & Co., a management consulting firm, conducted a study of quality programs in the United States and Europe that showed as many as two-thirds were stalling, failing, or being dropped.

Numerous other studies showed that quality programs failed to have a significant impact on either reducing defects or improving competitiveness.

Though the basic principles of improvement programs are usually sound, implementation is often flawed. This list of problems demonstrates how difficult—and yet how vital—sophisticated employee relations programs are today in engaging workers to meet the challenges of global competitiveness.

1. **American executives have short attention spans,** and as *Newsweek* magazine reported, management plans often have the "shelf life of cottage cheese." Like many other management trends (management-by-objectives, zero-based budgeting, excellence, one-minute managing), TQM was often treated as just another managerial fad without the commitment to follow through.

2. **Many improvement programs are generic,** canned, or inappropriate for American organizations. One size does *not* fit all.

3. **The emphasis on process** (statistical measurement, meeting quotas, charting, graphing, indicator reviewing) can become a "whipping boy" and divert attention from the primary focus of all these efforts—which is customer service.

4. **Oftentimes top management gives lip service but fails to act as role models.** Or, after their enthusiasm wanes, they delegate responsibility and soon a bureaucracy develops—TQM had quality directors, quality councils, quality departments, quality committees, and so on.

5. **Middle managers can feel disenfranchised or fearful of losing their role,** which can derail efforts to enhance greater employee participation. The transformation from autocrats to "coaches" is not easy, yet almost every improvement program demands it.

6. **Sometimes work teams aren't connected** by any coordinating strategy or mechanism, creating islands of improvement without bridges.

7. **In many companies, rewards are still tied to the bottom line,** not to quality work—or individuals are rewarded, rather than the teams on which the improvement process is usually based.

8. **Some organizations treat improvement efforts as just a *program,*** doing it for marketing purposes rather than because a focus on quality is the right thing to do for customers. Quality and customer satisfaction have to be the goals, not just slogans.

ONE SIDE-EFFECT OF RECENT IMPROVEMENT PROGRAMS: DOWNSIZING

As the economy fluctuates and organizations speed up their quest to stay competitive, so too changes the face of business. Therein lie the opportunities for public relations practitioners. The days of the colossal company are disappearing, and many organizations must pare down their workforce to produce quality work eliminating unneeded tasks. This new trend comes under many names—downsizing, reengineering, or right-sizing.

Reengineering (another short-lived managerial fad) attempted to combine these basic virtues:

➤ Zero-based restructuring: How would we do things if we were starting this organization from scratch?

➤ Among employees, it encourages cooperation instead of turfing, individual decision-making responsibility, and self-managing work teams.

➤ Its stimulus is the renewed drive to increase productivity. People need to work smarter not harder.

➤ Emphasizes keeping people broadly trained instead of narrow specialists, to greater facilitate productivity.

➤ Takes most of the good ideas of preceding fads and gives them unified application.

➤ It attempts to achieve the original goal of organizational redesign, QWL (quality of work life).

Downsizing—laying off workers to cut costs or because they're no longer needed—is a major employee relations challenge. ∎

QUESTIONS FOR DISCUSSION

1. Note how much farther a program like total quality management goes than mere employee newsletters. Does this suggest that the need for such standard communication vehicles will diminish, or maybe even die out?

2. In a zero-defects culture such as a TQM program, how do you create an atmosphere in which people feel it's ok to take risks (i.e., make mistakes) and at the same time feel the pressure to deliver perfection? What is the public relations role in resolving this conflict?

3. List all the instances in this case where public relations could have played a role, whether or not it actually did.

4. Bridging between principles and applications, which of the seven common denominators, or characteristics, to be found in almost all public relations programs (listed in Chapter 1) are clearly evident in this case? Are not evident?

5. Outline the interplay between external communication efforts and internal communications in this case. Did they affect each other? How?

CASE 3-4 KODAK'S SNAPSHOTS

The early 1990s were troubled times for Kodak. Pressed by changing technologies, international competition, and fickle consumer behavior, the Rochester, New York-based photo giant found itself struggling to maintain its legendary leadership in consumer photography.

In 1993, Kodak hired CEO George Fisher to lead a turnaround. He and his management team undertook an aggressive campaign to make Kodak more competitive and performance-driven. The backbone of this campaign was a "one-on-one" communication strategy designed to increase morale and productivity.

Kodak developed this strategy of speaking one-on-one with its 100,000 employees around the globe to resolve a problem it uncovered in late 1994: Employees were unclear about what was expected of them and their business units during a time of rapid change.

Though Fisher got broad employee approval, opinion surveys showed employees were confused and unable to see the big picture. "It's obviously difficult to build a performance-based culture if we fail to share expectations for performance with those charged with delivering the results," Fisher said.

As a result, the decision was made that managers and supervisors throughout the organization would meet quarterly with their work groups for a face-to-face briefing. Corporate performance information—including financial results as well as customer and employee satisfaction—would be communicated, providing a context for local unit information. It would also provide opportunities to educate employees and

managers about significant business news and key performance indicators. The proposal was endorsed and rolled out a month later. In 2001, the *Snapshots* program continues to bring supervisors and/or managers together with employees for regular face-to-face communication.

RESEARCH ON THE IMPORTANCE OF ONE-TO-ONE COMMUNICATION

1. Kodak best practices research shows **employees prefer direct interaction with supervisors.** This interaction also significantly increases understanding and reinforces the leadership responsibility of supervisors.
2. Employee surveys revealed skepticism and lack of confidence in Kodak managers—indicating a pressing need to build their credibility both as messengers of company information and leaders guiding the direction of change.
3. Two-thirds of production, technical, and clerical employees relied on outside sources like local news reports for company information. The leading sources for professional employees were supervisors and the company newspaper.
4. The communication rollout of major benefit reductions in the fall of 1994 was an important test of the face-to-face approach. For the first time, Kodak used direct management conversations to reach all U.S. employees with this news.
5. Post roll-out surveys of nearly 3,000 employees showed 84 percent felt the

meetings were a good way to communicate this information, and 74 percent understood why the changes were being made. Just as important, the process helped put a face on local leadership throughout the company.

OBJECTIVES OF THE "SNAPSHOTS" PROGRAM

1. **Establish a communication infrastructure** that helps employees see the "big picture" in a way that (1) fosters management credibility and (2) mitigates negative surprises.
2. Enable employees to understand Kodak performance expectations and act to achieve company objectives.
3. Clarify corporate and unit goals by answering "What does this mean to me?" and "What actions should I take?"
4. Stimulate regular, two-way communication between supervisors and employees.

HOW IT'S DONE

1. **A cross-disciplinary team**—including employee communication, human resources, finance, corporate research, and representative business units—develops the information to be put into the system.
2. **This team assembles the Snapshots package** for managers worldwide, which includes briefing charts and bullet-point scripts. In recent years, more effort has been placed on providing a "news" section along with the standard measures each quarter. This section includes topics of worldwide interest and impact, such as Kodak's consumer digital strategy, introduction of Kodak's new president, and an update on Kodak's online services business.
3. **Quick cycle time is a priority,** so briefing packages are prepared and approved within two days of receiving quarterly performance measures. The package is posted on the company's intranet, which is a big time and cost saver, eliminating all out-of-pocket costs for the corporate package.
4. **Grassroots pull** is created by "watch-for" messages in Kodak's employee media.
5. **Managers and supervisors are expected to meet face-to-face with employees** to present Snapshots information—but they are given a high degree of discretion in how they choose to do this.

RESULTS

Evaluation is built into the process, including quarterly attendance reports and post-meeting employee opinion surveys. Key findings have included:

1. **Attendance at voluntary briefings** increased from 57 to 81 percent in the first year. At many sites it approached 100 percent. These gains are a vote of confidence in the program. In 1999, five years into the program, 88 percent of employees attended a Snapshots session regularly or occasionally.
2. **Communication survey results** have been strongly positive. Employees agreeing Snapshots "helped me understand the company better" jumped from 71 percent in the first quarter to 81 percent in the fourth quarter. In 1999, 80 percent said the meetings provided useful information about the company's performance and 70 percent said the meetings helped them understand how successful Kodak is in meeting its goals.
3. **Opinion surveys** tracked gains in employee confidence in Kodak

management. Employees agreeing "Kodak is well managed" jumped from 29 percent in 1994 to 49 percent at the end of 1995—a 20 percent increase. At Kodak Park, the principal manufacturing center, where attendance is among the highest in the company, the increase was 23 percent.

Going forward, one of Kodak's biggest opportunities for communicating internally is to develop some adjunct training or orientation for managers and supervisors who are the presenters, to explain their role in gathering, presenting, and discussing local information. Given feedback received from internal research, employees want to understand more about their unit's role and performance. This tailoring of the package, however, must be done at the local level. Regardless how this program evolves, Snapshot's greatest significance is that it establishes a **permanent infrastructure for regular face-to-face communication between managers and employees.** ■

QUESTIONS FOR DISCUSSION

1. In today's "wired" world, why is face-to-face communication a better option than a broadcast e-mail, fax, or voice mail?
2. How does effective communication affect morale?
3. How can a communication program address problems created by falling stock prices, dwindling market share, and even layoffs?
4. Do you see a correlation between the attendance at the Kodak briefings and the people who say they have a better understanding of the company?
5. How would you prepare supervisors to better communicate with those reporting to them?

PROBLEM 3-A What Price "Good" Employee Relations?

Safeplay, Inc., has competed in the sports and recreation equipment market for more than twenty-five years. The market is hotly contested.

One of the programs for employee morale and productivity long used by Safeplay has been the retention of former athletes of national repute on its payroll at each of its five manufacturing plants. Although the athletes are part of the personnel department staff, they are made available by the public relations department for news interviews, to conduct sports clinics at schools, and to sit on committees for newsworthy civic events.

One of the Safeplay plants is located in the small city of Westward, which has a population of 20,000 and is located on the outskirts of a metropolitan city. This plant, with an average of 900 employees, specializes in leather items such as baseball gloves, golf gloves, basketballs, footballs, soccer balls, and leather carrying bags for sports clothing.

This plant has a former professional baseball star on the payroll as an assistant personnel manager. He is good copy on occasion, can speak with authority about the products, and directs a recreation program for employees.

A Tolerant Attitude

At Safeplay plants and in sales offices, there is some pilferage of products by employees. There is a company policy that any employee removing company property from the premises without authorization is subject to dismissal. So far this policy has never been invoked where products are concerned. The unspoken attitude of management is much the same as exists in many consumer product companies, particularly those that make food, confections, or inexpensive clothing items. It is tolerant, treats it quietly as a minor cost written into the price of products, and looks the other way rather than confront employees, with the risk of possible repercussions if someone is falsely accused. Put another way, management reluctantly concludes that the cost of a baseball mitt taken home in a lunch pail or paper bag to a kid on occasion is not high if employee turnover is low and working enthusiasm is high.

As a means of trying to discourage pilferage, Safeplay offers employees a discount on any products they buy from the store in the personnel office, and on the tenth birthday of any employee's child the employee can select any product priced under $20 and take it home free.

Tolerance Abused

Recently, however, the "mysterious disappearance" of sports items has gone beyond the boundaries of normal pilferage and management tolerance. Whole containers of items in the stockroom and in the shipping area have disappeared. Inventory records have apparently been doctored.

Obviously distressed, the home office has sent in a private detective agency. The agency's preliminary investigation and analysis are disturbing. It appears that there is an organized thievery ring involving as many as twenty-five of the Westward plant's employees. It appears, also, that the former athletic star on the payroll is somehow involved, but to what extent is not clear. Someone on the inside, not yet identified, deals with an outside "fence," and someone else on the inside, also not yet identified, handles the payoff to all the cooperating employees. Some of the involved employees are members of the union, and some are in the office "white-collar" jobs.

The Decision Process

At an executive decision-making meeting, you, as director of public relations, have been called in, along with the director of personnel and a company lawyer from the home office. The three of you have been asked to assess the repercussions if the town's police are called in and legal action is taken. You are asked to offer any other resolution that would "better serve the interests of all involved."

The lawyer says that as soon as an airtight case can be accumulated, including photographs and eyewitness accounts of products being removed, being transported to a "fence," and an actual money transaction completed, she favors appropriate law enforcement action and legal redress against those involved.

The personnel manager prefers, he says, to bring charges only against the leader or leaders inside and all those involved on the outside. He prefers to handle the cooperating employees individually, possibly allowing some sort of plea bargaining to keep the employees the company considers of real value on the payroll. He feels this approach will adequately frighten all employees, halt the activity, and avoid having to replace some trained and competent employees.

It is your turn to speak, using whatever notes you have taken while the others stated their positions. What is your view, taking into account the impact not only on internal relations, but on other publics directly or indirectly involved—including families of employees involved, neighbors, and the community generally, local law enforcement, news media in the trade, the Westward community, and shareholders of Safeplay, Inc.? Are there others?

What actions, and in what sequence, would you propose and why?

How would you deal with the recommendations of the lawyer and the personnel manager without setting up an adversary situation?

PROBLEM 3-B Keeping Merger Havoc at Bay

You are the vice president of public relations for a computer manufacturing company. The CEO called you and the vice president of human resources in for a meeting. Your company is planning to merge with another computer manufacturer.

You are aware of the havoc mergers inflict on employees. You also know that unhappy, disgruntled employees don't perform their tasks as well, can damage customer relationships, and can ultimately wreak havoc on a company's profits. You are worried about how to present this merger to the employees.

Communication with employees currently is done through an intranet site called "What's Happening." It's read by most employees, but not regularly as not all have access to a computer. A newsletter goes out periodically—at least quarterly, but more often if needed. The CEO meets with upper management weekly to be informed of goals and how well they're being met. He is a friendly, people kind of person, not afraid to speak before large groups, and thinks well on his feet. He enjoys the weekly meetings with upper management. He has from time to time thought about being more available to all employees but till now neither the time nor the motivation has been enough to bring that about.

The CEO has said he does not want anyone to lose his or her job. Some may need to be retrained but no one will be let go. The merger will take place in two weeks but the timeline for blending the organizations will be over several months.

He is asking that you and human resources work out the employee communication details and report back to him in two days.

Put together the key messages you want delivered to employees, and who will deliver them and how. Also plan the timing of the messages in conjunction with when the merger will actually take place. If you plan to use two-way communication, through what vehicles will employees communicate and to whom? Who will respond to their comments and questions? Is there a way to measure effectiveness?

4 | COMMUNITY RELATIONS

A community is a social organism made up of all the interactions among the residents and the organizations with which they identify. As a social organism, a community can take pride in its scenery or in its high school basketball team; it can be factionalized on the basis of who lives on which side of the railroad tracks, or who is well-off or poor; it can be a heterogeneous collection of suburban residents drawn together only by a common desire to escape living within a metropolitan area.

It is necessary for organizations to live by the community's ordinances and social mores. Permits must be sought to expand facilities, dig up utilities, change traffic flow, or even to operate at all.

A neighborhood, town, city, or state is obviously a human community. Like organizations, they require positive interrelationships among all members in order to function smoothly and efficiently. Because a company, hospital, school, or other organization would have difficulty operating effectively in a community that is disrupted or inefficient, it is necessary for them to accept the responsibility of corporate citizenship.

Therefore, mutual trust engendered by positive public relationships is essential in order for both the community and organizations located there to function in a reasonable manner. A community is not merely a collection of people who share a locality and its facilities.

THE OLD-FASHIONED VIEW OF COMMUNITY RELATIONS

Traditionally, employers have tended to regard their relationships with home communities as being extensions of their employee relations. The idea was that employees who were treated decently would go into the home communities singing the praises of their employer. In this traditional viewpoint, employers felt that their dollar payroll, their local tax payments, the occasional loan of a facility for a meeting, and the annual contribution to the United Way discharged their community obligations.

Their attitude seemed to say, "Look what we are giving: jobs, taxes, meeting facilities, and charitable donations." Employers who held this view tended to assume that with little more than a snap of their fingers they would be provided the practical necessities for efficient operations: streets, sewers, water lines, power and telephone, police and fire services, recreational areas, health care centers, schools, shopping centers, residential areas, cultural and religious facilities, and all the rest. The viewpoint tended to say, "These are what we are entitled to in return for what we give. The community owes us these."

This attitude has changed. Employers now know that they must have more than a general concern for the efficiency and adequacy of community services for themselves and for their employees. They have learned that they must become involved in specific community decisions and actions concerning fiscal policies; honesty in public offices; attracting new businesses and holding older ones; planning for the future; and generating the enthusiasm of volunteers in charitable, cultural, fellowship, educational, recreational, business, and patriotic endeavors. In general, they must apply the collective talents of the organization to the community in which it operates. The combination of these concerns involves having representatives in the policy-making structure of the community, sometimes directly and openly, sometimes behind the scenes.

- Community relations, as a public relations function, is an institution's planned, active, and continuing participation within a community to maintain and enhance its environment to the benefit of both the institution and the community.[1]

COMMUNITY ISSUES

Community relations (CR) work is a dynamic aspect of public relations. If there were no other reason, the changing physical and social makeup of communities would make it so, but there are many other contributing factors. Among them, few people stay in the communities where they are born. Families move not once, but several times. Community communications programs must deal with this constant turnover of residents. Also, employers move. Sometimes they move from a congested central city area to a suburb. When they move, both areas are disrupted. A manufacturer may move a headquarters or a manufacturing facility from one city to another, mortally wounding the economy of one and perhaps starting a boom in the other. Branches of businesses and institutions are opened in areas of growing population and closed in areas that are shrinking or that are poorly managed. A new interstate highway bypasses a community formerly dependent on travelers for its trade. Undesirable elements get control of government. A community also undergoes change when there is a movement for reform or rehabilitation.

Almost all the needs of a community as a desirable place to live and work can be put into ten categories:

1. Work for everyone who desires it
2. The prospect of growth and new opportunities
3. Adequate competitive commercial enterprises
4. Competent municipal government with modern police, fire, highway, and other services

---

[1]Wilbur J. Peak, "Community Relations," in *Lesly's Handbook of Public Relations and Communications,* Chicago: NTC/Contemporary Publishing, 1998, p. 114.

5. Educational, cultural, religious, and recreational pursuits
6. Appropriate housing and public services
7. Provision for helping those least able to help themselves
8. Availability of legal, medical, and other professional services
9. Pride and loyalty
10. A good reputation in the area and beyond

THE ROLE OF PUBLIC RELATIONS

Public relations work of a basic nature is involved in at least nine areas of an organization's community relationships:

1. Issuing news of interest to the community and providing top officials of the organizations with information on the status of community relations
2. Representing the organization in all sorts of volunteer activities, including fund drives—and getting employees to do likewise
3. Managing the contributions function—giving donations if a corporation, raising funds if a nonprofit organization
4. Counseling management on contributions of employees as volunteer workers or board members; arranging for use of facilities and equipment by community groups
5. Functioning as the organization's intermediary with local governmental, civic, educational, and ad hoc groups concerned with reform, social problems, and celebrations
6. Planning and helping to implement special events such as ground breaking or dedication of new facilities, change in location, anniversaries, reunions, conventions, or exhibitions
7. Preparing advertising or position papers aimed at residents or local government as needed or desirable
8. Preparing publications for distribution to resident groups
9. Planning and conducting open houses or tours as needed or desirable

With the dynamics of change mentioned earlier, public relations work is becoming less concerned with "routine" and more with the unusual: controversies between factions in the community; activism on social issues; and dealing with calamity, crisis, and governmental regulations as they affect the local community or as they are echoed in local ordinances affecting an organization.[2]

CAN COMMUNITY RELATIONS BE THE CORE OF PR PROGRAMMING?

Yes, community relations can be the core of public relations programming because it sets the tone of what an organization stands for—not in words (rhetoric) but in actions (behavior). Today, how organizations conduct themselves in the communities where

---

[2]For an example of a sudden and drastic change in local relationships, see news accounts of the oil spill of the *Exxon Valdez* in Alaska in March 1989.

they do business is driven by two factors that make it more than just "getting the house in order":

1. Instant communication, encompassing burgeoning information networks that go far beyond news media data gathering. It has the capacity to capture and transmit home behavior far and wide.
2. Global competition and the "global village" have created interest in such information, at least by competitors, activists, government agencies, and others who have reason to broadcast it.

Three strategic levels need to be planned:

1. **Defensive:** guarding against negative acts, or acts of omission
2. **Proactive:** being a leader in positive acts that appeal to key publics
3. **Maintenance:** finding ways to retain relationships with publics not currently key, but still able to influence a company's reputation by forthright expression of their perceptions of it

This approach is far different from "doing nice things for the community." Assigning community relations to indifferent or inexperienced staffers because it's "easy" no longer suffices—and of course misses the centrality of community relations today.

TWO TYPES OR LEVELS OF PROGRAMMING EMERGE

Standard community relations involves basic, arm's-length, "good corporate citizen" activities that reach out, invite in, create awareness, and let facilities be used. For example:

1. **Membership network,** assigning, "official" representatives to all important community groups
2. **Speakers bureau,** placing talks to key groups on topics vital to the organization
3. **Make facilities available**
4. **Open houses,** visitations, tours
5. **Programs around holidays**
6. **Service on boards** of directors
7. **Take part** in public events and back "must-support" causes

The second level of community relations involves becoming part of the fabric of the community by placing people throughout its planning and decision-making networks:

1. **Ambassador or constituency relations** programs
2. Hold regular **opinion leader briefings** or idea exchanges
3. Set up local **community relations advisory boards**
4. **Employee volunteer programs**
5. **Community research,** jointly with a college perhaps
6. **Social projects** that tackle the real community needs as seen by your key publics
7. **Make expertise available**

Neither list is exhaustive, but the two suggest the differences in the types. In most cases, some of both levels are useful.

Other Considerations

Employee volunteerism has so many serendipitous benefits that it raises the issue of **spouse, family, and retiree** participation. Those organizations that do involve them generally report expanded impact and a widening network.

Feedback databanks may be the biggest opportunity, capturing what is heard and observed from opinion leaders and community members in a formal way. Use of databanks is *really* listening to the community for invaluable information, which is instantly actionable through community relations programs.

SUCCESSFUL COMMUNITY RELATIONS ARE PLANNED, ORGANIZED, AND SYSTEMATIZED

In community programs there should be five considerations:

1. **Targeting**
   - Which *groups* in the community must be targeted . . .
   - In order to motivate the *behaviors* needed?
   - What specific *activities* will achieve this motivation?
   - What *information* must be gathered and assessed before starting?
2. **Participate or own**
   If your reputation needs improving, working on projects with accepted partners can use their reputation to pull yours up; if yours is good, projects you can own offer more benefits and visibility without any dilution.
3. **Here versus there**
   Should a program be based within the organization, or should it be an outside program? Should it take place on-site or off-site?
4. **"Official" versus employee volunteer activities**
   If the latter, how will the organization get credit? Should employees be able to do some volunteer work "on the clock"?
5. **Reaching opinion leaders**
   What design will assure that this critical goal is met?

TURNING WORKERS INTO GOODWILL AMBASSADORS

People trust people, so turning employees into ambassadors within the community is an effective way to be known, spread goodwill, and develop relationships. Because it wanted to develop its community relationships, Shell Chemical's Geismar site in Ascension Parish, Louisiana, did an opinion poll of 600 residents. The poll showed that when it comes to news about the plant, people tend to trust nonmanagerial plant workers. Asked who they would believe in matters regarding a chemical plant's impact on health, safety, and the environment, 68 percent said they would believe plant workers "a lot" or "some." Only medical doctors and the federal EPA got more favorable ratings. This data was used to leverage a program to keep employees better informed of the company's activities—turning workers into goodwill ambassadors both inside and outside the plant.[3]

References and Additional Readings

Arnstein, Caren. "How Companies Can Rebuild Credibility and Trust." *Public Relations Journal* 50 (April 1994): 28–29.

Bagin, Don, and Donald Gallagher. *The School and Community Relations.* 7th ed. Needham Heights, MA: Allyn & Bacon, 2000.

Brion, Denis. *Essential Industry and the NIMBY Phenomenon.* Westport, CT: Quorum, 1991.

Burke, Edmund. *Corporate Community Relations: The Principle of the Neighbor of Choice.* Westport, CT: Praeger, 1999.

Chynoweth, Emma, et al. "Responsible Care: Listening to Communities: What Do They Want to Know?" *Chemical Week* 153 (December 8, 1993): 68–69.

Corporate Community Relations Letter published by The Center for Corporate Community Relations at Boston College, www.bc.edu/cccr.

Cutlip, Scott, Allen Center, and Glen Broom. "Corporate Philanthropy." Chapter 14 in *Effective Public Relations.* 8th ed. Upper Saddle River, NJ: Prentice Hall, 1999.

Frank, Helmut, and John Schanz. The *Economics of the Energy Problem.* Joint Council on Economic Education, 1212 Avenue of the Americas, New York, NY 10022. Pamphlet.

Hunter, Floyd. *Community Power Structures.* Chapel Hill, NC: University of North Carolina Press, 1953. A Community Relations classic.

Hussey, John. "Community Relations," in *Experts in Action Inside Public Relations.* 2nd ed., ed. Bill Cantor and Chester Burger (White Plains, NY: Longman, Inc., 1989): 115–125.

Kruckeberg, Dean, and Kenneth Starck. *Public Relations and Community: A Reconstructed Theory.* Westport, CT: Greenwood, 1988.

Lerbinger, Otto, and Nathaniel Sperber. "Community Relations." Chapter 6 in *Manager's Public Relations Handbook.* Reading, MA: Addison-Wesley, 1982.

Lundborg, Lolls. *Public Relations in the Local Community.* New York: Harper and Row, 1950. Continues to be definitive. By the public relations staffer who advanced to CEO of Bank of America.

Making Community Relations Pay Off: Tools & Strategies. Washington, DC: Public Affairs Council, 1988. Tells how companies are meeting the test of effective community relations.

McDermitt, David. "The 10 Commandments of Community Relations." *World Wastes* 36 (September 1993): 48–51.

O'Brien, Paul. "Changing Expectations of Community Relations." *Executive Speeches* 8 (Oct/Nov 1993): 33–36.

pr reporter Vol. 41 No. 49 (December 14, 1998). "Hyundai's 'Blind Date' with Community Improves (Part 2)": 2.

pr reporter Vol. 41 No. 48 (December 7, 1998). "'Blind Dates' with Communities Don't Work; Steady Courtships Do": 2–3.

pr reporter Vol. 41 No. 35 (September 7, 1998). "Even Superior Community Relations Not Beyond Reach of Entrepreneurial Trial Lawyers—But It Can Defeat Them": 1–2.

pr reporter Vol. 36 No. 28 (July 19, 1993). "Can Community Relations Be the Core of Public Relations?": 1–2.

pr reporter Vol. 36 No. 4 (January 25, 1993). "Model for Employee Participation and Outreach Programs": 1–2.

pr reporter Vol. 35 No. 15 (April 13, 1992). "Inviting the Public Inside Is Effective and

---

[3]*pr reporter* Vol. 42 No. 34, August 30, 1999, "Shell Chemical's Employee Ambassadors Add Personal Element to Community Relations—and Help Assure Plant Survival," pp. 1–2.

Unexpected Way to Deal with Community Issues": 3.

The Public Relations Body of Knowledge. New York: PRSA. See abstracts dealing with "Community Relations."

Rich, Dorothy. "Business Partnerships with Families." *Business Horizons* 36 (September/October 1993): 24–28.

Skolnik, Rayna, "Rebuilding Trust." *Public Relations Journal* 49 (September 1993): 29–32.

CASES

CASE 4-1 A CLASSIC: CHEMICAL INDUSTRY TAKES RESPONSIBILITY FOR COMMUNITY CONCERNS

TRADE ASSOCIATION TAKES THE INITIATIVE

The American Chemistry Council (ACC) is the trade group for the chemical industry. Its members represent 90 percent of the industrial chemical productive capacity in the United States. Dues are based on a percentage of a company's chemical sales.

Chemical companies must be constantly innovative to remain competitive in today's global marketplace. Like most trade associations, ACC helps members stay abreast of issues and techniques. It provides assistance in complying with laws and regulations. ACC also offers **leadership training** and **task force groups** to develop skills and knowledge in the managerial, legislative, technical, and communications areas.

Over the years, Responsible Care's[1] focus has evolved from a measure of process to one of improved performance. After initially focusing on shaping our companies' operating behavior practices and reaching "Practice-in-Place," we have stepped up our commitment to Responsible Care®. Our industry is now dedicated to a vision of no accidents, no injuries and no harm to the environment.

> TOM REILLY, CEO OF REILLY INDUSTRIES

We have said all along that we are not asking the public to *trust* us. We are asking everyone to *track* us, to monitor our performance and make suggestions that will help us improve.

> FRED WEBBER, PRESIDENT, AMERICAN CHEMISTRY COUNCIL

As public awareness of environmental health and safety issues has increased over the past few decades, the chemical industry has been scrutinized by activists, regulators, and consumers more closely than ever before. As environmentalists make louder protests, legislators respond with more stringent regulations.

Under the Superfund Amendments and Reauthorization Act (SARA), also known as the Emergency Planning and Community Right-to-Know Act, chemical manufacturers and other organizations are required to inform employees and the community about the nature and hazards of the materials with which they work.[2]

---

[1]Responsible Care® is a copyright of the American Chemistry Council. Thanks to Lisa Grepps, APR, Manager of Strategic Communications for Responsible Care® for providing extensive updated information on this program for the 6th edition of this text.
[2]Bernard J. Nebel, *Environmental Science.* Upper Saddle River, NJ: Prentice Hall, 1990, p. 290.

As pressures from legislation mounted and NIMBYists[3] began paying closer attention to environmental issues in their communities, the chemical industry realized that it needed to reach beyond one-way communication of its side of the story. It needed to do three things:

1. *Listen to and recognize the perceptions and fears* of the public, especially neighbors of chemical plants.
2. *Own up to any performance problems.*

3. *Take action* to correct problems and address perceptions.

PROACTIVE RESPONSE TO PUBLIC CONCERNS: RESPONSIBLE CARE®

ACC created an initiative in the United States called *Responsible Care*® in 1988 (See Figure 4-1). Modeled after a Canadian Chemical Producers Association program, Responsible Care® couples environmental, health, and safety improvements in individual

FIGURE 4-1   Shown here is the symbol of Responsible Care®.

Responsible Care®
Good Chemistry at Work

(Courtesy of ACC.)

---

[3]*Not In My Back Yard.* An update is *NOPE (Not On Planet Earth).*

plants with invitations for industry and public scrutiny. Many observers believe this to be one of the best strategic public relations programs, although the industry does not acknowledge it as such.

An integral part of the Responsible Care® program is its **six Codes of Management Practices** (See Figure 4-2). These codes established priorities for operating chemical plants. ACC places reduction of emissions, reduction of the waste that facilities generate, and sound management of remaining releases and wastes at the top of its priorities.

According to Richard Doyle, vice president of Responsible Care® at ACC,

Responsible Care® calls for continuous improvement by the chemical industry in health, safety, and environmental performance. Responsible Care® is not a quick fix or an overnight cure. It is not a public relations program. It is an ongoing process, and a call for action. . . . Its ultimate goal remains to *create a dialogue with constituents in order to educate and obtain input into how the chemical industry can most effectively improve its performance in a manner that is responsive to the public.* [Emphasis added.]

Responsible Care® is *proactive public relations.* Rather than waiting for an accident to occur, or the public to become fearful or upset, it actively *invites* people to learn which chemicals are produced at a plant, how the plant is operated, and what protective measures are in place should an accident occur.

Studies have shown that *fear* of an unknown event is more powerful than an

---

FIGURE 4-2 The six Codes of Management Practices turn guiding principles to practical application.

1. **Community Awareness and Emergency Response Code (CAER)**

   to reduce potential harm to the employees and the public in an emergency as well as bring the chemical industry and communities together

2. **Pollution Prevention Code**

   to improve the industry's ability to protect people and the environment by generating less waste and minimizing emissions

3. **Process Safety Code**

   to prevent fire, explosions, and accidental chemical releases

4. **Distribution Code**

   to reduce employee and public risks from the shipment of chemicals

5. **Employee Health and Safety Code**

   to maximize worker protection and accident prevention, through training and communications

6. **Product Stewardship Code**

   to ensure that the design, development, manufacture, transport, use, and disposal of chemical products is done safely and without environmental damage

(Reprinted courtesy of ACC.)

actual *bad occurrence*. In a study of a group known to have latent tendencies for developing Huntington's disease, the majority of those whose genetic tests showed they would most likely develop this incurable malady felt that knowing was beneficial. "Better to know than be always wondering." Those that knew they were likely to get the disease reported their quality of life and psychological health was better than those for whom testing was inconclusive.

This holds true for knowing and communicating about chemical risks as well. Most people can handle truth better than being left in doubt. Open communication shows respect for people by treating them like responsible adults. However, the Huntington study also indicates that all people do not react the same when learning of risks. About 10 percent had trouble adjusting to the news, even when it was good (i.e., they would probably not develop the disease). Apparently for some, just handling the change or believing the test is accurate was more impactful than the relief. As always, no rule fits everyone.[4]

Responsible Care® is comprised of 10 elements:

1. Guiding Principles: followed by every member and partner company
2. Codes of Management Practices: environmental, health, and safety guidelines
3. Dialogue with the Public: to identify and address public concerns
4. Self-Evaluation: annual reporting on a company's implementation of the Codes
5. Measures of Performance: to view progress of Responsible Care®
6. Performance Goals: company-specific goals reported on annually

7. Management Systems Verification: independent review of companies' implementation of Responsible Care®
8. Mutual Assistance: company-to-company dialogue
9. Partnership Program: helping companies to participate in Responsible Care®
10. Obligation of Membership: to participate in Responsible Care® and follow these elements

ACC member companies adhere to a list of ten guiding principles about safe plant operations and proper public communications. Figure 4-3 illustrates these principles.

RESPONSIBLE CARE®'S TARGET AUDIENCES

The goal of Responsible Care® is to continuously advance the level of chemical industry performance, demonstrating commitment to a better, safer world. This message is targeted to:

➤ The chemical industry
➤ Teachers and students
➤ Employees
➤ Federal and state officials
➤ The media
➤ The general public
➤ Plant neighbors
➤ Local and national interest groups
➤ Supply chain customers

BUILDING PUBLIC RELATIONSHIPS

Activities to Reach External Audiences

ACC member and partner companies use a combination of one-way and two-way

---

[4]*pr reporter* 36, May 3, 1993, pp. 2–3.

1. To seek and incorporate public input regarding our products and operations.
2. To provide chemicals that can be manufactured, transported, used, and disposed of safely.
3. To make health, safety, the environment, and resource conservation critical considerations for all new and existing products and processes.
4. To provide information on health or environmental risks and pursue protective measures for employees, the public, and other key stakeholders.
5. To work with customers, carriers, suppliers, distributors, and contractors to foster the safe use, transport, and disposal of chemicals.
6. To operate our facilities in a manner that protects the environment and the health and safety of our employees and the public.
7. To support education and research on the health, safety, and environmental effects of our products and processes.
8. To work with others to resolve problems associated with past handling and disposal practices.
9. To lead in the development of responsible laws, regulations, and standards that safeguard the community, workplace, and environment.
10. To practice Responsible Care® by encouraging and assisting others to adhere to these principles and practices.

FIGURE 4-3 ACC member companies adhere to a list of 10 guiding principles about safe plant operations and proper public communications.

(Reprinted courtesy of ACC.)

communication activities to invite external publics to communicate with their local plants. One-way (or information transfer) efforts include:

➤ **Brochures** featuring shelter-in-place messages and explanations of Responsible Care®

➤ **Annual Responsible Care® reports** that target the business community, as well as community stakeholders, and report on the company's environmental, health, and safety performance

➤ **ChemicalGuide.com** Web site featuring member and partner company Web sites detailing products and outreach activities, as well as Responsible Care® performance

➤ **Advertisements** on the local level

➤ **Community newsletters** sent to plant neighbors to keep them informed about the company and its activities

Two-way (or relationship-building) efforts include:

➤ **Community advisory panels** (CAPs), groups of citizens with diverse backgrounds and feelings toward the chemical industry. CAPs are sponsored by local chemical plants and encouraged to voice community concerns with industry representatives. Well-run CAPs provide dialogue between the plant and the community. To date, ACC members and partners sponsor nearly 300 CAPs across the country with great success. One example is the LeMoyne (Alabama) Community Advisory Panel, which works to improve emergency response service to the local community and sponsors an annual "Responsible Care® Night" at member company plants to help residents understand the initiative.

➤ **Hazardous material drills** involving plants and local emergency responder groups. These exercises help improve knowledge and response time in the event of an incident. For more information, visit www.transcaer.org.

➤ **Responsible Care® fairs/days/open houses** are sponsored by the plants or CAP groups. These events are opportunities for the community to tour the plant and learn about its operations.

➤ **Inviting state legislators and local and national activist leaders to speak at association meetings** and sending ACC delegates or scientists to meetings of environmental, regulatory, and community groups.

Activities to Change Behavior of ACC Members

To maintain ACC membership, companies are required to implement Responsible Care® guiding principles and codes of management practice. More than 1,000 executives and managers have attended ACC workshops on implementing the codes for Responsible Care®. Many have found creative ways to reach their new objectives. For example, some have tied managerial bonuses to achieved objectives. Others use peer pressure of recognition to moti-

vate and support the Responsible Care® initiative.

As codes are implemented, ACC requires every company to report its progress along the way. As of 2001, 110 members or approximately 95 percent of companies that have been implementing the initiatives for five or more years are at full implementation of the six codes of management practices.

EVALUATION: EXTERNAL PUBLICS

The National Association of Public Environmental Communicators commended Responsible Care® for its one-way and two-way communication vehicles.

EVALUATION: INTERNAL PUBLICS

Reductions in Chemical Emission

ACC members reported that total releases (occurring when a chemical is discharged into the land, air, or water) declined from 381 million pounds in 1988 to 139 million pounds in 1998. Air releases dropped more than 69 percent. Water releases were cut by 75 percent, and chemicals sent to landfills were reduced by 74 percent. Underground injection of chemicals was cut by 39 percent. Off-site transfers (excluding off-site recycling and recovery) decreased 47 percent.

Self-Evaluation

The ACC Responsible Care® initiative includes a self-evaluation process. Member companies are required to furnish ACC with an annual report of their progress in implementing the Codes of Management Practices. They have shown significant gains in Process Safety, Distribution, Community Awareness, and Emergency Response.

Although these results show improvements, ACC recognizes the fact that company self-evaluations are subject to challenges of credibility. ACC is now identifying additional code measurement systems that continue to meet objective public scrutiny.

Performance Measures

Performance measures exist to demonstrate the progress being made through Responsible Care® and are used to help drive performance improvement throughout the membership. The performance measures include Community Awareness and Emergency Response, Pollution Prevention, Process Safety, Distribution, Employee Health and Safety, and Product Stewardship.

Performance Goals

Member and partner companies are asked to:

➤ Establish at least one goal for a Responsible Care® performance result

➤ Make steady performance improvement toward that goal

➤ Publicly communicate the goal(s) and progress toward meeting that goal(s)

➤ Annually report to the Council the established goal(s), progress, and public reporting mechanism

This case demonstrates the trend of public relations programs to *begin with responsible action* by organizations, with public relations practitioners playing a key role in *design and strategy*. The *communications and relationship-building activities* then follow to gain recognition for the responsible action. ∎

QUESTIONS FOR DISCUSSION

1. Richard Doyle, then ACC vice president of Responsible Care®, said the initiative "is not a public relations program." What did he intend to convey? He said Responsible Care® is a performance improvement initiative and that ACC's members are striving for public input into this process. What do you think he meant, and how can this goal best be achieved? Do you think the community advisory panels in neighborhoods around facilities are beneficial?

2. To what extent can a voluntary performance improvement initiative by private industry forestall government legislation and regulation on environmental matters? Explain your position.

3. What else could ACC do to attain higher credibility for Responsible Care® with:

   ➤ The public
   ➤ Its own members

   ➤ Associated industries
   ➤ Legislators and regulators
   ➤ Activist groups

4. How could it measure an increase or decrease in credibility?

5. List other industries whose products or operations engender fear. What steps are you aware of that each is taking to allay public apprehension? How does Responsible Care® compare with what these industries are doing?

6. Imagine yourself living across the street from a chemical plant. List all the feelings you can think of that you might have about the plant—positive, negative, or neutral. What specific actions would representatives from the plant need to take to address your feelings?

7. Draft a letter from a chemical plant manager to those living near the plant announcing introduction of the Responsible Care® initiative.

CASE 4-2 COMMUNITY RELATIONSHIPS MAINTAINED DURING HOSPITAL CLOSING

Throughout the 1980s and early 1990s, business and the government trimmed whatever fat there was from the healthcare system. In 1997, Congress passed the Balanced Budget Act in an attempt to reform Medicare and trim waste from the system. But cuts went billions of dollars beyond expectation. Now, the healthcare system is in a financial crisis. Health premiums aren't paying for the cost of services. Hospitals are being squeezed by managed care companies that are having their own financial troubles. One consequence is the closing of hospitals.

MERCY HOSPITAL–DETROIT'S STRUGGLE

The east side of Detroit is among the most troubled urban areas in the United States, struggling with a multitude of social and economic challenges. Mercy Hospital–Detroit was an important anchor in this neighborhood, not only providing access to healthcare, but also security, employment, leadership, and a place for social interaction. It relied heavily on Medicare, Medicaid, and other government sources for its business—nearly 80 percent of its total admissions.

In the early to mid-1990s, Mercy Hospital–Detroit found it increasingly difficult to maintain its fiscal health; operating losses were supplemented by the hospital's parent company, Mercy Health Services (MHS).[1] Then, in 1997, the Balanced Budget Reconciliation Act severely reduced Medicare and Medicaid reimbursements. The already struggling hospital was devastated by the cuts. Losses of $1.5 million per month began to mount. The federal and state funding cuts similarly affected operating margins at Mercy's other hospitals. The MHS Board was faced with system-wide financial constraints that put the system's bond rating at risk. Operating losses at Mercy Hospital–Detroit totaled nearly $100 million from 1990–2000.

In the hope of finding a buyer, a series of discussions with major Detroit health systems ensued in 1999, but all were facing the same circumstances: increasingly ill patients with no health insurance and decreasing reimbursements from the government. The decision was made to close the hospital in December 1999. Mercy Hospital–Detroit quickly became a national example of the evolving healthcare crisis in the United States.

SEVERAL PUBLIC RELATIONS ISSUES EMERGED

➤ How can the hospital close without giving the impression of abandoning the city and its poorest residents?

---

[1]Renamed Trinity Health after a May 2000 merger.

➤ Is it possible to close the hospital while still maintaining the excellent reputation of MHS and its sponsor, the Sisters of Mercy?

➤ How can Mercy coincidentally acquire a similar-sized hospital in a predominantly white suburban community without attracting major criticism and, worse yet, accusations of "racism"?

RESEARCH

Preparations began as early as 1997 when Mercy Hospital–Detroit commissioned a research study to obtain community opinion and attitudes. The study showed that parent company MHS was held in high esteem and that the local community not only counted on Mercy Hospital–Detroit but saw it as an entitlement for the community.

Meanwhile, the commitment to the community from the Sisters of Mercy and the MHS Board led MHS management to conclude that it should donate the 10-year-old building to the community. Instead of simply selling the hospital campus to a developer for commercial use, MHS decided the hospital should be converted as a long-term community asset to enhance neighborhood revitalization, and the new owner(s) and users should share the mission and values of the hospital's parent, MHS. Additionally, MHS decided to keep a presence on the hospital campus by earmarking $2 million for a primary care clinic for the uninsured. In doing so, Mercy supported its mission of "care for the poor and underserved" while seeking a new owner for the larger block of property and buildings.

The next step was a major study in early 2000—just after the announcement of closure—consisting of personal interviews with 198 Detroit community and opinion leaders, including elected officials, clergy, and major business and social service agency representatives, to obtain ideas about how to "do the right thing" and "give back" to the community, rather than simply close the hospital and move on. The personal interviews provided valuable input on specific community needs, possible organizations that met the criteria as a new owner, and communication tactics for most effectively reaching the important audiences of key community leaders and area residents, many of whom are without transportation or telephones. The interviews also helped crystallize other audiences to target:

➤ Mercy Hospital–Detroit employees, medical staff, board members, and volunteers

➤ Mercy's leadership group (40 top management personnel nationwide) and other corporate office employees

➤ Community religious leaders

➤ Local physician leaders

➤ Regional and national partners

➤ Major insurers

➤ Archdiocese of Detroit and Bishops in all MHS markets

➤ Michigan's governor and staff

➤ Detroit's Mayor and key aides

➤ The Wayne County Executive and key aides

➤ Detroit City Council

➤ Trade and healthcare consortia

➤ 99,000 residents in the primary service area

THE PUBLIC RELATIONS PLAN

A public relations plan was developed to reach these audiences using a variety of tactics—not relying on advertising—including specific ways to obtain their input and feedback. Tactics in the plan included e-mail; a telephone hotline; staff and community town hall meetings; targeted letters to volunteers, community leaders, and others; the hospital newsletter; editorial board meetings with Detroit's two daily newspapers, weekly business newsmagazine, and African-American weekly; formal closure notices in community newspapers; direct-mail letters; and news releases, fact sheets, and backgrounders.

The **key messages** to communicate were: "Mercy can no longer tolerate this level of losses or be supported by others within the Mercy system," "Mercy is 'doing the right thing' by donating the property to help meet community needs," and "Mercy continues its ministry for the poor with a new primary care center for the uninsured—investing $2 million per year to make that happen."

PLANS WERE EXECUTED WITH PRECISION

Plans began with a carefully implemented effort to obtain balanced stories—as early as September 1999—about the difficult financial situation and the possibility that Mercy Hospital–Detroit may close. This was followed with a series of editorial board meetings with Detroit's two dailies, the weekly business newsmagazine, and African-American weekly. Similar meetings were later held with community leaders and the Detroit City Council. The generally fair and favorable editorials and news coverage resulting from the meetings helped educate Mercy's key audiences and would later help them understand the reasons for closing.

Media coverage reached a crescendo in January 2000 and has continued through March 2001, including NBC Nightly News and several national trades. A total of 10,000 letters were mailed to residents' homes within three eastside ZIP codes. All audiences received the news of Mercy Hospital–Detroit's closing and, although disappointed that Detroit's east side would

lose an acute care hospital, they were generally understanding of the situation.

Excluding a regulatory requirement to place a "Public Notice" advertisement in local newspapers, no other form of advertising was used to reach the audiences.

EVALUATION

In late 2000, the Mercy Hospital–Detroit building was donated to a multi-service community organization (SER Metro) and a Catholic organization serving youths and families (Boysville). Other new tenants on the former hospital campus include Mercy Primary Care Center to serve the uninsured, the National Council of Alcoholism and Drug Dependency, Head Start, Child Care Coordinating Center, the Detroit Fire Department, and McCauley Commons' independent housing. The revamped campus promises to continue providing a positive, major impact in the community. Balanced media coverage told the story fairly. Personal interviews with a sample of 20 (from the list of those previously interviewed) were extremely positive. Internal meetings were equally positive. Employees from Mercy Hospital–Detroit, many of whom would be without jobs, gave Mercy–Detroit's CEO a standing ovation after he explained the closing and transfer of the hospital.

The final test came when MHS announced the purchase of St. Mary Hospital, a 300-bed hospital in the Detroit suburb of Livonia, only four months after closing the inner-city Detroit hospital. Without the effective public relations program on the closing of Mercy Hospital–Detroit, the announcement to acquire a new hospital in a predominantly white suburb could have caused significant editorial scrutiny and community backlash that would surely damage MHS' reputation (just one month after its merger with another major national health system to create Trinity Health) and hamper its future growth. All internal and external audiences met the announcement of the St. Mary Hospital acquisition, except for minor exceptions, with support and encouragement.[2] ■

QUESTIONS FOR DISCUSSION

1. You are the public relations director of the closing hospital. Your public relations plan calls for a community town hall meeting. Some people in the community don't have phones or computers. How will you alert everyone about this meeting? When will you hold it? How many times? Who will attend from the hospital? What is your goal for the meeting and how will you achieve that? Put together a plan addressing these issues.

2. Many depend on the hospital for their own and their children's health needs. The plan calls for input and feedback from the community. What will you do with their feedback? What if your CEO is unwilling to listen?

3. Take as an example the hospital closest to where you live. Who do you think are the opinion leaders for that hospital? Make a list and identify them by their position in the hospital, how they would be contacted and what the message strategy would be.

---

[2]Thank you to Stephen Shivinsky, APR, vice president of corporate communications and public relations at Trinity Health for this case study.

CASE 4-3   THE STRUGGLE FOR NUCLEAR POWER

One of the most challenging public relations positions since the 1970s has been working for an electric utility with a nuclear plant—such as Seabrook Station, which became a national symbol of the nuclear power debate in the 1970s and 1980s. Located in Seabrook, New Hampshire, forty miles north of Boston (See Figure 4-4), it was built on New Hampshire's seventeen-mile North Atlantic coastline in an extensive salt marsh area. During the prolonged construc-

tion and licensing process, Public Service Company of New Hampshire (PSNH)—the original owner—encountered persistent opposition from various sources.

➤ Initially, opposition came from environmentalists who were concerned about the potential impact a "once-through" water cooling system would have on ocean temperature. Among other issues,

FIGURE 4-4   Seabrook Station, located near the seacoast in Seabrook, New Hampshire.

(Courtesy of Seabrook Station.)

they were worried about possible irreparable damage that warming ocean waters would have on the biological populations in and under those waters.

➤ As plant construction progressed, a broader section of the community became increasingly concerned about the safety of the reactor and the proposed evacuation plans.

➤ The cost of the plant and its possible effect on the region's electricity rates sparked additional opposition. Increased power costs were perceived as an obstacle blocking industrial development and the prosperity of northern New England.

➤ Some citizens protested the plant because they doubted New Hampshire's need for a new power source.

Perhaps the first sign of problems for Seabrook Station occurred when the proposal to build came before various official boards. The illustrated model showed the containment unit, with a proposed height of 250 feet, mostly hidden from view by trees. But redwoods don't grow in New England!

Seabrook Station encountered delays as activists started demonstrating. The opposition intervened in the Nuclear Regulatory Commission's (NRC) adjudicatory review boards. The legal case was led by the Seacoast Anti-Pollution League (SAPL), while other grassroots activists spearheaded by the Clamshell Alliance led protests. The Clamshell used grassroots organizing, group decision making, and affinity networking against public or private projects felt to be disruptive to an area. Its activities ranged from peaceful demonstrations to forceful attempts at site occupation with mass arrests.

After nearly eighteen years of licensing, construction, and regulatory review, Seabrook Station began regular full-power operation on August 19, 1990. "We realize that we may never be able to satisfy the core group of people who do not support nuclear power," said Richard Winn, Seabrook's communications counsel at that time, "but we do not ignore them either." Through the years Seabrook Station has become more sensitive to the needs and concerns of its

publics. At that time, according to Winn, Seabrook was doing something that a nuclear power plant does not have to do—that is, focusing on "the sorts of things that don't make electricity," such as community relations, public education, and environmental information.

THE OPPOSITION

The Audubon Society opposed Seabrook Station before safety became an issue—before Three Mile Island. Its concern was environmental. When Seabrook changed the design of its cooling systems in order to prevent interference with the ocean, Audubon withdrew its opposition. Today, Seabrook is partnering with the Audubon Society and NH Fish and Game to build an osprey nest on its site in the hope of attracting a pair of nesting ospreys.

After the Three Mile Island and Chernobyl accidents, safety become the main concern of opposition. Seabrook opponents did include many gate-bashers, the form of opposition that comes to mind where nuclear power is concerned. But many other activists sought a different route to get their message heard. Issues of opposition ranged from complete rejection of nuclear power to the location of Seabrook Station.

The Clamshell Alliance, one of the most visible opposing organizations, went door to door in towns affected by Seabrook Station to gather support for protest. They also staged large, nonviolent and occasionally somewhat violent demonstrations.

Some real estate agencies and banks were opposed to Seabrook. Individuals in these fields joined other activist groups. In general, they were opposed to the possible drop in real estate value.

The Seacoast Anti-Pollution League (SAPL), a small group of dedicated volunteers, legally pursued Seabrook's perceived lack of safety. Their purpose at that time was "to work toward the deferral of the proposed nuclear plant at Seabrook."[1] Members, in conjunction with their attorney, Robert Backus, worked through the NRC's judicial system to improve the evacuation plan. SAPL believed that the initial plan was not adequate to meet the needs of the neighboring communities. Indeed, only three roads—all two-lane—lead away from the beach area adjacent to the plant, where on a summer Sunday as many as 100,000 people congregate for swimming and other beach activities.

Now that Seabrook is on line, SAPL strategies still emphasize the risks associated with living near a nuclear power plant. SAPL works in coordination with the Massachusetts-based Citizens within a 10-Mile Radius (C-10) to monitor the levels of background radiation to see if any additional radiation is being emitted from Seabrook Station. Their efforts are directed toward discovering if there is a correlation between increased levels of radiation and increased health problems in the area.

SAPL members often visit local schools to speak about the dangers of nuclear power, and they set up question-and-answer booths at university fairs and other events. SAPL also responds to NRC regulation changes distributed by the Nuclear Information and Resource Service. Members receive newsletters encouraging them to write letters to the editors of local newspapers in an effort to notify people about how these regulatory changes affect the general public. To this day, some dedicate their lives to opposing nuclear power.

FINANCIAL TROUBLES PLAGUE SEABROOK

As a result of the mounting costs of Seabrook, PSNH was forced into bankruptcy. The company became financially strained when New Hampshire legislators passed the CWIP (Construction Work In Progress) law, which forbade the utility from including the cost of the plant's construction in consumer electric rates until the power was turned on. This law delayed the economic burden on New Hampshire citizens but added to the utility's interest costs on millions borrowed to finance construction.

Construction ceased temporarily in 1984. Then New Hampshire Yankee (NHY), a division of PSNH, took over the project and with the Seabrook Joint Owners[2] (other

---

[1]Henry F. Bedfore, Seabrook Station, Amherst, MA: University of Massachusetts Press, 1990, p. 67.
[2]Originally, Seabrook Station was jointly owned by a large number of companies with PSNH holding the largest percentage of ownership. In 2001, Seabrook Station was jointly owned by Northeast Utilities, which is the current majority owner, along with 10 other minority owners. Due to deregulation, however, the biggest change in ownership will occur in 2002 when the plant will be auctioned/sold, bringing about a consolidation and ownership change.

IDENTIFYING THE SEABROOK PUBLICS

The Seabrook communications staff identified important publics for Seabrook.

INTERNAL PUBLICS

- All Seabrook Station employees who live in communities around the plant site
- Employees who do not live in the area

EXTERNAL PUBLICS

- Massachusetts and New Hampshire residents living both inside and outside the Emergency Planning Zone
- Local and national news media
- The financial community

Seabrook community relations staff targeted, in the 23 New Hampshire and Massachusetts towns, public and private schools, day-care facilities, police and fire departments, local officials and opinion leaders, local media, advocacy groups, large (over 50 employees) and small businesses, chambers of commerce, network organizations such as the Lions and Rotary clubs and the local United Way, and citizens living within the 22-mile radius.

power companies with an interest in the plant) reaffirmed determination to complete Seabrook. People from PSNH were moved into top position at New Hampshire Yankee.

DEVELOPING STRATEGIES

NHY's community relations team focused on Seabrook's publics in the seacoast area (see *Identifying the Seabrook Publics*). The public relations team initially used reactive programming to address the opposition's concerns and to resolve cognitive dissonance.[3] They used one-way and two-way communication techniques to address these goals.

One-Way Techniques

1. Created a series of hard-hitting ads featuring Seabrook employees offering words of reassurance (See Figure 4-5).
2. Distributed a "safety kit" consisting of information on Seabrook, waste management, radiation, and safety systems.
3. Circulated *Energy,* a community-targeted newsletter, between 1988 and 1989 to all publics in the emergency area. The articles focused on issues related to energy.

Two-Way Techniques

1. In 1986, NHY formally invited the surrounding community to tour the nuclear plant. More than 7,000 people

---

[3]The theory of cognitive dissonance, first put forth by Leon Festinger in 1947, suggests a human desire for consistency between what people know and what they do. Any conflict creates a disturbance. See Glen Broom, Allen Center, and Scott Cutlip, *Effective Public Relations,* 8th ed., Toronto, Ontario: Prentice Hall Canada, 1999.

Geryl Jasinski, Quality Assurance Engineer At Seabrook Station, On Her Job And Her Commitment To Safety.

About Geryl Jasinski . . .

I grew up along the seashore and I've always been conscious of how people treat the environment. That's how I became interested in science and in learning more about my surroundings.

Today, I'm part of a group that is responsible for seeing that Seabrook's Quality Assurance Program really works. I feel that by assuring the plant's safe operation, we also protect the environment around Seabrook. We're confident that the plant's systems will run smoothly because we constantly take actions to assure they will. Through regular testing and surveillance, we know our equipment is top-notch.

Every day we're in the field observing how work is performed on pumps, motors, valves, sensors — you name it. In this way, we make sure that all safety-related equipment is maintained at the highest level of quality.

Our program works well, and that's been proven by excellent reviews from the U.S. Nuclear Regulatory Commission and the Institute of Nuclear Power Operations.

Quality is everyone's responsibility, not just ours. That's why our program is effective.

I'm a mother of two now; my new baby, Kristin, was born just six months ago. I'm back on the job and looking forward to making a contribution to my children's future. Through my work at Seabrook, I can ensure that a safe, reliable supply of electricity will be available when they need it.

☐ **YES!** I would like to learn more about safety at Seabrook Station. Please send me a free information kit

NAME _____

STREET _____

CITY _____ STATE _____ ZIP CODE _____

Clip and send this coupon to Seabrook Safety, (PAC) Box 300, Seabrook NH 03874. Or give us a call at 1 (800) 338-7482

～seabrook station

A SAFE INVESTMENT IN OUR ENERGY FUTURE

This message is brought to you by New Hampshire Yankee.

FIGURE 4-5   Example of ads featuring a NHY employee and "The Lesson of Chernobyl."

(Courtesy of Seabrook Station.)

from the surrounding New Hampshire and Massachusetts communities attended this event.

2. Seabrook Station's Science and Nature Center (See Figure 4-6) allows viewers to explore nature and science simultaneously. The Center displays information about electrical generation and contains an ocean aquarium 260 feet below sea level. A total of 30,000 people visit the Center annually.

3. According to NRC regulations, the state must inform the public in the 23 affected towns about emergency and safety procedures. NHY took this one-way task and made it into a two-way strategy. Public relations staff created a calendar decorated with photographs of the seacoast and mailed copies to all homes in the area. The calendars include public notification information, including which radio stations broadcast emergency

FIGURE 4-6 A brochure of the Science and Nature Center.

(Courtesy of Seabrook Station.)

bulletins and instructions. Employees hand-delivered calendars to approximately 4,000 of the 7,000 small businesses in the area. Only 2 percent of those businesses rejected the information.

Seabrook did encounter some heated public opposition to the evacuation plan, and that attracted a lot of media attention. Some schools were unhappy with the proposed evacuation plans because teachers would be required to stay with their classes even though their instinct would be to rush to their own families. These perceptions of the proposed evacuation plan's shortcomings forced many towns to reject the emergency procedures.

4. Communicators representing Seabrook met with school superintendents and business executives to educate them about emergency planning. They also developed relationships with Massachusetts emergency medical squads and fire departments.

5. NHY communications approached the media proactively. If a siren that

had nothing to do with Seabrook sounded off in a surrounding town or if a rumor about Seabrook was circulated, NHY called the media before the media called them.

These efforts helped Seabrook Station achieve on-line status. NHY won its contested case before the NRC's adjudicating boards.

THE NEED FOR PROACTIVE MEASURES

Seabrook public relations teams did not stop once the plant was on line. "We did the things we needed to do to get our license according to the rules and regulations. And then we went a step farther to be proactive and adopt a policy of 'management of expectations' for our community relations efforts," wrote Richard Winn.

Seabrook utilized strategy to build one-on-one relationships. Now that the plant was up and running, those relationships needed to be maintained. According to Seabrook research at that time, the greatest percentage of people were not definitively for or against nuclear power. Therefore, public relations staff believed it was vital that the public feel comfortable about contacting Seabrook whenever there was a concern.

REINFORCING RELATIONSHIPS

NHY took measures to reinforce the relationships it had established.

1. NHY continued to send out an Emergency Plan Information Calendar to all of its external publics. The calendar consists of 33 pages of emergency planning and safety information.
2. The Science and Nature Center was made accessible for school and

community-based field trips. The Center provides hands-on exhibits featuring energy and environment and the Owascoag Nature Trail— approximately one mile of preserved woods and marshlands with a variety of plants and animals.
3. NHY established a local hotline for citizens in surrounding communities to call and inquire about specific problems and concerns.

FOCUSING ON THE COMMUNITY

In 1991, Seabrook Station employees and volunteers participated in several community-oriented events and activities. The community relations department initiated at least one new program encouraging community involvement each quarter.

1. Employees participated in the Lion's Camp Pride, a summer camp facility offering educational and recreational overnight programs to children with special needs. Volunteers installed docks, stained and painted buildings, and cleaned and set up bunkhouses.
2. Employees participated in the seacoast's Seafood Festival. They raised money at the event by selling popcorn and donated all proceeds to My Greatest Dream, an organization that benefits terminally ill children.
3. Volunteers participated in Coastweeks, a nationwide celebration of the nation's coastal areas. NHY cleaned up Hampton Beach, a New Hampshire state park about two miles from the Seabrook plant.
4. Time and building materials were donated to Action Cove Playground, an innovative playground in West Newbury, Massachusetts. The children's area was designed for explorative and imaginative play.

5. NHY founded a local Project Homefront, an effort assisting families whose relatives were called to serve in the Persian Gulf War. A total of 163 volunteers offered services and assistance in transportation; auto, electrical and plumbing repair; carpentry; and babysitting. Employees also donated $1,135 to this project.

Other community endeavors aided organizations such as Wish Upon a Star, which provides anonymous Christmas gifts to needy children, and the Girl Scouts of America. According to Martha Netsch, Director of Communications for the Swiftwater Girl Scout Council, the Girl Scouts frequently visit Seabrook Station's Science and Nature Center, work with staff on scout education programs about solutions to today's energy problems, and recognize the Science and Nature Center as support for young women interested in mathematics, science, and technology.

Seabrook encourages employees to become involved in local civic organizations and in local government. Many are on town and city boards, volunteer emergency medical squads and fire departments; Rotary, Lions, and Kiwanis clubs; or are active in school organizations. Every year employees serve as judges at local science fairs.

THROUGH THE 1990S, INTO THE 21ST CENTURY

In 1992, control of Seabrook was bought by Connecticut-based Northeast Utilities, which earlier took over bankrupt PSNH. One of its subsidiaries, North Atlantic Energy Corporation, oversees the daily operation of the plant. From a business perspective, Seabrook Station was recognized as Business of the Year 1991 by *Business New Hampshire Magazine*.

Some activist groups continue to exist, however, though most are now peaceful in their approach. According to SAPL's Joan and Charles Pratt, both SAPL and C-10 work as watchdogs. Their mission is to make sure Seabrook complies with NRC regulations. The Citizens Radiological Monitoring Network acts as a support group that focuses on how to live with potential hazards. Its goals are to monitor every air and water emission from Seabrook, to hold Seabrook socially accountable for every emission, and to expect a responsible attitude from the station itself. All these awareness groups keep a close eye on Seabrook.

Despite the controversial issues, Seabrook employees, for the most part, maintain professional relationships with activist groups. There are still a small number of people opposing the plant who remain very reserved and refuse to speak to anyone who works at Seabrook Station. The plant's community relations department believes it is in their best interest to deal cooperatively with these groups. North Atlantic Energy Corporation has grown ever more sensitive to the concerns of all involved publics.

As Alan Griffith,[4] who currently heads the Seabrook Station Communications Team, notes, "A subtle community relations shift occurred at Seabrook Station as the plant became more accepted and proved itself to be a good neighbor. Initially, the value of a solid community outreach program in large part was to help support the plant's efforts to get licensed and begin generating power. Now that Seabrook has done that, our community outreach is just as important now as it ever was. In many ways, our community relations activities have

---

[4]Our thanks to Alan Griffith for providing updated information on the current status of Seabrook Station and its community relations.

become more of an extension of our own employees' personal lives and commitments to their neighborhoods."

Since 1990, Seabrook Station employees have raised over $1,000,000 for the United Way. The Seabrook Station Web site (www.seabrookstation.com) lists 50 organizations, charities, and town offices that it has served; it understands that it is important to have a very open and active dialogue with the community by meeting with town officials and consistently sharing information with the community stakeholders. As Alan Griffith characterizes it, "We make sure that Seabrook Station is not a faceless plant, but an organization of names and faces. This humanizes the plant and raises the confidence of our stakeholders who know us and feel comfortable with us."

The Seabrook Station Science and Nature Center, its "most valuable PR outreach vehicle," continues its efforts to educate people about nuclear energy. The Center also affords the opportunity to inform visitors about the many initiatives taken by the Station that helped transform a town dump into a thriving ecosystem.

EVALUATION

Has Seabrook Station prevailed in the court of public opinion? In one sense, it has in that it is now an accepted part of the community.

Public opinion has also changed nationally. According to Griffith, a recent national poll reports that 66 percent of Americans not only support nuclear energy, they also support the construction of new nuclear plants in this country. "This is a phenomenal turnaround that would have seemed inconceivable as recently as 15 years ago," he notes.

Seabrook Station continues its two-way communication efforts by upholding its good neighbor policy, offering ongoing educational information to the public, and through the involvement of its employees in their neighborhoods and community organizations—becoming Seabrook Station's ambassadors. "Relationships with stakeholders are personal. When there is a potentially challenging issue, we all know we'll be able to sit down and discuss it," explains Griffith.

North Atlantic also recognizes the future problems associated with the Seabrook plant's ultimate decommissioning, spent fuel rod disposal, and radiological emissions risk correlations. The company plans to deal with these issues in the same "honest, proactive way we've dealt with everything since NHY was formed" in 1984. Over the 20 to 40 year operating cycle for a nuclear plant, the role of sound public relations remains vital. ■

HISTORY OF SEABROOK STATION

1960S

- Plans for a nuclear plant in New Hampshire developed.

1972

- Two-unit power plant proposed for Seabrook, New Hampshire.

1973

- Application for construction permit filed. Concerns about environment arise.

1977

- The Clamshell Alliance and others form and mount protests; 1,400 people are arrested.

1978

- Peaceful demonstration on site is suggested to "The Clam" by an area public relations counselor, Isobel Parke, as more effective than another protest; 30,000 people attend an energy fair on plant grounds. No one is arrested.

1979

- Three Mile Island incident causes Seabrook to reconsider its design. Safety features and more emergency planning are added. Activists express concern through demonstrations.
- Interest rates skyrocket. Construction delayed because of financing difficulties.
- CWIP (Construction Work In Progress) law passed; causes more financial strain.

1984

- Changeover period. New Hampshire Yankee, a division of PSNH, takes over in June to manage completion of construction, licensing, and operation of the plant.
- Construction is temporarily suspended for three months.

1986

- Election year. Candidates' success depended on whether they were for or against Seabrook.
- Paul McEachern, Democrat, defeated by incumbent Republican governor John Sununu, over the CWIP issue.
- Construction of plant completed (July 31).
- Nuclear Regulatory Commission issues license for testing of reactor.
- Chernobyl disaster in USSR.
- More safety concerns and activist demonstrations.
- Massachusetts Governor Michael Dukakis, representing the six Massachusetts towns near Seabrook, pulls his state's support and vows to fight the plant's opening.

1988

- Public Service Company of New Hampshire (PSNH) files Chapter 11 bankruptcy in January.
- Atomic Safety and Licensing Board, an arm of NRC, approves state of New Hampshire's emergency response plan for the towns surrounding Seabrook.

1990

- NRC issues full-power operating license in March, and power is generated for the first time in May. Power level reaches 100 percent in July.

1991

- U.S. Court of Appeals rejects appeal of the NRC's decision to issue an operating license in January.
- Massachusetts Governor William Weld directs state officials to begin cooperative emergency planning with New Hampshire Yankee in March.

(*continued*)

(continued)

- U.S. Supreme Court lets the lower court's decision stand to uphold the NRC's licensing of Seabrook Station in October.

1992

- PSNH is acquired by Northeast Utilities. Seabrook operates at 77.9 percent of generating capacity for the year.

2000

- Seabrook Station celebrates its tenth anniversary.
- Acknowledged by the industry as one of the best-run nuclear plants in the nation.

QUESTIONS FOR DISCUSSION

1. What responsibilities does a business have to the community, if any?

2. Should a business that produces a controversial product or service have obligations that surpass legal and regulatory mandates? Why or why not? Does your answer depend on whether the product (or production of the product) is potentially hazardous or lethal to the environment or humans?

3. Seabrook offers an informational phone line for communities and employees to call whenever questions or concerns arise. This phone line accommodates the local towns surrounding Seabrook Station. Do you think this phone line would be more effective if it were a national 800 number, thus making it available to all U.S. residents? Why or why not?

4. Develop some strategies that could strengthen the messages or effectiveness of the remaining opposition.

5. Develop some proactive and reactive strategies that Seabrook will need when decommissioning the plant, disposing of the spent fuel rods, and if the radiological emission risk correlations show that the plant has become dangerous.

CASE 4-4   NUCLEAR WASTE GOES DOWN THE DRAIN

Every day people all across the country choose to do things that have a certain degree of risk—crossing the street, driving a car, flying in an airplane, bungee jumping, or eating foods they know do not constitute good nutrition.

What happens, though, when someone else controls the risks we face? Do we ask our friend to pull the car over so we can get out? Never fly unless we pilot the plane? What happens if an organization wants to take a risk in a community, such as dumping low-level nuclear waste, even if it may be smaller than the risks we take in everyday life?

More and more, organizations are facing strident opposition to their plans from groups and coalitions opposed to taking on more risk. Grassroots environmental concerns have fostered attitudes such as Not In My Back Yard (NIMBY) and Not On Planet Earth (NOPE) to limit any sort of activities viewed as at all risky. Yet, in many cases, organizations need to assume some risk in order to run their business, produce products, adhere to government standards, or make a profit.

Risk management deals with explaining and persuading a risk-averse public to allow the execution of necessary actions that may carry some risk (See Figure 4-7). But risk communication is more than explanation or persuasion. It must be process-oriented to allow interaction between the opposing groups—the public, proponents, experts, and regulatory officials—and allow each to identify the true issues at stake from its perspective. Only then can the average citizen form an intelligent judgment.

IS RISK COMMUNICATION A DIFFERENT BALL GAME?

As technology has changed, so have the type and amount of risks we face. Public reaction to risk can be varied, depending on each individual's mind-set and experiences. Each person perceives risk in his or her own personal context and with his or her own established biases for or against that risk.

In 1983, the National Research Council (NRC) completed a study on managing risk, leading to a report entitled *Risk Assessment in the Federal Government: Managing the Process.* Raised in this study was the realization that with risk management comes a new kind of communication, risk communication. The NRC chartered a committee, the Risk Perception and Communication Committee, to research how to communicate risks effectively to the public. The committee found that explaining risks in a logical manner was not effective for convincing a risk-averse public that the risks were nothing to worry about. People evaluate risks contextually, and their *perception* of that risk motivates their behavior.

ONE EXAMPLE

For many years, the city of Albuquerque, New Mexico, had an ordinance forbidding anyone—except hospitals and radiation treatment clinics—from disposing of low-level radioactive wastes in the city's sewer system. Low-level radioactive waste covers anything that may have been contaminated by radioactive materials, such as equipment, clothing, tools, and so on.

ANNUAL NUMBER OF DEATHS PER MILLION PEOPLE

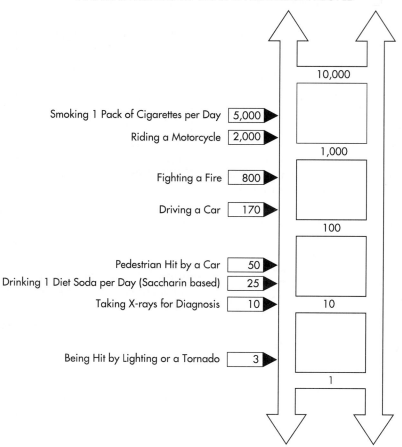

Source: Adapted from Schultz, W.,G. McClelland, B. Hurd, and J. Smith (1986), *Improving Accuracy and Reducing Costs of Environmental Benefits Assessment.* Vol. IV. Boulder: University of Colorado, Center for Economic Analysis.

WARNING! USE OF DATA IN THIS FIGURE FOR RISK COMPARISON PURPOSES CAN SEVERELY DAMAGE YOUR CREDIBILITY (SEE TEXT).

FIGURE 4-7 One tactic used by risk communicators has been to make risk comparisons in order to communicate the extent of the risk. But making quantitative risk comparisons with voluntary risk has proved illogical and damaging to the organizations who employ this tactic. Demonstrating it visually is more effective.

(Courtesy of the Chemical Manufacturers Association. From Vincent T. Covello, Peter M. Sandman, and Paul Slovic, *Risk Communication, Risk Statistics and Risk Comparisons: A Manual for Plant Managers* [Washington, D.C.: CMA, 1988].)

In 1991, Sandia National Laboratories (a facility of the Department of Energy, DOE) and Inhalation Toxicology Research Institute (ITRI) petitioned the city to dispose of their waste in the city sewer systems, as the hospitals were already allowed to do. Sandia initially made the proposal because it wanted to dump 50,000 gallons of low-level radioactive water (used to shield nuclear reactor fuel rods) into the sewer system. Radiation experts assured Albuquerque residents that the risk was minimal and their tap water had more natural or "background" radiation in it than the wastewater did.[1]

An amendment to change the city's sewer-use ordinance was put before the city council. The change would have allowed anyone licensed to use radioactive material to dump low-level radioactive waste into the sewers. Though more organizations would be allowed to dump, more stringent limits would be set on how radioactive the waste could be. They would be able to dump waste at only one-tenth the radioactivity standards established by the Nuclear Regulatory Commission.

After investigating, the city council found that its ordinance or any amendment to an ordinance regarding discharging radioactive wastewater does not fall under its jurisdiction. These regulations are set by the federal government through the Nuclear Regulatory Commission and DOE. Thus Sandia as a federal laboratory could ignore the city ordinance and dump anyway—that is, if its managers thought this was acceptable public relations policy. They did not, however, so the issue went to public debate.

A VOCAL OPPOSITION

Citizen opposition was immediate and outspoken. A group named People's Emergency Response Committee (PERC) began to organize. PERC was formed a year before the emergence of this issue, when those involved first became aware of Mayor Louis Saavedra's attempt to change the city's sewer-use ordinance. It is an ad hoc coalition of citizens' organizations made up of Hospital and Healthcare Workers Union 1199, Citizens for Alternatives to Radioactive Dumping, the South West Organizing Project, New Mexico Public Interest Research Group, the Albuquerque Center for Peace and Justice, Sierra Club, and the Labor Committee for Peace and Justice.

PERC immediately established its position with four fundamental statements:

➤ No other industries including Sandia National Laboratories should be allowed to dump radioactive wastes in the sewers.

➤ The existing Albuquerque sewer ordinance should be strengthened to control and monitor the radioactive wastes being dumped by hospitals and other medical treatment facilities.

➤ The DOE and private industries must develop long-range plans for dealing with their radioactive waste. These plans should not include dumping in the sewers as an option.

➤ All plans must include strategies on how these companies and the DOE will reduce the *generation* of radioactive waste in the first place.

Representatives of the group were at the first hearing regarding the change. They were concerned that the issue was more than obtaining permission to dump 50,000 gallons of waste. They saw it as a ploy to allow any business in the future to rid itself of radioactive waste. Concerns were raised about the water's path. Would it enter the Rio Grande and then affect towns

---

[1]Background radiation is naturally occurring radiation that accounts for more than half of the radiation we are exposed to. It is generated from cosmic rays, naturally occurring elements such as uranium, and radioactive chemicals in the body.

downstream from Albuquerque? This was not a risk that the citizens of Albuquerque and the surrounding towns were prepared to take, PERC felt.

PERC'S TACTICS

One communication tactic that PERC utilized was to publish a newsletter entitled Radioactive Pipeline to establish its position. Its focus was on the risks that residents perceived: that this could contaminate Albuquerque and that there was no telling if Sandia and the others could be trusted. This newsletter helped PERC get its message out to make people aware of the situation. The newsletters and flyers PERC distributed urged the citizens of Albuquerque and surrounding areas to take action and voice their concerns at community and city council meetings. Postcard campaigns were mounted by distributing preprinted cards so that citizens could easily send them to local city councilors expressing opposition to this ordinance. A petition drive was started, gathering more than 7,000 signatures.

OBSTACLES FOR SANDIA

Media coverage was not helpful for Sandia, either. While officials were explaining how safe the water was in one article, other articles in the newspaper reported some of Sandia's sewer violations and mismanagement of radioactive materials by DOE.

City council meetings were packed with citizens who came to voice their outrage. Sandia arranged for two radiation experts to speak in an attempt to reassure people of their physical safety, but this expertise did not address the underlying issues that made up a major part of this controversy.

➤ Many Americans have a **lack of trust** for the federal government and those organizations that are a part of it. When, or if, stories con-

cerning federal mismanagement and secret nuclear tests are uncovered, the public will remember them later.

➤ The effects of radioactive wastes are not completely understood. Some effects will not be apparent for a very long time, and this **uncertainty** is difficult for anyone to deal with.

➤ Many people already have **biases** against anything nuclear, especially if it is near where they live.

➤ Albuquerque residents were concerned with what this initial dumping would mean for the **future.** They were asking themselves: What else would be dumped, and how often would it happen?

THE SANDIA SIDE OF IT

Sandia's public affairs department did make an attempt to educate the public about this risk to try and allay public fears about radiation and radioactive materials. Some of their activities included:

➤ Organizing some of the public meetings to create the opportunity for citizens to voice their concerns and get questions answered.

➤ Reaching out to public officials and leaders who showed opposition to the proposal to give them the facts of the issue.

➤ Making public affairs people available for any and all questions that the public had about the issue.

➤ Arranging for television interviews with radiation experts to disseminate to the public the facts of radiation.

CAN THERE EVER BE AGREEMENT?

On November 5, 1991, the Albuquerque City Council voted against the proposal to change the city ordinance. The Council then formed a study committee to review important questions about radioactive dumping and offer recommendations in six months. Two years and two research studies later, the city council finally consented to the disposal of the wastewater in the sewer system.

For Sandia National Laboratories, the task of disposing of its waste became an ordeal. A simple task of applying for a permit had become an extended three-year controversy.

For all affected organizations, the question remains: What will we do with our low-level radioactive waste? What is often overlooked is the benefits that nuclear science offers. Do we abolish nuclear science altogether? NIMBYists demand that disposal not be done where they live. Where else, then? Will there ever be an acceptable alternative? For public relations practitioners, the challenge of communicated risk will only become greater as technology advances.

YUCCA MOUNTAIN—AN UNRESOLVED RISK MANAGEMENT PROBLEM

While Sandia National Laboratories was eventually successful in obtaining permission to dispose of its wastewater in the city sewer system, another Department of Energy (DOE) proposal for the disposal of radioactive materials continues to remain unresolved. The Yucca Mountain case is further complicated by issues of alleged environmental racism and the right to protect culturally sacred sites.

In 1982, Congress passed the Nuclear Waste Policy Act that set an objective framework for government officials to study and evaluate multiple potential repository sites for nuclear waste in the United States. The DOE faces the task of finding a geologic repository to permanently store 77,000 metric tons of high-level radioactive waste that is temporarily being stored at various locations around the country. About 90 percent of this waste is from commercial nuclear power plants; the remainder is from government defense programs.

The Nuclear Waste Policy Act Amendment of 1987—nicknamed "Screw Nevada Act" by residents there—(1) eliminated all but one of the potential repository sites, Yucca Mountain in Nevada, and (2) directed the DOE to study only that location for site suitability. The Amendment stressed that if, at any time, the Yucca Mountain site is found unsuitable, studies of the site will be stopped immediately. If the studies are discontinued, the site will be restored and the DOE will seek new direction from Congress.

Yucca Mountain is located 100 miles northwest of Las Vegas and sits on the western edge of the DOE's former nuclear-weapons test site. The proposed repository would sit 1,000 feet below the top of the mountain and 1,000 feet above the ground water.

In 1992, Congress passed the Energy Policy Act, which required the Environmental Protection Agency (EPA) to develop site-specific radiation protection standards for Yucca Mountain to protect public health and the environment from harmful exposure to the radioactive waste that would be stored there. The Nuclear Regulatory Commission (NRC) is responsible for implementing the standards set by the EPA. Ultimately the NRC would be responsible for establishing the process for deciding whether Yucca Mountain meets the EPA's standards.

From the beginning, the State of Nevada has firmly opposed the plan and is prepared to file lawsuits through all steps of

PR MESSAGES SET RISK PERCEPTIONS, AND RISK IS EVERYWHERE

All communications have become risk communications. Therefore, the rules for dealing with hazardous waste and cancer fears should be applied to every communication—to employees, shareholders, stakeholders, and customers, and surely to regulators, government entities, and the body politic.

Why? Because today publics are interested in two things: What can you do *for* me? And what, if I'm not careful, might you do *to* me? That second query—people's natural skepticism raised to new levels by today's troubled economy and quality-of-life—adds a risk perspective to every message or appeal.

INFLUENCING PEOPLE'S PERCEPTION OF RISK

Risk communication is proactive. Its goal is to improve knowledge and change perceptions, attitudes, and behaviors of the target public, write Leandro Batista and Dulcie Straughan, of the University of North Carolina at Chapel Hill.[1] They note, however, that changing risk perception—a necessary step for behavior change—is complicated. It can be:

1. *Objective:* product of research, statistics, experimental studies, surveys, probabilistic risk analysis, or

2. *Subjective:* how those without expert or inside knowledge interpret the research or the situation—which is based on their values and particular levels of experience and knowledge.

Thus experts and lay people build different mental models that lead them to interpret risk activities differently. One does it objectively, the other subjectively.

FORMAT OF THE MESSAGE

The format of the risk message forms the risk perception. For example, radon and asbestos have a 25-fold difference in *actual* risk to the population, but generate only a slight difference in *perceived* threat. The inaccuracy of people's perceptions of the relative risks of radon and asbestos can be explained by the similarity of the format of messages conveying the risks involved. Regardless of the actual content of the message, the idea that is usually conveyed is that "this is a technical area that you probably won't understand, but there is a *danger here.*" In other words, people will have similar responses to messages that are expressed in similar formats, even though the information may be different. Pubic relations teams can apply their knowledge of this aspect of human nature to formulate effective messages in a systematic way.

1. Each risk has its own identity (or risk perception), which is a specific combination of subjective risk factors (see box), or, as Neil Weinstein and Peter Sandman call them, "Outrage Factors."[2]

2. Some combination of these outrage factors leads people to be more upset about hazard X than hazard Y.

3. Not all factors are relevant for all risks, and there is no trade-off among factors-scoring high on one factor will not compensate for a low score on another (the

(continued)

(*continued*)

noncompensatory model). Factors are either on or off in the overall perception of that risk.

4. Therefore, it's important to understand the underlying dimensions that affect the perception of a particular risk—how the outrage factors combine to form a risk perception.

5. Messages should not be formulated until these underlying dimensions are understood.

SUBJECTIVE RISK FACTORS

Less Risky	**More Risky**
voluntary	involuntary
familiar	unfamiliar
controllable	uncontrollable
controlled by self	controlled by others
fair	unfair
not memorable	memorable
not dreaded	dreaded
chronic	acute
diffused in time and space	focused in time and space
natural	artificial

A final concept to keep in mind is the one that governs the decision-making process: With health or environmental risks, people will modify their behavior if a highly threatening situation exists (or is perceived to exist). Thus a minimum standard, or threshold, is set for risk acceptability. If a risk is greater than the threshold, action occurs; otherwise the status quo is preferred. In all probability, this concept is as true for risks of being overcharged, getting fired, or losing on investments as it is for nuclear discharges.

Peter Sandman's formula for identifying risk has become widely used by public relations practitioners: HAZARD + OUTRAGE = RISK PERCEPTION.[3]

---

[1]"Dimensions Influencing Risk Perception: The Case of Lung Diseases." Unpublished paper, n.d.

[2]Neil D. Weinstein and Peter M. Sandman, "Predicting Homeowner Mitigation Responses to Radon Test Data," *Journal of Social Issues* 48, 1992.

[3]Peter Sandman, *Responding to Community Outrage: Strategies for Effective Risk Communication*, Fairfax, VA: American Industrial Hygiene Association, 1993.

---

the process if Yucca Mountain is recommended as the permanent repository site. The state is supported in its opposition by more than 200 environmental groups.

Primary concerns with the plan to make Yucca Mountain the permanent resting grounds for the country's nuclear waste are: (1) The threat of earthquakes in the pro-

posed area which could cause leakage. Since 1976, over 600 earthquakes of 2.5 or more on the Reichter scale have occurred within a 50-mile radius of Yucca Mountain. In 1992, a 5.6 earthquake occurred on a previously unknown fault at Yucca Mountain. (2) There is evidence, uncovered by the Los Alamos Department of Energy Project in 1998, that

Yucca Mountain would not comply with guidelines regarding ground water flow. Data regarding rainwater infiltration of Yucca Mountain would have called for the immediate disqualification under set guidelines. However, Yucca Mountain was not disqualified. When the nuclear industry found that two of the DOE requirements were going to be violated, they lobbied Congress to change the suitability guidelines.

In November 1998, the opposition held a news conference. Many political representatives and members of consumer organizations and environmental groups introduced a petition from more than 200 groups opposed to the plan. They urged the DOE to "follow the law, disqualify the site because it could not meet the environmental guidelines under the current law." Despite the opposition, the evaluation of Yucca Mountain continues. In August 1999, the EPA released draft radiation protection standards for Yucca Mountain. It gave a preliminary approval of Yucca Mountain as a safe disposal site. After issuing its report, the EPA accepted written comments and held public hearings around the country "to ensure public involvement in the decision-making process."

In December 1999, a policy revision proposal for Yucca Mountain was released by the Federal government. The proposal eliminated safeguards regarding water flow on the mountain. Nevada Senator Henry Reid said the change contradicted Energy Secretary Bill Richardson's original goal that science, not politics, would drive the decisions regarding the disposal of nuclear waste.

Nevada Agency for Nuclear Projects sponsored a series of public workshops designed to encourage public participation and comment on the DOE's Yucca Mountain draft Environmental Impact Statement (EIS). The DOE was conducting public hearings on the draft EIS in ten Nevada communities. State-sponsored workshops were held in those same communities. Its goal was to prepare Nevadans to effectively comment on the draft EIS. The DOE is required to address the public's comments in the final EIS.

ENVIRONMENTAL RACISM IS INVOLVED

Opposition also comes from native rights groups and, more specifically, the Western Shoshone Nation because Yucca Mountain is a place of spiritual significance to the Shoshone and Paiute peoples. The Western Shoshone Nation contends that the government has no right to use the land since it was guaranteed to them by an 1863 treaty (18 Statutes at Large 689). Corbin Harney, a Western Shoshone spiritual leader, says "Even the mere study of the site is a violation of the treaty. The Shoshone people want the DOE off their land and their mountain restored to them."

Based on the history of the interaction of the United States government with Indian tribes, mistrust of the government is deeply instilled in most native people. In their view, another treaty violation and further dismissal of native participation in the process simply validates and exacerbates this mistrust. Many native and environmental groups believe that native lands are specifically targeted for nuclear waste disposal by the federal government and that these actions can be defined as environmental racism. According to Grace Thorpe of the National Environmental Coalition of Native Americans, the following factors make native lands an easy selection for governmental agencies:

➤ The lands are some of the most isolated in North America
➤ The lands and the populations are extremely impoverished

➤ The tribes are politically vulnerable

➤ Their tribal sovereignty can be used to bypass state environmental laws

A review of the government's Yucca Mountain Project Web site (www.ymp.gov) indicates that the spiritual concerns and land rights issues of the Western Shoshone Nation are given little, if any, consideration. Under a section entitled "Preservation through Conservation," the site states "the U.S. Department of Energy works to protect important cultural resources at the site . . . through the Yucca Mountain Project's Cultural Resources Program. As part of the Cultural Resources Program, delegates from the Project have met with tribal leaders . . . to gather cultural data for the Program." While this Program professes to endeavor to protect the "archaeological, botanical, and cultural resources," there is no mention of the spiritual nature of the land or acknowledgement of the 1863 treaty and, therefore, the alleged illegality of the presence of the Project in the Yucca

Mountain area. In fact, the Web site states "Nearly all of the land surrounding Yucca Mountain is federally owned."

Although the Yucca Mountain repository was originally scheduled to open by 1998, numerous technical and political delays have advanced that date. Spencer Abraham, Secretary of Energy, was expected to decide in 2001 whether to recommend to President Bush that Yucca Mountain be established as a nuclear waste repository site but that decision was further postponed by the September 11 terrorist attacks. The attacks put the safety of transporting nuclear waste from one location to another under further scrutiny. However, in January 2002, Secretary Abraham announced that he would recommend to the president that Yucca Mountain be used as a nuclear waste storage site. The president will then decide whether to recommend the site to Congress for approval. If approved, the DOE must apply for licensing from the Nuclear Regulatory Commission. The license would then permit the DOE to construct the facility and begin waste disposal in 2010. ■

QUESTIONS FOR DISCUSSION

1. If you were a public relations practitioner working at a local hospital that was dumping low-level radioactive waste into the sewers, what would you have counseled management to do during the Sandia attempt to gain authorization to dump its waste? Why would you recommend that?

2. Would it have been possible to convince the citizens of Albuquerque to allow the dumping of radioactive waste in the sewers? Why do you believe this? What tactics could Sandia have used to allay the fears of the public?

3. Why was PERC successful in gathering so much public support? What did it do differently than Sandia?

4. If you were the EPA's public relations director, what would you do to reach the opposition and communicate about the risks involved at Yucca Mountain? Do you think it's possible to reach a win-win solution? If so, how? Or must the government strong-arm its plan into place? If it pushes through its plan, what do you think will be the consequences?

CASE 4-5   GRASSROOTS EFFORTS SAVE A HISTORIC PIECE OF LAND

In the summer of 1995, a for-sale sign was placed on a small parcel of open but developable land in the heart of historic downtown Exeter, New Hampshire. Almost immediately, a small group of concerned citizens (including public relations firm Jackson Jackson & Wagner senior counsel Isobel Parke) began a grassroots effort to purchase the land and keep it as open space for everyone to enjoy. It was on this land that the original Town House of Exeter stood. And it was there, on January 5, 1776, that New Hampshire declared its independence from Great Britain—the first of the colonies to do so.

A total of $150,000 was needed to purchase this last parcel of open space in historic downtown Exeter. The grassroots effort had three phases:

1. Gathering over 50 signatures on a citizens' petition to place a warrant article before town meeting for $70,000 toward the land's purchase price.
2. Gaining a yes vote for the article at town meeting. This was a real challenge because the taxpayers union had won two-thirds support for changes in town government that it felt would restrain expenditures.
3. Raising, in three months, matching funds from private donations. This effort was a public-private partnership.

PUBLIC RELATIONS TACTICS

This grassroots effort successfully used the following tactics:

➤ **The information campaign began early to give those most likely to be interested a heads-up without alerting the opposition.** Soon after the for-sale sign appeared, the historic Perry-Dudley House (home of Jackson Jackson & Wagner), located next to the open space, participated in a town-wide open house tour. This provided an opportunity to talk with visitors about the importance of the adjoining open space. A flier handed out to over 250 visitors outlined the issue and suggested action steps, such as calling their selectman to express support for saving the open space.

➤ **A broad spectrum of well respected opinion leaders in the community were chosen to be members of the organizing committee.** Their connections and credibility helped to support the cause.

➤ **The committee concentrated on those most likely to offer support**—especially helpful when there are limited resources. They did not waste time trying to convert others. To gain support for the upcoming vote at town meeting, a mailing was sent to organizations most likely to be supportive: Exeter Historical Society, Conservation Commission, an area land trust, a local museum, and friends of the organizing committee—including a local walking club (of which one of the steering committee was a member) and a senior citizens community known to have strong environmentally aware residents.

Brief talks were given to local organizations such as the Chamber of Commerce and the Rotary. Personal visits were made to the chief of police and to the fire department—both situated opposite the open space.

➤ **The organizing committee was open and upfront with likely objections. This weakened the force of the opposition.** Through one-on-one research, the committee anticipated opposition from the newly formed taxpayers association, especially its concern that creating a park on the open space would remove the land from the tax rolls. The tax implications were explained in a flier sent to selected town residents and made available at the town meeting where the issue was discussed.

The leader of the taxpayers association opposed taking the land off the tax roll. On another project, however, he expressed support for the concept of the public-private partnership. Park proponents used the communication strategy of asking that his group remain at least neutral in discussion of the warrant article, since opposition was discourteous to fellow citizens willing to make the effort to raise private matching funds for this public-private partnership.

This soft tactic worked. The leaflet produced by the taxpayers association advised its members to oppose almost every warrant article up for vote at the town meeting, but omitted the park issue—even though it required the largest amount of money.

➤ **Despite negative predictions, the committee did not give up**—hoping that events over which they had no control might tilt the balance in their favor. Organizers had hoped for a small turnout with their supporters carrying the day. But due to special items on the agenda, the meeting was larger than anticipated. Many of the supporters for the open space were in their 60s, 70s, and 80s. Organizers had relied on the advice from town officials that the meeting would probably be a short one, over by lunch.

However, the contentiousness of the taxpayers association prolonged the discussion of the early items on the agenda, which made a lunch break necessary. Would the supporters for open space return after lunch? They did. Some of the taxpayers association supporters melted away because the two items on which they felt most strongly (and lost) were dealt with early in the agenda. The order of the agenda (which unexpectedly was changed) was extremely helpful to the open space cause. Without this change, the taxpayers association would have stayed to the bitter end.

All the articles adding to the town budget passed. The open space article was the last money article on the agenda. It came up at about 4 P.M. Shortly before the opening speech, the organizers decided to amend the article. This was a risk but it served them well in presenting a case for a downward cap on the amount of money requested. Rather than asking for $70,000, it was amended to ask for half the negotiated purchase price, not to exceed $70,000.

As expected, selectmen and the speakers from the floor raised the negative aspects of taking property off the tax roll. The committee's three speakers were brief and avoided going into the kind of detail, especially financial, that usually confuses and leads to disaster in town meeting situations. Feeling that the meeting was ready to vote, the "cleanup" speaker decided not to speak, knowing well that many good causes have talked themselves to death. The initial voice vote was indecisive. A hand vote showed the motion carried by a safe majority of 106 to 78. Given the inauspicious environment of the voters and the opposition of the selectmen, the committee was pleasantly surprised.

➤ **The committee avoided the media because organizers were uncertain of the media's stand on the open space issue.** During the period of town elections, an initial visit was paid to the editor of the local paper. His support seemed uncertain, especially since he gave editorial support to the successful bid for office by the leader of the taxpayers association. No news releases or media interviews were given until after town meeting. This avoided giving the opposition a target.

During the fund-raising period, the committee also worked "under the media radar" until one-third of the money was raised. Then, members of the media were given an informational kit and two members of the committee were designated to act as spokespersons for the fund-raising committee.

➤ **Fund-raising audiences were carefully targeted.** Forty potential donors able to give $5,000 or more were targeted for personal calls by members of the committee who knew them. Letters were sent to 2,100 taxpayers with property valued over $100,000. Others were invited to participate through a sign posted on the open space and an advertisement in the local newspaper. Gifts from more than 400 individual donors, businesses, and foundations raised more than $163,000—this did not include the $70,000 from the town of Exeter. Money remaining after the sale of the land was used for beautification of the park and the establishment of a maintenance fund.

➤ **Fund-raising materials were carefully matched with the values of the community.** They were simple, no pictures, one-color ink on white or colored paper, no gloss, and designed to use one first-class postage stamp.

The half-acre public park was purchased, completed, and dedicated 18 months after the plan to create the park began. It is simply landscaped with low-maintenance perennial flowers, trees, and bushes that bear spring flowers and offer shade in the summer and rich color in the fall. Brick walkways, benches, and a picnic table make it an inviting green space for people to enjoy. ■

QUESTIONS FOR DISCUSSION

1. Consider the efficacy of a "stealth" campaign. What conditions must be present for a stealth campaign to be the best option?
2. Was the inclusion of "opinion leaders" on the steering committee beneficial? Why? How?
3. Evaluate the tactic of not attempting to convert those opposed to the park. Is this a risky move? Why? What can be done to reduce any risk this strategy carries?
4. Evaluate the role "small-town America" played in this campaign. Would these same tactics succeed in New York? Los Angeles? Your hometown? Why?
5. What could proponents have done if the opposition and media took a vocal, opposing stance to the park?

CASE 4-6 ONE COMPANY'S BATTLE RESURRECTED IN A HOLLYWOOD MOVIE: WHAT IS THE BEST DEFENSE?

Having your company name featured—or even mentioned—in a Hollywood movie starring top-name actors is a public relations practitioner's dream—if the focus is positive. But what happens when your company is portrayed negatively?

W. R. Grace faced this challenge when *A Civil Action,* a movie starring John Travolta and Robert Duval, opened on Christmas Day 1998. You may remember the case. It was the subject of a book also titled *A Civil Action* published in 1995 based on a lawsuit involving W. R. Grace. In the suit, Grace was accused of contaminating drinking water in the Boston suburb of Woburn. The case gained national attention after the book became a bestseller. Unfortunately for W. R. Grace, that attention was resurrected with the release of the film three years later. How W. R. Grace handled the situation is the focus of this case.

A COMPANY WITH DEEP ROOTS

W. R. Grace is a $1.6 billion global supplier of specialty chemical, construction, and container products. The company was founded in 1854 in Peru by William Russell Grace, and relocated in 1865 to New York City. In 1880, Grace was elected mayor of New York City for two terms, and in 1885, he accepted the Statue of Liberty from the people of France.

Over the years, the company expanded, and the Grace name became well known around the globe. In 1914, the Grace National Bank was established, later to become Marine Midland Bank. That same year, Grace sent the first commercial vessel through the Panama Canal. Later that decade, Grace Line passenger ships were drafted into war service to ferry troops.

THE STAGE IS SET

From 1960 to 1988, Grace operated a machine manufacturing plant in Woburn. In the early 1980s, a leukemia cluster was discovered in the town. The families of those who died of the disease filed a lawsuit accusing W. R. Grace and a second firm, Beatrice Foods, of polluting the town's water supply with industrial solvents. They believed the chemicals contaminated their drinking water and caused the deaths of many innocent people.

W. R. Grace admitted to dumping some chemicals, including trychloroethylene (TCE), in an area of Woburn but adamantly denied that the chemicals entered the families' water systems. The legal case created a controversy in the community and heartache for the families involved for many years. In the end, the families received an $8 million settlement, although W. R. Grace claimed no responsibility for the deaths. The companies are today engaged in a 50-year, $70 million clean up.

A VALUABLE—BUT COSTLY—LESSON

Grace received much criticism by professionals for its public relations strategy during the Woburn case. It strongly asserted its innocence throughout the trial and refused to talk about the case publicly. It chose instead to focus efforts on cleaning up the polluted sites and building relationships with the community. Unfortunately, the company's efforts didn't include some key publics. "We did a bad job of communicating with employees, and paid a heavy price for it," explained Mark Stoler, former director of environmental safety and health at W. R. Grace. "We also made mistakes in not addressing the concerns of community and government agencies."

According to Stoler, Grace was determined to use the lessons learned from the Woburn trial to build relationships with employees and government agencies. The company set up social responsibility programs with local schools and provided training and equipment to help the fire department better respond to hazardous materials handling. In the years following the Woburn case, the Environmental Protection Agency praised W. R. Grace's efforts as setting "a new standard for accelerating the pace of Superfund cleanup."

THE CASE THAT WOULDN'T DIE

But the case was not closed in the eyes of the media. In 1998, 12 years after the Woburn trial ended, Disney announced the upcoming release of *A Civil Action*. The film would be based on a book of the same name about the Woburn trial. The book, written by a previously unknown author, Jonathan Harr, became a bestseller.

When W. R. Grace executives found out about the planned movie, they tried to contact Disney producers to give them their side of the story—to point out what they perceived as untruths in the book, and to promote their progress in making amends with the Woburn community. Grace representatives said they received no response from Disney representatives.

A MEDIA CAMPAIGN IS BORN

Grace public relations executives felt they had no choice but to launch an offensive against the movie, especially in light of their previous mistakes. "We didn't talk for 10 years," explained Stoler. "Under these circumstances, we felt we had to stand up and say something."

Grace employed several tactics to prevent or counteract potential negative publicity the movie might generate:

- ➤ CEO Paul Norris sent a letter to the press giving his opinion of the movie—but he did this before he even saw the movie.
- ➤ The company developed a Web site titled "Beyond A Civil Action: Woburn Issues and Answers."
- ➤ Press kits were distributed at the movie's opening in Los Angeles and New York.
- ➤ Grace representatives appeared on talk shows and in newsrooms to tell the public about the company's efforts to clean up the environment.

➤ A glossy, 30-page press kit was mailed to newspapers, magazines, and radio and TV stations around the country.

Grace attempted to "get ahead" of the issue and provide the media with information on its activities since the case was settled, hoping to generate attention on the positives rather than the negatives. Unfortunately, it neglected an important public relations tenant: *Understand the opposition's strategy before making a move.*

Subsidiaries of the other company in the suit, Beatrice Foods (which disbanded after the trial), chose to sit back and wait it out. Interestingly, Beatrice Foods was barely mentioned in the media coverage. Boston Herald reporter Dan Kennedy, who covered the trial for years, said Grace overreacted to the film. "They're really almost an afterthought in the film," he said in a *Boston Globe* article following its release.

A MORE EFFECTIVE APPROACH

Perhaps Grace would have been well served to more thoroughly determine exactly what it was up against. The company focused little attention on two of its key publics: Woburn residents and its own employees. Through pre- and post-focus groups, could the company have assessed its publics' opinions on the film and developed a more targeted path of action? Its hands-off approach motivated key players to retry the case in the media, who, thanks to the information pro-

vided in Grace's press kits, were more than willing to listen.

In a similar case, Dow Corning was deep in the silicone breast implant controversy (See Case 10-4) when the company learned of a made-for-television movie about it. After determining the film contained inaccuracies, they decided to take a stand. Dow communicated with all of its publics, and focused particular attention on the hometown community. It organized a town meeting at the local high school where the company's CEO, president, and bankruptcy counsel commented on the situation, and then opened the floor to questions. The executives stayed until every question was answered.

ANOTHER CHAPTER

Just six months after the release of the movie, W. R. Grace found itself involved in yet another confrontation with citizens in one of its operating communities. Residents in a Cambridge, Massachusetts, neighborhood felt the company's measures to contain the release of asbestos during the construction of a hotel, two office buildings, and a retail space were inadequate. For years they had been trying to persuade W. R. Grace to investigate and clean up the contamination and abandon its plan to develop the area. "The problem is," said City Councilor Kathleen Born at a meeting on the issue, "W. R. Grace does not have a trust relationship with this community." ■

QUESTIONS FOR DISCUSSION

1. Environmental issues like those addressed in the Woburn and Cambridge incidents have become hot topics. What are some of the

behaviors driving the key players on both sides of these situations?

2. Your public relations firm was hired by W. R. Grace to handle the company's

strategy around the release of *A Civil Action*. What are some of the situational factors that would have been important to evaluate before developing a plan?

3. Keeping those issues in mind, what would be the main objectives of your plan, and what tactics would you use to achieve them?

4. List the positive steps, then the negative ones, W. R. Grace took in this case, and be prepared to defend your decisions.

PROBLEM 4-A Helping Isn't Always Easy

You are a member of a civic organization that has 300 members locally and is the local chapter of a national organization. Most of the membership is well educated and falls into the middle- and upper-income brackets. The local organization has a reputation of civic involvement—working for better schools, increased voter registration, and equal rights for minorities and women.

About eighteen months ago, the executive committee made a presentation to the organization on illiteracy in your city. Studies show that 25 percent of the adult population is "functionally illiterate." By the year 2001, the number of functional illiterates is projected to reach more than one-third of the population. Although the problem is spread throughout the population, the percentage of minorities in this group is high.

Soon after the executive committee's presentation, the organization votes to establish a literacy council for adults in the city. The primary function of the council is to solicit and train volunteers to act as tutors and match these persons with individuals wanting to learn to read and write. The organization is able to generate heavy news coverage of the council and public service announcements about the need for tutors and students. Despite the coverage, very few persons have volunteered to tutor, even fewer persons have requested the service.

Because of your expertise as a communicator, the organization has asked you to become involved in this program. Your review of the program indicates there is general agreement among individuals that something has to be done, but no one is quite sure what. Your organization sets an objective of obtaining and training 50 volunteer tutors and matching these with 50 students in the next six months.

As a well-trained public relations professional, you recognize that your organization has fallen into the trap of believing that widespread and positive publicity will influence behavior. You agree to help the cause but stipulate that research is essential to discover why the program hasn't taken off.

Describe how you will design and budget (in time and money) a research program to give you the information necessary to implement a successful recruiting program for students and tutors.

PROBLEM 4-B Adjusting to a Change in Command

For ten years, George Loyal has been a one-person public relations department at Siwash, a college of 3,500 students in Ohio. They have been 10 good years in terms of George's working conditions. There has been plenty of publicity material to pump out, and there has been cooperation on the part of news media.

A main factor assisting George has been the attitude of the Siwash College president. He takes an open stance publicly. He is articulate, handsome, and personable. He has been effective in attracting quality faculty, activating alumni support, and adding notable trustees who have been important in raising funds and making sure that Siwash is favorably regarded by legislators in the state capital.

But all these good things seem to have come to an end. The president was struck down by a massive heart attack and suddenly passed away. The trustees moved quickly to name a successor, who turned out to be a senior member of the Siwash faculty. He is a professor of anthropology, a scholar who is well published, quiet, and nonpublic.

The new president, in the month since his selection, has not informed George that he is not going to be active in alumni affairs, visible at sports events, or available to talk with news media whenever they want him to. He spends most of his time closeted with a few of the older faculty members. His secretary seems to feel that her job is to protect him from intrusions or outside visitors. He has not sent for George or sent him a memo about any specific job to do or any change in his responsibilities.

George's work has almost come to a standstill except for routine news releases. He frankly is not sure where he stands. The cooperative relationship he has had with news media seems to be threatened. The director of alumni relations is as baffled as he is. Two trustees have quietly indicated that they are stepping aside rather than stand for reelection when the time comes. The local sports editor has tipped George off that the newspaper's managing editor plans to ask for a meeting with the new president soon if he doesn't "come out of his shell."

The question before George is, What options does he have in trying to preserve the gains in public relations attained during the past 10 years?

1. What would be the most effective way of establishing a proactive relationship with the new president?
2. What would be your overall strategy for maintaining the college's relationships with its important stakeholders?
3. Given the personality of the new president, what role would you allot to him in maintaining the college's reputation?
4. How would you gain support for this strategy?

PROBLEM 4-C Bringing the Community to Consensus

You are an employee of a public relations firm that focuses on raising money for the fine arts. A large client of the firm wants to find funding in order go relocate the city's largest Center for the Arts within a yet-to-be-built state-of-the-art facility. You meet with your peers and discuss taking on this large assignment.

There are several key factors to consider; most important is how the community will react to such a change. The Center's current home is legendary, dating back to when the city was first built. It has held many memorable performances. Parents love to bring their children to the plays and musicals that are performed there; many enjoy its opera and classical music performances. Film festivals and dance performances have also been presented there.

However, the Center is old and in need of repair. Estimates for the needed repairs and for long-term upkeep are high. This client feels it would be more financially sound to build a new facility than to pour more money into the old building. The advantages for building a new Center — state-of-the-art acoustics, up-to-date technology, expanded and more comfortable seating, etc. — weigh greatly against the community's desire to keep the old building and find funding to repair it in future years. There is also the matter of convincing the board of directors. Some of the members are in favor of keeping the old building and feel that, historically, it is too valuable to abandon.

Knowing that you need to sway opinion within the community as well as the board of directors, how would you begin? What information do you need and how would you get it? What specific audiences would you target? Which audience must you reach first? How do you propose to reach all the various audiences? How would you use two-way communication in your plan? Would opinion leaders work here? If so, how would you find them? Consider also the future use of the current building. How can that become part of your plan?

5

INVESTOR
RELATIONS

Financial investment is no longer the purview of the wealthy alone. With the advent of the IRA, 401(k), ESOP (Employee Stock Ownership Program), and online trading, the body of investors has swollen with middle-class wage earners looking to a more secure future. These people follow the market with the same fervor as traditional institutional investors, and probably suffer more over the ups and downs of the market than any high rollers.

One aspect of financial affairs that increasingly affects the national mood is U.S. investors' evaluations of the corporations in which they have invested. The major measurements are dollar sales volume, profit, the increase or decrease in interest or dividends paid, and whether the price of the stock or bond has increased or decreased from the original purchase price. Other factors include the rank of the company among competitors in its field and what percentage of dividends is paid in comparison with the purchase price.

Experts in the financial world who make a living, and sometimes a fortune, by analyzing and trading equities for themselves and for customers have to be aware of changing conditions in the money supply, raw material prices, international monetary affairs, national economies around the world, and much more. They use sophisticated measurement tools such as stock market trend lines, a company's management capabilities, debt to asset ratio, and several others.

In addition, there is the element of government finance-borrowings by the Treasury Department, municipalities, or state agencies in the form of bonds or debentures.

Today, with stock market news and international monetary or economic status constantly reported and talked about, public relations practitioners also must keep abreast of these topics. A small percent of practitioners will specialize in investor or financial relations. However, *all* practitioners need to be familiar with the economic climate and its impact on the organizations they represent—corporate, governmental, or nonprofit.

THE PUBLICLY OWNED CORPORATION CONCEPTUALIZED

In the U.S. business system, as an ideal, the publicly owned corporation's mission, performance, and behavior represent the consent granted, and the consensus of views held, by all those who have a stake in its financial success. This concept embraces shareholders, employees and their pension fund, community neighbors, suppliers, and certainly customers. On the sidelines, appropriately, are those associations and governmental agencies designated to encourage, oversee, referee, or discipline in the name of all taxpayers, or the voters. In this idealization, publicly owned corporations might be seen as instruments of a people's capitalism. In actuality, such a concept is simplistic, and does not exist, for these companies quickly take on the personalities of those who manage them—competitive, greedy, self-serving, or just the opposite.

A publicly owned business is created and managed to be profitable and to be competitive with others that sell the same product or service. In order to get started at all, there must be capital or credit, and a product or service for which a market is perceived or waiting to be created. Prudent use of capital and skill in producing and marketing the product or service become the province of a small group that manages the enterprise day by day. Survival comes first. Beyond that, growth, diversification, and expansion make up goals that fuel ambition and drive all participants on the payroll. Profit, what's left over after all expenses are paid, makes everything else possible.

Given these realities, it is simply not practical for all those who have a stake in the outcome of an enterprise to take an active part in a forum for major decisions or as links in the decision process. Apart from being largely inaccessible, the stakeholders of a publicly owned corporation are too diverse in their self-interests and in their views of what a business should do, except for a few public issues such as quality of environment, to rally and force action. Given the realities, it should not be surprising that profit, and the power it brings, frequently leads to excesses, abuses, and corruption. These bring investigation, prosecution where indicated, and regulatory measures to preclude recurrence, in the name of the ultimate public interest.

REALITY HAS A LONG HISTORY

Corporations are not ordained by Mother Nature but are a creation of the state. Until the early 1800s, someone starting a business had no "corporate shield" but put all his or her assets at risk. If the business failed, the owner was personally responsible for all debts to the point of personal bankruptcy. Because this situation discouraged the formation of new business, laws were enacted allowing for the formation of **corporations**—business entities in which shareholders risk only the amount of their investment.

What the state creates it can regulate. Regulatory measures started a long time ago. In addition to regulations in interstate commerce mandated by the U.S. Constitution, the federal government began to institute more stringent controls over business. In 1890, the Sherman Antitrust Act was passed, aimed at concentration or monopoly within several industries. This act was supplemented by the Clayton Act in 1914, and in the same year, the Federal Trade Commission Act set up a mechanism to keep channels of interstate trade open to competition. The 1929 stock market crash and the Great Depression of the 1930s stimulated legislative and regulatory actions in the investment area. First was the Securities Act of 1933, requiring a corporation to publish a prospectus (a preliminary printed statement that describes an enterprise and is distributed to prospective investors) when it prepares to sell securities to the public. Then came the Securities Exchange Act of 1934, creating the Securities and Exchange Commission (SEC) and dealing with the conflict of interest involved when a corporate official reaps personal financial gain on information not known to the public. Rule 10b-5 in 1942 tightened the act, prohibiting fraudulent and deceptive practices in the purchase or sale of securities.

THE MATURING OF FINANCIAL PUBLIC RELATIONS

In spite of the Teapot Dome scandal and other problems stemming from over-control of many economic areas by the so-called robber barons, financial public relations didn't spring up in the 1920s, but publicity specialists such as Ivy Lee and Ed Bernays were called in at that time for their expertise.

Financial relations in the 1930s was recognized by employers as a useful communications element, but secondary to the publicity and special events that supported marketing efforts as the economy struggled out of the depression. It gained no ground in the pecking order and earned no particular voice in the decision process during World War II, when the corporate focus was on employee morale to achieve the productivity necessary to arm the Allies and on war bond sales to finance the effort. After the war, with so much pent-up consumer demand to be satisfied, it was hard not to be successful and keep stockholders satisfied, so financial relations specialists were not needed.

A financial relations breakthrough came in the 1960s, in a classic situation of insider trading, where a single news release was deemed by a court to be the critical factor in whether the investing public had been misled (See Case 5-1). Out of the case came—in the determination by the SEC, the New York Stock Exchange, and corporate officials—that financial communications were important and could create or obviate legal liabilities for the corporation. Shingles labeled "Financial Public Relations" appeared by the thousands. Qualified practitioners began to sit in on the financial decision-making process of their corporations.

AT THIS JUNCTURE

Corporate growth has become almost a religion in U.S. industry. The means of getting to heaven has involved huge investment in research and technology, diversification of products and services, acquisitions, mergers, conglomeration, and multinationalization. From these actions has come an increasing concentration of corporate ownership among a few thousand very wealthy individuals, investment funds, and banking and insurance interests, both U.S. and foreign. Boards of directors of huge corporations have been woven in a crisscross pattern of a few thousand individuals whose views of the system are similar and whose posture is dependably reactive when the system comes under criticism of any kind.

In the 1970s and into the 1980s, conditions were not reassuring for the small investor or average wage earner. Inflation helped wages but hurt buying power. Borrowed money for car or home was at high interest rates, mortgaging the future. Available jobs for traditional functions shrank as corporations went abroad for cheap labor and automation displaced people. Savings decreased or disappeared for a great many.

In the latter 1980s, conditions were ripe for the rich to get richer and for the high-rolling risk takers and arbitrageurs to find market manipulation and insider trading irresistible. The mood seemed to be that "anything goes if you don't get caught." Each new rumor of a corporate raid, takeover, issuance of junk bonds, or bit of privileged information spurred speculation.[1]

Black Monday came in October of 1987. It was a rude awakening as the market's Dow Jones average plummeted some 500 points, taking with it some of Wall Street's big dealers. In the wake, a Tender Offer Reform Act was proposed as an amendment to the Securities Exchange Act of 1934. Too little, too late.[2]

Things quieted down, but not completely or permanently. In 1988, another case made financial headlines when a young trainee in Morgan Stanley's mergers and acquisitions department was alleged to have fed material information to a wealthy Hong Kong customer, who then traded on that information, garnering $19 million in gains. Then for the next several months it seemed each week brought a new Wall Street scandal, making the names of such men as Michael Milken and Ivan Boesky infamous.

The 1990s saw the government, through the Securities and Exchange Commission, get tough on insider trading issues. With an outpouring of public comment—nearly 6,000 comment letters and the vast majority from individual investors in favor of adopting Regulation Fair Disclosure (Reg FD)—the SEC adopted the ruling. Reg FD's intent is to end the special relationship that existed between public companies and analysts and brokers—to level the playing field for *all* investors. Prior to Reg FD, analysts and brokers often received information from companies that was material to investment decisions but was not shared with the general public. As one comment letter noted: "The explosion of the Internet provides ways for information to reach all investors. Analysts are one way, and in the past they were the principal conduit. But now that's changing."

On October 23, 2000, the new ruling took effect with cries from the analyst community that it would chill communications from companies. In fact, it has both promoted and inhibited corporate communications. A survey by the National Investor Relations Institute of its membership finds that 28 percent are providing more information to investors than before the new rule, 48 percent are issuing about the same amount, and 24 percent are providing less information. NIRI is concerned about that 24 percent. Further study is needed to determine the reasons and what can be done about it.

---

[1]Elliot D. Lee, "Takeover Predators Now Share the Prey," *The Wall Street Journal*, April 29, 1988. Article lists takeover activity at the time, including Campeau Corp. buying Federated Stores for $6.6 billion and GE acquiring Roper Corp. from Whirlpool. William Celis, "Low Stock Prices Spur Takeover Flurry," *The Wall Street Journal*, March 1, 1988, revealed six takeover transactions in a single day, totaling $5.4 billion in assets. Among those involved were Homestake Mining, Media General Inc., and USG Corp. A chart showed total value of transactions increasing from $10 billion the first two months of 1987 to $28 billion in the same period of 1988.

[2]George Getschow and Bryan Burrough, "Pickens, Acting Bitter, Finds Takeover Game Isn't Much Fun Now," *The Wall Street Journal*, April 5, 1988. Detailed profile of Texas oil man T. Boone Pickens, who said in 1983 he wanted to take over Gulf Oil Corp; later decided not to go ahead, but made a $518 million pretax profit when speculators bid up the price of Gulf stock on the basis of his intent. In 1988, he was weary and bitter, lashing out at investment bankers, advisers, local and national news media, and many others.

NIRI's survey also found that, prior to the new ruling, 60 percent of its member companies were providing full public access to their conference calls to discuss quarterly earnings results and guidance. After Reg FD, 89 percent are doing so, mostly through webcasts. Eighty-four percent of companies are notifying investors and the media of their upcoming conference calls in a news release, 75 percent post a notice on their company's Web site, and 55 percent are using "push technology"—directly notifying interested investors who want an e-mail alert.

The one-on-ones between companies and analysts and investors are continuing, according to NIRI's survey, contrary to the fear that these might be severely cut back for fear of violating Reg FD. However, there is important information, much of which is nonfinancial, that companies can and should discuss with analysts and investors. This nonfinancial information offers important measurements of a company's well being, which can directly affect the bottomline. Analysts may have to do more work now with Reg FD. No longer can they be guided in their analysis by the companies. Information will be distributed equally. Knowledge and the ability to analyze data are key.

AN ENVIRONMENT OF STRONG VIEWS

Financial relations present a worthy challenge to the practitioner. As prime audiences, you have millions of small investors fighting to be on an equal footing with those who "control" the market (such as pension funds, mutual funds, and other money managers) and leaders of publicly owned corporations who can make decisions that are helpful or harmful, choosing short-term expedients or long-haul public interest. Then there are the regulators—and the ever-inquiring media, economists, and legislators—who can make and change the rules.

The positive views small investors have of the corporate world stem in part from good news such as dividends or appreciation in the value of their investments, bullish forecasts by corporate and investment spokespersons, and profiles of company leaders portraying them as intelligent, honest, and planning for future success.

Their negative views are formed in part by information in proxy statements about lavish executive salaries, bonuses, and stock options not based on the health or performance of the corporation. Investors read news items about costly indulgences such as private aircraft, executive dining rooms, limousines, club memberships, and junkets, all in the name of incentives or customer relations, that are recovered in higher prices for the products or services. And they are not reassured when such free-spending corporations, unable to compete with foreign products, run to the government for protection.

Large investors—directors chosen to guide the corporations and the people hired to manage the businesses—constitute a relatively small audience with some deeply ingrained convictions in common. They claim that the system works well. Criticism or threats of regulation tend to harden their positions and to render spokespersons less flexible rather than more open and accessible. When challenged, this posture provides an example of the *artificial censorship principle*. At times, unwelcome criticism or questions concerning economic matters are labeled as expressing an unacceptable political viewpoint—thus the strategy or tactic of *changing the issue*.

A LANGUAGE OF ITS OWN

A generation ago, practitioners had to learn new financial semantics. Terms such as *privileged information, conflict of interest, insider trading, timely and adequate disclosure, due diligence,* and *a material fact* became part of communications as well as legal language.

An infusion of words appeared during the late 1980s and early 1990s. Practitioners needed to understand *arbitrage* and *arbs, junk bonds, payment in kind* (PIK), *green mail, raiders, programmed trading,* and *hostile takeover.*

Today, new lingo continues to emerge on the Street, for example, Regulation Fair Disclosure (see page 121).

- The role of the corporate financial relations specialist or consultant tends to be that of *interpreter and mediator* between the prime audiences. He or she usually comes on as a moderate or neutral in economic and political philosophy. The position requires skill and objectivity in representing the average investor, the middle-class unsophisticated citizen, while representing private enterprise and conservative views publicly.

Among the intervenors financial relations must take into account are the financial news media, those who run and support nonprofit institutions such as education, and those charged with making and enforcing the securities laws.

THE SPECIFICS OF THE FUNCTION

The financial public relations role can be summarized as:

- Communications strategy appropriate to management goals in investor relations
- Preparation of public literature, including reports required by law and establishing press contacts
- Managing relationships with the financial community, including analyst meetings, tours or visits, and so on

Among the specific situations requiring communication are:

1. A company goes public, splits its stock, or arranges added financing.
2. A corporation wishes to make a tender offer to acquire another corporation, to merge with another corporation, or to head off or oppose an unwanted offer. An acquisition or merger may result in a change of identity such as name, logo, headquarters location, or ownership.
3. A timely announcement is needed for significant new products, services, expansion, or acquisition, which might affect the price of the company's stock.
4. Periodic reports of financial results are issued, including an annual report.

5. Arrangements are required for meetings with investors and for public reports of proceedings, including the annual meeting—and, in some enlightened corporations, an employee annual meeting.
6. Special literature is required, dealing with a corporation's philosophy, policies, and objectives; its history or anniversary; and its scope, "identity," or "culture." Any of these may also be the subject of advertising.

References and Additional Readings

Berkeley, Alan. "Stand by for Change: The Future of Investor Relations." Address at University of Texas, April 30, 1987. Synopsis in *pr reporter* 30 (August 17, 1987).

Berle, A. A., Jr. *Power Without Property*. New York: Harcourt, Brace and World, 1959. A classic book.

Cheney, Richard. "What Should We Do About Takeovers?" *tips & tactics, pr reporter* 25 (supplement, April 6, 1987).

Cutlip, Scott, Allen Center, and Glen Broom. "The Practice: Business and Industry." Chapter 14 in *Effective Public Relations*. 8th ed. Upper Saddle River, NJ: Prentice Hall, 1999.

Dobrzynski, Judith. "The Lessons of the RJR Free-for-All." *Business Week* (December 19, 1988). Raises and answers questions about the battle for RJR Nabisco.

"Four Barometers Analysts Apply in Measuring Management Performance." *Investor Relations Update* (October–November 1992): 15. Summary in purview, supplement to *pr reporter* (February 15, 1993).

Holliday, Karen Kahler. "Understanding Investor Relations." *Bank Marketing* 24 (August 1992): 22–25.

Leeds, Mark, and Bruce Fraser. "Why Wall Street Matters." *Management Review* 82 (September 1993): 23–26.

Lees, David. "A Strategy That Pays Dividends." *Management Today* (March 1994): 5.

Lerbinger, Otto, and Nathaniel Sperber. "Financial Relations." Chapter 7 in *Manager's Public Relations Handbook*. Reading, MA: Addison-Wesley, 1982.

Metz, Tim. *Black Monday: The Catastrophe of October 19, 1987 . . . and Beyond*. New York: William Morrow, 1988. A chronology of the stock market drop of 500 points and theory concerning the mystery of it.

Miller, Eugene. "Investor Relations." Chapter 11 in *Lesly's Handbook of Public Relations and Communications*. 5th ed. Chicago, IL: NTC Business Books, 1998.

Moore, Philip. "Ciba Takes Investors into Account." *Euromoney* (September 1993): 37–38.

National Investor Relations Institute offers a wealth of information, including *IR Update,* a monthly newsletter. National Investors Relations Institute, 8045 Leesburg Pike, Suite 600, Vienna, VA 22182; 703/506-3570; www.niri.org.

The *Public Relations Body of Knowledge*. New York: PRSA. See abstracts dealing with "Financial and Investor Relations."

Seely, Michael. "Hit the Financial Bull's Eye with Well-Aimed IR Programs." *Corporate Cash Flow* 14 (July 1993): 26–30.

CASES

CASE 5-1 A CLASSIC: ON WALL STREET, INSIDE INFORMATION IS PROFITABLE

For nearly 30 years after the enactment of the Securities Exchange Act in 1934 prohibiting manipulation and deception in the financial world, the role of public relations in stock transactions was not taken seriously by corporate management and the relevant sectors of the Securities Exchange Commission (SEC). As a result of a landmark court case involving Texas Gulf Sulphur Company, the role of public relations changed drastically.[1] This case is definitive in understanding some of the problems and requisites in the performance of financial relations.

➤ At the heart of the case was a single news release drafted by a public relations consultant and the vice president of Texas Gulf. The manner in which the news was released to the media raised questions of whether the content was deceptive.

PRECEDENTS

Until 1942, inside trading, or using private information, had not been outlawed. In fact, this device helped create many personal fortunes. It was said that advance information of the Duke of Wellington's victory at Waterloo was a key to the Rothschild wealth, and in the United States early news that the War of 1812 was coming to an end enabled John Jacob Astor to reap an enormous financial harvest. During the industrial

Section 10 of the 1934 Securities Exchange Act, and Rule 10b-5 promulgated by the SEC in 1942, state that persons may not "make any untrue statement of material fact or . . . omit to state a material fact" that would have the effect of misleading in connection with the purchase or sale of any security.

A precondition would be that a person did, in fact, possess information whose disclosure or nondisclosure could have an effect on the value of a security. Thus, "insider" information, the disclosure of such information, and the purchase or sale of securities are mutually involved. Private gain is implicit.

---

[1]The name was subsequently changed to Texasgulf. In 1981, the company was acquired by the French corporation Elf Aquitaine Inc. for $5 billion and then purchased by Potush Corporation of Saskatchewan in 1995 for more than $800 million.

development of the United States, advance information concerning the allocation of railroad rights fed the growth of some real estate fortunes. Discoveries of raw materials, whether coal, iron, or oil, were traditionally hushed and even hidden from all but a few people for investment, and having inside knowledge to gain an advantage in stock trading was generally regarded as "the way the chips fell."

Questions of integrity or ethics went largely unasked publicly until the Sherman Antitrust Act was passed in 1890. Even after the Securities Exchange Act was passed in 1934 and Rule 10b-5 was made public, the laws were not enforced and went untested for two decades. Exceptions were instances of such blatant abuse that disapproval came even from corporate executives for whom insider trading was regarded as nothing more than a smart, low-risk move or a reward for their past efforts.

THE TEXAS GULF SULPHUR CASE

The Texas Gulf Sulphur (TGS) scenario started with some late 1950s exploratory activities for minerals in eastern Canada.[2] Aerial, geophysical surveys over a large expanse of land were made until potential drill sites were selected. The people who participated in the surveys included:

➤ **Richard D. Mollison,** a mining engineer and later a vice president of Texas Gulf Sulphur (TGS)

➤ **Walter Holyk,** a Texas Gulf geologist

➤ **Richard H. Clayton,** an electrical engineer and geophysicist

➤ **Kenneth H. Darke,** a geologist

They selected a segment of marshland near Timmins, Ontario, that showed sufficient promise to indicate a survey on the ground. This land was not owned by TGS. One of the first problems was to get title or drilling rights, via an option from the owners. Contact with the owner of part of the desired area was first made in 1961.

Eventually, in mid-1963, some land was acquired and drilling began in November. On visual inspection, the sample—obtained by diamond core drilling—seemed to contain sulphides of copper and zinc.

On Sunday, November 12, 1963, Darke telephoned his boss, Walter Holyk, at his home in Connecticut with an optimistic report. Holyk called his boss, Richard D. Mollison, nearby in Old Greenwich, and later that evening called Dr. Charles F. Fogarty, TGS executive vice president, also nearby in Rye, New York. Holyk, Mollison, and Fogarty subsequently went to the site—called the Kidd 55 tract—to see

---

[2]The narrative and facts that follow were gleaned from some of the same sources that formed public opinion during the period when the events in this case took place. Among the sources are a complete text of the court's opinion in the U.S. Court of Appeals for the Second Circuit, No. 296, September term 1966 *SEC v. TGS*, 446 F.2d p. 1301 (2nd cir 1966); an article by John Brooks, "Annals of Finance: A Reasonable Amount of Time," in *New Yorker* magazine, November 9, 1968 (and from a critique of the John Brooks piece provided by TGS public relations consultant William H. Dinsmore); *The Wall Street Journal* articles, "Big Boards Expands, Tightens Standards on Timely Disclosure of Corporate News," July 18, 1968. "Texas Gulf Ruled to Lack Due Diligence in Minerals Case," February 9, 1970; "Rise Detected in Use of Inside Information to Make Stock Profits," October 31, 1972; "Most Executives Say They Won't Give Insider Data to Analysts," August 16, 1968; "New Structure Prompt Firms to Revise Policies on Disclosure of News," October 9, 1968; and "Rules on Disclosure Don't Bar Exclusive Interview, Cohen Says," October 9, 1968; and "No Comment—A Victim of Disclosure," the *New York Times*, August 25, 1968. Also helpful was an analysis provided to officers of Motorola, Inc., by its legal counsel, entitled "Corporate Information Releases." We also drew on several references in issues of the *Public Relations Journal*, *PR News*, *pr reporter*, and other business and professional publications. An appeals brief for the defendants was requested of attorneys but was not received.

for themselves. The group concluded that the core was indeed promising and should be shipped to Utah for chemical assay.

A LID ON THE INFORMATION

Pending the results, they wanted the acquisition program for other desired land in the area to proceed as quickly as possible. They knew obtaining rights might be difficult. To facilitate matters, TGS president Claude O. Stephens instructed the group to keep the unconfirmed results a secret . . . even to other officers, directors, and employees of the company. Following traditional prospecting and camouflage customs, the first hole was marked and concealed, and another one, *barren,* was drilled and left in sight.

CALENDAR OF EVENTS: 1963–1964

- ➤ November. Seven TGS employees were the "keepers" of significant information. In the same month drilling began, and Fogarty, Clayton, Mollison, and Mrs. Holyk bought TGS stock totaling 2,050 shares at $17–$18 a share.

- ➤ December. The chemical assays of the test core came back, largely confirming the TGS estimate of copper and zinc content, as well as discovering a silver content. TGS scheduled the resumption of drilling in March.

- ➤ January–February. Inside informers and those they gave "tips" to owned 8,235 shares. At this point there were also 12,300 calls (options to buy a specified amount of stock at a fixed price) to buy TGS stock.

- ➤ February. The company issued stock options to 26 of its officers

and other employees, 5 of whom were the insiders on Kidd 55. The option committee and the company's board of directors had not been made aware of the find.

- ➤ March 31. The company resumed drilling.

After further drilling of three more holes by April 10, there was evidence of a body of commercially minable ore. (The accuracy of the estimate later came into contention between SEC experts and TGS officials).

LEAKS AND RUMORS

By this time, there had been enough activity at the Kidd site that rumors of a possible major ore strike were circulating in Canada. A press item on February 27, in the *Northern Miner,* reported rumors of Texas Gulfs "obtaining some fat ore indications" from its work north of Timmins. On March 31, Texas Gulf invited the publication to visit and see the exposed, barren site for itself, and a date was set for April 20. Then on April 9, the *Toronto Daily Star* and the *Globe and Mail* carried stories. The *Globe and Mail* headline read, "Wild Speculation Spree on TGS: Gigantic Copper Strike Rumored." The phone lines and the conference rooms at TGS headquarters, 200 Park Avenue, New York, were busy on April 10. According to John Brooks, writing later in the *New Yorker* magazine,

President Stephens was sufficiently concerned about the rumors to seek advice from one of his most trusted associates, Thomas S. Lamont, senior member of the Texas Gulf board . . . and bearer of a name long venerated on Wall Street. Stephens asked what Lamont thought ought to be done about the "exaggerated" reports.

"As long as they stay in the Canadian press," Lamont replied, "I think you might be able to live with them." However, he added, if they should reach the papers in the United States, it might be well to give the press an announcement that would set the record straight and avoid undue gyrations in the stock market.[3]

PUBLIC RELATIONS CALLED IN

The stories in Canada were picked up and printed on Saturday, April 11, by such U.S. media as the *New York Times* and the *New York Herald Tribune,* with the rumor of a major copper strike. Robert Carroll, a Doremus & Co. public relations consultant, helped Dr. Fogarty, the executive vice president, draft a news release over the weekend, and it was released at 3:00 P.M. on Sunday, April 12, to appear in Monday morning's papers.

NEWS MEDIA AND STOCK MARKET REACT

The Monday *New York Herald Tribune,* an important financial medium, headlining its story, "Copper Rumor Deflated," quoted passages from the TGS press release and hedged on the optimism in its earlier story out of Canada.

On the New York Stock Exchange, TGS stock price on April 13 ranged between 30⅛ and 32, closing at 30⅞. When compared with an $18 high in November the $30 price represented a 65 percent rise in five months. Meanwhile, the internal, nonpublic reports from Timmins became so rosy that an official announcement confirming a major ore strike was readied for April 16.

There was a problem in the synchronization of communications. A reporter for the *Northern Milner,* a Canadian trade journal, had interviewed Mollison, Holyk, and Darke and had prepared an article confirming a 10-million-ton strike for publication in his April 16 issue. The story, submitted to Mollison, was returned to the reporter, unamended, on April 15. Separately, a statement drafted substantially by Mollison was given to the Ontario minister of mines for release on the air in Canada at 11:00 P.M. on the fifteenth, but was not released until 9:40 on the sixteenth. Also, separately, in the United States an official statement announcing a strike of at least 25 million tons (2½ times the Canadian trade-journal story) was read to the financial press in New York from 10:00 to 10:15 A.M. on April 16, following a 9:00 A.M. directors' meeting. The news showed up on the Dow Jones tape at 10:54 and on Merrill Lynch's private wire 25 minutes earlier at 10:29, another peculiar circumstance.

THE TRIAL AND APPEALS

An SEC complaint indicated that company executives had used privileged information to trade in the company's stock before the information had been disclosed publicly. In May, the complaint was argued before Judge Dudley B. Bonsal of the Southern District Court at Foley Square, New York. He ruled in favor of all the defendants except David M. Crawford and Richard H. Clayton, who had engaged in TGS stock purchase after the first press release on April 12 and before the second one, on April 16, was public knowledge.

The lower-court judge dismissed the case against the defendants who had purchased

---

[3]J. Brooks, "Business Adventures," New York: Weybright and Talley Division, David McKay. Originally published in "Annals of Finance," *New Yorker* magazine, November 9, 1968.

THE PRESS RELEASE: APRIL 12, 1964

NEW YORK—The following statement was made today by Dr. Charles F. Fogarty, executive vice president of Texas Gulf Sulphur Company, in regard to the company's drilling operations near Timmins, Ontario, Canada. Dr. Fogarty said:

> During the past few days, the exploration activities of Texas Gulf Sulphur in the area of Timmins, Ontario, have been widely reported in the press, coupled with rumors of a substantial copper discovery there. These reports exaggerate the scale of operations, and mention plans and statistics of size and grade of ore that are without factual basis and have evidently originated by speculation of people not connected with TGS.
>
> The facts are as follows. TGS has been exploring in the Timmins area for six years as part of its overall search in Canada and elsewhere for various minerals—lead, copper, zinc, etc. During the course of this work, in Timmins as well as in eastern Canada, TGS has conducted exploration entirely on its own, without the participation by others. Numerous prospects have been investigated by geophysical means and a large number of selected ones have been core-drilled. These cores are sent to the United States for assay and detailed examination as a matter of routine and on advice of expert Canadian legal counsel. No inferences as to grade can be drawn from this procedure.
>
> Most of the areas drilled in Eastern Canada have revealed either barren pyrite or graphite without value; a few have resulted in discoveries of small or marginal sulfide ore bodies.
>
> Recent drilling on one property near Timmins has led to preliminary indications that more drilling would be required for proper evaluation of this prospect. The drilling done to date has not been conclusive, but the statements made by many outside quarters are unreliable and include information and figures that are not available to TGS.
>
> The work done to date has not been sufficient to reach definite conclusions and any statement as to size and grade of ore would be premature and possibly misleading. When we have progressed to the point where reasonable and logical conclusions can be made, TGS will issue a definite statement to its stockholders and the public in order to clarify the Timmins project.[1]

[1]From the appeals court opinion, *SEC v. TGS*, 446 F.2d, 1301 (2nd cir 1966).

stock prior to the evening of April 9, on the grounds that information they possessed was not "material," that their purchases or tips to others were educated guesses or hunches, and that executives should be encouraged to own shares in their own company. As for trading by insiders following the April 16 directors' meeting, and whether they had waited a "reasonable time" for the disclosure to become public knowledge, the judge decided the controlling factor was the time at which the release was handed to the press, not when it appeared on the Dow Jones stock market tape.

PUBLIC RELATIONS INVOLVEMENT

The trial court judge gave a big lift to the public relations profession because a public relations consultant had been involved. The judge decided that because corporate executives had sought the advice of public relations counsel, they had exercised reasonable business judgment.

As for the news release itself, a major point of contention in the hearings was whether it was encouraging or discouraging to investors. A Canadian mining security specialist said that they had had a Dow Jones (broad tape) report that TGS "didn't have anything basically." A Midwest Stock Exchange specialist in TGS was "concerned about his long position in the stock" after reading the release. TGS defense attorneys contended that the financial media had been at fault in not publishing the full text of the controversial release. The trial court stated only, "While in retrospect, the press release may appear gloomy or incomplete, that does not make it misleading or deceptive on the basis of the facts then known."

THE COMPLAINT MOVED UP THE COURT LADDER

The SEC appealed all dismissals, and the case was argued in the court of appeals. In essence, the appellate decision reversed the lower court's findings on the important issues, except for the convictions of Crawford and Clayton, which were affirmed.

The case was remanded to Judge Bonsal of the lower court for the "appropriate remedies." He:

➤ Ruled that Texas Gulf Sulphur Co. and its executives failed to exercise "due diligence" in the April 12 news release.

➤ Ordered certain defendants to turn over to TGS profits made by trading on inside information.

➤ Issued injunctions against Crawford and Clayton, barring

them from further purchases or sales based on "undisclosed" information.

➤ Denied a request by the SEC that TGS, as a corporation, be enjoined from issuing false, misleading, or inadequate information, pointing out that there was no "reasonable likelihood of further violations."

➤ Because there was no "reasonable likelihood," did not issue injunctions against Darke, who had left the company; Holyk, chief geologist; Huntington, a TGS attorney; Fogarty, then president of TGS; and Mollison, a vice president.

➤ Noted that Coates, a director, had paid $26,250 in an approved settlement, including $9,675 said to be profits to several "tippees," and that Crawford returned "at his cost" the stock he purchased.

➤ Assessed paybacks of $41,795 from Darke personally and $48,404 for his "tippees," $35,663 from Holyk, $20,010 from Clayton, and $2,300 from Huntington.[4]

SOME OF THE ECHOES

In the immediate wake of the TGS settlement, several predictable measures were taken to avoid a repetition. Publicly owned corporations reexamined their practices of disclosing financial information to be sure they were in compliance. The New York Stock Exchange expanded its policies regarding timely disclosure and issued new pages for its company manual.

---

[4]Extracted from the opinion rendered in 65 Civ. 1182 by Judge Dudley J. Bonsal, United States District Court, Southern District of New York, February 6, 1970.

Financial news media, somewhat defensively, placed responsibility for the published information on the corporate sources of such information without permitting those sources to control what was published. While insisting on the media's right to edit financial releases according to the news values perceived in them, some comments by financial editors suggested that corporate practitioners constituted obstacles rather than facilitators in getting out all the relevant facts.

Corporate financial relations people, for their part, undertook with notable success to exercise a more important and outspoken role in corporate decisions regarding the "what, when, and how" of significant information to be released publicly via press or controlled media. This meant a seat in management councils for financial relations people when decisions were made regarding whether a particular item of information was newsworthy and whether it was capable of influencing the value of the corporation's shares in the stock market. This also meant attendance at meetings with groups of analysts where material information might inadvertently be introduced, calling for immediate broad disclosure.

New counseling shingles were hung out, with the words "Financial Public Relations." The trade literature abounded with analyses of the risks and requirements implied by the TGS case.

A SUBJECT THAT WOULD NOT QUIT

Despite effects by the SEC and the stock exchanges[5] and disciplinary procedures by corporations, the temptation for individuals to make a profit on secret or "privileged" information continued to be too great for some individuals. Incidents involved executives in many large national corporations such as ITT, Faberge, Liggett and Myers, Bausch and Lomb, Occidental, Penn Central, and Stirling Homex, and touched some smaller ones, too, such as Rheingold and Carl's Jr. restaurants.

Inevitably, insider trading allegations would include public relations professionals alerting the calling to its vulnerability. In one episode an SEC complaint aimed at Pig 'n Whistle Corp. named the firm's former counsel, Financial Relations Board, as the defendant.

The **Public Relations Society of America (PRSA)** reviewed and strengthened its Code of Professional Standards, a document that then dealt almost entirely with relationships between members of the society and employers or clients, not with behavior outside those relationships.

A few years later, the head of a Detroit consulting firm was under SEC investigation for alleged insider trading in the stock of a client company. After the SEC filed formal charges, the matter was settled with a "consent decree" (an accused, without admitting or denying charges, agrees, henceforth, not to do what was alleged). This episode was magnified within journalistic professional circles, partly because the individual under investigation had assumed the presidency of PRSA; subsequently he resigned office. The embarrassed society had to reshuffle topside.[6] As a result, in 1988 PRSA passed a stronger Code of Ethics and disclosure requirements for officers and committee members. The code has

---

[5]See Robert W. Taft, Hill, and Knowlton, "New Disclosure Rules: More Public Information," *Public Relations Journal*, April 1972, and "Disclosure: What A Year," in the April 1973 issue. Also see Cutlip, Center, and Broom, *Effective Public Relations*, 8th ed., Upper Saddle River, NJ: Prentice Hall, 1999.

[6]The incident involved Anthony Franco in 1985.

since been changed. In 2000, a new Code was adopted (See the introduction to Chapter 10). Its focus changed from enforcement to education. It also dropped the previous official interpretation of the Code as it applied to financial relations.

ON WALL STREET, THE WORST WAS YET TO COME

In the 1970s, instances of insider trading did not headline the economic news. Public attention was fastened more on unemployment, continued inflation, and rising interest rates. Government kept business under the gun on those matters. In the 1980s, government sought to rev up business as the best way to slow the rate of inflation, put more people on payrolls, and bring down interest rates. In the good times that resulted, mergers and acquisitions in the name of "efficiency" and "international competition" became the order of the day. Yuppies were in. "Get-while-the-getting-is-good" was in. The stock market was ripe for excesses if not illegalities. Speculators and manipulators did not let the opportunity get away. As one bit of evidence, there were more than fifty prosecutions under the provisions of Rule 10b in the 1980s.

In one of them, W. C. Clark, a lawyer, was convicted of fraud, tax evasion, and lying to regulators about insider trading conspiracy. That made sizeable news partly because he had used the *Wall Street Journal* stories for some of his information. In 1985, Dennis B. Levine, a managing director of Drexel Burnham Lambert, was charged with using insider information to make more than $12 million illegally over a period of years, found guilty, and sentenced to two years. He implicated Ivan Boesky, a promi-

nent arbitrageur—one who buys and sells securities simultaneously in order to profit from price fluctuations—who admitted that the insider trading world had grown to staggering size. Boesky then tagged Martin Siegal, a former Kidder Peabody executive, who in turn named Richard Freeman, a head of arbitrage at prestigious Goldman Sachs, Richard Wigdon, a vice president at Kidder, and Timothy Tabor, a former Kidder officer. It was like a line of dominoes falling over.[7]

In 1987, Kidder Peabody agreed to pay $25 million to settle government charges. Ivan Boesky agreed to plead guilty to conspiracy, to pay back $100 million of his ill-gotten gains to the government, and to continue spilling information about many of those who had played loose with other people's money. Much of Wall Street went into a crouch waiting to hear whose names were called.

As for Boesky's punishment, Judge Morris Lasker, reputed to be lenient in matters that "after all, are only money," commended Boesky's cooperation, gave him a three-year sentence, and in light of the $100 million he had already paid to the government, waived his fine of $250,000 and then set him free on bail. Boesky served the full three years of his term. However, his troubles did not end with his parole from jail. Boesky faced another lawsuit in 1992 and settled out of court for $50 million with Maxus Energy Corp., a company Boesky had bilked out of millions by his insider trading.

The doings and ordeal of junk bond king Michael Milken were yet to come. His illegal use of this high-risk financial instrument had—like most Wall Street crimes—cost investors millions of dollars

---

[7]For a synopsis, see Richard B. Stolley, "The Ordeal of Bob Freeman," *Fortune*, May 25, 1987, pp. 66–72. For an Ivan Boesky summary, see the Associated Press story "Boesky Pleads Guilty to Violating Securities Laws," April 24, 1987.

while he and his clients made billions. By any definition, such activities do not promote positive relations in society—and are therefore of concern to the public relations profession.

RELEVANCE TO PR PRACTICE

With the dollar stakes involved in the stock market so large today as to seem almost fictional, the day-by-day practice of public relations may seem remote or unrelated. It is neither.

Every large corporation, bank, brokerage firm, charitable foundation, and other financial institution has public relations counsel or staff. The professionals providing counsel and implementing the communications involved in financial affairs can qualify legally as "insiders." They can be found guilty, as individuals, of knowingly releasing financial information that is false, deceptive, or misleading or of trading on privileged information. In court cases, it has been evident that financial relations practitioners are not in the clear by pleading "I only did (or said) what the client told me to." Practitioners must make reasonable efforts to verify facts disseminated. "Hold harmless" clauses no longer constitute a shield. ∎

QUESTIONS FOR DISCUSSION

1. Drawing on the information in the case, and having the benefit of knowing how it all came out, what should the public relations executive have counseled TGS officers to do differently, or to communicate publicly, at some point before TGS executives were found to be trading in the stock?

2. Apart from the TGS case, try a different situation. Suppose that a weekly financial magazine column "Tips and Rumors" regularly got into some people's hands a day before each issue of the magazine came out, and some of the stocks mentioned were suddenly traded heavily and run up in price. Suppose also, it turned out that a clerical person in the magazine's public relations department privately had been giving an advance rough draft of the column as a favor to a friend at a brokerage firm. Neither that clerk nor the friend at a brokerage firm traded or made any profit. As you understand SEC's Rule 10b, who is legally liable? Put another way, where does common sense tell you the responsibility for the privacy of material facts belongs?

3. Objectively, was the initial TGS news release about the ore strike at Timmins misleading on the basis of what was known *at the time the news was released?* Or did it go only as far as a cautious, prudent management was willing to go for fear of overstating and getting in trouble for that? Or, what else does your objective evaluation say might have been the determining consideration?

4. A reputation for being honest in economic matters, civil in social relations, and honorable in character has long been said to be a precious and fragile possession. And the reputation of communications people is generally perceived by critics and supporters alike as being a reflection of those they serve and associate with. If we accept both premises, how can we stay clean and honorable, earn a good living, and advance in a career when we are cast in an atmosphere that many moralists, historians, intellectuals, journalists, and some government officials describe as a "moral morass"?

CASE 5-2 A CLASSIC: NADER TAKES ON GENERAL MOTORS

THE OPPONENTS

A small group challenging a company such as General Motors (GM) sets up a bantamweight-heavyweight, David and Goliath situation. Not only is GM a Goliath in sales and earnings, but in 1987 it had more than 315 million shares of stock around the world in the hands of some 830,000 shareholders. The company takes in more money every year than all but a handful of sovereign nations!

Without doubt, the majority of shares were in the hands of a few hundred shareholders and their representatives who held views similar to corporate management's. Rounding up a majority of opinion opposing GM management on any business issue seemed unrealistic.

But not to Ralph Nader and his associates, the challengers in this case. "The Nader group versus GM" is a classic example of minority shareholders expression. The group owned only 12 shares of General Motors stock but sought to induce modifications in the corporation's management policies.

THE NADER PAST WITH GM

Nader had a prior experience tangling with GM in 1965. He had written a book, *Unsafe at Any Speed,*[1] which criticizes the auto industry in general, and in particular denounced the early Corvair autos built by GM.

At that time, GM's legal department ran an investigation on Nader that focused on his private life. To Nader this was a form of harassment invading his right to privacy. Nader brought suit. The company settled out of court for $425,000 and GM's board chairman apologized for the harassment. Nader said the money would be used to establish a "continuing legal monitoring of General Motors' activities in the safety, pollution, and consumer relations area."

Shortly before the settlement, Nader created an organization of young lawyers called the Project on Corporate Responsibility. Ralph Nader, the spokesman, announced at a Washington press conference that the project's efforts would be directed at "the establishment of enduring access to corporate information, effective voice for affected social and individual interests, and thorough remedy against unjust treatment."

THE NADER-SIDE STRATEGY

In 1970, Nader took on GM again, this time to make changes regarding General Motors' investor relations.

In conjunction with formation of Project on Corporate Responsibility, the Nader group announced "Campaign GM," which would "seek to persuade GM shareholders to demand stronger 'public interest' efforts by GM, such as reducing air and water pollution and making safer cars." Campaign GM, the announcement said, was going to

---

[1]Ralph Nader, *Unsafe at Any Speed*, New York: Grossman, 1965.

THE POWER OF A SHAREHOLDER

The shareholders of a corporation collectively own it. In theory, they are collectively "the boss" and should have a voice in policy making and an active part in the decision-making process. Shareholders express their independent decisions most often through their votes on matters submitted to them. Votes are allocated on the basis of one vote for each share owned, *not* one vote for each shareholder.

In actual practice, the directors and top management of a corporation (who may also own shares) have the authority to run the corporation the way they feel will best benefit shareholders collectively. They must also look after the other publics, such as customers and employees, on whom the corporation depends for its success. A shareholder with a few shares feels powerless. The only choices minority shareholders have are to write complaint letters, accept whatever decisions are made, or sell their shares. Minority shareholders historically have rarely raised questions or expressed discourse. Consequently, most corporate annual meetings have traditionally been formal, scripted, cut-and-dry, rubber-stamp affairs.

THERE HAVE BEEN EXCEPTIONS

There are, however, some perennial critics who make a point to attend meetings and raise questions. On occasion, individuals in positions to speak for many small shareholders, and persons owning large blocks of stock who share a different viewpoint than the management, have banded together and spoken with a single voice. Small shareholders try to change a policy or attitude by making a proposal for inclusion in the proxy statement. This statement is voted upon at the annual shareholders' meeting.

Whether the proposal is adopted or not, small shareholders have alerted the corporate management and the financial news media (the media are usually present at the major company annual meetings) to their opinions and perhaps attracted others who share common views. Examples of questions raised have been environmental and safety issues, overextended salaries for corporate management, and minority employment. The outcomes of these efforts are considered a gain for those who represent the small shareholders in the same sense that the expression of a minority viewpoint in a Supreme Court decision is a gain for the losing side. Winners can't ignore the existence of the minority view.

seek public and private support, climaxing at GM's annual meeting of shareholders with three proposals offered as resolutions:

➤ **Proposal number 1** would add three public representatives to GM's twenty-four-member board: The campaign's candidates were to be the former consumer adviser to a U.S. president, a Pulitzer Prize-winning biologist and member of a President's Advisory Committee on Environmental Quality, and a minister who was then a Democratic party committeeman from the District of Columbia.

➤ **Proposal number 2** would create a Committee for Corporate Responsibility with representatives from the company and from conversationist, union, civil rights, consumer, and religious groups.

➤ **Proposal number 3** would deal with the amending of the company's corporate character to specify public interest requirements.

In addition, Campaign GM created six additional proposals included in the proxy sent to shareholders before the meeting.

The Securities and Exchange Commission (SEC), on inquiry from GM, decided that seven of the total of nine proposals could be omitted from the proxy statement and that the project's Campaign GM should amend one of the two remaining proposals to make it suitable for its inclusion. The surviving proposals were for expansion of the board of directors and establishment of a Committee for Corporate Responsibility.

Nonetheless, the campaign's strategy called for rousing the support of institutional investors and their constituents. Nader appealed to shareholders as "citizens and consumers, victims of water pollution, congested and inefficient transportation, and rocketing repair bills for shoddy workmanship."[2]

THE GM-SIDE STRATEGY

The GM vice president for public relations wrote during the months between the project's Campaign GM proposals and the annual meeting:

February and March were extremely busy months for us. As the days passed, it became obvious that the Project was having little trouble getting all the media coverage it wanted. For us, there was the question of whether we should fight the Project at every point or whether the better course was to "play it cool" and not increase the opportunities for rebuttal headlines. In the end, our response could be characterized as walking the middle ground—answering all the charges but avoiding response which would provide a further forum.

The spring saw the first Earth Day and the first teach-ins on the environment. Seminars and discussions at high schools and colleges throughout the nation focused attention on environmental problems. General Motors sent speakers to 116 or these teach-ins . . .

The Project attempted to capitalize on this college environmental movement in order to generate attention and support for its cause. It tried to form students into pressure groups to force the

---

[2]In preparing this case study, and again in preparing the revision, we wrote to Mr. Nader, asking for information that would tell the "Nader side of the story." Both invitations went unanswered, even though it was made clear that the information was wanted for classroom use.

universities to back the Project and vote endowment shares against GM management. Generally, its efforts failed.

Amid all this public controversy and discussion, the owners of our business, the stockholders, were taking the challenge rather calmly. Only 264 letters, or 12 percent of the 2,200 comments received prior to the annual meeting, dealt with one or both of the Project's two proposals. This surprised us, because we thought the publicity which had been given the Project's activities would generate a greater stockholder response.

While our stockholders weren't strongly motivated to write us about the proposals, they did write in far greater numbers for tickets to the annual meeting. We received 3,500 requests for tickets.[3]

THE ANNUAL MEETING

The meeting itself, starting at 2:00 P.M., went on for more than six hours, with the GM chairman presiding. In the course of the meeting, contrary to precedent, some 67 shareholders and proxy holders spoke. (See Figure 5-1).

Before that happened, a motion picture was shown depicting how the company was meeting some of its social responsibilities. (This film subsequently went into the company's film catalog, and in its first three

FIGURE 5-1 A packed house for annual meeting of shareholders in world's largest industrial corporation the year Campaign GM began.

(Courtesy of General Motors.)

---

[3]Anthony DeLorenzo, "Round Three," also from speeches to public relations professionals and corporate secretaries.

years was shown 11,348 times to an estimated total audience of 337,938.)

The prepared remarks by the chairman covered the deaths of a GM executive and a United Auto Workers (UAW) top official; retirement of two directors; introduction of 20 directors present; the trend of sales and earnings, influences on them, and problem ahead, the matter of social responsibility and GM activities in that area; introduction of the film; and introduction of the proposals in the proxy statement.[4]

Of the five proposals on the agenda, the first one, the selection of independent public accountants, was overwhelmingly ratified. The other four—to limit executive compensation, to provide cumulative voting in the election of directors, to establish a responsibility committee, and to increase the number of directors—were defeated by massive majorities. The last two of these were the proposals of the Project.

The chairman made a closing statement pledging socially responsible conduct by the corporation. At a press conference immediately afterward, he was asked whether he though GM had achieved a "victory." His response was, "I don't think we won a victory. I think we won a vote of confidence from our shareholders. I think we could lose that vote of confidence very quickly unless we respond in the way our shareholders expect us to—and that's what we intend to do."

IN THE WAKE OF THE MEETING: ROUND ONE

One move came within two months. A five-member Public Policy Committee was formed as a permanent standing committee of the board to "inquire into all phases of the corporation's operations that relate to

public policy and recommend actions to the full Board." On the committee at the outset were the chairman of the Mellon National Bank and a trustee of Carnegie-Mellon University; the chairman of the corporation of Massachusetts Institute of Technology; the chairman of Allied Chemical Corporation and former Secretary of Commerce; the trustee of Meharry Medical College; and the president of Marshall Field, who was also a trustee of Northwestern University.

At the beginning of the next year, the board elected the first African American to membership—the originator of the Opportunities Industrialization Centers of America. In April, a professor of mechanical engineering at the University of California (an expert in thermodynamics and air pollution) was hired as vice president for environmental activities, to coordinate work in automobile safety, emissions, product assurance, and industrial air and water pollution control.

Spurred by the Public Policy Committee, a Science Advisory Committee, chaired by a Nobel Prize winner, was formed to assist in technological and scientific matters involving basic and applied research.

SHIFT IN STRATEGY

According to the vice president, after evaluation GM's public relations people decided to return to and review the second step in the process, strategic planning. After review, they felt sure Campaign GM would hammer away at the responsibility theme. They decided to swing from their reactive "cool-it" tactics to a proactive advocacy.

Implementing a proactive approach, the company's news relations section stepped up the number of interviews by financial, popular, and trade media with senior GM

---

[4]Extracted from *Report of the 62nd General Motors Stockholders' Meeting,* a company booklet.

officials. There was an all-day conference at the GM Proving Ground for newspaper publishers. This event was repeated for prominent educators and representatives of foundations and investment institutions. The range of subjects was wide, even getting into such sticky problem areas as abandoned cars.

These meetings, important in themselves, additionally provided the substance for a booklet to shareholders, employees, and business and community leaders. Concurrently, there was no letup in communications efforts; television shorts were shown, as just one example. The company's next annual report contained a report of progress in areas of social concern.

THE NEXT ANNUAL MEETING: ROUND TWO

Campaign GM, in round two at the next year's annual meeting, offered three proposals:

➤ **Proposal number 1** termed "stockholder democracy," would permit the listing of shareholder nominees for the board in the company's proxy.

➤ **Proposal number 2** on "constituent democracy," sought board positions for representatives of employees, auto dealers, and consumers.

➤ **Proposal number 3** on "disclosure," would require disclosure of policies, activities, and expenditures in the areas of pollution, safety, and minority hiring in the annual report.

All three proposals were put into the proxy statement by GM, and the corporation's opposition to all three was clearly stated, not because of their cost, but because they would "do more harm than good."

Those hoping for fireworks at the meeting were disappointed. The project's proposals were overwhelmingly defeated by majorities of more than 95 percent.

How Public Relations Became an Issue

Regarding the GM public relations function, one shareholder proposed to nominate a public relations counselor to serve on the board of directors. This item on the agenda was reported in the postmeeting report in these words:

The Chairman said that General Motors has its own public relations staff and utilizes outside consultants in this area. He also said that directors were chosen for general as well as specialized abilities and it would not be in the best interests of the Corporation to reserve board memberships for persons identified with particular occupations or professions. A stockholder supported the proposal, saying such a director would be able to assist in meeting public relations problems. A proxy-holder recommended a woman as public relations counselor and said for too many years GM has been interested only in dividends, to the exclusion of other considerations. The chairman replied that General Motors has been concerned with many other aspects of society and business. A stockholder said the need for a public relations counselor or director at all corporations, including GM, should be obvious.

The vote on this proposal was 95.73 percent opposed and 4.27 percent in favor.

Questions raised at the meeting generally ran the same course as those the previous year. They were pleasantly received and answered with courtesy and patience. The most emotion-laden issue proved to be a proposal from the Episcopal Church to discontinue GM's operations in South Africa. The black GM director spoke for the proposal, the first time in the corporation's experience that a director had publicly opposed the announced position of the board.

ROUND THREE

The project was back at it a third year. Meantime, GM again stepped up its proactive efforts to take its position out publicly to the working, buying, investing, and voting public. Speeches, magazines, and newspaper advertising and network television were used.

In an extensive magazine article, the vice president for public relations raised what he termed, from GM's standpoint, a basic question: "What is the Project really trying to do?" He cited GM's answer in a booklet sent to shareholders. "The Project is using General Motors as a means through which it can challenge the entire system of corporate management in the United States."

A spokesman for the Nader group, Susan L. Gross, explained the selection of GM this way: "We haven't chosen GM because it is all bad, but because it epitomized all corporations. And we have found that if you can get GM to change, other corporations will follow."

The GM vice president for public relations termed the project a "time-consuming distraction from a basic reevaluation of goals and responsibilities which has been under way for several years."[5] Regarding the criticisms and reacting to them,

The real danger is that through misinformation or a reluctance to tell our side of the story, our political system will overreact to the critics' charges. Some critics of business exaggerate, misquote and make statements which are flatly and purposely misleading. Businessmen are not venal, money-grubbing villains who each day do their best to deceive and cheat the consumer. On the other hand, we can't complain if people hold that view of us if we don't try to tell our side of the story.

The vice president quoted from the chairman's address to GM's divisional and central office public relations people:

At various times in the history of General Motors, different staffs have been called upon to make vital contributions to our company. Today it is you public relations men [*sic*] who are being tested.

GM public relations has more visibly and aggressively taken the corporation's human side to its constituency in controlled media and messages.

AT THE MARKETPLACE

In mid-1988, GM decided to use a combination of marketing and public relations pizzazz in a campaign to regain its image as the invincible leader on top of the world auto industry. The campaign was launched with a lavish exhibit called "GM Teamwork & Technology—for Today and Tomorrow," staged in New York's Waldorf Astoria, and coupled with eight-page inserts in magazines such as *Reader's Digest*, at a cost of $20 million. Streamlined design, getaway speed, power, and luxurious fittings were their evidences of image and leadership.

---

[5]This and other quotations cited are from the speech "Round Three" presented by Anthony DeLorenzo, vice president for public relations at the time.

AS FOR CORPORATE STATESMANSHIP . . .

The company's 1993 Public Interest Report devoted 26 pages to internal matters considered to be in the public interest, 10 pages about its programs to foster community relationships, 3 pages about GM's role in the economy, and 3 pages about its efforts in minority activities. The chairman's overview stressed the need that GM has to be competitive by "maintaining the highest standards of corporate responsibility in products, services, and processes, and in our relationships with stakeholders and communities" (See Figure 5-2).[6]

BRINGING A CONTINUING STORY UP TO DATE

In succeeding years, groups with which Ralph Nader has been associated have kept tabs on GM. From GM's standpoint, that should not have been all bad, because the corporation has had repeated opportunities to tell its story with a wide audience paying attention.

At one point, GM and Nader were on the same side. The Center for Auto Safety (a Nader spin-off) felt that the Environmental Protection Agency was favoring Chrysler and Ford because they were not in the same financial shape as GM.

Nader and GM differed over a housing issue regarding the Poletown renovation (a district in Detroit) and reconstruction including a Cadillac plant. Nader joined a citizens group in opposition. At the time, GM reverted to its "cool-it" stance and froze in it by refraining from comment. Not long after, Nader was reported to be working on a book forecast as "a revealing look at corporate power."

Ralph Nader was named among "The 100 Most Important Americans of the 20th Century" in the fall 1990 issue of *Life* magazine. According to *Life,* Nader "is a crusader who became backseat driver for a nation." Twenty-eight years after publication of *Unsafe at Any Speed,* there are safety standards and air bags in cars. Nader has fathered legislation from the Freedom of Information Act to the Safe Drinking Water Act. He has also headed federal agencies such as Occupational Safety and Health Administration and the Consumer Product Safety Commission. He has inspired people to act on their rights. "Many a tenacious idealist is called a Ralph Nader, symbol of the citizen's right to know."[7] ■

QUESTIONS FOR DISCUSSION

1. Considering what you know about GM and about Ralph Nader, and what you read in this case study, what, if any, reform or change in GM attitudes toward its public responsibilities would you credit to the activities of the Nader group? If there are some, would you conclude that small investors do have a say in the policies and decisions of corporate management, or was the Nader campaign an aberration? Should small investors have any more say than is represented by the small size (number of shares) of their holdings measured against the size of the holdings held by investment trusts, foundations, and wealthy people, including GM officers and directors?

---

[6]*GM Public Interest Report* is available to students and others on request. GM Corp. General Motors Bldg. 3044 West Grand Blvd. Detroit, MI 48202.
[7]*Life,* Fall 1990, p. 19.

"FOCUSED ON IMPROVING COMPETITIVENESS

we recognize that this process must include maintaining the highest standards of corporate responsibility in our products, services and processes, and in our relationships with our stakeholders and the communities where we live and work."

FIGURE 5-2 The 1993 *Public Interest Report.*

(Courtesy of General Motors.)

2. There is an ancient concept, *noblesse oblige,* holding that those of noble birth, wealth, or power have a moral obligation to act with honor, honesty, and generosity, the inherent elements of leadership. Does it follow that General Motors, one of the world's largest and perhaps most powerful corporations, in its decisions, uses of power, and gestures of charity, sets the standards of character for all lesser corporations, whether it chooses to do so or not? If you think it does, how is GM doing as a true leader in the public interest?

3. GM's 1993 Public Interest Report covering 1992, a 48-page booklet, devotes 10 pages to philanthropic activities, 3 pages to programs for minorities and women, and 1 page of statistics to Equal Employment Opportunity data. Under philanthropy, GM donated $58 million. That was about 1.6 percent as much as its net income. The biggest beneficiary was education, getting $36 million, $22 million was given to other beneficiaries such as health and welfare, cultural organizations, urban development and community action, United Way, cancer research awards, and the National Concerto Competition. The Equal Employment Opportunity tables showed that total GM employment had gone down from 382,498 in 1987 to 365,877 in 1991. Do you think that GM would be benefited by seeking broad public disclosure of its social responsibility activities, or would the corporation be better served by quietly "cooling-it," as was done in dealing with Ralph Nader?

4. A black eye on almost all large corporations is negative public reaction to the lavish salaries, bonuses, stock options, perks, and golden umbrellas given to management, in good times or bad, whether line workers are being laid off, jobs are going abroad, or assets being sold off. Do you think such executive rewards can be justified on the basis that some rock singers, professional athletes, film and television entertainers, and network anchorpersons also reap golden harvest? What approach would you suggest to this real-world problem with which corporate professional people have to wrestle?

CASE 5-3   A CITY DIVIDED:
SDG&E TAKEOVER

In a society where organizations must recognize the interest of stakeholders as well as stockholders, investor relations often goes far beyond stock issues and earnings reports. This abbreviated case shows how public many topics once reserved only for stockholders have become.

The late 1980s left California in a serious recession. The real estate and banking industries suffered miserably, thanks to falling property values and the S&L scandals. Southern California Edison, a power utility headquartered in Rosemead, a suburb of Los Angeles, experienced financial difficulties and was a victim of a depressed economy. The population growth of Los Angeles had begun to slow, but San Diego, served by San Diego Gas & Electric, was the fourth largest growing city in the United States. Edison, the larger of the two utilities, licked its chops at the thought of eating SDG&E for dinner in a hostile takeover.

On July 26, 1988, Edison pounced on SDG&E with a hostile takeover bid of $2.03 billion in Edison stock. SDG&E officials initially resisted the offer, continued to reject the augmented bids of $2.1 billion and $2.15 billion, and eventually asked the state to stop the Edison takeover attempt. Suddenly on November 30, SDG&E directors turned enemies into allies and embraced an Edison proposal of $2.5 billion.

City officials and civic leaders of San Diego were unnerved. Mayor Maureen O'Connor and several civic leaders challenged the merger. There was even discussion of a municipal takeover of SDG&E. SDG&E dropped out of the greater San Diego Chamber of Commerce. Two board members at SDG&E resigned in protest of the merger. Rumors circulated that SDG&E officials were being offered positions by Edison, and a poll revealed that San Diegans opposed the Edison/SDG&E merger by a two-to-one margin.

GROUPS PROMOTING THE MERGER

Three groups were promoting the merger.

1. San Diegans for the Merger, a grass-roots organization funded by Southern California Edison, was an "impartial" front group composed of stockholders and SDG&E employees (current and former) who felt that the merger would improve stock value. San Diegans for the Merger distributed literature and held informational meetings.
2. Southern California Edison.
3. Members of management and the board of directors at San Diego Gas & Electric.

GROUPS OPPOSING THE MERGER

Four groups opposed the merger.

1. The Coalition for Local Control (CFLC), a diverse organization representing business interests, environmental and consumer issues, and organized labor concerns, was created in early 1989 when the president of The Greater San Diego Chamber of Commerce, Lee Grissom, persuaded

Gordon Luce of Great American Bank to form a merger opposition committee from both public and private sectors. The CFLC was funded by contributions from concerned citizens and vehemently opposed the merger. Subsequently, the group launched a public relations campaign against it.[1]

2. San Diego Mayor Maureen O'Connor, the spearhead of the opposition, gained more respect than she had previously enjoyed by defending the independence of SDG&E. She was a major spokesperson against the proposed merger.

3. City Attorney John Witt and his legal staff.

4. The majority of employees at San Diego Gas & Electric.

THE COALITION FOR LOCAL CONTROL

The CFLC was headed by executive director Bob Hudson, who coordinated the talents and skills of a diverse group of people to unite against Edison. This coalition was formed "to convince the majority of the PUC [Public Utility Commission] members [three of five] to rule against the merger through a groundswell of opposition."[2]

A BROAD-SPECTRUM COALITION BROUGHT TOGETHER UNLIKELY BEDFELLOWS

The conservation coordinator of the San Diego chapter of the Sierra Club, the business manager of the International Brotherhood of Electrical Workers #465, a mayor from the nearby city of Chula Vista, the executive director of the Utility Consumers Action Network, a public relations professional, and many others worked together to represent San Diego in a fight for the control of SDG&E. They adopted a vision statement that was accepted by the entire coalition by June 19, 1989.

If we are successful San Diego would have preserved its quality of life and controlled its own destiny.

➤ SDG&E will remain healthy, local, and investor-owned.

➤ SDG&E will be supporting the community with civic leadership and philanthropic support.

➤ SDG&E will provide economic vitality and responsiveness to the community.

➤ SDG&E will enhance its record of effective management.

➤ SDG&E rates will continue to be competitive with other Southern California utilities.

KEY MESSAGES FROM SOUTHERN CALIFORNIA EDISON

In its struggle against the mayor and the CFLC, Edison argued that:

1. The merger would prove cost-effective by eliminating duplicative functions (e.g., billing departments, public relations departments, and so on).

2. The community would benefit from price advantages, namely a promised 10 percent rate reduction.

---

[1]We thank Nuffer, Smith, Tucker, Inc., public relations counsel, for the information provided for this case.
[2]For setting rates and ruling on other issues, the PUC is often the agency that decides whether something is in the best interest of the public.

Prioritization of Decision Makers

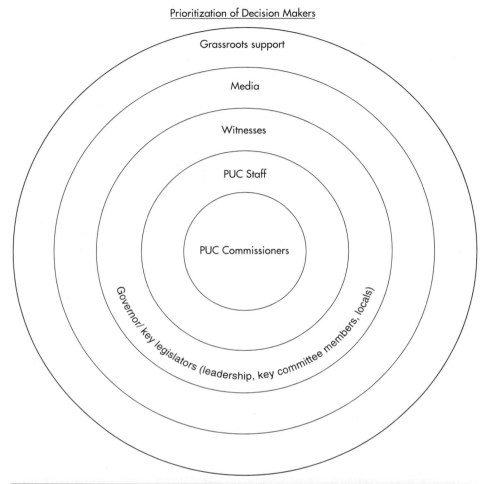

FIGURE 5-3 The CFLC devised its strategy by prioritizing which decision makers would be most receptive to its message.

(Courtesy of CFLC.)

3. The environment would be saved because SDG&E and Edison wouldn't need to invest in and construct new power facilities.
4. The merger would benefit shareholders, who would partake of the savings.

KEY MESSAGES FROM CFLC

CFLC countered with their own arguments:

1. A relocation of the utility's central headquarters to Rosemead would create a loss of corporate presence in San

FIGURE 5-4 The CFLC "working group" celebrates its victory for the citizens of San Diego after a 32-month fight against the merger.

(Courtesy of CFLC.)

Diego. The city had just lost Pacific Southwest Airlines corporation, and there was speculation that another loss could psychologically damage San Diego's independence.

2. Downsizing and transfers in both companies could sacrifice between 1,000 and 1,600 jobs.
3. The pollution level of Los Angeles could increase even further.
4. The magnitude of the combined utilities would be reminiscent of the 1930s, when utility trusts had to be broken up.

BOTH SIDES TAKE ACTION

Edison and its front organizations spent more than $2.2 million on advertising and publicity campaigns, pamphlets, and flyers. (Legal fees brought the total Southern California Edison expenditure close to $100 million.) San Diego and the CFLC spent their far smaller budget (approxi-

mately $80,000) on a different public relations strategy—reaching the decision makers by focusing on third-party advocates who had influence with the PUC.

The CFLC distributed its own facts refuting the claims made by Edison. Its activities began by assessing receptivity to the CFLC mission of the publics that influence the Public Utility Commission (the PUC commissioners, PUC staff, the governor and legislators, the media, and grassroots support) (See Figure 5-3). The role of the mayor as a prominent spokesperson in this campaign increased media attention on the issue and brought the story out of the business section into the general news pages. Predictably, it had a similar effect on the grapevine and coffee-break discussion.

THE RESULTS

On May 8, 1991, after a three-year battle, the PUC unanimously denied Edison's proposed merger with SDG&E. After several investigations by state and federal authorities, it was determined that the merger would not benefit San Diegans through lower pollution and electric rates.

An overwhelming percentage of the public opposed the merger because of the media and public relations efforts by the mayor and the CFLC. The Greater San Diego Chamber of Commerce welcomed the SDG&E utility back to the Chamber in a sincere effort to begin the healing process for themselves, the utility, and the San Diego community (See Figure 5-4). ■

QUESTIONS FOR DISCUSSION

1. Was it fair to SDG&E stockholders, who might have benefited financially by selling their stock in the proposed takeover, for other parties to intervene? Why or why not?
2. Make a point-by-point case, pro or con, on a situation in which people who own shares in a company nonetheless have a voice in its destiny. Justify your position with comparative examples in other areas of public policy.
3. Compare the key messages from CFLC and Edison. How are they dissimilar or similar? What is the specific strategy behind each of the messages? What publics might find each appealing or persuasive?
4. How was the public served in this case?
5. How ethical was Edison's decision to fund San Diegans for the Merger?

CASE 5-4   THE SEAMLESS WEB: HOW RELATIONS WITH OTHER PUBLICS AFFECTS INVESTOR RELATIONS

Whether a publicly held corporation is trying to sell clothing, automobiles, houses, or homemade sausage, it needs three essential ingredients for success: excellent products, quality staff, and a high profile as a valuable investment. If one of the three is lacking, the entire organization is affected.

A corporation needs investors—persons willing to invest healthy sums of money and ideas to support growth. In order to attract and keep them, investor relations is a key function. Bob Evans Farms, Inc. uses a quality approach to investor relations. The bottom line is always quality—the best products, strong employee relations, superior consumer relations, and quality investor relations—because, after all, stockholders invest in all of these items.

BOB EVANS FARMS, INC., MISSION STATEMENT

"To provide quality products and services to meet our customers' needs, allowing us to prosper as a business and to provide a reasonable return for our stockholders."

HISTORY OF BOB EVANS FARMS INC.

In 1946, Bob Evans was operating a small, 24-hour restaurant in Gallipolis, Ohio. At that time, he couldn't find sausage good enough to serve to his customers, so he started making his own. Evans invited guests to his farm in Rio Grande, Ohio, to taste the sausage. Visitors became so numerous that the company built its first restaurant, The Sausage Shop, right on the farm. The Sausage Shop became the basis for a corporation now operated by 38,500 employees, which includes nearly 470 full-service, family restaurants in 22 states and distributes food products to 30 states.

MARK FOR CHANGE

Today Bob Evans Farms (BEF) connotes success, but this level of achievement came only after the mid-1980s. At that time the company's performance was sluggish. Earnings were down, and stock was lacking. According to Mary Cusick, Senior Vice President of Investor Relations and Corporate Communications, strategic planning was not used effectively.[1] Executives decided that the center of these problems, the stagnancy of the organization, needed to be researched and tackled. Why wasn't the corporation progressing?

Bob Evans implemented a series of initiatives to strengthen investor and consumer

---

[1]We thank Mary Cusick, Senior Vice President of Investor Relations and Corporate Communications, and Mandy Jordan, Restaurant Media Relations Administrator of Bob Evans Farms, Inc., for the information provided for this case.

relations. BEF's internal research found that management, employees, and investors were directly affected by BEF's lack of strategic planning. Employee job performance was affected by a lack of communication and information. Investors felt the brunt of this communication gap as well. As a result, management decided that employees and investors needed better communication regarding all aspects of the business.

THE NEED FOR CHANGE

During the past decade the company has continued to refine its approach to business. Management incorporated good communication between consumers, investors, and employees because the satisfaction of those audiences affected all aspects of the business. Its ongoing goals are:

1. Target product development to focus on items that represent the brand yet put a twist on home-style food (See Figure 5-5)
2. To meet annual profitability levels set by management
3. To strategically grow the company through same-store sales increases, market expansion, and new products
4. Be more responsive to investors, customers, and employees
5. Strategically consider acquisitions

THE EXTERNAL PUBLIC: THE PERCEPTION PROBLEM

Executives worked together and implemented an "involved strategic planning process—bringing things such as changing consumer needs to the forefront," explains Cusick. The company started with consumer relations because customer perceptions were at the heart of the problem—if BEF's products were not being purchased, investors would pull out, employees would lose their jobs, and the business could fail.

Through various ongoing research methods including customer surveys and strategy meetings, BEF executives have continued to develop ways that the company can freshen and promote the brand:

1. Upgrading facilities throughout the system. In fiscal 2001, Bob Evans rebuilt 13 restaurants and remodeled 33 current restaurants. All new restaurants include a Carry Home Kitchen, which allows carryout customers to order, park, and pay more easily, and a "Corner Cupboard" retail area. (See Figure 5-6)
2. Maximizing the usefulness of its point-of-sale computer system and utilizing sales data received to enhance the ability to collect information on buying patterns and consumer behavior.
3. Increasing use of technology without taking away from the brand through the Bob Evans Web site, in-store customer survey kiosks, retail ordering systems, Web-cast conferences, and online employment services.
4. Adding seasonal entrees to the menu in order to add variety to the menu, generate news about the new items, and further reinforce the focus on value and taste.
5. Developing new retail products and line extensions to grow presence in grocery stores and appeal to customers.
6. Directing focus to families with children to generate awareness and develop brand loyalty.

THE INTERNAL PUBLICS: THE EMPLOYEE SATISFACTION PROBLEM

Corporate communications set up new ways to improve communications with employees. Bob Evans Farms' communications

FIGURE 5-5   Bob Evans Farm distributes pamphlets that let the public know a little bit more about it and healthy recipes that use its main product, sausage.

(Courtesy of Bob Evans Farms, Inc.)

team recognized the detrimental effects of "word-of-mouth." Executives had to better inform the midlevel managers so that these supervisors could serve as a reference for others. They could answer and clarify questions that employees might have. To do this, corporate communications created:

1. "The Almanac," a new quarterly video news magazine, which gives managers updated news on all aspects of the company.

2. "The Homesteader," a quarterly employee newsletter mailed to the 38,000 employees' homes containing relevant company information from surveys to upcoming events.

3. The B.E.S.T. Bulletin, a bimonthly bulletin distributed to all restaurant units. The bulletin emphasizes pertinent information for restaurant employees regarding cleanliness, performance, safety, and other areas of importance for the units.

FIGURE 5-6 This is one of the 486 family-style restaurants in 22 states owned and operated by Bob Evans Farms, Inc.

(Courtesy of Bob Evans Farms, Inc.)

4. An intranet containing information such as benefits, a bulletin board, and weekly newsletter to inform corporate employees of activities and updates within the company.
5. Availability of an employee stock option plan, dividend reimbursements, and stocks as incentives and rewards. The idea is that if employees own part of the company, they will value it and support its initiatives.
6. A communications audit every two years to reevaluate the effectiveness of current communications programs.

TARGETING INVESTOR PROBLEMS

Bob Evans Farms also realized that it needed better communication between investors and the business. The corporation now:

1. Continues to send annual reports and SEC filings to investors by traditional mail and make them available electronically.
2. Works with the Ohio business press and financial media and uses the company's Web site to disseminate information to stockholders.
3. Invites stockholders to attend restaurant openings in their area.

4. Promotes stock through speaking engagements to financial analysts and other institutional investors.

EVALUATION

In 2001, the company reached a milestone when in surpassed $1 billion in net sales. According to Mary Cusick, the organization had 39,490 stockholders as of June 2001. Approximately 37 percent are individual owners and 98 percent are residents of Ohio. Bob Evans Farms recognizes the key to a company's survival—the whole is only as good as the sum of its parts. ■

QUESTIONS FOR DISCUSSION

1. What other strategies can you suggest top maintain current investor satisfaction and encourage new investment in Bob Evans Farms, Inc.?

2. Review the actions taken by management to address the external and internal publics problems. What have they got to do with *investor* relations? What effect might they have on investors, if any?

3. List elements of investor relations that will be different for a company such as BEF—a smaller, locally held company with mainly individual investors—than for a giant creature of Wall Street. Which do you think presents the greater challenge for its public relations practitioners?

CASE 5-5   THE MAKING OF A DPO AND THE ROLE OF PUBLIC RELATIONS

For many Americans, starting up a business is a dream come true. Small businesses pop up across the United States every year, but few survive the challenge of entering the world of stocks. An *initial public offering* (IPO) is the standard procedure for selling stocks in the business world. An IPO is "a first and one-time-only sale of publicly tradable stock shares in a company that has previously been owned privately," according to a definition on whatis.com. Specialized companies normally manage an IPO because of its complex place in the stock market. Many big corporations sell their stock in this manner.

Helping small business emerge across the United States is the *direct public offering* (DPO), which started in 1976. With a DPO, the company sells shares directly to the public instead of working through brokers. "DPOs work best for businesses whose customers have a natural attraction to their product," says Drew Field, a San-Francisco attorney specializing in DPOs.

Several success stories prove that small companies can accomplish the "American Dream" by approaching investor relations in this way. Some of these include Internet companies such as Yahoo! and Amazon. com as well as the company that is the topic of this case study: Annie's Homegrown.

ANNIE'S HOMEGROWN

In 1985, on a farm in Hampton, Connecticut, a small business phenomenon was born. Ann Withey and then-husband Andrew Martin had an idea to capitalize on the health food craze and create their own unique white cheddar cheese popcorn—Smartfood—which they sold to PepsiCo/FritoLay. After success in the snack food industry, Withey had another idea—to add the white cheddar cheese to pasta. Four years later, Annie's Homegrown Inc. was born.

Many aspects of Annie's Homegrown make it a unique business. Some say its products make it unique: 12 varieties of macaroni and cheese, 4 kinds of vegetarian canned pastas, and 8 Indian cuisine entrées. Others mention the fact that it is one of the few all-natural pasta and cheese dishes on the market. But what makes Annie's Homegrown stand out above the rest is its treatment toward investor relations.

With only eight employees, the company has grown highly competitive. It is the leading "all-natural" brand and ranks second to Kraft in the total macaroni and cheese category, according to Information Resources, Inc. Two main ingredients contribute to the company's success: its strong consumer relationships and its direct public offering (DPO).

ANNIE'S HOMEGROWN DPO

Annie's Homegrown was sure of one thing when it decided to go public in 1995: the company had very loyal customers. This was due to a superior product and personal contact with customers. Withey opens every customer letter (many are received) and personally answers those she feels warrants a personal response. "I really try to connect with the person. I try hard not to just write form letters." This often inspires customers to write back. So, over the years, Withey has accumulated "quite a few pen pals."[1]

After six years as a solid pasta-producing business, Annie's Homegrown decided to undertake a $3.6 million DPO in August 1995. "Our whole thinking was to make our customers our owners, and to enlist them as a marketing team, because they care about our company," explained Deborah Churchill, former vice chairman of Annie's.[2]

The approach was rather simple. The company (1) stuffed one million DPO flyers into its pasta boxes asking customers to call, write, or fax for a prospectus; (2) sent 40,000 letters to customers from its mailing list; (3) advertised in the magazine *Mother Jones*; and (4) posted a notice on its Web site.

Going public with a DPO was a logical step, not only because of the company's loyal following, but also for financial reasons. One unique aspect of DPOs is that they don't require securities underwriters, who on average receive 13 percent of the money raised in a public offering. Also, many DPOs can actually generate between $300,000 and $4 million. Annie's offered 600,000 shares at $6 a share. The minimum purchase was 50 shares and with 2,435 investors, the company was $1.5 million richer. Revenues for Annie's Homegrown were $5.5 million for the 1996 fiscal year.

ANNIE'S HOMEGROWN CONSUMER RELATIONS

A 1997 *Boston Globe* article described Annie's Homegrown as, "a folksy, socially conscious marketer that some might call the Ben & Jerry's of macaroni and cheese." The approach of the all-natural Annie's Homegrown to consumer relations is unique and very smart. The company stands by its mission to be "socially responsible." By utilizing word-of-mouth marketing, instead of advertising, Annie's establishes a personal relationship with its consumers. Annie gave out her home phone number for customers to call and ask questions or make comments until a few years ago, when the volume of calls became too large. She continues to faithfully answer customers' letters.

The Annie's Homegrown Web site (www.annies.com) is also a good tool for its customer relations. The site sells its food products and other merchandise; tells about the company and its commitment to the environment; describes its socially responsible programs; and offers recipes, coloring pages, and "links we like." An entire section is dedicated to Annie's pet rabbit, Bernie—who is gone now, victim of a too-powerful antibiotic—but his memory lives on in the company.

Other consumer relations approaches that Annie's uses include:

➤ Folksy notes on the pasta box
➤ Donations to nonprofit organizations for children, women, education, and the environment
➤ Scholarship information program
➤ Environmental Studies Scholarship Program—giving away 25 $1,000 scholarships annually
➤ Free case of Annie's to students who earn a 3.8 grade-point average
➤ Discount coupons
➤ Free "Be Green" bumper stickers

---

[1]*Country Journal*, July/August 2000.
[2]Carol Steinberg, "Direct Public Offerings Turn Customers into Investors," *Success*, March 1997.

➤ E-mail newsletter distributed free to customers who request it

➤ Will ship a case of pasta to a friend as a gift idea

For Annie's Homegrown (and other similar companies—See Case 5-4), the relationship between customer and shareholder is close, making communication both easier and more important. With the bulk of your stock in the hands of those who consume your products, the pressure is on to satisfy both "stakeholders" at once. Product performance and financial performance always go hand-in-hand, but never so closely as when the customer and the shareholder are one. ■

QUESTIONS FOR DISCUSSION

1. Why was a DPO a logical option for Annie's Homegrown rather than an ordinary IPO?
2. What role did public relations play in this decision to use a DPO?
3. What factors come into play when deciding which route to take to "public" status?
4. Would the 42 percent subscription rate achieved by Annie's Homegrown DPO make you rethink the value of such a procedure? Why?
5. Is Annie's Homegrown approach toward public relations and investor relations suitable for all publicly held companies? Why?
6. Is there any conflict of interest between the shareholder/investor and customer/consumer?

CASE 5-6   MANAGING CORPORATE MARRIAGES—TWO DECADES OF LESSONS LEARNED

Merger mania swept the corporate world through the 1990s. Almost daily, business sections of major news publications were filled with stories on Wall Street's latest mergers and acquisitions—often known as M&As. Along with the news of mergers, however, came the news of slowed starts and dramatic disappointments. In fact, studies have found that an unbelievable 50 to 75 percent of all merging companies are unable to retain their book value two years after they combine, due in many cases to culture clash and loss of top talent. Ultimately, failed mergers result in profit losses and, typically, falling stock prices.

In a society where organizations must recognize the interest of stakeholders as well as stockholders, investor relations often go far beyond stock issues and earnings reports. The following case study shows the importance of developing relationships with all publics when managing the marriage of two companies.

The 1997 merger between two global companies—Boeing and McDonnell Douglas—was successful. In fact, the combined company's merger program won the Grand Prize for Excellence in the International Public Relations Association (IPRA) Golden World Awards. Crucial to its success was its focus on building unity within the combined company.

Before the merger was announced, management researched other merged companies. It found that in most cases, workers did not receive much, if any, attention in planning the merger. As a result of this research, a strong employee communication strategy was adopted right from the start. Just after the public announcement of the merger between the two aviation firms, 21 employee focus groups were conducted to (1) determine levels of understanding and (2) refine the type, scope, and nature of ongoing communications.

The sessions included various levels of supervisory management with Boeing, McDonnell Douglas, and Rockwell (Rockwell was acquired by Boeing a week before the McDonnell Douglas talks began). Management heard three important messages:

1. "Communicate, communicate, communicate. Even when you don't know the answer, tell us you don't know."
2. "Treat the merger as a celebration, not a funeral."
3. "We're not ready or willing to start working together as a team."

From these key messages, management realized it had a lot of work to do to show employees that they were a priority in the merger. Communications teams were formed and facilitated by members of each company.

Management had just five days between the final sign-off of the proposed merger and the announcement to the public. CEOs and communications staff immediately began developing preliminary programs to get underway before the press announcement was made. Five million dollars was spent on complicated communication materials that explained the merger to employees. It was imperative that these materials be ready for distribution when the merger was approved by the U.S. government, shareholders, and the European Union.

Execution of the merger during the transition period leading up to the merger approval was a crucial period. The merger was announced on a Sunday and, by 8 A.M. on Monday, complete packets of information were on managers' desks to be distributed to employees. In addition:

> ➤ Twenty-eight "Transition Bulletins" were issued, videos and internal TV programs were aired, and company newspapers offered weekly updates.
> ➤ Company Web sites carried daily information; the sites merged on Day 1.
> ➤ The Boeing corporate logo was restructured to include the history of McDonnell Douglas.
> ➤ Both CEOs were heavily involved in public appearances and usually appeared together to promote the "We Are One Company" theme.
> ➤ Media tours were provided to background reporters and provided them with internal reactions.

During the first week of the merger, all 220,000 employees received—at their homes—information packages including:

> ➤ Two videotapes: one of the CEOs discussing the significance and vision of the merger and another highlighting products, capabilities, and programs

> ➤ A 30-page color brochure featuring products, etc.
> ➤ A lapel pin to introduce the new company logo

An employee-only town hall meeting was held in Washington, D.C. A select group of employees and guests attended a telecast from the National Air and Space Museum and a press conference with the new CEOs, "Phil and Harry." Employees all over the world gathered in 52 plant locations to view the telecast from Phil and Harry prior to the public announcement. The Washington news conference was broadcast live on giant screens in factories and on tarmacs. In some locations, air shows and parachutists were featured in the celebration.

Fourteen hundred banners announcing "One Company, One Vision" were created and delivered in person by "Phil and Harry's Excellent Adventure," a five-day visit to employees in 14 cities. They walked through production areas, greeted employees, signed autographs, and answered questions. At one plant, employee applause lasted seven minutes, surprising even the CEOs.

Post-merger focus groups were used to evaluate the communications programs. The majority of employees appreciated the efforts made by management to include them in the program. Employees almost unanimously believed the merger was a good idea. The McDonnell Douglas C-17 production line experienced one of its most productive days ever—despite an hour of down time the day CEOs Phil and Harry visited that plant.

Overall, management felt that the time and energy put into the employee communications was well placed and will show dividends over the long term. ■

QUESTIONS FOR DISCUSSION

1. Why is it important that merged companies be concerned with "connecting" with all their employees?
2. Assess the outcome of the focus groups. How should management deal with the position that the workers were "not ready to start working together as a team"?
3. Was the strategy of mailing information to the homes of 220,000 employees a good one? Why?
4. Is management justified in thinking the communication program will "show dividends over the long term"? Why?

PROBLEM 5-A Can an Annual Report Please Everyone?

Preparation of the annual report for a publicly owned corporation is probably the most frustrating, if not the most difficult, communications literary task generally assigned to the corporate communications staff. This statement is true whether the job is handled internally or with the aid of outside counsel.

As the "report card" of management to those who own the company as shareholders, and to those in the financial community who can influence others for or against owning shares, it is an ultrasensitive and personal document. In many cases it is an ego trip for the head of the firm, for the top financial officer, or for officers hoping one day to become CEO.

The top official, when the company has had a good year, both competitively and in operating results, may want a lavish four-color booklet. The senior financial officer may prefer one or two colors (the second being silver or gold), demonstrating prudence as well as success. The heads of operating divisions, wanting to broaden the circulation to customers and prospects, may want lavish product or service pictures, particularly of the products or services of their particular division or subsidiary. The director of personnel will probably want pictures showing how happy the employees are at their jobs. Systems analysts will want their latest cost-reducing equipment shown. If the corporation is international in scope, the export department will want to emphasize "hands across the seas."

Shareholders who may receive dividends of $1 per share of stock may receive an annual report that costs $1 to $2 per copy to produce, not counting the time to put into it by executives and members of the communications staff. In many corporations, thinking about the next year's report starts as soon as one year's annual report has come out and been distributed, feedback has been received, and the annual meeting of shareholders has taken place. Given the high vanity quotient involved; the diversity of views within a corporation; the inherent "competition" for attention, recognition, and prominence among corporate divisions; and possibly financial results that are not the best, public relations has its work cut out for it.

Persuasion, compromise, and reconciliation are needed. See how you would go about this task: Select a corporation and acquire an annual report. Assume that you have to plan for the next year's report.

1. What questions will you ask and what research will you do before you start your basic strategic plan for the report?

2. Your research indicates the desirability of some major changes in the content and design of the report. Draw up a formal outline of your approach, including:

- Overall theme in words and graphics (with your rationale)
- Table of contents indicating obligatory information
- Preliminary concepts for cover and layout
- Photography needs or other visual techniques with costs
- Printing costs, including number of copies
- A timetable with deadlines

3. How will you suggest reducing the cycle time required to produce the annual report?

PROBLEM 5-B Here Comes That Man Nader, Again

The article shown in Figure 5-7 appeared in the national newspaper *USA Today.*

You are newly hired, a business school graduate with an emphasis in public relations, in the shareholder relations section of a department in one of the 10 companies named in the news story. (Take your choice.)

After the story appeared, there were a few well-chosen expletives expressed in your company regarding Nader and his associates, but there was no request from

FIGURE 5-7 Ralph Nader's group nominates 10 companies for hall of shame.

Ralph Nader's group nominates 10 companies for Hall of Shame

They won't tell you, so we will.

They are 10 major USA companies, and what they won't tell you is they've been named to the 1983 Corporate Hall of Shame.

For outstanding achievement in "unethical conduct, narrowness of vision, lack of foresight, and unwaveringly steady focus on the short-term bottom line," Ralph Nader and the Corporate Accountability Group bring you:

■ Dow Chemical Co.: Refused to settle charges brought by Vietnam veterans claiming Agent Orange injuries.

■ Eli Lilly and Co: Said it acted "responsibly and ethically" when marketing arthritis drug Oraflex in the USA, although the public already knew that Lilly knew of Oraflex-related deaths overseas.

■ FMC Corp.: Led a nationwide effort to enact laws curtailing victims' rights to just compensation for injuries inflicted by defective products.

■ General Motors Corp.: Lobbied to defeat auto safety standards requiring USA automakers to put airbags or passive belts in all autos by last fall.

■ General Public Utilities Corp.: Pushed for federal OK to restart nuclear generators at Three Mile Island just after GPU's operating unit was indicted on charges of falsifying 1979 safety-test results at TMI.

■ Manville Corp.: Used the bankruptcy process to avert financial responsibilty for asbestos-related injury claims.

■ Mellon Bank: Loaned millions of dollars to Japanese steel makers while foreclosing on USA steel company loans.

■ The Nestle Co. Inc.: Ignored the World Health Organization by aggressively marketing infant formula in the Third World.

■ Sperry Corp.: Overcharged the Air Force $325,000 for missile guidance work.

■ Upjohn Co.: Continued to campaign for government approval of Depo-Provera — a suspected carcinogenic contraceptive the company wants to market in the USA.

How 'bout a big hand for the winners.

(Reprinted with permission of *USA Today.*)

senior financial officers or top management that any responsive or reciprocal action be taken. Your immediate boss asked nothing of you, and the vice president for public relations made no request of him. The position of your employer, apparently, is much the same as the "cool-it" posture of GM when Nader's Campaign GM was on. There is a new development, however.

A letter has come in, addressed to Director of Shareholder Relations. The letter includes these passages:

> My husband was a successful businessman. His success is the reason I am able to live comfortably on my investments, one of which is ownership of 1,000 shares of your stock. I might say that I own more of your stock than some of the people on your board of directors.
>
> Having more of my money invested in your stock than some of your directors who get paid fees concerns me somewhat. But my major concern is that you do things that invite attention and distrust because they appear unethical, illegal, short-sighted, or just plain greedy, and contrary to what investors and consumers are entitled to expect. Isn't this a legitimate reason to question the justification for the huge salaries, bonuses, and stock options you give yourselves?
>
> I know I have the alternative of removing my funds from the company and investing them elsewhere. The news article, however, suggests that the standards you set for your conduct, and your performance, are typical of all big business. That leaves me no place to go except to foreign businesses, or to government with demands that they regulate you more strictly, or take over your industry and run it for the benefit of everyone. Frankly, your speeches complaining about regulation leave me a bit cold.
>
> Isn't it high time that those in business take the lead in self-discipline so that government and everybody else will have real leadership to follow?

This letter has been passed down the line, and it stops with you. The note of instruction on it reads: "We may get a bundle of letters pretty much like this one. Upstairs [the president's office] they want a reply, to be signed by the president. Let's see what you can come up with."

1. What will you do before you fire up your computer to write the letter?
2. Write a draft of the letter with a cover sheet explaining to the president the rationale for your approach.

PROBLEM 5-C Planning the Annual Meeting with a Twist

You work for the corporate communications department of a major corporation in California. Your duties vary on what projects come up, but your focus as of late has been internal. As a function of your job, your department is responsible for arranging the annual meeting of shareholders. Your corporation has decided to merge with another leader in the industry and the company has decided to release this information at the annual shareholder meeting.

Planning the annual meeting is a large task to take on, but with the added information that will need to be communicated, you realize that you have a huge job on your hands. This merger will have a significant effect on many aspects of the corporation. First, it will be a larger operation. As you are already a leader in the industry, this merger will put your company at the top and possibly put it in the *Fortune* 500. Second, the company will expand its services and products and will have to make changes internally to support the new business that it will be taking on. Job descriptions will need to be changed as well as departments consolidated so that they may become more cohesive as to what their new concentration will be. Third, many jobs will be eliminated from both companies to complete the final merger. Some of the company's shareholders are employees; some of them might lose their jobs in this process.

Knowing all of this, how will you communicate this information to shareholders at the annual meeting? Would you make a presentation to employees separate from shareholders and allow them to voice their concerns? What media outlets would you use to relay this information to the public outside of the company? In what sequence would you release this information?

Public relations practitioners often play the role of interpreter or mediator in situations like these. What recommendations will you make to the CEO that might help her present this news in a positive light?

CHAPTER

6 | CONSUMER RELATIONS

"Who are the three most important publics?" asks an old trick question. The answer is "customers, customers, and customers." If you don't succeed in attracting and then building continuing relationships with them, you'll be out of business and nothing else will matter.

During the rise of marketing as a cure-all in the mid-1980s, this view frequently prevailed in corporations. Hospitals, universities, public agencies, and even churches adopted marketing as a response to the increasing competition for people's interest and dollars. On balance, the marketing revolution was helpful to many organizations—particularly large or very successful companies, which had often forgotten that it is the customer who pays the bill, and to nonprofit entities, who often treated users of services as a nuisance to their routine, rather than the reason for their existence.

Ironically, while this trend reestablished a key point of public relations philosophy, it sometimes pushed public relations departments into a secondary role to marketing. A much-debated point was whether public relations is a part of marketing or vice versa or whether they are both essential strategic services and thus equal factors.

The question was prominent because marketing became a part of organizations that traditionally did not use marketing concepts. Hospitals in particular began marketing their "products" in an effort to gain their share of the healthcare market. Their patients began making it clear they did not want to be sold health care, and hospitals retreated—putting the function back into perspective.

Marketing and public relations share some fundamental concepts. These include analyzing market opportunities (research), selecting target markets (publics), developing a marketing mix (communication and action plan), and managing the marketing effort (evaluation).

The sharing of these concepts illustrates the close working relationship of the two fields. Despite these similarities, keep in mind that marketing is ultimately product-specific or service-specific. Public relations is so much broader a discipline. *pr reporter* illustrated the differences, stating that public relations as a strategy does four things marketing cannot do:

- Public relations is concerned about internal relations and publics.
- Public relations cares about noncustomer external publics and the environment in which the organization operates.

163

- Public relations operates on the policies of human nature (what makes the individual tick), whereas marketing focuses on consumer behavior (purchasing and economics, often expressed in number-crunching research).
- Public relations may work to stabilize or change public opinion in areas other than products.[1]

In the 1990s and into the twenty-first century, the functions have come close together, as demonstrated by the dominant customer relations strategy: relationship marketing. As the name suggests, this approach adopts public relations principles such as personalized, one-on-one dialogue regarding marketing of products and services.

The buyer-seller relationship concerns every public relations department and every public relations counselor. Ideally, the role of the public relations counselor is to help create conditions of understanding so that the objectives of sellers can be attained by satisfying needs of consumers. As a landmark conference between public relations and marketing leaders concluded,[2] public relations must both (1) help motivate purchases and (2) create a hospitable environment for the organization to sell product and services.

HISTORICAL BACKGROUND

Starting in the late 1940s, following an almost universal base of hardship during the Great Depression, consumer "wants" were for material possessions, labor-saving devices, convenience, ease, and luxury. To producers and sellers, these were seen as consumer "needs." In the succeeding decades of increasing prosperity and affluence, it followed that if a product or service could be sold, it "deserved" to be sold. If a desire for it could be induced, it was what the people "wanted." Wants translated with adept interpretation into needs. A hula-hoop, a Frisbee, a pair of jogging shoes became "needs" for wholesome recreation or health.

For product and service sellers, the 1950s were happy times, as they were for marketing, promotion, advertising, and publicity personnel. The economy was based and dependent on increasing consumption. Trading in one's car annually, building a summer home, discarding clothes for each fashion change, engaging in fads, buying on time with credit cards, maintaining a big mortgage, stocking a basement with appliances, using hair tonics and electric shavers—these were "marks of distinction." Buying was promoted as though it were patriotic. Communications served these times well, especially when television came on the scene to give printed and audio media rough competition.

In this set of conditions, it was inevitable that sellers would stretch the boundaries of quality, service, and safety in products and services. They would exceed the limits of truth and accuracy in their claims and would abuse the privilege of using the public media. On occasion, through inadequate concern for quality, they would kill and injure some people and alienate many others.[3]

---

[1] *pr reporter*, Vol. 27, January 2, 1984, p. 3.
[2] "A Challenge to the Calling: Public Relations Colloquium 1989" held at San Diego State University on January 24, 1989, sponsored by Nuffer Smith & Tucker.
[3] For further insight, see Earl W. Kintner, *A Primer on the Law of Deceptive Practices,* New York: Macmillan, 1971.

The first significant government restraint in the 1960s came in the Kefauver-Harris Drug Act in 1962. Through the decade, other federal laws were passed, involving abuses in packaging, labeling, product safety, drugs, and truth in lending. Early in the game, Ralph Nader showed up with his *Unsafe at Any Speed* (See Case 5-2). Regulatory agencies became more active and aggressive.[4] A presidential assistant was appointed to represent and help protect the consumer. A tough adversary relationship was established for business.

Meanwhile, business approaches to the consumer were shifting. "Share of mind" superseded "share of market" for many national product advertisers. Programs spoke more about "benefits" and "value." Publicists were engaged more in concepts to sell "an idea," "industrial statesmanship," "a good company to do business with," or the "philosophy" or the "personality" rather than the sheer pleasure of owning the product or enjoying the service.

In public relations programming, there was an increasing shift to use of public service hitched to marketing. Recipes were provided for home economists; commemorative events were tied to products; dinosaur models went on exhibit; cars were tested by the loan of one to each family in a small town; a blimp roamed over public events, aiding national telecasts. The introduction of a new line of sports equipment endorsed by a celebrated athlete might be accompanied by a personal appearance. On tour, the athlete might sign autographs in stores, be interviewed by local writers on controversial sports subjects, be photographed at bedside in children's hospitals or wards, and conduct free clinics on sportsmanship at a local school.

- Today this approach has become the rule: People want to be *served,* not sold.

Further business response to growing consumer protectionism and advocacy came in the activation of ombudspersons, 800 numbers, understandable warranty statements, devices for improved listenership and response, calls to customers to check satisfaction after purchase, quick settlement of injury claims, and product recalls. This attitude gave even more importance to public relations and its implementation, but it did not stop all the abuses.

Television commercials were louder by several decibels than entertainment broadcasts. Among the largest advertisers were makers of products that were the most profitable but among the least necessary to human survival or uplift—cosmetics, liquor, and tobacco, to name a few. Going into the 1970s, consumer disenchantment with sellers, their wares, and their words expressed itself as more awareness of alternatives and here and there a boycott.

In 1970, Federal Communications Commission (FCC) Commissioner Nicholas Johnson raised and answered his own question of alternatives. "How can we make life in the corporate state more livable and more human?" His personal approach was to plan an "ideal day." In it he found fundamental elements to be love, beauty, contemplation of some kind, personal analysis, creative expression, contact with nature, and some participation in the support of one's life. He included such measures as riding a

---

[4]Early cases of Federal Trade Commission intervention and decisions include Carter's Little Liver Pills in the 1950s and Geritol in the 1960s. There are many more recent cases.

bicycle; throwing away expendable things in the house; and using bicarbonate of soda for toothpaste, gargle, mouthwash, burn ointment, stomach settler, room freshener, fire extinguisher, refrigerator cleaner, children's clay, and baking powder—at less than 25 cents a box.

He jotted down his thoughts on the basic elements of life. One of his observations was that "when people live their lives in ways that take them too far from these basic truths, they begin to show up in the rising statistics indicating social disintegration, crimes of violence, alcoholism, drug addiction, suicide, mental illness, and so forth."[5]

THE LINK BETWEEN REPUTATION AND MARKETING

In the 1980s, a new rash of crises shared the front page; they involved violence, drugs, greed, pollution, and lack of integrity. Business has adjusted to this situation. Advertising and publicity talk about reforestation, human dignity, education, rehabilitation, and "caring." Projects and speeches focus on safety, health, and the minority, neglected, and handicapped groups in society.

There are other problems. Conglomeration and divestiture tarnish traditional identities. What happens when Armour, not only a prestigious name on a pound of bacon but a landmark at the Chicago stockyards and a family intertwined for generations in the culture and society of the city, is swallowed into a bus company, also with a well-known name, Greyhound? Or when Twinkies becomes a product of International Telephone and Telegraph? Or when the Bell System disappears and spawns Nynex, U.S. West, and Sprint, among others?

Multinationalism is another matter. Does anything significant happen in consumer relationships when a company that has proclaimed its "loyal American heritage" goes abroad to manufacture because wages are lower?

In the 1990s, savvy consumers made buying decisions based on how companies ran their businesses, according to a 1995 survey by pr firm Porter/Novelli.[6] Five major influences on buying habits were (1) product quality, (2) the company's method of handling consumer complaints, (3) the way a company handles a crisis in which it *is* at fault, (4) challenges by a government agency about product safety, and (5) accusation of illegal or unethical trading practices. Communication with consumers began moving from a product or service focus to information about how the organization operates and what values guide its decisions.

THE ROLE OF PUBLIC RELATIONS

Technically, both marketing and public relations support the sales function. "Nothing happens until a sale is made," says an old bromide. The difference is that marketing is totally engrossed in selling, whereas public relations is more holistic. It supports sales to customers, but also is concerned with relationships with all other stakeholders of the organization.

---

[5]Nicholas Johnson, "Test Pattern for Living," *Saturday Review*, May 29, 1971.
[6]*pr reporter*, October 2, 1995, pp. 3–4.

Originally, public relations supported sales almost exclusively through media publicity, promotional events, and consumer information programs. The objective was to make people:

1. Aware of the product or service in the first place
2. Knowledgeable about the benefits and advantages of the particular product or service
3. Constantly reminded and reinforced in favorable feelings toward the product or service

Such activity ties in with advertising and authenticates product claims. Media used include newspapers, magazines, radio, television, features, photos, planned events, sponsorship of sports or musical activities, and many other venues for promotion. These are one-way communication vehicles touting the name and claims of the product or service.

Although the emphasis on marketing pushed some public relations departments back to this role, the changing conditions of the marketplace also brought forth several new activities, such as:

1. Forming user groups (as computer makers did) or customer service departments (as some automakers and utilities did) to personally build customer loyalty
2. Adopting customer satisfaction programs in which the entire organization is focused on delivering not just a product or service but also the quality and personal interactions consumers expect when making a purchase (as retailers, utilities, and brand manufacturers did)
3. Concentrating the publicity and promotion activities on taking customers away from competitors (which the beer and cigarette makers state as their primary reason for publicity and advertising)
4. Protecting the reputation of the product or service, and of the organization, in a period of consumer activism, government regulation, competitive predation, global marketing, and similar conditions that bring a continual bevy of public issues to bear on every organization and industry

CUSTOMER DELIGHT REPLACES CUSTOMER SERVICE

Yet even as organizations trimmed and shaped themselves to meet their customers' needs and values, two problems surfaced: (1) how to discipline and motivate the organization (and its employees) so it (2) delights customers who then become regular, repeat, and loyal.

Grant Medical Center (GMC) of Columbus, Ohio, succeeded in satisfying its customers by involving its employees. Out of its experience evolved a four-step customer satisfaction model.[7] GMC found its emergency room was ranked in the third

---

[7]"Action Research Unites Staff And Management in Satisfying Customers," *pr reporter*, May 23, 1994, pp. 1–2.

percentile in terms of satisfying customers—97 percent were doing better than GMC. The process undertaken to correct this involved:

- Phase 1: Staff held brainstorming sessions to draft a model of a satisfied customer from the viewpoint of those who deliver it, and the barriers that prevent them from delivering it.
- Phase 2: The staff then went to customers to learn what they want. This research gave them a model of what satisfies customers designed by customers and a baseline of data on which to measure future progress.
- Phase 3: These results were taken to senior management for prioritizing as to what could get done today, in several months, and not at all. Results were revealed to staff and they began to frame the recommendations. What resulted was a matrix divided by customer, any required action, who is responsible for implementing it, and the current status.
- Phase 4: Ongoing evaluation to make sure operational changes are happening, tracking survey data, and continuing to update the plan.

Results of this process were dramatic. GMC's customer satisfaction ranking climbed. Senior management, convinced of its success, expanded it.

Further proof of the importance of customer service is shown in recent research of a major national company. It found that 64 percent of surveyed customers were perfectly satisfied with the product or service, but changed because of the way they were treated. Seventy percent chose a particular organization, not because of its product/service (which they know they can also get elsewhere) but because of how they were treated.

Organizations that compete for customers know that the goal has shifted to *delighting customers*—the ultimate competitive edge. Even if competitors satisfy customers, your organization can prevail by delighting them. Elements in designing a customer delight program include:

1. **The Promise:** A plainly stated vision of benefits for customers. Take care that these benefits are not undermined by employee actions or by ad copy that promises the moon.
2. **Customer Expectations:** These arise chiefly from (a) your actual promise, (b) competitors' delivery of delight, and (c) customers' perceptions of service quality in general.
3. **Delivery:** The gap between promise and delivery is frequently huge. Management must recognize that frontliners—those who actually serve the customers—are not the bottom rung of the organization, but its most important resource. Keeping those frontliners motivated means using teamwork, continuous training, employee evaluation and reward systems, and a method for measuring customer delight.
4. **Aftermath or Maintenance:** This is where reputations are sealed as shown by the classic study[8] that shows satisfied customers tell 4 or 5 others, while dissatisfied customers whose cases are not resolved tell 10 others.

---

[8]*pr reporter*, November 9, 1981.

References and Additional Readings

Aaker, David. *Managing Brand Equity.* New York: Free Press, 1991.

Broom, Glen, and Kerry Tucker. "Marketing Public Relations: An Essential Double Helix." *Public Relations Journal* 45 (November 1993): 39–40.

Crispell, Diane. "What's in a Brand?" *American Demographics* 15 (May 1993): 26–32.

Cutlip, Scott, Allen Center, and Glen Broom. "Consumer Affairs and the 'Marketing Mix.'" Chapter 14 in *Effective Public Relations.* 8th ed. Upper Saddle River, NJ: Prentice Hall, 1999.

Davidson, Kenneth. "How to Improve Business Relationships." *Journal of Business Strategy* 14 (May/June 1993): 13–15.

Degen, Clara, ed. *Communicators' Guide to Marketing.* New York: Longman, 1990.

Feeman, Laurie. "Direct Contact Key to Building Brands." *Advertising Age* 64 (October 25, 1993): S2.

Felton, John. "Consumer Affairs and Consumerism." Chapter 16 in *Lesly's Handbook of Public Relations and Communications.* 5th ed. Chicago, IL: NTC Business Books, 1998.

Hardesty, Monica. "Information Tactics and the Maintenance of Asymmetry in Physician–Patient Relationships." In D. R. Maines and C. J. Couch, eds., *Communication and Social Structure.* Springfield, IL: Charles C. Thomas, 1988: 39–58.

Harns, Thomas. *The Marketer's Guide to Public Relations.* New York: John Wiley & Sons, Inc., 1993.

International Customer Service Association (ICSA) has a variety of materials related to the total quality service process and encourages professional dialogue in the achievement of customer satisfaction. For more information, contact ICSA, 401 N. Michigan Ave., Chicago, IL 60611-4267; www.icsa.com.

Kotler, Philip. *Principles of Marketing.* 9th ed. Upper Saddle River, NJ.: Prentice Hall, 2000.

Lerbinger, Otto, and Nathaniel Sperber. "Consumer Affairs." Chapter 4 in *Manager's Public Relations Handbook.* Reading, MA: Addison-Wesley, 1982.

Mazur, Laura. "A Consuming Ambition." *Marketing* (January 13, 1994): 23–24.

McManus, John. "Disaster Lessons Learned: Customer's Lifetime Value." *Brandweek* 35 (January 24, 1994): 16.

Murphy, John. *Brand Strategy.* Upper Saddle River, NJ: Prentice Hall, 1990.

Ott, Rick. *Creating Demand.* Richmond, VA: Symmetric Systems, Inc., 1999.

pr reporter Vol. 43, No. 46 (November 20, 2000). "Relationship Marketing: What Precisely Is PR's Role? Creating the Environment, Counseling, Running the Show?"

pr reporter Vol. 37 No. 12 (March 21, 1994). "Elements on Making Your Organization Customer-Friendly."

The Public Relations Body of Knowledge. New York: PRSA. See abstracts dealing with "Marketing, Marketing Support, and Consumer Relations."

Rich, Judith. "Public Relations and Marketing." Chapter 14 in *Lesly's Handbook of Public Relations and Communications.* 5th ed. Chicago, IL: NTC Business Books, 1998.

Sanford, David, and Ralph Nader, et al. *Hot War on the Consumer.* New York: Pitman, 1969.

Wilcox, Dennis, et al. *Public Relations: Strategy and Tactics.* 6th ed. New York: Longman, 2000.

Zandl, Irma, and Richard Leonard. *Targeting the Trend-Setting Consumer.* Homewood, IL: Business One Irwin, 1991.

CASES

CASE 6-1   A CLASSIC: THE CHANGING KINGDOM OF COORS

Times change. Organizations change in structure, in the products or services they provide, in their scope, in the values projected by their leaders, and in the public impression they wish to convey. Sometimes change is evolutionary, as with organizations committed to clothing fashions, automobile design, or nutritional and health values. Sometimes change is sudden or drastic, as in bankruptcy, change of owners, or a catastrophic event.

The public relations function, by whatever name, is an agent for change within an organization. Two-way interpretation of the organization's relationship to the greater public good, and the use of two-way communications to adjust an organization to the publics on which it depends for success or failure, can be expected to change over time in form and emphasis. The necessity for interpretive input and output, and for reconciliation of public and private interests, never goes out of style.

Change and adjustment characterize the dynamics of almost any organization, large or small, local or national, competitive or nonprofit, private or governmental. Making adjustments to changing conditions will constitute part of every practitioner's career regardless of the organizations served. For our classic example of a company's adaptation to change, we turn to the Adolph Coors Brewing Company, a consumer-oriented organization with a philosophical mind of its own. Its basic product is widely known and consumed.

A MAVERICK AMONG BREWERS

For many years Coors operated contrary to some of the most widely accepted textbook ideas about what constitutes success in financing and running a business and in marketing its products. The differences were enough to raise some eyebrows—and some envy—within the beer industry, and in business circles generally, not to mention the consternation caused among politicians whose approach to public issues was generally moderate and safe. Coors, as a company and a family, was outspoken. The prognosis by qualified analysts was not optimistic. Yet few products in America can claim the mystique of Coors beer. Demand was so great that until the "Beer Wars" of the late 1970s—when marketing came into the staid industry in a big way—Coors actually had to ration its beer to wholesalers. Travelers to states where it was sold brought it home in their luggage as treasured contraband. A popular 1977 movie, *Smokey and the Bandit,* was about a trucker illegally bootlegging a whole trailer of Coors into a state where the company did not distribute its products.

IMAGE VERSUS REPUTATION

An *image* is false, not real. Consider a snapshot, which is an image of the person photographed and not the person. *Reputations* are based on experience with a product, service, or company—or the expression of trusted comrades. Which would you rather have—a good image, or a good reputation?

THE COORS STORY FROM THE BEGINNING

The original Adolph Coors—a quiet, private man—was born in Rhenish Prussia in 1847. He was taken to Westphalia and at the age of 15 was apprenticed as a bookkeeper. Five years later, he left and worked for breweries in Berlin and Kassel. Orphaned, he set out for the United States in 1868. He worked off his passage in Baltimore, went to Chicago and worked first on the Illinois-Michigan Canal. Later he became a brewery foreman in nearby Naperville, Illinois. In 1872, at age 25, he was attracted to Denver, where he entered business bottling wines and beer. Before the year was out, he sold that business. He and Jacob Schueler purchased a brewery site in Golden, Colorado, in the Rocky Mountain foothills a few miles west of Denver. The brewery was opened in 1873, three years before Colorado joined the Union.

Times were lean from 1917 to 1933 partly because of prohibition and the Depression but the company survived by producing malt and other items. When prohibition was repealed, Coors was ready.

Adolph Coors, Sr., died in 1929, but family management continued. By 1958, Adolph Coors III had become chairman of Adolph Coors Brewing Company and its subsidiary, Coors Porcelain. In 1960, however, Adolph III died at the hands of a kidnapper. His brother William, second son of Adolph Jr., and president of Coors, took command. His brother Joseph headed the Coors Porcelain Company. By this time, Coors had become the fourth largest U.S. brewer.

SUCCESS IS WHAT YOU MAKE IT

Some characteristics set Coors apart from other family businesses:

1. Coors had been a regional company, limiting its sales to 11 states. The brewers ahead of it were national in their distribution. Thus, for Coors to attain fourth rank nationally, its acceptance in those 11 states had to be phenomenal, running as high as 40 percent of the market.
2. A barrel of beer weighs more than 260 pounds. Nearly 11 million barrels, traveling an average distance of 900 miles each, add up to a lot of transportation expense. Still, Coors had one brewery, the world's largest, in Golden, rather than several closer to major market areas.
3. In attaining its size, the company had refused to borrow money. Growth had been financed out of earnings.
4. Coors production was remarkably integrated vertically; the firm built most of its own packaging, brewing, and malting equipment and produced its own beer cans. It also operated a

major transportation company to move its beer to market and a small railroad to move items around its extensive plant site.

5. Coors's management style was informal, to the point that employees called the president by his first name. Bill Coors resembled a professional football coach in the off-season, working with cuffed shirtsleeves in a spartan office that contained an extra desk for his brother Joe.

6. Employee tenure was long, with attitudes generally characterized by pride and loyalty, in a family spirit. Supervisory employees didn't "go to work at Coors," they were "with" Coors. Executives were "Coors executives," almost as if indentured. Salaries were good, "for the locality." There were not some of the usual fringes such as bonuses associated with profitability. Promotion from within was the policy. All eleven members of the company's board were full-time employees. The use of outside experts tended to be avoided.

7. The company hewed to its own value standards and spoke its mind in public issues. Coors family values—austerity, dedication to hard work, honesty, pride in the best-quality product possible, and a rugged individualism that valued highly personal and corporate prerogatives—had been handed down from generation to generation. Sometimes, however, these values led to misunderstandings and accusations.[1]

8. When it came to the use of communications for marketing, Coors admitted that its Coors Banquet Beer was "the most expensively brewed beer in the world" and felt that this fact kept the demand greater than the supply without shouting about it. Its advertising had been "less than $1 a barrel," or a fraction of what major competitors spent. Here again, the do-it-yourself philosophy prevailed. An in-house staff prepared what ads and promotional pieces were used.

COORS PRESS AND PUBLIC RELATIONS

Coors's public relations was inhibited by a tight-lipped, reactive attitude where financial or competitive information was involved. Because the company was family-owned and sought no outside funding, there was no need for management to reveal these matters and no self-interest benefit. The few investors to whom an accounting had to be made could, theoretically, gather for dinner at Bill's or Joe's house.

The policies of promoting from within and avoiding the use of outside experts tended to eliminate publicity or public relations projects that might have the objective of attracting executive recruits. The employment of thousands in Golden, coupled with the Coors family's civic and charitable contributions in the Golden-Denver area, left little for public relations professionals to deal with in community relations.

In public affairs and on public issues, the brothers were both "the corporation"

[1]On one occasion, the FTC had charged Coors with some heavy-handed sales techniques when they refused to sell draft beer to bars unless they carried it exclusively and in insisting that wholesalers not cut prices. Referring to this episode, *Fortune* magazine said, "Bill Coors is astonished that anyone would challenge his control over his product, and he vows to fight all the way to the Supreme Court." Later, the FTC ruled that the company had "illegally restrained competition." At that time, Bill Coors put his position to a *Wall Street Journal* reporter this way: "If we have to, we'll take over distribution ourselves, and Coors will become the biggest beer distributor in the world."

and the "corporate view." They need not wait for a consensus, nor need they use indirect channels in addressing the community, the trade, or local or federal officials.

In product marketing, with one product, the publicity thrust was to enhance the mystique of success. Elements of production were mountain spring water, Moravian barley, Californian and Southern rice, modern brewing equipment, shipment under refrigeration, and the resulting light pilsner brew.

By putting all this together, or perhaps by a process of elimination, the public relations function could properly have been called the "public service information function," performed if, as, and when requested.

A SHIFT OF TACTICS IN THE MAKING

By the mid-1970s, there was good reason to conclude that Coors had better make some changes in attitudes and tactics or go down the competitive tube. Events had hit Coors like a series of jabs to the face and body. Among them:

1. A union boycott starting with a strike had harmful echoes due to contentions that Coors discriminated against African-Americans, Hispanics, and females in employment.
2. Anheuser-Busch, by aggressive marketing, had cut deeply into Coors's domination of some major markets such as California. Other brewers responded to Budweiser's and Miller's bold marketing—and the "Beer Wars" were on. Initially, Coors declined to join in, which resulted in loss of market share.
3. Light, lower-calorie beer had caught on, and Coors had no entry in the field.
4. Coors had come up with a punch-top can opener that gave customers more

problems than the familiar flip-top openers of competitors.
5. The trend was to fewer brewers, mainly national in scope, as local beers fell by the wayside.
6. Anticipating the inheritance tax requirements, the company had to go public, raising the possibility of outside shareholder voices in its decision-making process. All voting stock, however, remained with the family.
7. Some of management's right-wing views, expressed mainly by President Joe Coors (a member of Ronald Reagan's "kitchen cabinet"), and widely reported in the news, were of no help in broadening public support in the consumer market.

SYMPTOMS OF A TURNABOUT BECOME VEHICLES

Led by public relations and marketing departments, several significant actions were taken to reverse the business downslide and bid for broad public support. A lengthy *Wall Street Journal* article put it this way:

> The company has embarked on an elaborate image-building campaign, running nostalgic ads about corporate history and messages beamed at ethnic minorities, homosexuals, union members, women's rights activists and others who may be harboring ill will against Coors.
>
> The campaign also includes a telecommunications course for Coors executives—traditionally distrustful of the media—who are subjected to intense baiting by communicators simulating "obnoxious reporters." The notion is to condition the managers to project charm, humility and control for real interviews.[2]

---

[2]John Huey, "Men at Coors Beer Find the Old Ways Don't Work Anymore," *The Wall Street Journal*, January 19, 1979.

Another tactic was the disarming public admission of past arrogance, articulated by the new generation of Coors management, Jeff, then president of operations, and Peter, then president of marketing and administration.

On the product front, Coors introduced a low-calorie light beer. An outside advertising agency was retained, and a budget of some $87 million was allocated for advertising and promotion. It has since grown to over $200 million.

This new approach encouraged the company to become more involved on the public relations front. Candor and visibility replaced "no comment" and low profile. Coors was out in the open competitively, and on the record publicly.[3]

A Corporate Public Affairs Division took shape. Its charter, publicly stated, was to

> appraise employee, public and government attitudes, problems and opportunities . . . initiate and improve programs developing an economic, social and political climate which will assist [in operating] profitably, thereby enabling employees and community neighbors to work, enjoy life, and prosper.

Implementation of the charter in the form of charitable contributions and donations, as one example, was explained in a booklet (See Figure 6-1).

Coors's ultimate objective was linked to public relations—*to building, or rebuilding, relationships that would let its products speak for themselves in the marketplace.* For public relations staff, the goal was "removing the political litmus test" that seemed to surround all the company's actions. The focus was on the boycott.[4] As with any program seeking to attain a turnaround of 180 degrees, there were bound to be some communications hitches along the way.

THE BOYCOTTS

The first boycott started in 1960 when the Coors family donated a helicopter to the Denver Police Department, which was under criticism (as were many white majority city police departments) for allegedly trying to keep minorities in the ghettos. For a variety of reasons, Coors employees voted to decertify their union. In 1977 the AFL-CIO called for a boycott of Coors products supposedly because of the company's practice of using lie detector tests in employee investigations and hiring. Several contractual issues were mentioned as well— because the unions wanted to regain their position at the company. This boycott ended in 1987 when labor agreed to stop it if Coors would hold a union certification election. (Workers voted not to have a union.)

In 1984, Chairman Bill Coors seemed to put a blemish on some of the views that they had worked so hard to change. Speaking off the cuff in a speech at a seminar of the minority Business Development Center in Denver, Coors said that Africa's economic problems stemmed from a lack of intellectual capacity. This comment caused a furor in some quarters and reenergized the boycott. Coors sued the *Rocky Mountain News* because the headline that made the charges was not supported by facts in the story itself. (An out-of-court settlement resulted.)

---

[3]By 1984, outside counseling services used had included Manning, Selvage and Lee; Carly Byoir and Associates; The Johnston Group; and Jackson Jackson & Wagner.

[4]Of special interest, in 1983 Coors welcomed the CBS *60 Minutes* program to look into allegations of bias toward unions and minorities long plaguing the company. Host Mike Wallace found the charges against the company basically untrue. Public relations director Shirley Richards and her staff had shown how to defang the tiger by openness and absolute candor.

Making an Impact On Illiteracy—One Person At A Time. If not for the Los Angeles Urban League Milken Family Literacy Center, Ralph Lee might very well be unemployed today. The 39 year-old Los Angeles native initially read at the 3.5 grade level, but thanks to his tutors at the Center, he now reads at the 7th grade level and was able to qualify for a full-time maintenance job at the Los Angeles Free Clinic. Lee looks forward to taking math and English classes at a junior college and is interested in writing poetry, things he never imagined he would be able to do.

Literacy tutor Liz Moseley listens as student Ralph Lee reads during sessions at the Los Angeles Urban League Literacy Center.

The Center's counselor began work with Lee by determining what he wanted to get out of the class. "I just wanted to learn how to read," says Lee, who attends tutoring sessions at least twice weekly. Having grown up in a large family, he recalls a sense of becoming lost in the crowd during his early teens, both at home and at school.

Lee works on a one-to-one basis with his volunteer tutors and has nothing but praise and appreciation for them. Liz Moseley is one of his tutors and has worked with Ralph Lee for about a year. Upon moving from San Francisco to Los Angeles in 1980, she found herself without family or community ties. "Helping others is something so basic to me. It is so easy to give," says Moseley, who began by working with children. Moseley says it is gratifying to see her students develop more self-confidence in the supportive environment offered by the Center.

Moseley is described by Literacy Coordinator LaVone Barnett as one of a number of consistent, core volunteers who gives her time and has been instrumental in planning and implementing special programs and activities for the classroom. She has volunteered over a hundred hours, and donates class supplies and materials to assist her learners.

Moseley is also involved in a mentoring program at a local junior high, and is a member of the Los Angeles Chapter of Young Black Professionals, for whom she produces a newsletter each month.

Both Lee and Moseley were honored for their achievements when Coors hosted them and their guests at the 19th Annual Whitney M. Young, Jr. Award Dinner. The two were joined by Dale Blow, who entered the program in 1990 as an elementary student learner. Dale is now in junior high school and has improved his reading and math levels by two full grades.

The Literacy Center, through funding from corporate sponsors such as Coors, provides services in reading, math, writing, listening and problem solving to disadvantaged youth and adults. Since opening its doors, the center has helped more than 800 students·improve their reading skills.

FIGURE 6-1   Coors's community giving program has flourished and expanded, addressing many community needs.

(Courtesy of Coors Brewing Company.)

Many distributors and marketers felt the boycott was thwarting their best efforts. Historically, however, product boycotts are rarely effective. Company research found that very few beer consumers were even aware of the boycott. Even those who knew about it were seldom persuaded to avoid the product, except in certain union areas where anti-Coors activities made the brand socially unacceptable. Fewer than 4 percent of retail accounts were refusing to sell the brand.

Furthermore, among those who were brand avoiders, the labor issues were much less often the reason than were the allegations of discriminatory practices against minorities. The AFL-CIO made these issues the centerpiece of its campaign, and though Coors and its workers strongly denied the accusations, they had some effect in the African-American and Hispanic communities, which are important markets for beer.

Still, sales were rising. Coors moved into new states successfully despite AFL-CIO activity to discredit them there. (By 1989, the company served all fifty states plus several foreign markets.) Public relations counsel concluded: "The boycott is not working in the marketplace, but it is very successful in the headquarters at Golden, Colorado." Stronger efforts were called for.

THE NEW APPROACH PAYS OFF

The sequential phases of disarming critics, going public, and reaching out for the national market had major punctuation marks:[5]

1. Coors signed a National Agreement with a Coalition of Hispanic Organizations, giving assurances of employment, training for management roles, increased number of Hispanic distributorships, increased use of Hispanic vendors and services, and a minimum of $500,000 annually to be spent in public service programs in the Hispanic community.

2. Earlier, Coors had entered into a National Incentive Covenant with the National Black Economic Development Coalition with much the same assurances and objectives. In both cases, company actions were linked to assistance in its marketing efforts from the other party—quid pro quo.

3. The company undertook diversification into gas and oil exploration, snack foods, transportation, and occupational health.

4. New products included Coors Extra Gold, George Killian's Irish Red Ale, and Herman Joseph's Original Draft.

5. Plans were announced for the creation of a second brewery, located in the Shenandoah Valley of Virginia (See Figure 6-2) which began operations in 1987. The company added another brewery in 1990, which is located in Memphis, Tennessee.

6. An annual report displayed a statement of corporate philosophy. It was titled "Our Values" and summarized as "Quality in all we do and are." This became the theme of communication efforts.

7. Coors's V.I.C.E. Squad volunteer program (Volunteers In Community Enrichment) was recognized as a model for linking employees, retirees, and their families with community

---

[5]Typical of the openness in present-day public relations at Coors, we were supplied a generous bundle of information for this case. There were no questions designed to make sure we were a "friendly" medium and no defensive ruse such as "we'll be glad to check your case study for accuracy." We are indebted to Marvin "Swede" Johnson, Vice President of Corporate Communications for the information provided for this case.

FIGURE 6-2   The Shenandoah Valley brewery at Elkton.

(Courtesy of Adolph Coors Brewing Company.)

needs. So well received was the activity that a new adjunct group was established for people who had no connection with the company.

8. Coors' Wellness Program, created in 1981 by Bill Coors, was honored in 1992 with the C. Everett Koop National Health Award for commitment to health and wellness as a priority for employees.

9. The 10-millionth visitor took the company's highly personalized plant tour in May 1988.

10. In 1987, Coors became the first brewer to target women specifically in full-page magazine ads (See Figure 6-3). A major women's program that increased awareness about breast cancer won awards and showed that allegations of bias were unfounded (See Figure 6-4).

There was more. The year 1987 was a busy one in Coors's public affairs. Joe Coors took a turn as a witness in the Iran-Contra Congressional hearings and testified that he had contributed $65,000 to Colonel North's supply operation for the Nicaraguan rebels (or freedom fighters, if you prefer). Finally, the AFL-CIO was persuaded to call off its 10-year boycott in negotiations, led by Peter Coors, based on carefully crafted public relations strategy that has served to deter any follow-up national boycotts to date. Joe Coors, Sr., announced near year end that he was planning to step down from day-to-day operations. He remained within earshot as vice chairman, while his brother Bill remained chairman. But actual management was passed to Peter and Jeff, both sons of Joe. Joe Jr. began moving up into top ranks.

These new faces have been well received, and under their management the company

FIGURE 6-3 Settings for women in Coors ads suggest energy and activity, not necessarily sensuality or submissiveness.

(Courtesy of Adolph Coors Brewing Company.)

I never shower alone.

And neither should you. Because simply by hanging this free card in your shower, you could save your own life.

You see, this shower card will show you how to do monthly breast self-examination. And remind you to do it. This is vitally important. Because even though 1 in 10 women will develop breast cancer, 90% of those cancers are controllable if detected early.

So send for your free Coors/High Priority Shower Card today. Then put it in your shower and use it. And if you're over 35, ask your doctor about getting a mammogram. Because in the fight against cancer, we're not alone.

For your free Coors/High Priority Shower Card, send this coupon to the AMC Cancer Research Center at: Shower Card, Box 1987, Denver, CO 80201.

NAME
ADDRESS
CITY   STATE   ZIP

One card per coupon, offer good while supplies last.

Cher, High Priority Charter Member

FIGURE 6-4   Coors's breast cancer awareness program, High Priority, encouraged women to do monthly breast self-examinations.

(Courtesy of Adolph Coors Brewing Company.)

PERSONALITY, VIEWS, AND PRODUCTS

A recurrent question in organizational public relationships is the extent to which the personality (abrasive or charming), the political affiliation (liberal, moderate, or conservative), or the views on controversial issues (such as birth control, privacy, and the public's right to know) influence consumer purchase decisions. Do they or don't they?

Domino's Pizza experienced a boycott similar to Coors's. The National Organization of Women (NOW) claimed that Domino's CEO Tom Monaghan discriminates against women, by funding programs that attempt to eliminate reproductive choices. This allegation arose when Monaghan donated $50,000 to a Michigan ballot measure outlawing tax-funded abortions. NOW spokeswoman Madeline Hansen emphasized awareness as the focus of the boycott. "We're not telling people not to buy his pizza, but we are telling them where their money goes when they do."[1] In response to this charge, Domino's defense was that Monaghan's donation was a personal contribution.

In every locality, there are prominent, outspoken individuals whose conduct of their businesses, views on public issues, and displays of personality and character constitute mixed, if not confused, public images. It would be helpful to their public relations counsel to know whether, and under what circumstances, their expressions and actions unrelated to business adversely influence customer purchases of their products or services. Research among customers, noncustomers, and critics might provide a clue.[2]

[1] *pr reporter,* Vol. 32, May 29, 1989: pp. 2–3.
[2] Refer to Case 9-5, Dayton Hudson, for further study.

---

has prospered despite a bad economy and a flat beer market. Coors is now the third largest brewer in the United States. Not too bad for a company some predicted a few years earlier would fail when it was targeted for the longest-running boycott in recent history. ■

QUESTIONS FOR DISCUSSION

1. List all the reasons you can think of why a company's reputation, or its executives', influence the sale of its products or services. Then list all the reasons why it does not. Do you conclude that when people reach for a Coors they are thinking of the company's reputation—or merely concerned with quenching their thirst? Or both?

2. Some companies, such as Coors and Ford, have the founding family's name on the door. What discipline does this identity demand from members of the family, especially in terms of public relationships? What problems might

be created for public relations staff? Overall, is this situation an advantage or a disadvantage in operating the enterprise successfully?

3. What types of reactive strategies could have been developed by Domino's in response to NOW's allegations of dis-

crimination? What proactive strategies would help prevent future crises?

4. Can a prominent businessperson, whose fortune came from the business, distinguish "personal" actions from those of the company? Why or why not?

CASE 6-2 TEXAS CATTLEMEN VERSUS OPRAH WINFREY

On April 16, 1996, Oprah Winfrey, host of America's top syndicated talk show, featured a former cattle farmer named Howard Lyman, who was invited as part of the Humane Society's Eating with Conscience Campaign. On the show, Winfrey and Lyman discussed the Bovine Spongiform Encephapathy (BSE) disease—a deadly disease that had been found in British cattle. Just a month before the show, the British government had announced that 10 of its young citizens had died or were dying of a brain disease that may have been a result of their eating beef from a cow sick with mad cow disease, a similar dementia. An article in *The Nation* magazine quoted a scientist who headed the British government's Spongiform Encephalopathy Advisory Committee saying that millions of people *could* be carrying the disease, and that it is fatal and undetectable for years. When it does appear, it emerges as an "Alzheimer's-like killer."

In the Winfrey interview, Lyman compared BSE with AIDS and raised the possibility that a form of mad cow disease *might* exist in the United States. He also explained that the common practice of grinding up dead cows to use as protein additives in cattle feed *may have* contributed to the outbreak of BSE.

Winfrey seemed clearly shocked by what Lyman said. At one point she asked, ". . . you say that this disease could make AIDS look like the common cold?" Lyman replied "Absolutely." Winfrey replied, "It has just stopped me cold from eating another burger."

The audience applauded in approval. But Wall Street did just the opposite: The price of cattle futures dropped and remained at lower levels for two months.

The cattle industry was enraged at Winfrey and Lyman for what they viewed as defamatory and libelous remarks. Texas rancher Paul Engler of Amarillo, Texas, along with a group of other beef ranchers, immediately filed a $12 million lawsuit against Winfrey, her production companies, and Lyman, claiming they violated the Texas disparagement law, otherwise known as the "veggie libel law." Passed in 1995, the law attempts to protect farmers and ranchers against false claims about their products that could unnecessarily alarm the public and hurt industry sales. According to the law, the plaintiff must prove two things: that the statement(s) made were false, and that the person who made them knew they were false.

There has long been an adage advising against making war against "those who buy ink by the barrel" and it should be extended to those who have hours of television time at their disposal every week. While the case against Winfrey and Lyman proceeded through the courts of law, it really heated up in the court of public opinion.

Battle lines were drawn early and included comments from industry groups such as the National Cattleman's Beef Association and the American Feed Industry Association supporting the cattlemen and consumer groups venting via publications ranging from *USA Today* and *The Nation*. Issues such as "free speech" and the First

Amendment to the Constitution were bantered about against those who would prevent "economic havoc caused by sensational and untruthful reporting by the media."

The ranchers, and the city of Amarillo, were not fully prepared for a battle with Oprah Winfrey on either front. When the trial dates were set, Winfrey put her national popularity and fame to work, moving her show to Amarillo to "avoid interruption" of her daily taping. Once there, she continued her daily shows while her crack legal team fought the battle in court.

With each airing, the American public was reminded once again that the show was in Amarillo because its host was being sued by Texas cattlemen who didn't like her opinion that she would not eat hamburger again. Cast in that light, the legal effort was disparaged without even so much as a mention. Public opinion was clearly in the corner of the popular talk show host.

Legally, things were not going much better for the plaintiffs. Lyman's opinions were just that—opinion—even if misguided opinion. Winfrey's declaration was just that—her vow that she would not again eat hamburger meat. Proving those statements to be false would be difficult because they were personal opinions. The legal grounds for the suit, even under a law established to protect agriculture from disparaging comments, seemed weak.

Consumer groups said the laws prevented critics from making any statements that might anger the food and cattle industry. An article in *USA Today* the week before the trial reported "Critics say the laws, enacted as consumers' concern over food safety is at an all-time high, are an effort to squelch debate on public health issues." According to the magazine *The Nation*, "Winfrey had the right to broadcast it and hamburger lovers have the right to know it . . . even if Winfrey's program gave a one-sided perspective on things, cattlemen have obvious remedies: They could have published and disseminated point-by-point critiques of Lyman's statements, they could have challenged him to open public debates and they could have hired the best experts money could buy. After all, the meat industry already spends hundreds of thousands of dollars a year hawking its products; its opinions and promotions and celebrity spokespeople dominate the commercial airways."

The jury found the defendants not guilty. Right after the verdict, the president of the National Cattleman's Beef Association said in a statement "The good news for the American consumer from this trial is that all the scientific experts testified that America has the safest beef in the world."

The Winfrey/Cattleman episode clearly shows the peril of confusing legal and public relations issues. Under libel and slander laws (to which the veggie law is similar) legal redress is limited and difficult to achieve. Proving statements false is one thing; proving state of mind of the speaker is another. Courts tread lightly on such slippery slopes, and appellate courts are even more careful. Initial verdicts rarely make it through the appeals process, meaning remedy in the courts of law is illusive, indeed.

The court of public opinion, however, is another thing. When individuals or industries have a grievance with public utterances, the better avenue of remediation is usually via public opinion. Here the public relations practitioner is the "attorney" and the affected publics are the "jury."

As the apple industry did when attacked by media driven by the Natural Resources Defense Council in the Alar "scare,"[1] the cattle feeders might have used

---

[1] See Case 7-2.

the "facts" to their advantage in a public relations response to the Winfrey/Lyman assertions. The facts are BSE is not the equivalent of AIDS, nor does it "make AIDS look like the common cold." (Editors note: The common cold is still much more common and less fatal than AIDS.)

The cattle-feeding industry might have called in favors from its end-users—McDonald's, Burger King, Wendy's, etc. The popularity of Winfrey's show is unquestioned, but millions of American consumers are satisfied customers of hamburgers every day. This personal experience will prevail over the opinion of even the most famous celebrity.

In the end, the cattlemen did get across a message that American beef is safe—if anyone was listening. In the end, Winfrey's show and its popularity remain intact. The American consumer still buys hamburger meat in copious quantities. The City of Amarillo still stands, even if its mayor at the time had to confess, "I didn't realize the depth and breadth of Winfrey's popularity."

The American public has a relatively short memory. This issue, like most others, can and did pass without lasting damage—the lesson to be learned in handling similar cases in the future. ■

QUESTIONS FOR DISCUSSION

1. Assess the wisdom of legally challenging a national icon such as Oprah Winfrey. What are the pros and cons?

2. Comment on Winfrey's strategy of moving her entire broadcasting operation to Texas for the period of the trial. What was she hoping to accomplish? Did she succeed?

3. What limits are there to First Amendment rights?

4. What other ways could the Texas cattlemen have considered to handle this issue?

5. Do American consumers adopt or change behaviors based on what they see on a television show?

CASE 6-3   A CLASSIC: TYLENOL RIDES IT OUT AND GAINS A LEGACY

The Tylenol tragedy, Johnson & Johnson's responsive reaction, the product's reissue and comeback, and the nation's applause, add up to a classic case study of how a corporate crisis can be dealt with using effective public relations strategy.

This story has been told in a variety of special and public media. It has been interpreted for its merits in the practice of management, marketing, and public relations, and for the blend of what is admirable in all three.[1]

In 1982, some Tylenol capsules, laced with cyanide, were discovered to be the cause of seven persons' deaths in the Chicago area. It was discovered that the packages had been tampered with, and the cyanide added by a person, or persons, unknown. In 2001, the crime remains unsolved. All supplies of the product in stores nationwide were pulled off the shelves by the parent company, Johnson & Johnson, at a cost exceeding $50 million. After due time and investigation, the product was reissued in tamper-resistant containers, and a sealed package of capsules was offered free to consumers who had discarded the suspect supplies in their possession. The company became a champion of tamper-resistant consumer product packaging.

In the echoing events, Tylenol recovered more than the share of market it had held before the tragedy. The company gained credibility, public trust, and esteem. The Food and Drug Administration of the Department of Health and Human Services (HHS) tightened its regulations regarding packaging (See Figure 6-5).

PRACTICAL REALITIES

It is relevant here to set "what-if" questions aside in favor of a realistic situation analysis. Why was it that Johnson & Johnson, specifically, was able to weather this storm—indeed, to turn adversity into gain? Among the factors that appear instrumental:

1. The company benefited from a long history of success and service in a field of "beneficial" and "worthwhile" healthcare products.
2. The company took pride in its public visibility and its reputation for integrity.
3. The company benefited by having had a strong founder who believed that "the corporation should be socially responsible, with responsibilities to society that went far beyond the usual sales and profit motives."[2] High ethical standards were set in place early on to be continued as a tradition or as a legacy.

---

[1]For accounts that address these issues further refer to *pr reporter*, February 13, 1983; *Public Relations Journal,* March 1983; *Public Relations Review*, Fall 1983; "The Tylenol Comeback," Johnson & Johnson, undated booklet; "Tylenol's Rebound," *Los Angeles Times*, September 25, 1983; "Tylenol Deaths Still a Mystery," Associated Press, September 26, 1983; and "Tylenol's Miracle Comeback," *Time*, October 17, 1983.
[2]Lee W. Baker, *The Credibility Factor*, Homewood, IL: Business One Irwin, 1993, p. 54.

FIGURE 6-5 Tylenol case leads to federal regulation on tamper-resistant packaging.

(Courtesy of The Food and Drug Administration.)

4. There was a credo, a "For this we stand" on paper, on which succeeding generations of executives have built and interpreted in terms of changing times and challenges. The credo was brought out during this episode for the world to see (See Figure 6-6).

5. In its relations with employees, neighbors, investors, customers, and government agencies, there was a candor consistent with competitive and financial security. Company spokespeople—including the CEO—showed leadership and authority.

6. There was a recognition of the public interest and its legitimate representation by news media. Information, whether good or bad, was forthcoming as rapidly as it developed (See Figure 6-7).

7. The corporate public relations function was part of management, participating in the decision process and in the implementation when communication was involved.

8. There were mechanisms for feedback from constituent publics, and a high value was placed on public input.

These virtues, some of which derived from the company's history, graced the behavior of Johnson & Johnson in its emergency. This is not to say that their behavior was without agonizing, great risk, or debates within the management task force set up to make decisions (See Figure 6-8).

JOHNSON & JOHNSON WAS NOT ALONE

In the crisis, public attention was focused heavily on Johnson & Johnson, the parent company, which took over for its McNeil Consumer Products subsidiary, which makes and sells Tylenol. However, many other entities were involved, some in a major capacity.

It is instructive to look at the public information actions of one of them, the Food and Drug Administration (FDA).

Over a period of several days the FDA's press office was busy keeping the public informed about this incident. Constant communication about this crisis characterized its behavior. It issued several updates about the initial recall of 93,000 bottles of Tylenol on September 30, 1982. In addition, it reported on the total national recall of the drug that Johnson & Johnson installed five days after the first local recall. Finally, on November 4, the FDA released its new uniform standards for nonprescription drug manufacturers in providing tamper-resistant packages. This constant flow of information from an objective third party helped to quell any consumer panic.

DEALING WITH A SEQUEL

Four years after the first poisoning episode, there was a recurrence. In February 1986, a stenographer in Westchester County, New York, died of cyanide poisoning from Tylenol capsules that had been purchased at an A&P store in Bronxville. Johnson & Johnson, well-prepared for the crisis, halted capsule manufacturing and offered to refund or exchange all capsules on the market for tablets or caplets. A few days after the stenographer's death, five poisoned capsules were found in a Woolworth store. Johnson & Johnson took action to withdraw Tylenol capsules entirely from the market at a cost of $180 million, which covered "inventory handling and disposal, *and communication expenses* to reassure consumers of the safety of noncapsule Tylenol." The action fitted the public image of Johnson & Johnson, and the news media coverage was positive.

By the late 1980s, competition in the pain-easing medicine business returned to normal. Entries such as Advil (American

Our Credo

We believe our first responsibility is to the doctors, nurses and patients,
to mothers and all others who use our products and services.
In meeting their needs everything we do must be of high quality.
We must constantly strive to reduce our costs
in order to maintain reasonable prices.
Customers' orders must be serviced promptly and accurately.
Our suppliers and distributors must have an opportunity
to make a fair profit.

We are responsible to our employees,
the men and women who work with us throughout the world.
Everyone must be considered as an individual.
We must respect their dignity and recognize their merit.
They must have a sense of security in their jobs.
Compensation must be fair and adequate,
and working conditions clean, orderly and safe.
Employees must feel free to make suggestions and complaints.
There must be equal opportunity for employment, development
and advancement for those qualified.
We must provide competent management,
and their actions must be just and ethical.

We are responsible to the communities in which we live and work
and to the world community as well.
We must be good citizens — support good works and charities
and bear our fair share of taxes.
We must encourage civic improvements and better health and education.
We must maintain in good order
the property we are privileged to use,
protecting the environment and natural resources.

Our final responsibility is to our stockholders.
Business must make a sound profit.
We must experiment with new ideas.
Research must be carried on, innovative programs developed
and mistakes paid for.
New equipment must be purchased, new facilities provided
and new products launched.
Reserves must be created to provide for adverse times.
When we operate according to these principles,
the stockholders should realize a fair return.

Johnson & Johnson

FIGURE 6-6 The well-publicized credo.

(Courtesy of Johnson & Johnson.)

FIGURE 6-7 Employees got the word fast in company publications. This is the cover of a booklet that Tylenol published to keep employees informed about the situation.

(Courtesy of Johnson & Johnson public relations.)

FIGURE 6-8   The corporation used news, such as this news conference, as well as ads to communicate with the public.

(Courtesy of Johnson & Johnson.)

Home Products), Ecotrin (Smith Kline), Bufferin (Bristol Myers), Anacin (White-hall), Panadol (Sterling), and some others matched and countermatched each other's claims in consumer media advertising and publicity to get a bigger piece of the very large and profitable market. If the tragic incident befalling Tylenol was a negative for the product, that didn't show in a 1986 poll of consumers about the same time as the second incident. Some 76 percent of those queried said they thought the company had done enough to ensure that its products were not tampered with. Apparently, much of the public had come to realize that iso-

lated acts of violence and terrorism cannot be totally avoided.

THE PUBLIC MATTERED

The importance of corporate responsibility to the public is illustrated vividly by the Tylenol crisis. Although the company did not specifically have a plan before to deal with crises such as this one, its commitment to the credo "the first responsibility is to the customer" helped Johnson & Johnson to bounce back and contain the tragedy without sacrificing credibility. "Johnson & Johnson developed and geared activities to protect and communicate with its customers, to react to their fears, and provide what consumers needed."[3] A study conducted by Johnson & Johnson emphasized the importance of recognizing a responsibility to the public and maintaining positive public relationships. Companies that gave special attention to the public and their needs enhanced their profitability.[4]

James Burke, then chairman stated, "I think the lesson in the Tylenol experience . . . is that we as business men and women have extraordinary leverage with our most important asset—*goodwill*—the goodwill of the public. *If* we make sure our enterprises are managed in terms of *their obligations to society,* that is also the best way to defend this democratic capitalistic system that means so much to all of us."[5]

ALMOST ABOVE IT ALL

Regaining its competitive lead was not the only positive result for Johnson & Johnson. In 1986, the Council on Economic Priorities gave the company its "American Corporate Conscience Award." In that same year, a public relations exclamation point was added by then-public relations vice president Lawrence Foster who authored a book entitled *A Company That Cares,* honoring the company on its hundredth anniversary. Throughout the 1990s, Johnson & Johnson received numerous industry honors including two more awards from the Council on Economic Priorities for its achievements in corporate social responsibility in 1998 and 2000, the "Best corporation reputation" award from The Reputation Institute in both 2000 and 2001, and

was voted one of the World's 100 Best-Managed Companies by *IndustryWeek* magazine in 2000. It is evident that the Tylenol brand name regained its reputation as a safe product because Johnson & Johnson successfully launched numerous Tylenol-based remedies since the late 1980s. The company reported $29.1 billion in sales in 2000.

However, it has not been all smooth sailing for Johnson & Johnson. Since the beginning of 2000, it has had to insert additional warning language on two of its pharmaceutical products (*Propulsid* and *Sporanox). Propulsid* was eventually taken off the market due to serious side effects.

By the end of 2000, Johnson & Johnson faced a severe blow to its reputation. One of its units, LifeScan Inc., pled guilty to federal criminal charges related to its marketing, for several years, of a *knowingly* defective diagnostic test for diabetes patients. It agreed to pay $60 million in fines. This decision also sets the stage for lawsuits already filed on behalf of the thousands of customers who used the device and who will likely seek hundreds of millions of dollars in damages.

Johnson & Johnson's response to this problem is in sharp contrast to its immediate recall of Tylenol in the 1980s and its much heralded crisis management at that time. Ralph S. Larsen, chairman and CEO, issued a statement concerning the LifeScan situation saying that no one at the company "engaged in intentional wrong doing or intentionally sought to mislead customers or the governments [FDA] . . . [but] mistakes and misjudgments were made . . . We fully acknowledge those errors and sincerely apologize for them."[6] Time will tell if

---

[3]Eileen Murray and Saundra Shohen, "Lessons from the Tylenol Tragedy on Surviving a Corporate Crisis," *Medical Marketing and Media*, February 1992.
[4]*pr reporter*, Vol. 27, February 6, 1984, p. 3.
[5]Ibid.
[6]See Ron Winslow, "J & J Unit Pleads Guilty After Marketing Probe," *The Wall Street Journal*, December 18, 2000.

this statement of acceptance of corporate responsibility will help to maintain a feeling of goodwill with the public, current customers, and potential future customers in the twenty-first century. ■

QUESTIONS FOR DISCUSSION

1. Business is said to be a game of hardball most of the time, and competitive success requires that the cards be played close to the chest. The pharmaceutical business is no exception. How, then, can you defend Johnson & Johnson's traditional adherence to a "do-gooder" credo written by its founder or the open and candid way the company went about dealing with the problems posed by a small number of poisoned Tylenol capsules in Chicago?

2. Tylenol is a product of the McNeil Consumer Products wing of Johnson & Johnson. When the deaths occurred, the parent organization moved in and took over both responsibility and spokesmanship. What are the pros and cons to that strategy as far as the CEO and the communications people in McNeil are concerned? What about the news media?

3. Although the functions of marketing and public relations are often confused as one and the same, or as part of each other, what do you see as distinguishing one from the other? Use this case as an example.

4. Which of the following conclusions do you feel can properly be drawn on the basis of your personal familiarity with the Tylenol incident?
   a. The episode (diminishes/enhances) Johnson & Johnson's claim to competitive leadership in its industry.
   b. The episode illustrates that marketing and public relations are (much the same/different) in values and priorities.
   c. The episode shows that having a sterling character can (help/hinder) the bottom line.
   d. Public relations (has/does not have) a significant voice in the decision process during a crisis when big money is at stake.

CASE 6-4 INTEL PAYS HIGH PRICE FOR LOSING FOCUS

Getting customers to try a product is important. But maintaining their loyalty is just as vital—if not more so—to a business' bottom line. It's a relatively well-known fact in the management world that it takes five times as much to attract a new customer as it does to keep an existing one.

Intel Corporation spent years—and millions of dollars—convincing consumers that its microprocessor chips are the brains of personal computers. With its campaign, "Intel Inside," the company managed to make its brand a household name in regard to computers. By 1994, 80 percent of personal computers contained Intel chips. But after spending so much time and money winning over customers, the company, made up mainly of engineers and mathematicians, failed to take the next step—keeping customers happy.

RELEASE OF THE FLAWED PENTIUM CHIP

In the spring of 1993, Intel released its Pentium series of chips—the company's most advanced microprocessor. About a year later, the company began receiving complaints from some high-tech users concerned with erroneous calculations. About the same time, the company discovered that the chip contained a flaw—a bug that affected complicated computations. Believing that the flaw affected mainly high-end theoretical math problems and that there was no impact on the average personal computer user, Intel decided not to alert customers about the problem. Intel continued to sell the flawed chip until October of 1994 (18 months later) when a new chip was designed and distributed.

On October 30, 1994, a mathematics professor at Lynchburg College in Virginia reported the problem in an Internet message. The story spread quickly, at first through the computer industry, then among the general public. Intel's initial reaction was mainly defensive. Company spokespeople claimed the problem was so minor that it would affect a computer's calculations only once every 27,000 days (that's more than 70 years). They also pointed out that most computer chips, by their very nature, have some type of flaw or bug when they are released. Experts acknowledged the truth in that, but admonished Intel for failing to let the public know about the flaw and letting customers make their own decisions on whether or not it was a big deal.

INTEL TAKES A DEFENSIVE STANCE

For weeks, Intel maintained its defensive position. The company had the facts on its side and thought the facts mattered. Intel engineers didn't know that it is how the facts are presented that matters to the public. In that light, it offered a replacement chip *only* if consumers could prove that the flaw affected them.

For several weeks, Intel managers held 8 A.M. daily meetings to work on the crisis. Each member of the group reviewed news stories that covered the Intel issue and discussed reports that contained information from sales representatives in the field and from the customer hotline set up to handle customer questions. The group met again at 5 P.M. each day, sometimes staying until late in the night. After two weeks, calls to the hotline slowed down. Intel executives began to think the worst was over.

IBM DEALS A DEADLY BLOW

In reality, the worst was yet to come. On December 12, IBM announced that its scientists determined that the flaw could affect users once every 24 days instead of every 27,000 days as Intel claimed. As a result, IBM suspended shipments of computers containing Intel chips.

The news stunned Intel. In a *New York Times* article, Intel's then CEO Andrew Grove said that was when he started to realize "an engineer's approach is inappropriate for a consumer problem."

In addition to the IBM announcement, consumer advocacy groups were concerned:

➤ Attorney generals in two states asked Intel to level with customers.

➤ The GartnerGroup, a well-known and respected consulting group, said companies would be wise to put off purchasing computers containing Pentium chips.

➤ On the Internet—where news of the flaw was initially released— more than 10,000 messages were posted.

➤ Engineers and computer writers wrote harshly about Intel's reluctance to replace the flawed chip.

AN ABOUT FACE FOR INTEL

On the Tuesday after the IBM announcement, Intel ran ads in major newspapers containing an apology for the way it han-

dled the flaw. It offered to send a new chip within 60 days to those who requested one, and to help install the chip or pay to have someone do it.

Intel continued to dispute IBM's findings that the flaw would affect users on an almost monthly basis. Grove told *USA Today,* "We hope to convince them, engineer to engineer, that they're wrong." But some analysts thought politics were behind IBM's decision to stop shipments. At that time, top PC makers were concerned with Intel's dominance in the market. Some were busy developing their own chips.

Whatever the case, Intel was faced with a serious public relations crisis. From the beginning, CEO Andrew Grove spoke for the company. An engineer by nature, he told *USA Today* he was shaken by the episode. "I feel personally responsible for the decisions," he said. "These are harsh lessons to learn. We made a lot of mistakes. But we can't replay history."

Wall Street was immediately pleased by Intel's change in its replacement policy for the flawed chip and its public apology. Intel's stock was the second most actively traded stock that day, rising $3 to just over $61 a share. Explained Drew Peck of Cowen & Co in *USA Today:* "Rightly, analysts and investors see this as stopping the crisis."

A HIGH PRICE TO PAY

If only the crisis could have been avoided. When final figures came out in January, Intel may have realized how expensive its mistakes were: The company took a $475 million charge against its fourth quarter earnings to cover expenses incurred from replacing the flawed chip. Analysts had anticipated the charge would be between $50 million and $300 million. Fortunately for the company, net income fell just slightly for the year.

NOT INTEL'S LAST RECALL

In his book *Only the Paranoid Survive,* Andrew Grove wrote that this incident, Intel's first recall, was a defining event for the company. Since then, Intel has been forced to recall other products. It has also felt the pressure of consumers regarding product design. Pentium 4 was introduced in November 2000 *without* the controversial PSN (Processor Serial Number) that was in Pentium 3. Its presence in Pentium 3 caused consumers to boycott Intel because they feared an invasion of consumer privacy, according to the organization Big Brother Inside. Intel's push to be first in this market—to beat out its competition—is continually being tempered by consumers' needs and expectations. ■

QUESTIONS FOR DISCUSSION

1. Would formal research helped Intel's strategy? How?
2. What can go wrong with an "engineer's approach" to a "consumer problem?"
3. What value is there to the "engineer-to-engineer" approach?
4. When facts and perceptions clash, which usually prevails? Why?
5. Should Andrew Grove have acted as spokesman throughout this crisis? Why? Why not?
6. Did the $475 million cost of the recall affect Intel's decision to not recall?
7. Why did IBM challenge Intel, za valued supplier, during the crisis? What impact did that have on the outcome?

CASE 6-5 CUSTOMER SATISFACTION: HOW WAL-MART AND L.L. BEAN TRANSLATED IT FROM BUZZWORD TO BEHAVIOR

Customer satisfaction has become a buzzword. With competition between businesses increasing every day, more organizations are looking to distinguish themselves by professing that they offer unsurpassed customer service. Ultimately, they are focusing on how they can build a long-term relationship with customers that will keep existing customers loyal and attract new customers. The result: Customer satisfaction has a direct impact on an organization's bottom line, both from the view of *increased productivity* (an organization's opportunity to become a least-cost producer when employ-

ees are running the show smoothly) and an *established good reputation,* which is the best marketing tool you can have.

So pronounced has this become that now, to stay ahead, organizations are talking about customer *delight!*

WAL-MART: A COMMITMENT TO CUSTOMERS

In 1962, the first Wal-Mart Discount City was opened in Rogers, Arkansas, by Sam and Bud Walton. Three decades later, their commitment to customers has paid off. The

---

INTERNAL AUDIENCE (EMPLOYEES) ARE KEY TO EXTERNAL RESULTS WITH CUSTOMERS

The best way to achieve customer satisfaction is to make sure that employees—ambassadors of your organization who are closest to your customers—have been properly trained to serve customers and adhere to the philosophy that the customer comes first.

A survey by Citi-Corp of 17 companies known for excellent service showed that service *training costs for front line employees, managers, and executives averaged 1 to 2 percent of sales.* According to Jack Pyle of Face-to-Face Matters,

vertical cross-training (employees learning jobs above and below their own level) and **horizontal cross-training** (employees learning other jobs at their level) greatly contribute to customer satisfaction.

According to Pyle, these training strategies allow job switching and create better understanding of how the organization operates. They also help employees more easily solve customer problems, and they increase employee self-esteem.

THE CUSTOMER SATISFACTION MODEL

Jackson Jackson & Wagner's four-step customer satisfaction model speaks to the need to define customer satisfaction internally, then *conduct customer research* to come to a consensus on a definition *that includes customer feedback.* It is then important to develop an *action plan* addressing the revised definition—and build in a mechanism for ongoing evaluation.

PHASE I: DESIGNING A DRAFT MODEL INTERNALLY

1. **Department training and preparation.** Hold a session with the department staff to outline the purpose of the customer satisfaction program, background, and related theory to create understanding and acceptance of the process.

2. **Prioritize lists of internal and external customers.**

3. **Develop a profile of a satisfied customer.** Identify specific behaviors, actions, and reactions.

   Steps 1–3 set benchmarks for research with customers and departmental goal setting.

4. **Identify obstacles to delivering customer satisfaction.** This step empowers staff by considering areas for change in the process and in attitudes that may be needed to deliver customer satisfaction.

The end product of Phase I is a draft model of what constitutes customer satisfaction from the viewpoint of *those who must deliver it.*

PHASE II: CUSTOMER REVIEW OF THE DRAFT MODEL

Conduct research with a representative group of customers to critique and correct the model developed in Phase I and identify the current status of customer satisfaction. This research can be achieved via *focus groups* or *brief survey research,* via telephone interviews made by staff.

This phase is an opportunity to *identify the status of customer satisfaction* and let customers critique the staff's model, thereby drafting *their* model of a satisfied customer. The end products of Phase II are a model of what satisfies customers designed by those customers themselves and a baseline of data against which to measure progress.

PHASE III: STAFF DESIGNS AN OPERATIONS PROCESS THAT WILL CARRY OUT THE MODEL

Department sessions are held to:

1. **Present the results of the model** as adjusted by customer panels and research.

2. **Design an action plan for "closing the gap"** between the model (ideal) and current status (reality).

3. **Work through steps** in implementing the plan and follow up to assure successful use by all staff.

The end product of Phase III is a *staff-designed* step-by-step action plan linking operational procedures and staff behaviors to delivering customer satisfaction.

PHASE IV: ONGOING EVALUATION OF PERFORMANCE

1. **Replicate research** (entire study, or just pieces) to measure improvements in customer satisfaction levels over time.

2. **Staff reviews the model** to determine achievability and update action plans to reflect new goals.

company now operates over 2,000 Wal-Mart stores, warehouse-style Sam's clubs, and Hypermart USAs (combinations of groceries and general merchandise, which include a variety of fast-food and service shops to create "one-stop shopping" for the customer) (See Figure 6-9).

Much of that success can be attributed to the company's founder, Sam Walton, and his forward-thinking philosophies on the treatment of two key constituencies—employees and customers.

Guiding Principles Focus on Customers

What is the secret of Wal-Mart's success? The three basic principles that have guided the company since its founding are aimed at customers or publics that directly influence customers.

> ➤ **Principle 1:** *Provide Value and Service for Customers.* Wal-Mart's pledge is to always offer quality merchandise at the lowest prices. Because they claim to offer consistently low prices—and have

successfully communicated that perception to consumers—they don't have to spend as many dollars on advertising circulars as competitors. That cost savings is passed on to the customer.

> ➤ **Principle 2:** *Partnership with Associates.* Employees, or "associates," are considered part of the team at Wal-Mart. They enjoy a family environment and a chance to participate in every way, from making suggestions to posing as fashion models for circulars. They have a personal stake in the store's success, because employees benefit financially through Wal-Mart's profit-sharing plan.

> ➤ **Principle 3:** *Commitment to Communities.* Each store has a community-involvement project. The dollars they raise on a local level are matched by the Wal-Mart Foundation. Associates are encouraged to participate in

FIGURE 6-9 One of the many Wal-Marts in the United States, located in Somersworth, New Hampshire.

(Photo courtesy of Jenna Wilson.)

campaigns for the United Way, Children's Miracle Network, and other causes—once again emphasizing a "caring and sharing" attitude. Foundation dollars are also available to qualifying industrial and economic development programs. Wal-Mart knows it is in the company's best interest for stores to operate in communities that have a strong economic base.

Doing Something About the Issues That Affect the Community

The issue of foreign competition taking business away from the United States, resulting in the loss of American jobs, was its manufacturing partners to improve products and packaging. It used recycled paper for stationery and provided an outlet for customers to recycle goods, including an automobile battery-recovery program to ensure proper disposal.

Looking Ahead to Continue to Provide Top Service

Often a pioneer in technology, Wal-Mart is constantly looking for ways to improve products and services. It was the first retail chain to be equipped with scanner cash registers in all facilities. Today, each store is tied into the Bentonville, Arkansas, home office by computer for easy communication and quick replenishment of supplies.

> We want to ALWAYS have the best customer service. We want to ALWAYS have the best prices every day. Our commitment to the customer is ALWAYS—in everything we do. (David Glass, Wal-Mart President and CEO)
>
> The People Greeter program is a unique form of customer service that was implemented in 1983, on the suggestion of an associate. At every store, there is an associate greeting and welcoming customers and offering assistance if any is needed. As a customer once said, "They treat you like they want you to be here."

of concern to Wal-Mart and its customers. Its "Buy American" program was launched in 1985 with the goal of converting from foreign sources to American manufacturers. It was a cooperative effort between retailers and domestic manufacturers to reestablish a competitive position in the price and quality of American-made goods in the marketplace.

Since 1985, Wal-Mart says it has converted or retained almost $2 billion in purchases that could have been placed for production offshore. This figure translates into 40,000 direct American jobs and 30,000 related jobs, according to company calculations. In 1989, Wal-Mart took on another cause important to its constituents—improving the environment. It challenged

A new program, VideOcart network, serves two purposes—promotion and research. One thousand electronic shopping carts displays flashing promotional messages change as consumers go through the store. VideOcart also tracks where the customer is going—providing important information on shopping patterns and consumer buying habits.

L.L. BEAN: NOTHING IS MORE IMPORTANT THAN A SATISFIED CUSTOMER

When Leon Leonwood Bean founded the now-famous L.L. Bean in 1912, he may not have realized that his "golden rule" would lead to a catalog, retail, and manufacturing success story that would result in more than $743 million in annual sales in 1992 (See Figure 6-10).

His golden rule was, "Sell good merchandise at a reasonable profit, treat your customers like human beings, and they'll always come back for more. "With its Freeport, Maine, stores open 24 hours a day, seven days a week, and offering customers a 100 percent satisfaction guarantee on merchandise whether purchased there or by mail order, L.L. Bean is often acknowledged for the management practices that have led it to become a prime example of customer satisfaction. Two important elements of L.L. Bean's success are research and training.

Ongoing Research

As in any service-based organization, listening to constituents is key. L.L. Bean's many mechanisms for keeping in touch with customers include:

➤ **Feedback form,** printed on recycled paper and signed by Leon Gorman, president, requesting suggestions and ideas for improvement (See Figure 6-11).

➤ **Market surveys** that provide a demographic profile of customers. As a result, the company has developed 22 different catalogs that are tightly targeted to fit the customer profiles.

FIGURE 6-10 "L.L." Bean demonstrates to a customer the benefits of his Maine hunting shoe, the product that got it all started for him over 80 years ago.

(Courtesy of L.L. Bean, Inc.)

Please share your comments with us.

To our valued customer,

Your comments on our service and products are always welcome. We'd like to hear from you if you have suggestions or ideas to help us do a better job. If you need more space, please use the back of this form.

TIME AND DATE OF YOUR VISIT

_____

_____

_____

_____

_____

_____

_____

_____

                                    Thank you, Leon A. Gorman
                                         President, L.L.Bean

(Mr. Mrs.
Miss Ms.)
NAME

ADDRESS   APT. #

CITY   STATE   ZIP
(   )
AREA CODE   PHONE

L.L.Bean®
For the outdoors inside each of us

Printed on recycled paper.

FIGURE 6-11 Customer feedback is one of the many ways that L.L. Bean strives for customer satisfaction.

(Courtesy of L.L. Bean, Inc.)

➤ **Toll-free customer service number,** separate from the number to call for ordering merchandise, for instant two-way feedback and service.

➤ **Heavy focus on customer research, surveys, panels, and focus groups.** "We try to get a lot closer to customers and be as responsive as we possibly can," notes Gorman.[1]

➤ **Internal test marketing.** "We try to get out as much as we can at Bean, and do the same things that our customers are doing, use our own products so that we have a better idea of how they're performing. We can identify better with our customers' experiences and needs."[2] Employees and owners are encouraged to give feedback just as customers are.

Training and the Internal Customer Concept

L.L. Bean's search for "total quality" is continual. Thousands of employees attend two or three days of "total quality" training each year. Employees are taught from day one the concept of "internal customers" as an important part of the corporate culture.

According to Gorman, "The internal customer concept means that each of us identifies who we deal with in our responsibility areas, and who are the customers for whatever we do. And it's getting together with your customers one-on-one and just discussing what they really need from you, and what they're not getting that they should be getting, and how to better serve their interests."[3]

This concept highlights the need for *internal customers to work together effectively* before *external customers can be effectively served.* ∎

QUESTIONS FOR DISCUSSION

1. The policies and programs that Wal-Mart and L.L. Bean employ are management decisions. What is the role of public relations in them, if any? Why are these cases included in a public relations book?

2. Apply the customer satisfaction model to a real or hypothetical situation. Why does such "modeling" of how a public, such as customers, might feel, think, or behave have value in public relations practice?

3. Every department store once had greeters, known as floorwalkers. Part of their job was to move around the store and offer assistance to anyone who might need it. Today only Wal-Mart continues the practice. What public relations concepts are embodied in the idea?

---

[1]Eric Moody, "L.L. Bean, Inc., Beyond the Maine Hunting Shoe," *Southern Maine Business Digest,* August 1991, 2D.
[2]Ibid.
[3]Ibid.

PROBLEM 6-A Wine Bar Needs Positioning

"Berry's" is a wine bar in a southwestern U.S. city with a population of 400,000. In fact, it is the only full-fledged wine bar in the city. While many other bars serve wine, none specialize in fine wines of the United States and Europe as Berry's does. The fact that it is the only wine bar in the city is its problem. Although the city has ample well-educated middle-income people, wine has not developed a following as it has in some larger cities. Because no other wine bars are available, wine drinkers have become used to ordering wine at regular bars rather than at "specialty shop" wine bars.

Berry's location is good—downtown near some fine hotels and in an area that is being revitalized, further emphasizing the upscale image. The interior is pleasant and has wine vaults for persons who want to store their wine there and have it available whenever they come into the bar. All of these vaults have been rented.

The wine bar has been open for only six months. It has a good lunch business, but needs a better evening business (especially during the week).

The total budget for creating new business is only $11,000. Mr. Berry comes to you because he knows you have just opened your own communications firm. He says, "I know it's not a lot of money, but it's a lot for my business. I can't afford to just buy ads—what do you suggest?"

Consider what type of research you would use to determine how to manage customer satisfaction—how to attract new customers and how to retain the loyalty of existing ones.

On the basis of your research, prepare a one-year strategic marketing plan that prioritizes your publics and uses a mix of one-way and two-way communication activities with evaluation methods built in. Provide a budget that allocates the $11,000 between research and customer relation activities.

Finally, what issues should Berry's be speaking out on, considering the enormity of alcoholism and driving-while-intoxicated problems, so much in the news today? Think about how to position Berry's as a socially responsible drinking establishment.

PROBLEM 6-B Good Intentions, Bad Results

Earlier this year, when you graduated from college, you were fortunate. You had a job waiting for you at Bart's Cartmart Inc., the largest distributor of motorized vehicles and accessories in Amarillo. The firm's slogan is, "Speed Up with Us!" Bart (Cartwright), the owner, happens to be your father. That saves having to work your way up. Besides, you've already helped out summers, when you weren't using one of the products playing golf, cruising off-road, or mowing the lawn.

This job has great promise. You're an only child, and your Dad has long had in mind that you would be taking over the business some day. In preparation, you majored in marketing, minored in public relations, and took several elective courses including one in business law.

To start you out full-time, your dad put you in charge of customer relations. It has been fun and challenging. This first year, you've devised a follow-up program in which you or an assistant called on each customer a week or so before the warranty period for the product purchased expired. You asked whether anything was needed by the customer that you could supply within warranty. Customers praised and liked that attention. And you've had Bart's Cartmart sponsor the winners' awards in one of the major competitive events at the annual Stock Breeders' Exhibition (motor vehicles as well as plaques and ribbons, of course).

This week, the Annual Harvest Festival is on, and acting on a request from the committee running it, you have loaned six used golf carts for the festival events.

Your father has been most tolerant about your activities. He obviously wants you to enjoy your job and to relish growing with the company. At the same time, Bart is no softie. He came off a farm and up in business the hard way. He knows what he wants and is determined to get it. At times he can be tough, if he feels he has to, and even dictatorial.

When you got to work recently, you were handed a morning newspaper by the receptionist. In it there was a story about a 12-year-old boy, the son of a local farmer and Harvest Festival official, who was driving one of your carts around late yesterday afternoon for fun. Something happened, and the cart tipped over on his leg, mangling it, with possible permanent damage. The kid, in the hospital, told his parents, and they told the newspaper reporter, that he "didn't know what happened." He was "just going along fine," when he felt a bump and he couldn't turn the steering wheel. Next thing he knew, the cart was headed for a big harvest machine. He tried to turn the wheel, but it wouldn't work and he became jammed between the cart and the machine. The newspaper carried a head shot of the boy. He was cute. The story indicated that the cart had been borrowed from Bart's Cartmart.

You sought out your father immediately. He said he'd gotten a call from the newspaper late in the evening, but there was no reason to disturb you. He had called the boy's father and mother, with whom he was acquainted, to express concern and sympathy. They were very upset. When he'd mentioned to them that these heavy carts weren't really made for handling by little kids, the father had made some critical remarks about lending out used carts that might have something wrong with them.

"I don't like it," your father said to you. "People don't react reasonably when their own flesh and blood is involved. I doubt we've heard the last of it." You asked him what you could do. Should you send someone in the shop with a trailer to bring the cart back and have it inspected, send the boy a book to read, arrange to retrieve all the loaned carts, or what? "We shouldn't touch that cart," your father said, "not until I can talk to our lawyer. Just sit tight for a few hours, and we'll know where this thing is going."

Within the hour, a lawyer representing the injured boy and his family called the company to say he had requested that local authorities "inpound" the cart, and indicated he would want to talk with Bart soon. Also within the hour, your father had talked with the company's lawyer, the agent of the firm handling the company's insurance, and with a person at the police department who said they would hold the cart. Your father's lawyer, he said, would be talking with the legal department of Rundo, the manufacturer of the carts.

Before the day was over, you and your father talked again in some detail. "This is the kind of thing you dread in a business like this," he told you. "And with so damn many ambulance-chasing lawyers around, good intentions and fair dealing don't always come out the way you had in mind. With the newspeople looking for things to blow up into headlines, I can see this thing heating up into a court case and a local issue where people who should be minding their own business stick their noses into ours and choose up sides."

You assure your father that the good intentions in loaning the carts will come out in the end and that if you're open with the newspeople they'll be fair in whatever they write or say. He says, "We'll see. If you have any ideas as this thing goes along, come tell me. I'll welcome them. But don't go off half-cocked talking with others in the newspaper, the Festival Committee, or the next door neighbors. Come see me first."

Obviously, you are anxious to help, to apply what you learned in four years, and to retain the conviction that if you treat others fairly, that's what you get in return.

Given the four-step planning process, and the aforementioned events, what might you set as your objective, your strategy, and your main tactics in helping resolve the problem before it boils over into the community and into a courtroom? What might you recommend to your father regarding the do's and don'ts of customer and community relations in the future, and communications about those relations?

PROBLEM 6-C Turning Customer Complaints to Customer Delight

Eagle's Wings Airlines is a young company that flies no-frills flights within the United States. You work for its public relations department. Winter holiday time is approaching and flights are booked but customer complaints are increasing. For now, the cheaper ticket prices are keeping reservations high, but if the level of complaints continues, customers will be lost. In fact, you have just been informed that Eagle's Wings has been named the worst in customer service. The number of customer complaints has been piling up on your desk. Flights continually arrive and depart late due to the inefficiencies of airport crew members and the on-flight crew has received poor ratings because of rudeness.

To add to this pressure, flight attendants and pilots are complaining about being overscheduled. They want time off to enjoy the holidays at home with their families, not in some remote location as they wait for a flight back—a result of poor scheduling, which has been happening more frequently.

The number of customer complaints is growing as are employee complaints. You do not have responsibility for human relations but you can see that it impacts customer relations. The head of human relations is very busy and understaffed but she has agreed to meet with you tomorrow. In the meantime, you need to get a plan formulated because you can't afford to further antagonize customers. In fact, you want to delight customers. How will you do that knowing what you know about this situation? What is your immediate plan of action?

Then put together a one-year strategic plan to build consumer relationships outlining possible problems and solutions. Put into action an evaluation process that will help you to gauge the minds of your consumers as well as your employees. This will make it easier for both sides to communicate what they like, don't like, and would like to see improved. You hope this will bring about improvements and repeat customers, which will help business in the long run.

7 | MEDIA RELATIONS

The biggest misunderstanding in public relations concerns the mass media: what its role and power really are in modern society and how important media relations is in building effective public relationships.

A few practitioners still go to the extreme of *equating* public relations with publicity. So, unfortunately, do some managers. Others find contemporary journalism so unbalanced in its emphases and its audiences so fractionated that, except in unusual circumstances, they prefer to avoid the media. Fortunately, many scholarly studies have given us an objective look from which to devise workable strategies. They find that:

1. **Media influence is cumulative and long-term.** A single news report, even if covered by media across the country, or an item in a single medium, even if it's the evening news, usually causes little if any behavior or attitude change. But when many media cover a subject over the years, perhaps expressing a viewpoint on the topic, whole generations can be influenced. For example, most of us have no personal experience whatsoever with communism, yet we strongly oppose it—because all our lives it has been a subject portrayed in a negative way in our media.

2. **The main power of the media is to make us aware**—of products, services, companies, and ideas—and to provide information about them. By itself, awareness rarely moves us to action or even shapes an opinion. But as a first step in the decision-making process, it is vital. If we don't know something exists, we can't do anything about it. Scholars call this the *agenda-setting role of the media.* (See Figure 7-1.)

3. **The media concentrate on reporting bad news**—the errors, accidents, and scandals of human society. As an early American political figure said, "In a republic based upon public opinion, it is necessary to excite a spirit of inquiry—to furnish public men with information of their errors."[1] Today, this statement is true not only of elected officials but of all executives and all organizations as well. As educator Scott Cutlip said, "There are no private organizations today, even if they are totally owned by one or a few persons, because all must abide by the rule of public consent." But research shows we prefer to hear about bad news,

---

[1]William Plummer, U.S. Senator, several times governor of New Hampshire and historian, in an article titled "To the People," published widely, May 23, 1820.

FIGURE 7-1 Even members of the media, such as the creator of this popular cartoon, recognize the changes that have occurred in news gathering and dissemination.

(Reprinted with permission from Universal Press Syndicate. All rights reserved. Calvin and Hobbes copyright 1994 Watterson.)

rather than good news, by a factor of seven to one. In their own marketing interest, then, it follows that the media would feature bad news. It's what their customers demand.

Clearly the challenge is to create relationships with journalists and media figures—as with *all* publics—that will permit them to rely on our organizations when we are the focus of interest. If reporters and editors have learned that they can trust an organization and its public relations staff, they are likely to (a) report on the information of which we need to make our publics aware and (b) give us a fair chance, or at least balanced reportage, when we're on the hot seat.

Though the generalized relationship between journalists and practitioners may forever be characterized as adversarial, we must remember that the two professions share one basic tenet—the First Amendment—and in pursuit of protecting this license, we are united.

WORKING WITH THE MEDIA

An important part of the practitioner's job often is working with the media. This relationship depends on practitioners providing information that newspeople consider to be of public interest—is it newsworthy?

A close and friendly working relationship is relatively easy between small or local organizations and the community, trade, or professional media. In such situations, and there are many thousands of them, the media have small staffs and need "free" newsgathering help. Public relations practitioners provide it.

> That word *media* still puzzles. It is plural. Newspapers in Cincinnati are the local print *media,* but the *Cincinnati Post* is a *medium.* Yet we often use this plural word as a collective noun and so treat it as if it were singular. How often do we read "media is" rather than "media are"? Further complicating the lexicon of public relations is that *all* communication forms are also called media. Technically, we ought to differentiate between the *news* media or *mass* media (radio, television, newspapers) and *communication* media (newsletters, group meetings, speeches, letters, videos, and so on). This chapter deals with the former.

Personalized, mutually supportive relationships have become extremely difficult, however, between the mass media and the giant enterprises and institutions. Both entities tend more and more to conglomeration and automation, as the former bends to exposé journalism and the latter turns to controlled advocacy—and as animosity grows between the private and public sectors.[2]

---

[2]Ben H. Bagdikian, *The Media Monopoly*, Beacon Press, 1997. When first published in 1983, 50 corporations owned most of American media. According to *Advertising Age* (August 20, 2001), the top 10 leading media companies in 2000 were AOL Time Warner, Viacom, AT&T Broadband (AT&T Corporation), Walt Disney Company, NBC-TV (General Electric Company), Gannett Company, Cox Enterprises, News Corporation, Tribune Company, and Clear Channel Communications. These rankings were based on the net revenue generated from each company's U.S. media properties.

The old image of "press relations" with a publicity-seeking "flack" wining and dining an underpaid newsperson is passè. Most major media have ethics codes that prohibit their journalists from accepting favors. The notion that it is helpful to have a buddy or a relative as a reporter, columnist, editor, publisher, news director, or producer is no longer always true. It can be suspect or even function as a handicap, particularly as media ethics codes become more common.

THE FUNDAMENTALS

Stripped down to basics, the mission of the news media is to inform audiences quickly, accurately, and fully on matters in which audiences express an interest and on matters that affect them significantly, whether or not the audiences have expressed interest, or are even aware.

In simple terms, the mission of the public relations function is to build working relationships with all of an organization's publics. When appropriate, doing so may require making use of news media when viewpoints or activities are newsworthy.

Along with the opportunity and capability possessed by journalists and public relations practitioners to shape public opinion go the obligations of truth and accuracy, under the law. A high degree of ethical responsibility involving moral standards and integrity is implicit in serving the ultimate best interests of the public.

The freedom of the news media to inform the public and to interpret information without bias is assured by the First Amendment to the Constitution. Abuse of that freedom could lead to loss of credibility with the audience, loss of revenue from advertisers, and public censure. Thus, while news prerogatives are jealously guarded, journalistic education and practices emphasize self-discipline. News media, owned privately and operating competitively for profit, are admittedly careful. When they interject their own views, they are expected to label them as "editorial," "opinion," "analysis," "commentary," and so on.

The public relations function comes under the freedom of speech provision in the First Amendment. Practitioners have the choice of telling their story in paid space or time or offering it as news, subject to editing or rejection by the media. The penalties for abuse of free speech rights by a private organization can be loss of supportive constituents such as shareholders, employees, neighbors, customers, members, or donors, as the case might be. Then, too, there is monitoring by the FCC, FTC, and other federal agencies, as well as professional and trade societies. Within the professional practice of public relations, the penalties can be expulsion from membership to professional groups such as the Public Relations Society of America (See Chapter 10) or exposure by the news media. The penalties to the individual practitioner for being "clever" in manipulating facts, being "devious" in dealings with journalists, being "unavailable" when sought by the media, or being "unauthorized as the spokesperson" for an employer can be reaped in loss of credibility and integrity in the eyes of the media and consequently loss of some functional value to the employer. The sword has an edge on both sides of the blade.

A DIFFICULT, DELICATE TASK

The practitioner serves two masters. One is the employer. The other is the public interest. Often, the news media stand between the two. The practitioner travels a precarious and rather thin line. The employer wants his or her best foot put forward in public. There are bound to be times when public exposure can be damaging to a campaign, a product, or a reputation. At these times, employers would prefer no publicity. Then there are times when the truthful and accurate response to a press inquiry is simply not known (the facts have not been ascertained). There are times when an organization's policies, or legal or competitive considerations, give precedence to its "privacy" over the "public's right to know." At such times, the forbearance of the media is desired—but rarely forthcoming.

If a practitioner is not able to handle the flow of information so that favorable news is covered and adverse news is at least treated fairly, the practical value of the practitioner to the employer is somewhat limited. However, practitioners must make it clear to employers and clients that they cannot control the media.

GUIDELINES THAT HAVE SURVIVED

Although, as we said earlier, it is risky to draw generalizations about media relations, a number of guidelines are widely followed.

1. Start with a sound working knowledge of the methods and the technology involved in gathering potential news, evaluating it, processing it editorially, and putting it into the best format and mode for newsprint, magazine, and broadcast electronic media. Be able to fit into the process.
2. Be sure that the employer has a designated spokesperson available on short notice. It may be you.
3. Have spokespeople be as candid as possible in response to inquiries—within the limits of obvious competitive and national security and of compassionate consideration for those hurt by the news.
4. Play the percentages, as in a long successful partnership, taking the instances of bad news in stride with a record of good news coverage achieved.
5. Continuously educate and train employers and spokespeople on how to handle themselves when in contact with news media.
6. Generate good news situations as a track record to offset instances of undesired news. Do not simply wait defensively for bad news.
7. Advocate an employer's views on public issues among the organization's natural constituencies and in the news media receptive to them.
8. Expect the unexpected and be prepared for it. In particular, have a crisis or disaster plan for every foreseeable circumstance.

CONSIDER CREATING A "SURGICAL" MEDIA STRATEGY

Because there is no evidence that visibility in the media motivates behavior or influences attitudes and because more managements are expecting behavior change or motivation rather than merely wanting to dump information on unwilling publics, a new media strategy is needed.

A "surgical" strategy means just what the term implies: placements in exactly the right media for your purpose. It requires knowing which media your target publics actually read, watch, or hear. Assumptions are dangerous, so intelligence work is needed. In issue cases or legislative support, it may mean targeting a single key person and placing a story in the medium she reads (or has clipped for her). A single such placement is worth a folder of untargeted clips.

Example: You're working on a regulatory matter and Sen. Jones from Louisiana is key. Don't expect her to see, be shown, or believe what the *Washington Post* or *New York Times* write. Place something in the *New Orleans Times-Picayune,* however, and you can rest assured the staff will clip it for her—because it was also seen by her constituents. Give the story a local angle, or a local person, and that's good surgical media use.

STRATEGY FOR THE NEW CENTURY

In today's environment, people want to be served, not sold; involved, not told. Where does the media fit in when reaching out to and involving these stakeholders? Here's a five-point strategy:

1. **Build relationships face-to-face.** Earning trust through relationships motivates behavior. Ironically, when a relationship is formed, people will accept and pay some heed to your communications.
2. **Make internal publics top priority**—inreach before outreach. Only satisfied employees can deliver customer delight.
3. **Consider an "under-the-radar" approach to bypass media.** As journalists become entertainment-oriented voyeurs and media credibility and reach continue to decline, rarely can media help, even if disposed to do so. They can hurt, because in skeptical times it is easy to sow doubt, and bad news travels the grapevine fast. Instead, go direct to key publics, and don't make yourself overly visible since that may attract media snooping.
4. **Use accountable, focused, measurable programs.** Once called "soft," these pr programs incorporate value-adding efforts. Strategic philanthropy, value-added and cause-related marketing, and loyalty programs are prominent examples. The former "we're just nice people" approach never jibed with other organizational behaviors and was not trusted.
5. **Expand research**—far beyond statistical surveys. Research has gone beyond lip-service to be the backbone of programming and strategy setting. Top research techniques are participative: focus groups, panels, delphi studies, and gap research.

Public relations practitioners know now that one-way information transfer is insufficient. We must pursue the ideal of two-way dialogue. Involving stakeholders and offering them service information or events is the key.

References and Additional Readings

Cutlip, Scott, Allen Center, and Glen Broom. "Media Relations." Chapter 9 in *Effective Public Relations*, 8th ed. Upper Saddle River, NJ: Prentice Hall, 1999.

Dilenschneider, Robert. "Use Ingenuity in Media Relations." *Public Relations Quarterly* 37 (Summer 1992): 13–15.

Evans, Fred. *Managing the Media: Proactive Strategy for Better Business* and *Press Relations.* Westport, CT: Greenwood, 1987.

Foundation for American Communications (FACS) is an organization that seeks to improve mutual understanding between major American institutions and the news media. For more information write: Foundation for American Communications, 85 S. Grand Ave., Pasadena, CA 91105; 626/584-0010; facs@facsnet.org; www.facsnet.org.

Freedom Forum offers a variety of programs and publications exploring the field of mass communication and technological change. It funds two independent affiliates, the Newseum (Arlington, VA) and the First Amendment Center (Vanderbilt University, Nashville, TN). For more information write: The Freedom Forum World Center, 1101 Wilson Blvd., Arlington, VA 22209; 703/258-0800; news@freedomforum.org; www.freedomforum.org.

Glynn, Carroll, and Robert Ostman. "Public Opinion About Public Opinion." *Journalism Quarterly* 65 (Summer 1988): 299–306.

Greenburg, Keith Elliot. "Radio News Releases Make the Hit Parade." *Public Relations Journal* 48 (July 1992): 6.

Grunig, James, and Todd Hunt. *Managing Public Relations.* New York: Holt, Rinehart and Winston, 1984. See chapters 11, 19, 20, 21, and 22.

Lerbinger, Otto, and Nathaniel Sperber. "Media Relations." Chapter 3 in *Manager's Public Relations Handbook.* Reading, MA: Addison-Wesley, 1982.

Lesly, Philip. "Publicity in TV and Radio." Chapter 25 in *Lesly's Handbook of Public Relations and Communications.* 5th ed. Chicago, IL: NTC Business Books, 1998.

Lukaszweski, Jim. *Influencing Public Attitudes.* Leesburg, VA: Issue Action Publications, 1993.

Marquis, Simon. "Media Speak: Mutual Respect Fosters Healthy Media Relations." *Marketing* (December 9, 1993): 21.

Mundy, Alicia. "Is the Press Any Match for Powerhouse PR?" *Business and Society Review.* (Fall 1993): 34–40.

Newsom, Doug, Dean Kruckeberg, and Judy Vanslyke Turk. "Communication Channels and Media." Chapter 11 in *This Is PR: The Realities of Public Relations.* 7th ed. Belmont, CA: Wadsworth, 1999.

Powell, Jody. *The Other Side of the Story.* New York: William Morrow, 1984. Media seen by a presidential press secretary.

pr reporter, Vol. 41 No. 18 (May 4, 1998). "Items to Consider in Creating A 'Surgical' Media Strategy."

pr reporter Vol. 39 No. 28 (July 15, 1996). "Strategy Now: People Want To Be *Served,* Not Sold; *Involved,* Not Told."

Public Relations Body of Knowledge. New York: PRSA. See abstracts dealing with "Media Relations, Including Crisis Management."

purview, pr reporter supplement (April 4, 1994). The "new aggressiveness" in media relations; public relations learns new tricks.

Rafe, Stephen. *Mastering the News Media Interview.* New York: HarperCollins, 1991.

Raley, Nancy, and Laura Carter, eds. The *New Guide to Effective Media Relations.* Washington, DC, Council for Advancement and Support of Education, 1988.

Reardon, Kathleen, and Everett Rogers. "Interpersonal Versus Mass Media Communication: A False Dichotomy," *Human Communication Research* 15 (2) (Winter 1988): 284–303.

Reilly, Robert. "Publicity." Chapter 6 in *Public Relations in Action.* 2nd ed. Upper Saddle River, NJ: Prentice Hall, 1988.

Shoemaker, Pamela, ed. *Communication Campaign About Drugs: Government, Media, and the Public.* Hillsdale, NJ: Lawrence Erlbaum Associates, 1989.

"Technology Transforms Media Relations Work." *Public Relations Journal* 49 (November 1993): 38–40.

Trahan, Joseph III. "Media Relations in the Eye of the Storm." *Public Relations Quarterly* 38 (Summer 1993): 31–32.

Trahan, Joseph III. "Building Media Relations During a Crisis." *tips & tactic*, a *pr reporter* supplement, December 14, 1992. Lessons learned from Hurricane Andrew.

Tucker, Kerry, Doris Derelian, and Donna Rouner. *Public Relations Writing: A Behavioral Approach.* Upper Saddle River, NJ: Prentice Hall, 1996.

Tucker, Kerry, et al. "Managing Issues Acts as Bridge to Strategic Planning." *Public Relations Journal* 38 (Fall 1993): 41–42.

Van Leuven, James, and Michael Slater. "How Publics, Public Relations, and the Media Shape the Public Opinion Process." *Public Relations Research Annual*, Vol. 3. Larissa Grunig and James Grunig, eds. Hillsdale, NJ: Lawrence Erlbaum Associates, 1991: 165–178.

Walsh, Frank. *Public Relations Writer in a Computer Age.* Upper Saddle River, NJ: Prentice Hall, 1986.

Wilcox, Dennis, and Patrick Jackson. *Public Relations Writing and Media Techniques.* White Plains, NY: Longman, 2000.

CASES

CASE 7-1   NASSP: NEWS MEDIA AS A FEEDBACK SOURCE

Thoughts about education reform abide in the minds of teachers, principals, and politicians because of the many challenges that exist in our school systems. But one essential question persists: What lies behind these education challenges? In an effort to find out and at the same time build relationships with its publics and the media, the National Association of Secondary School Principals (NASSP) investigated.

THE PROBLEMS OUR EDUCATION SYSTEM FACES

Many American students lack the resources and the motivation to score higher than their European and Asian peers on assessment tests. Yet Americans have not found a solution. These lower scores could affect the future of American business. American businesses might fall behind countries that are more competitive because their work forces are better trained.

Schools are also filled with social and cultural problems. Many students are unmotivated, wrapped up in drug and alcohol problems, trapped by poverty, angry, and uninterested in coping with everyday life at school. Many skip school or cheat on tests and assignments. Controversy over whose responsibility it is to teach sex education takes priority in many schools across the nation. Many other problems exist. The question is: Who will solve them, and how?

Teachers have been underpaid for years and many feel that, with minimum pay, they should not have to do more than teach. In an effort to answer these questions, educational organizations, state and federal governments, teachers, and parents are looking for solutions—and many are finding some.

NASSP TAKES ACTION

NASSP is an organization of 40,000 high school and middle school principals, assistant principals, and aspiring principals from the United States and more than 60 other countries. Its focus is on professional development, as well as promoting the interests of education in Congress and conducting research on issues critical to middle and high schools. Its vision statement reads:

In a profoundly changing global society, schools must be responsive to the needs and aspirations of an increasingly diverse student population. Principals, as the educational leaders, are essential to ensure the successful flow of change. They must be the primary agents of change for effective learning and teaching.

NASSP, as the pre-eminent organization for middle level and high school administrators, will assert itself locally, nationally, and internationally in addressing school quality and the professional leadership needs of school administrators. In setting the educational agenda for the twenty-first century, NASSP will assist principals and other school leaders in improving the conditions under which schools are organized for effective teaching and learning.

NASSP's research found that one of the major problems embedded in our education system is communication between parents and secondary school principals. One survey, conducted by Roy R. Nasstrom, found that principals are not perceived as instructional leaders and that many dislike contact with parents. The survey found further that these principals need to understand the value of discussing school issues with parents and other community members, because parental contact is the "major source of dissatisfaction" among secondary school principals.

With these problems in mind, NASSP decided to set up a telephone hotline at its 1989 annual meeting in New Orleans to give principals an opportunity to talk to parents from around the nation. In setting up this hotline, NASSP decided to achieve four goals:

1. To disseminate information about schools.
2. To position principals and assistant principals as knowledgeable instructional leaders.
3. To strengthen principals' knowledge about problems in the school system and make them aware of the concerns that members of the school community have about these problems.
4. To strengthen NASSP's positive relationship with the newspaper *USA Today,* an important national medium for NASSP's long-term public relations program.

NASSP STUDIES ITS PUBLICS, PLANS ACTIVITIES

In order for the hotline to succeed, NASSP needed a plan. To begin the process, it first determined its publics. These included:

1. **Potential volunteers** to answer the phone (made up of the best-quality principals, personally invited, and who were attending the convention)
2. **Interested members of the public** who needed information and would ask questions
3. *USA Today* **staff** with whom NASSP needed to maintain a reputation of credibility

NASSP's first test was to find enough volunteers—108 principals and assistant principals—to answer the phone for the four-day period at the annual meeting. This goal became a priority because without volunteers other goals could not be achieved.

To ensure that the overall goals would be met, NASSP determined its immediate objectives:

1. Provide volunteer principals with a news release format to promote the event with news media in their communities.
2. Have at least 90 percent of the principals indicate after the project that they enjoyed the experience.
3. Have at least one of the state affiliates consider replicating the hotline as a state project.
4. Receive at least 1,000 phone calls during the four-day period.
5. Receive news coverage on the project for the four-day period that would encourage people to call.
6. Receive coverage in at least one-third of the 91 Gannett newspapers (parent company of *USA Today* and the

largest newspaper chain in terms of circulation).

7. Have members of the *USA Today* staff in some observable fashion indicate their pleasure with this hotline after its completion.

8. Have *USA Today* seriously consider conducting a second education hotline at the 1990 NASSP convention.

NASSP believed working closely with *USA Today* would be key to making the hotline a success. One advantage NASSP had in the beginning was that *USA Today* was making education a priority in selecting stories. However, a problem could have arisen had *USA Today* decided to do the hotline with another educational organization that also was having an annual meeting at the same time as NASSP. From a media relations angle, therefore, suggesting the idea to them was a risk.

HOMEWORK IS ASSIGNED

To accomplish its goals, NASSP undertook the following activities:

1. Wrote a pitch letter for use when soliciting principals to participate and to assure that all potential volunteers received the same information.

2. Contacted each volunteer individually to ascertain his or her commitment to the project.

3. Developed a schedule of volunteers who agreed to participate.

4. Sent letters to all volunteers, with background materials to help them handle questions about subjects that were anticipated as high interest. It also expressed the organization's appreciation and reminded them of their day and times to answer the hotline.

5. Attached reminders to every volunteer's convention registration badge

to ensure that the volunteers wouldn't forget their time commitment.

6. Prepared and published articles in the daily convention newspaper, including a list of principals and assistant principals who volunteered to answer phones. This measure served as a reminder and as recognition of the volunteers.

7. Distributed a national news release to approximately 780 news outlets throughout the country. In addition, it published an article in the NASSP *NewsLeader*, a monthly newsletter for members.

8. Sent thank-you letters and a post-survey form to all volunteers to evaluate the success of the hotline and to learn what concerns callers voiced to the volunteers.

9. Sent letters to volunteers' superintendents recognizing the principals for their efforts.

10. Sent post-project news releases to all NASSP state-affiliate newsletters.

NASSP AND *USA TODAY* RECEIVE AN "A" FOR A SUCCESSFUL PROGRAM

More that 1,500 people (500 more than projected) called from throughout the United States. Principals gained valuable insights to problems that secondary schools are facing and also provided some helpful answers to concerned parents, grandparents, and students.

Volunteers learned about the problems within the education system from an external perspective. They had an opportunity to offer suggestions for improvement, as well as answer the questions of those people who called the hotline. The volunteers discovered new approaches for handling educational problems, gained insights on concerns of community members, and returned to their state and local schools with ideas for making programs more sensitive to public concerns.

Budgeted at less than $500, plus staff time, the program achieved most of its goals and objectives. The total number of volunteers exceeded 108 principals, which was the original goal. News coverage reached, at best, 22,898,169 *potential* newspaper readers. Two *USA Today* staff members most closely involved wrote letters commending the project and indicating an interest in doing the hotline in subsequent years. *USA Today* not only replicated the hotline for two more years, but it also added two telephones and a fifth day to the event for the second and third years (See Figure 7-2).

In the words of Lew Armistead, former director of public relations for NASSP, as he told the authors:

"There are very few instances where people can be moved to action through use of newspapers. At best, newspaper coverage makes people aware of a concern. This program goes beyond that. It involves newspapers in a real public relations effort. This program provides a way for people to get answers to their questions so they can take action in their local communities. Typically, newspapers are one-way mass media vehicles. But this program turns *USA Today* into a two-way communication vehicle." ■

FIGURE 7-2   The hotline was run for the third year in 1991.

OUR HIGH SCHOOL HOT LINE:

800-777-2596

9 a.m.-9 p.m. EST/6 a.m.-6 p.m. PST, today, Tuesday; TDD for the hearing impaired only: 800-331-1706

More than 60 high school principals will answer USA TODAY's hot line being conducted from the National Association of Secondary School Principals' convention in Orlando, Fla. Call about:
► Courses your child should take in high school.
► Problems between a student and a teacher.
► Coping with peer pressure.
► Preparing for college.
► Dealing with drugs and alcohol.
Or any other subject that you would like to discuss with a high school principal.

(Copyright 1991, *USA Today*. Reprinted with permission.)

QUESTIONS FOR DISCUSSION

1. Can you think of other one-way communication vehicles that may be turned into a two-way communication vehicle as NASSP did with *USA Today*? How could NASSP have utilized them in order to accomplish its plans?

2. Was NASSP corrupting the integrity of channels of communication by cosponsoring this event with *USA Today*? How could a *USA Today* reporter remain objective and write a balanced story about this program?

3. If you were the director of public relations for NASSP, how would you advise a principal who was featured in a national news article for his participation on the hotline but was later criticized by local parents for his inaccessibility? They claim he can't be reached on the phone and seldom returns their calls. Would you give him the same advice if he were the president-elect of NASSP?

CASE 7-2   ALAR AND PR: GETTING TO THE CORE OF THE APPLE PROBLEM

This is the story of the fall and rise of the American apple industry in 1989. Though it happened over a decade ago, it serves as an excellent example of public relations' role in bringing about a change in public perception and in redefining the problem. This case was precipitated by a forceful public relations and publicity campaign that brought discredit and disfavor to apples and apple products. The ensuing problem was met by an equally forceful rebuttal campaign with the result that, today, apples are being consumed in normal fashion.[1]

THE SITUATION

Apples have been part of a healthful diet for centuries. An apple a day kept the doctor away. An apple for the teacher was appreciated, even if apple-polishing students were not. A favorite person was "the apple of my eye," and being "as American as apple pie" was as patriotic as one could get.

That's why the nation was shocked to hear, in February 1989, that people (especially small children) eating apples were jeopardizing their health. What had happened to change the shiny cure-all to a carcinogen? Alar and pr; *60 Minutes*, and the national media.

Since 1968, apple growers had used a chemical called daminozide (trademark Alar) to slow the ripening process and retain the red color. However, in 1985, scientists reported Alar and its residue, UDMH, could cause cancer in animals. Many growers stopped using Alar at that time[2] and in 1986 a self-designated public interest group called the Natural Resources Defense Council (NRDC) began a study of pesticides and resultant risks to preschool children.[3] (See Figures 7-3 and 7-4.)

The Environmental Protection Agency (EPA) began a regulatory process to consider banning the pesticide and, in early February 1989, announced that the process was being sped up, possibly as a result of efforts by NRDC. There was no rise in consumer awareness of Alar-related problems at that time.[4]

On February 26, however, the CBS show *60 Minutes* aired a segment entitled "A Is for Apple," which characterized the risk, especially to preschoolers, of getting cancer from eating apples and apple products as "intolerable."[5] It based the report on a white paper from NRDC, "Intolerable Risk: Pesticides in Our Children's Food."

NRDC followed the CBS report with a major news conference in Washington, D.C.,

---

[1]Thank you to Steven Rub, a student at the University of Central Florida, who developed this case study under the direction of Frank Stansberry, APR, who teaches at UCF.
[2]"Apples Without Alar." *Newsweek*, October 30, 1989, p. 86.
[3]"Intolerable Risk: Pesticides in Our Children's Food," a report by the National Resources Defense Council, February 27, 1989.
[4]"The Alar Scare: Rebuilding Apple Consumption During the Alar Crisis," a report by Hill & Knowlton (undated).
[5]*60 Minutes.* Transcript "A Is for Apple," broadcast February 26, 1989.

**Intolerable Risk:
Pesticides in our Children's Food**

Summary

**A Report by the
Natural Resources Defense Council**

February 27, 1989

FIGURE 7-3 The NRDC published a 141-page report in 1989 that examined the types and amounts of pesticides that are in foods.

(Courtesy of the NRDC.)

the next day, augmented by regional news conferences in a dozen cities around the country.[6] In short, a major publicity effort had begun.

National awareness of the "danger" of eating apples rose from virtually nil at the first of the month to 95 percent at the end of the month, as all news media jumped on this journalistically enticing story.

Faced with that type of public awareness and concern, the members of the International Apple Institute voluntarily stopped using Alar on their crops.[7] In June, Uniroyal, maker of Alar, announced plans to discontinue sales of the pesticide in the United States.[8]

Meanwhile, apple growers began to fight back. Spurred by the Washington State Apple Commission, the industry hired the public relations firm Hill & Knowlton (H&K), to mount the counterattack. H&K had been monitoring public opinion since

---

[6]*The Wall Street Journal*, October 3, 1989, an op-ed article on the Alar issue.
[7]*New York Times*, May 16, 1989, pp. 1, 19.
[8]*New York Times*, June 30, 1989, pp. 1, 11.

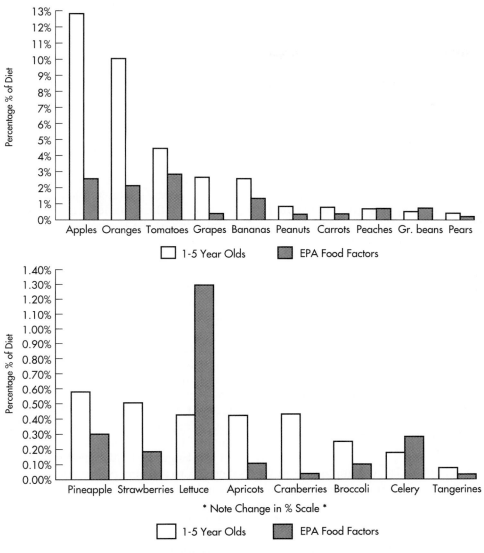

NOTE: Current preschooler consumption estimates were derived from the CSFII — *Nationwide Food Consumption Survey: Continuing Survey of Food Intakes by Individuals, Women 19–50 Years and Their Children 1–5 Years, 6 Waves,* 1985, and are average intakes of all forms (*i.e.* raw and processed) of each produce type for all children included in the 1985 Nationwide Food Consumption Survey. Food Factors were obtained from EPA, Toxicology Branch, Revised Average Food Factors, May 1, 1978.

FIGURE 7-4   The report of NRDC examined pesticide intakes by children and noted the large consumption of apples by children.

(Courtesy of the NRDC.)

before the first volley from NRDC. Its research showed that "purchase intent" for apples had gone into a "deep decline."

In its report, "The Alar Scare: Rebuilding Apple Consumption During the Alar Crisis," H&K noted that the media blitz from Alar's critics "led to a widespread panic, and a firestorm of negative reporting on the safety of apples. Moms across America began dumping apple juice down the drain. Cancer hotlines were deluged by calls from anxious parents. The message they were getting everywhere was 'don't feed your kids apples, its not worth the risk.'"

The strategy for gaining back the lost confidence was threefold—to get the facts about the safety of apples to worried consumers; to discredit the NRDC report as "bad science," and to get key sources (government regulatory bodies, scientists, the medical community) to reaffirm apples' wholesomeness and nutritional benefits.

The plan worked; by fall 1989, per capita consumption of apples had returned to an all-time high, a trend that continues today.

THE FACTS

The facts about Alar and apples are pretty clear. Alar is a plant growth inhibitor. Without Alar, apple growers will have to pick the crop four to six days earlier, before the apples drop. Thus, some varieties may go to market a little "green" and may lack perfect visual appeal. Shelf-life may also be affected.

Alar, as one of many products produced by Uniroyal, contributed only $4.6 million in sales at the time of the controversy, which accounted for about six-tenths of one percent of Uniroyal's total sales. It was not a major player in the overall sales picture.

Before 1985, about 35 percent of all "eating" apples were treated with Alar, including most red apples and some Golden Delicious. By 1989, the industry estimates of Alar usage were between 5 and 15 percent.[9] Most growers stopped using Alar after EPA investigations in 1985.[10]

Risk factors from Alar-tainted apples are less clear. In a table released by NRDC as part of the "Intolerable Risk" report, apples fell at the midpoint of 26 fruits and vegetables rated by frequency of detectable levels of pesticides. Strawberries were ranked first (63 percent with detectable levels). Apples and spinach (29 percent) were in the middle, and corn and bananas (1 percent) were at the bottom.

Uniroyal continually said its pesticide was safe as used. Support for this position was widespread and broad-based. Canadian health officials noted pesticide residues only one-thirtieth of safety levels and commented that a child would have to eat 250,000 apples a day for Alar residues to impose a threat to health.[11]

In England, British health officials saw "no risk to consumers," noting that an infant would have to consume 150 times a normal amount to reach even a "no effect" level of UDMH.[12]

Even Consumer's Union, through its publication *Consumer Reports,* said, "Apples treated with Alar are not necessarily unsafe to eat, since daminozide itself has not been firmly shown to cause cancer."[13] Later, in a letter to the editor of another consumer's

[9]"Where the Daminozide Is," *Science News,* June 14, 1985, p. 169.
[10]"Law & Legislation," *Newsweek,* February 13, 1989, p. 65.
[11]"An Apple-Spray Scare," *Macleans,* March 20, 1989, p. N-8.
[12]"Upsetting the Apple Spray Cart," *Chemistry and Industry,* January 1, 1990, p. 2.
[13]"Bad Apples," *Consumer Reports,* May 1989, p. 287.

magazine, *Consumer's Research,* the editors of *Consumer Reports* acknowledged, "The statements that 'Apples are safe to eat,' and that 'The EPA should ban Alar' sound contradictory, but they are not." *Consumer Reports* further said that current data suggest that Alar, per se, probably is not a carcinogen, but that its breakdown product, UDMH, probably is.

Thus, the risk is associated more directly with processed apple products than with raw apples (UDMH is released when apples are heated or otherwise processed). *Consumer Reports* saw the risk if UDMH levels rose to 45 parts per million and said, "While large enough to justify EPA regulatory concern, . . . there is no need for public panic over a risk this size."[14]

The federal agencies, EPA, Food and Drug Administration (FDA), and the U.S. Department of Agriculture, agreed to issue a joint statement on March 16, 1989, which said, "The federal government believes that it is safe for Americans to eat apples."[15]

Mothers and Others (a spin-off group from NRDC) said in a "fact sheet" that "chances are very slight that an individual child will get cancer from consuming apples or apple products," even when Alar was in use.[16] (See Figure 7-5.) And *Consumer Reports,* in a sidebar to its "Bad Apples" story,[17] tested 44 brands of apple juice for daminozide levels and found only four (all regional brands unique to the New York area) unacceptable.

UDMH, however, continued to pose a problem. *Consumer Reports* said, "The likely carcinogen is UDMH, which appears when juice from daminozide-treated apples is cooked to produce the concentrate from which commercial juice is made."

This perception of danger, dramatized by major new outlets, was what caused the public to panic. The impact on apple growers was immediate and substantial. Apple growers lost an estimated $100–150 million on the 1988 crop, which was being sold at the time. Most of this economic impact was felt in Washington State, where growers lost between $100 and $140 million on that year's crop. Washington supplies 60 percent of the fresh, or "eating," apples consumed in the United States.[18]

Apple juice sales in 1989 fell as much as 22 percent at one point and finished the year down about 14 percent,[19] while overall apple sales were down 20 percent for the year.[20]

THE PUBLIC PERCEPTION

The facts notwithstanding, the public was not buying apples. The media images of danger were too clear. For example, the *60 Minutes* story that kicked off the scare was entitled "A Is for Apple," but it showed a skull and crossbones superimposed over a shiny red apple. The *Consumer Reports* story carried the title "Bad Apples."

Urged and directed by NRDC, actress Meryl Streep took to the airwaves and popular magazines to say she was "furious" to discover that two of her children's favorite foods, apples and strawberries, might be

[14]*Consumer's Research*, July 1989, p. 28. Letter from editors of *Consumer Reports* in response to article, "Does Everything Cause Cancer?"
[15]"Fruit Fights," *The Wall Street Journal*, March 17, 1989, p. A-14.
[16]Mothers and Others, "Fact Sheet: Alar," undated.
[17]"Apple Juice: A Long Way from the Tree," *Consumer Reports*, May 1989, p. 293.
[18]Reuters, "Agencies: Alar Scare Nearly Over," *Orlando Sentinel*, November 4, 1989, p. 12.
[19]A. C. Nielsen and Co. report to Florida Citrus Commission, October 1989.
[20]"Avery's Uniroyal Ends Alar Sales in U.S.; Apple Product Imports Still Worry Critics," *The Wall Street Journal*, June 5, 1989, p. B3.

Mothers & Others
for a livable planet

40 West 20th Street, 11th floor • New York, New York 10011

phone: 212-727-4474 • fax: 212-675-6481

Fact sheet: Alar

Mothers & Others is frequently asked about Alar, the chemical that was removed from the market in 1989 after a campaign by Mothers & Others and the Natural Resources Defense Council to call attention to problems of pesticides in children's food. Here, we address some of the facts and myths surrounding this controversial chemical.

Our children are safer with Alar off the market. In 1989, public pressure led the manufacturer of Alar (which was used on apple crops to control growth and enhance apples' red color) to take the product off the market. The U.S. Environmental Protection Agency (EPA) later banned Alar for use on food products—*years after the agency first acknowledged the chemical's potential to cause cancer.* After concluding its review of the scientific data in 1992, the agency reiterated that Alar and its "breakdown" product, UDMH, should be classified as "probable human carcinogens," and that long-term exposure to Alar posed unacceptable risks to public health. (UDMH was formed when apples containing residues of Alar were processed into things like applesauce and apple juice.) Children eat significantly more apples and apple products, relative to their body weight, than adults do, and therefore received relatively greater exposure to Alar/UDMH. What's more, because their physiological systems are still developing, children are usually more susceptible than adults to the toxic effects of a contaminant. So children were *even more at risk* from exposure to Alar and UDMH than the general public—and are better off with Alar off the market.

There is NO truth to the claim that a child would have to eat 28,000 pounds of apples a day to be at risk from Alar. The chemical industry makes this claim based on high doses of UDMH fed to laboratory animals. Animals are routinely tested at very high doses, and a majority of the scientific community endorses the high dose method as a valid basis for regulating human exposure to chemicals, rather than waiting for actual proof of carcinogenicity in humans. However, the *human* risk from Alar was not based on the assumption that children would ingest an equal amount of UDMH as lab animals—risks to people are always figured on real exposure levels. In the case of Alar, exposure estimates were based on actual pesticide residue levels found on apples and on actual consumption data for pre-schoolers, which the USDA says is one ounce of raw apple and two ounces of apple juice per day.

FIGURE 7-5 Mothers and Others distributed a specific fact sheet about the Alar chemical.

(Courtesy of Mothers and Others.)

hazardous to their health because of Alar.[21] *Newsweek* entitled its report "EPA Is Looking for a Few Bad Apples."

The result was what publicist David Fenton described as "a sea of change in public opinion." *The Wall Street Journal* reported that "apples and apple juice have been going down garbage disposals all across the country." The school boards of New York City, Los Angeles, and Chicago, among others, banned apples from the lunch programs. (Fenton later said that effect was one not recommended by NRDC.)

The NRDC report highlighted the risk to children, who, because of their size and tendency to eat more fresh fruit than adults, seemed more at risk. "Children ingest so many apples for their size," Fenton said, "that the legal federal standard is unsafe." Reuters reported "Many consumers and school lunchrooms stopped buying apples," after hearing or seeing the report. "The negative messages about the safety of Alar and apples left the public unsure about what to believe," the Hill & Knowlton report said. "This led to a startling decline in intent to purchase apples."

The public was faced with cognitive dissonance—wanting to believe that apples were healthful, yet besieged by messages that apples would cause cancer. "The scare, though short-lived, was nearly everywhere," reports Lee Baker in his book *The Credibility Factor*.[22] People phoned the International Apple Institutes to see if apple juice should be disposed of in a toxic waste site!

Merchants, too, were worried. "Consumer reaction to the program [*60 Minutes*] was explosive, prompting many retailers to proclaim they would no longer sell Alar-treated apples or apple products." The

International Apple Institute said at the time that consumers' concerns about the health effects of Alar had probably cost apple growers more than $100 million, a figure that proved to be conservative.

Competitors, however, were delighted. A representative of the A. C. Neilson Company reported to the Florida Citrus Commission that "lingering effects of the Alar scare" in 1989 helped orange juice widen its lead over apple juice as the fruit beverage of choice in American homes.

THE PUBLIC RELATIONS PROBLEM

Although the facts about apples and Alar weighed heavily in favor of the industry, the emotions were all negative.

The bulk of the communication, however, targeted apples and Alar in general—*without regard to the secondary role of UDMH.* Perception had been shaped in a way that left apples—all apples—tainted by association with the pesticide. Changing that perception was the challenge of the industry and its public relations counsel.

THE PUBLIC RELATIONS IMPACT

Public relations techniques created the problem for the apple growers and processors, and public relations techniques helped get them back on their feet. David Fenton, public relations counsel to NRDC, outlined his program in a lengthy memo. In his memo, Fenton said that the situation was created "because of a carefully planned media campaign," based on NRDC's report "Intolerable Risk." Participation by actress Meryl Streep "was an essential element."

Fenton said that the goal of his campaign was to "create so many repetitions of

---

[21]"Ms. Streep Goes to Washington to Stop a Bitter Harvest," *People Magazine*, March 20, 1989, p. 50.
[22]Lee Baker, *The Credibility Factor*, Homewood, IL: Business One Irwin, 1993, pp. 120–127.

NRDC's message that average American consumers could not avoid hearing it. The idea was for the story to achieve a life of its own, and to continue for weeks and months to affect policy and consumer habits." This goal, Fenton says, was met. "A modest investment by NRDC repaid itself many-fold in tremendous media exposure and substantial, immediate revenue for further pesticide work." Other revenue-producing elements of the program were "self-published book sales . . . and a 900 phone number."

The timing of the campaign was to grant *60 Minutes* an exclusive "break," then to hold the Washington and satellite press conferences the following day. The *60 Minutes* broadcast moved the needle of public awareness to 45 percent, while subsequent coverage moved it to nearly 95 percent. (But both numbers are highly questionable; for initial exposure to reach 45 percent of *any* public, to say nothing of the food-consuming public, is virtually impossible. The total audience for *60 Minutes* proved to be a tiny fraction of this group.)

Fenton played the "Streep" card a week later fanning the flames. Her group, Mothers and Others for Pesticide Limits, would lobby citizens to seek changes in pesticide laws and ask for pesticide-free products at retail outlets. Other celebrities joined the bandwagon as the story gained momentum. Schools began dropping apples from the menu; retail stores began rejecting Alar-tainted fruit. Alar was withdrawn from the market and the EPA, USDA, and FDA issued statements saying that apples were safe.

The media relations work done by Fenton and NRDC was thorough. In breadth and depth, the coverage generated and the resultant outcry met Fenton's goals.

In fact, the media took the story so strongly that, to some, the coverage became advocacy rather than reporting of factual information or news. This is often the case in contemporary journalism, as audiences and advertising decline and coverage becomes more and more sensational in an attempt to recapture them.

At a Smithsonian Institution conference for environmentalists and writers, Charles Alexander, science editor of *Time* magazine, said, "I would freely admit that, on this issue, we have crossed a boundary from news reporting to advocacy." Later, David Brooks, editorial writer for the *Wall Street Journal*, wrote, "somehow the idea has gotten around that the environment isn't just a normal political issue, but a quasi-religious crusade. As a result, public discussion of the environment has been about as rigorous as one experts from a jihad . . . The reporters who became advocates seem to think they are doing the environment a favor."[23]

Andrea Mitchell of NBC said, "Clearly, the networks have made that decision now, where you'd have to call it advocacy."[24] "Usually, it takes a significant natural disaster to create this much sustained news attention for an environmental problem," Fenton wrote in his memo. "We believe this experience proves there are ways to raise public awareness for the purpose of moving Congress and policy makers."

THE APPLE GROWERS RESPOND

Apple growers would probably characterize the Alar scare as an "unnatural disaster." According to Hill & Knowlton, the producers of *60 Minutes* had promised the apple industry a "balanced look at the pesticide

---

[23]"Alar PR," *Chemtech,* May 1989, p. 264.
[24]Ibid.

issue," but what occurred was later characterized by the *Wall Street Journal* as "fright wig treatment of Alar." Apples, not Alar, took the center stage.

With overnight telephone surveys, H&K followed the decline in apples' reputation. The public wanted to be assured that apples were safe before sales could rebound. What industry leaders hoped could be a low-profile response shifted into a higher gear. The truth would be the chief weapon.

While Washington State apples were hardest hit, and those growers would be the principal financial backer of the defense effort, it was decided that a national organization should represent the industry. Therefore, the International Apple Institute was identified as the nominal leader for the program funded by the Washington Apple Commission.

The strategy was threefold: (1) to get the facts out about apples' safety (and to separate apples from Alar); (2) to discredit the NRDC research as being based on old, discredited data; and (3) to get key influencers—government, scientific, medical—to stand up for the safety and nutritional benefits of apples and apple products.

Key publics were (1) governmental agencies, (2) industry insiders including growers, (3) the food industry including retailers and wholesalers, (4) the medical and scientific community, (5) schools, and (6) the news media.

The results were good. Consumer awareness of the Alar "danger" remained high, but by the third week of March 1989 (less than one month after the first *60 Minutes* broadcast) the decline in intent to purchase had reversed.

Sales bottomed out and began a slow climb upward until, by early May, shipments were "setting seasonal highs." By fall, per capita consumption of apples hit an all-time high. During the 1989–1990 apple season, the average American ate 21 pounds of fresh apples.

WHERE THE ISSUE IS IN 2001

It has been 12 years since the beginning of the Alar controversy and the EPA ban on the chemical. However, proponents from both sides of this issue continue to debate the dangers of Alar in the media. The debate has switched away from apples specifically to the alleged dangers or safety of Alar because the apple industry succeeded in separating its product from the Alar issue. It met its goal of changing the public's perception of the problem—from apples to Alar.

One of the legacies of the Alar debate was the passage of "agricultural disparagement" laws by at least 12 states. These laws, also called "veggie libel laws," establish liability if someone knowingly makes false and disparaging statements about perishable food products that result in damages. The state of Texas passed an agricultural disparagement law in 1995. This law was the basis of an unsuccessful lawsuit brought against talk-show host Oprah Winfrey in 1996 by Texas cattlemen for an on-air comment she made concerning beef.[25]

Opponents of the veggie libel laws say that the laws violate the First Amendment, stifle public debate, and discourage people from speaking out or filing complaints with government agencies. More than 15 states now have anti-SLAPP (Strategic Lawsuits Against Public Participation) laws in place, which prevent bringing a lawsuit based on an agricultural disparagement law. Anti-SLAPP legislation is not in response only to the veggie libel lawsuits but is a measure to

---

[25]See Case 6-2 in Chapter 6.

prevent any meritless litigation that is aimed at suppressing free speech.

There continues to be numerous articles, studies and reports published that offer evidence that Alar is safe as well as unsafe. Representatives from both sides of this issue continue to resolutely maintain their positions.[26] Despite the removal of Alar from the marketplace in 1989, many in the food and chemical industry are committed to reiterating that the Alar "scare" caused an unnecessary panic and that Alar will always be synonymous with "hoax." As soon as one article appears that supports the harmlessness of Alar, another follows, documenting the hazards of the chemical. The apple industry carried out a successful counterattack to maintain the healthy image of apples. But advocates on both sides of the issue of Alar's safety continue to keep that debate alive in the media. ■

QUESTIONS FOR DISCUSSION

1. To carry out its work, a public interest organization such as NRDC must maintain a staff of administrators, scientists and researchers, lawyers, public relations practitioners, and others—as either employees or consultants. Because NRDC has no products or services to sell, in the usual sense, funds must be raised through memberships, contributions, and events to cover its budget. To what extent might this consideration influence the preparation, release, and promotion of a highly visible, controversial report such as the one on Alar? Do you think that the public that is the target of such campaigns—which are carried on by all public interest organizations as an important part of their *illusions*—is aware of this possible self-interest? If the public should be aware, whose responsibility is it to make them so?

2. Why would the public listen to an obvious nonexpert such as Meryl Streep on a scientific topic like this? Critics of such celebrity involvement in issues called her a "Hollywood toxicologist." Are you aware of any similar incidents?

3. Among its target publics, Hill & Knowlton listed the news media. Are the media a *public?* Or a communications *vehicle?* What are the strategy implications of according them status as a public?

4. Does David Fenton's campaign for NRDC raise any ethical issues? Check the PRSA code in the introduction to Chapter 10.

5. Is it possible that the attention focused on apples by the Alar scare played a part in the fact that Americans are now consuming the fruit in record numbers? Attempt to make a case for the position that it did.

---

[26] See "Ten Years Later, Myth of 'Alar Scare' Persists," Environmental Working Group report (www.ewg.org/pub/home/reports/alar/alar.html) and "The Alar 'Scare' Was for Real," Elliott Negin, *Columbia Journalism Review*, September/October 1996.

CASE 7-3   GM VERSUS NBC: A CORPORATE CRISIS OF EXPLOSIVE PROPORTIONS

"An error only becomes a mistake when you fail to admit it." Those were John F. Kennedy's words as he witnessed the infamous Bay of Pigs invasion of Cuba come to a disastrous end.

That statement will surely echo in the thoughts of former NBC News President, Michael Gartner, as he recalls the events connected to the *Dateline NBC* report on GM trucks. Gartner calls the aftermath of that broadcast "the worst week of my life."

THE SITUATION

On November 17, 1992, television viewers saw an old car being pushed by another vehicle along a narrow road in rural Indiana and colliding with a pickup truck—a collision sparking a fire that sent shock waves across the airwaves. This was the scene *Dateline NBC* broadcast that evening in a story showing a crash test of a GM truck that produced surprising results.[1]

The estimated 17 million viewers of that *Dateline NBC* program were likely shocked as they witnessed a General Motors C/K pickup truck bursting into flames after being hit in a crash test. The implication was clear; GM trucks were unsafe and should be recalled immediately.

ABC, CBS, and other media outlets subsequently broadcast similar newscasts citing NBC's material evidence and expert witnesses. If it were not for an outside tip, GM's battle might have been lost from the start. Pete Pesterre, editor of *Popular Hot Rodding Magazine,* wrote an editorial criticizing the *Dateline NBC* story. Soon afterward, a reader of that publication located a firefighter who had been present at the filming of the crash and had recorded his own video of the incident. GM's excellent relationship with the general media likely contributed to its acquisition of the firefighter's video.

There was only one concern on GM's part now—to clear its good name.

THE FACTS

The NBC crash demonstration was a sham, rigged in every way from start to finish. The claims broadcast to millions were blatantly fraudulent. GM would have to embark on a meticulous investigation to research the facts of the NBC demonstration and expose the falsified report.

The ensuing actions of GM are unprecedented in American corporate history. Abiding by the old adage that says, "never pick a fight with a guy who buys ink by the barrel" would have seen GM letting this extinguish itself. Instead, they were taking on NBC, a Goliath in the media industry.

GM designated a unique team to tackle the crisis; it included one public relations

[1]This case was prepared by University of Central Florida student, Paul Smith, under the supervision of UCF instructor, Frank R. Stansberry, APR, Fellow PRSA.

professional, four attorneys, and two engineers. The team obtained the firefighter's personal video that proved to be the turning point of GM's efforts. The video clearly documented that the test was rigged. The prop trucks used in the broadcast were located at a salvage yard in Indiana, and the GM investigators purchased them for examination. In one of the trucks, a used model rocket engine was found and the gas cap was not present.

With the video revealing that the test took place under abnormal conditions, the evidence was quickly stacking in favor of GM. Between November 1992 and January 1993, four letters were sent to NBC by GM. In that time, they did not receive an adequate response or explanation. Even after threat of a lawsuit, NBC News President Michael Gartner continued to defend the network's claim, insisting the story "was entirely accurate."

In February 1993, GM filed a lawsuit against the National Broadcasting Company, charging that *Dateline NBC* had rigged the crash and falsely reported the results. GM was now fully in crisis mode.

THE PERCEPTIONS

The key public relations principle at work is that perception is truth, and the media creates that perception following a crisis. In most cases, the perception is established in the first few hours after an incident. Bill Patterson, head of crisis communications and media training practices at HMS Partners of Columbus, Ohio, has discovered that there is an unfortunate trend for most management teams at this stage of a crisis:

➤ Top management invariably says it is the public relations persons' problem.

➤ Worse yet, the organization may have no PR person or staff to rely on or blame.

➤ The company may have a "crisis plan" but it turns out to be two pages with phone numbers of people to be notified.

➤ Management decides that it is "an internal problem" and endorses the stonewalling philosophy.

➤ The official policy is "no comment."

The trade journal, *PR News*, cites a survey that says 65 percent of the public interprets "no comment" as an admission of guilt. GM could have chosen to take no direct action and let the situation play out in the press, but once it established that its claims had merit, the team instead fought hard to defend the company's reputation.

Taking an adversarial approach to this media relations problem was never an option. Unlike doctors and lawyers, journalists have no official oversight committee, board, or organization. When one is offended or harmed by a doctor or a lawyer, a case can be made before a medical board or bar association. The first amendment clearly outlines freedom for the press so it has become nearly impossible to successfully sue them for libel or slander. This is the state of affairs GM would have to come to terms with in pursuit of fairness and accountability.

The perception of the questionable safety of GM trucks was only heightened when the National Highway Traffic and Safety Administration (NHTSA) opened an independent investigation of GM. Responding to public pressure, due in part to a well orchestrated campaign by NBC's attorneys, NHTSA launched this probe just one month after the initial broadcast. Consumer concern was at its highest level.

THE PROBLEM

GM's crisis communications program was managed by two members of a recently reorganized communications staff: William

J. O'Neill, then the director of communications for GM's North American Operations (NAO), and Edward S. Lechtzin, director of legal and safety issues for the NAO communications staff. Initially, O'Neill had, in fact, agreed that GM would participate in the original *Dateline NBC* program but had not been notified during the interview session about NBC's taped test.

Lechtzin's boss, GM General Counsel Harry J. Pearce, was selected to face off with the media. At the heart of the team's public relations effort would be a press conference, conducted by Pearce. The crisis communication team further made a conscious decision to target television as the key medium to deliver GM's message that they weren't going to settle for this. At GM, there was never any doubt that this deception should be publicized and as widely as possible. Briefed during an inaugural event for President Clinton, GM President Jack Smith told his public relations executives, "Don't overplay it, but do what's right."

A primary concern was to discredit NBC's supposed expert witnesses. The claims made by these individuals went to the heart of the case. It is no secret that adversary journalism relies on information from partisan or interested sources. That's no scandal in itself. Equally clear, though, is that unless the press brings a skeptical intelligence to bear on its partisan sources, as we see NBC did not do, its reputation will be at those sources' mercy.

What kind of experts did NBC use? Byron Bloch, for one, has a peculiar list of professional specialties. On one hand, he is a frequent network consultant on auto safety. When not doing paid media consulting, however, Bloch is perhaps the single best-known hired expert witness in injury lawsuits against automakers. He doesn't challenge reports that he lacks formal training in auto safety or engineering, and he acknowledged in a 1980 case that his résumé listed a degree he didn't have. Still, he's appeared in court to testify about alleged defects not just in cars but in products ranging from coffee pots to railroad cars.

Next there was Bruce Enz of The Institute for Safety Analysis (TISA). He frequently testified against GM and evidently against every other major car manufacturer in the U.S. market. He's not an engineer, nor, he says, are any of the 25 staff members of his institute, which is a for-profit organization.

Then there's Ben Kelley, another frequent witness. Kelley has enjoyed a successful career of providing crash-test footage to TV producers. When CBS's "Street Stories" questioned safety-belt reliability, it relied heavily on Kelley's Institute for Injury Reduction. Marion Blakey, head of NHTSA, flayed the resulting coverage as "factually inaccurate," not to mention that Kelley's group was founded and continues to be largely supported by a small group of trial attorneys. GM would have to scrupulously discredit the credentials and objectivity of the so-called safety experts. This objective headed the list of topics to be addressed in the press conference.

THE PUBLIC RELATIONS IMPACT

Harry Pearce was scheduled to take the stage in the GM showroom at 1 P.M. on February 8, 1993. The only uncertainty now was what the media's reaction would be.

From the moment Harry Pearce stepped to the podium until the time he concluded more than two hours later, the assembled media personnel, numbering nearly 150 journalists and 25 camera crews, were mesmerized.

"What I'm about to share with you should shock the conscience of every member of your profession and mine, and I believe the American people as well," began Pearce. "I will not allow the good men and women of General Motors and the thousands of independent businesses who sell our products and whose livelihood depends upon our products to suffer the consequences of NBC's irresponsible conduct transmitted via the airwaves throughout this great nation in the November *Dateline* program. GM has been irreparably damaged and we are going to defend ourselves."

For the next two hours, calling on years of trial experience, Pearce systematically shredded any semblance of defense that NBC might have had. He concluded with a statement issued earlier in the day by NBC, "We feel that our use of those demonstrations was accurate and responsible." His reply was a challenge, as if to a jury. "Well, you decide that one, and that's going to prove your mettle within your own profession. It's sometimes most difficult to police abuse in one's own profession."

At the center of the Pearce press conference was a repeat of NBC's 55-second crash demonstration. After the replay of the segment, Pearce carefully commented on the credentials, or lack thereof, of NBC's so-called expert witnesses.

Ultimately, no source, not even the internal report generated by NBC after the affair, fully explained what the crashes of two aged Citations pushed into the sides of two Chevy pickups were supposed to prove. Certainly, it wasn't that the trucks were dangerous since the performance of the trucks impacted at 39 and 48 miles per hour respectively was superb considering the conditions. Even with the use of incendiary devices, the only fire produced was a 15-second grass fire caused by escaped gasoline from an incorrectly fitted gas cap. NBC's own investigative report summarized it best:

We believe that the combined effect of the shot from the bullet car and the slow motion film creates an impression that the flames are about to consume

the cabin of the truck. These images in the edited tape convey an impression quite different from what people saw at the scene. The fire was small, it did not consume the cabin of the truck, and it did not last long.

GM's news conference brought NBC to its knees. On the day after Pearce's press conference appearance, NBC initiated a negotiating session that lasted for 12 hours. GM would accept nothing less than a full public retraction of its prior broadcast.

On February 9, 1993, a day after the GM press conference, *Dateline NBC* co-anchors Jane Pauley and Stone Philips read a four-minute, on-air retraction that put the blame solely on NBC and apologized to GM.

In the aftermath, three *Dateline* producers were fired, the on-air reporter was demoted and reassigned, and ultimately, NBC News President Gartner resigned in humiliation. NBC agreed to reimburse GM all expenses incurred during the three-week investigation. In exchange, GM agreed to drop the defamation suit it had filed against NBC.

Following this incident, GM increased its public relations offensive to counter concerns about the safety of its trucks. It sought to show that the plaintiff's attorneys had a vested financial interest in nurturing the idea that the trucks were unsafe. Another consideration was that the experts were found to have been either financed by the plaintiff's attorneys or served as expert witnesses in mounting legal action against the company.

Seventeen-year-old Shannon Mosely had recently died in a fire when his GM pickup truck was side-impacted by a drunk driver. The *Dateline NBC* video was made in conjunction with the hearing of that case. The attorney's trying the case in Texas obviously stood to gain from testing that would implicate GM's trucks. With that in mind, the fact that the testing and production of that video was partially financed by a group of attorneys (the plaintiff's bar) indicates that this misrepresentation would afford the opposing legal team a very unfair and fraudulent advantage over GM's lawyers. All involved, of course, had not counted on such swift and effective public relations.

NHTSA still demanded that GM voluntarily recall its pickup trucks while it completed its own investigation. The company refused. In April 1993, GM sponsored briefings in which Pearce explained to key members of the media why the company wouldn't recall its trucks and why NHTSA's conclusions were false.

The Executive Summary of NBC's internal report concluded, "The story of this ill-fated crash demonstration and its aftermath is rather a story of lapsed judgment—serious lapses—by persons generally well-intentioned and well-qualified. And it is a story of a breakdown in the system for correction and compliance that every organization, including a news organization and network, needs."

IDEAL PR IMPACT

An unprecedented effort resulting in the desired outcome could not fairly be called anything other than successful. Historically, there is really no standard to measure GM's actions. The company put together a unique response team that effectively handled all decisions in its public relations offensive. Even though the team reacted superbly in this matter, its effectiveness might have been maximized if a crisis plan outlining such a situation had already existed.

These members were selected after the onset of the crisis, and the president was briefed while on leave in Washington. Had there been a plan in place, GM's actions might have been swifter in mustering its team and delivering the fatal blow to NBC's fraudulent broadcast.

Another consideration is that GM did not necessarily have to dignify the report with a response and could have attempted to let it fizzle out in the media untouched. Many respected professionals still argue strongly in favor of this tactic. The writers and editors of Pat Jackson's *pr reporter* were some that shared in this school of thought during the events of this incident. Even though NBC reimbursed GM for all costs, the investigation lasted nearly a month and GM suffered $2 million in expenses while in pursuit of vindication. Not acknowledging the story might have seen the company arriving at the same results without incurring such high expenditures.

A truly proactive role would have seen GM conducting its own safety tests prior to putting a different product on the market. Certainly there are considerations regardless of where the fuel tank is located when it comes to various types of accidents, but the "side-saddle" design begs to have a side-impact test conducted before leaving the company open to the scrutiny it soon found. The company could surely have afforded a voluntary experiment by NHTSA when the new design was unveiled. Tests on record at GM could have readily dismissed NBC's claims as soon as they emerged as well as avoided the confrontation they ultimately had with NHTSA.

GM's excellent understanding of the media and its positive relationships with them came to the team's aid in this scare. Harry Pearce's trial experience was also key in establishing GM's innocence, but more importantly its perceived innocence in the court of public opinion.

NBC NOT THE FIRST, JUST THE FIRST TO GET CAUGHT

An "electronic Titanic" is how Howard Rosenberg of the *Los Angeles Times* characterized it. It was heralded as an unprecedented disaster in the history of network news and considered the biggest TV scam since the Quiz Scandals. NBC was actually a latecomer to this sort of safety-exposé game, and it is believed that its decisions were made under cost-cutting pressures.

CBS and ABC were quoted by another *Los Angeles Times* reporter as having said, "Their standards forbid the sort of staging that got NBC into trouble." An investigation of past network auto-safety coverage reveals that both CBS and ABC have run the same sorts of grossly misleading crash videos and simulations, withheld similar sorts of material evidence, and relied on the same dubious experts GM discredited as being tied to the plaintiff's attorney.

In June 1978, ABC's *20/20* reported "startling new developments" showing that full-size Fords, not just the sub-compact Pinto, would explode when hit from behind. The network aired film tests from a UCLA demonstration in 1967 that showed researchers under contract with Ford simulating a rear-end collision into a Ford sedan at 55 miles per hour. The end result was the vehicle bursting into a fireball.

ABC insisted that it had analyzed a great number of Ford's secret rear-end crash tests, and anyone who owned a Ford of any kind was at risk of suffering the same outcome displayed in the film. If ABC had really analyzed those UCLA test reports, it had every reason to know why the Ford in the crash film burst into flames: There was an incendiary device under it. As the UCLA researchers explained in a 1968 report published by the Society of Automotive Engineers a decade before the ABC broadcast, one of their goals was to study how a crash fire affected the passenger compartment of the car; to do that, they obviously needed a fire. It clearly revealed that the testers had tried on multiple runs to produce a fire without an igniter and failed.

The coverage seen on ABC gave plenty of credit to the network's expert, Byron Bloch. He is the same expert from the *Dateline NBC* program and his defense in the GM case was very similar to the defense he gave concerning the ABC broadcast, "There was nothing wrong with what happened in Indianapolis. The so-called devices underneath the pickup truck are really a lot of smoke that GM is blowing to divert you away from any punitive damages." While NBC refused to acknowledge that the rocket engines started the fire, they did admit that they shouldn't have put them in and that their presence should have been revealed to the audience.

After NBC's downfall, Don Hewitt, CBS *60 Minutes* executive producer, was frequently quoted in the media that such things were unheard of at his show. "I'd be looking for a job tomorrow," he insisted if that happened under his watch. However, CBS already had a history of producing several similarly tainted reports on vehicles.

In December 1980, *60 Minutes* reported that a small army-style Jeep was dangerously prone to roll over, not only in emergencies but "even in routine road circumstances at relatively low speeds." The footage was of tests run by the Insurance Institute for Highway Safety and was produced in collaboration with a CBS film crew. It shows "CJ" Jeeps going through a series of standard maneuvers. From a distance, the audience watched as CBS repeatedly flipped the Jeep. In test run after test run, the camera shows J-turns and evasive maneuvers to avoid obstacles in the roadway all result in an overturned Jeep.

The catch is that the viewers might have benefited from knowing that the testers had to put the Jeeps through 435 runs just to produce eight rollovers. Make a car skid repeatedly and you predictably degrade tire tread and other key safety margins, Chrysler later said.

Also key in these tests is that the Jeeps were piloted by robot drivers who were turning the wheel through more than 580 degrees of arc in these supposedly "fairly gentle" maneuvers. In one case, the wheel was rotated more than five turns per second. An unrelated study by GM revealed that average drivers even in emergency conditions only turn the wheel around 520 degrees per second. The robot drivers in these tests were operating at rates from 1,100 to 1,805 degrees per second. Unless you plan on investing in a dangerously high-tech chauffeur, the conditions represented here were anything but real world.

NHTSA later found that the Jeeps had been loaded with weights in key areas and were shown under "abnormal test conditions and unrealistic maneuvers."

In March 1981, CBS produced an Emmy-winning *60 Minutes* segment revealing how the most common type of tire rim used on heavy trucks can fly off, killing or maiming bystanders. What their expert, Ben Kelley, failed to mention is that they had to shave off 70 percent of the rim and remove the locking caps before they could get it to separate from the tire. Again, this is the same Ben Kelley, supported by trial attorneys, who appeared in the GM program.

There is still another account of a *60 Minutes* attack on the Audi 5000 in 1986. "Sudden acceleration" had viewers puzzled by a car that was apparently possessed. What it was actually possessed by was a tank of compressed air or fluid attached by a hose to a hole that was drilled in the transmission.

The history of dubious safety journalism goes on and on in the other networks, but both ABC and CBS insist there was no wrongdoing on their parts at any time. This might leave NBC to be considered the moral front-runner. The network got burned, and it apologized, which is more than its rivals have done. Former NBC News head Michael Gartner secures his spot in infamy with this last statement. "I saw that I had been too ready to believe our so-called experts, without trying to find out who they were . . . I realized we were just plain wrong." ∎

QUESTIONS FOR DISCUSSION

1. Assess the value of positive relationships with the media to General Motors in handling its problems with *Dateline* and NBC.
2. Is "fighting back" a good strategy for media disputes in general? Why?
3. Do media reporters and producers have a responsibility to investigate their sources as well as to investigate the targeted organizations?
4. What other options might GM have considered in rebuttal to NBC/*Dateline*?

References

"Exposing the Experts Behind the Sexy Exposés; How Networks Get Duped by Dubious Advocates." *The Washington Post,* Sunday "Outlook" (February 28, 1993).

"It Didn't Start with *Dateline NBC.*" *National Review* (June 21, 1993).

"The Most Dangerous Vehicle on the Road." *The Wall Street Journal* (February 9, 1993).

"Crisis Advisor Says Only 10 Percent of Corporations Have Plans." *PR News* (October 16, 1995).

"A Chink in the Armor." Bill Patterson, Director of Crisis Communications and Media Training

Practices, HMS Partners. www.media-relations.com/articles.htm.

NBC self-generated internal report, "Report of inquiry into crash demonstrations broadcast on *Dateline NBC* November 17, 1992."

The Practice of Public Relations. 6th edition. Upper Saddle River, NJ: Prentice-Hall, Inc., 1995.

CASE 7-4   A CLASSIC: BUILDING MEDIA RELATIONSHIPS THAT PAY

In the late 1970s the domestic car industry was threatened by the rash of imports that flooded the country. The imports were fuel-efficient and better built than many American cars. These qualities, coupled with the economy that was hard hit by a suffocating recession, served to jeopardize the very existence of the three top U.S. auto makers. Chrysler was one car manufacturer that decided to fight back—but did not expect the media problems that would come along with the fight.

Chrysler Motors[1] had several problems at once. Its cars did not appeal to many buyers and its sales lagged behind those of the two major competitors in the United States, Ford and General Motors. In 1978, the corporation was listed in *Fortune* as the year's "biggest loser," selling the "wrong kind of cars for the wrong kinds of buyers."

SITUATION ANALYSIS

Fortune magazine described Chrysler's problems in this way:

1. The demographics of Chrysler product owners showed that they were more conservative, older, blue-collar people less inclined to buy cars loaded with options, and people who got hurt first in an economic downturn.
2. Product engineering dominated the planning and marketing of cars.
3. Auto designs were considered "stodgy."

4. The corporation was on the move to non-automotive ventures around the world, many of which were not profitable.
5. Government regulations on mileage, safety, and emissions were things with which all manufacturers had to contend.[2]

Just at this downturn, Chrysler executives decided to launch a new product, the Dodge Omni, and its twin, the Plymouth Horizon. They were the company's first venture into the subcompact car line and also the first medium-priced cars with front-wheel drive manufactured in the United States.

The new products were introduced to the news media in two phases: The "long lead" preview for writers and editors of monthly magazines was held at the Chrysler proving grounds in Chelsea, Michigan. The "short lead" preview for daily newspapers, weekly news magazines, and radio and television stations was conducted in San Diego.

News kits timed for simultaneous release with the short lead preview were sent to all major U.S. daily and weekly papers, minority papers, and dealers.

Radio cassette actualities, featuring top sales executives and special feed from the preview site, were offered to all radio stations. Television networks were offered footage with and without sound, and a television crew was available on site for stations requesting special material.

---

[1]In 1998, Chrysler Motors merged with Daimler-Benz of Germany and the company is now known as DaimlerChrysler.
[2]*Fortune*, June 19, 1978, p. 55.

The crucial part of the introduction, however, was the test driving of the Omni and Horizon by the reporters and editors present at the short lead preview. Approximately 43 of them drove the cars from the proving grounds to their home cities.

Chrysler received extensive and glowing coverage from the news media. The News Analysis Institute, a Pittsburgh-based company hired by Chrysler, reported the publication of 904 news stories, totaling 16,646 column inches in newspapers with a combined total circulation of over 137 million. News/Sports Radio Network reported 12,888 radio broadcasts of the story to 136,022,600 potential listeners. About 78 television stations reported that they had aired stories and visuals to an average audience of 18,448,000. Glowing reports came from the automotive publications:

Auto Week: Hell of a nice car. Got a lot of favorable attention on the highway, especially from the foreign car guys. It's just what you need. Well worth waiting for.

Car and Driver: Fine little car.

Automotive News: It's a fine car, beautiful. Even at top speeds I was getting 31 mpg. Car handled fine.

Auto World: I was impressed. At 70, it handled beautifully. We averaged 31 mpg at the higher speeds. It's a beautiful little car.

Motor Trend, a magazine for automobile enthusiasts, gave the car its "Car of the Year" endorsement.

Fortune magazine reported that the cars had "scored well in the marketplace."

CRISIS HITS SIX MONTHS LATER

On a Tuesday, six months after the introduction of the cars, Chrysler was conducting another of its long lead previews at its Chelsea proving grounds. Fifty-four

monthly magazine editors and photographers from such diverse publications as *Hot Rod*, *Medical Economics*, and *Vogue* attended.

The entire public relations department was geared toward building a responsive two-way relationship with the news representatives. They coordinated product seminars, set up interviews, ensured that the writers were involved with ride and drive programs, and arranged models and props for special photographs.

Consumer Reports, a monthly product testing and rating magazine, turned down Chrysler's invitation to the long lead preview, even though one of its reporters had attended a preview from another automobile manufacturer the week earlier.

Sometime in the afternoon that Tuesday, a reporter from the *Washington Post* called a Chrysler public relations executive: "I would like to get Chrysler's reaction to Consumers Union's finding your Omni/Horizon car unacceptable." (See Figure 7-6.) The question hit like a bombshell. The reporter insisted that the charge was true; having heard it from a reliable source within Consumers Union. He also said Consumers Union would hold press conferences to announce their findings the following day, in New York and Washington D.C. By late that afternoon, Consumers Union confirmed that the press conferences would be held, but refused Chrysler admission.

CONSUMERS UNION'S CHARGES AGAINST CHRYSLER

Consumers Union's charges against Chrysler had been related to a test procedure that the Union said was performed routinely at auto proving grounds to check a car's directional stability: "ability to center itself and return to its original course when it is deflected abruptly from a straight path." The test is made by driving at steady

FIGURE 7-6 Photo from *Consumer Reports*. The new Chrysler cars are branded as "not acceptable," although earlier the cars had been rated very highly by the persons who had used the car.

(Courtesy of *Consumer Reports.*)

"expressway" speed, turning the steering wheel sharply to one side and then letting go of the steering wheel with both hands. The Union claimed that in such tests, most cars waver from side to side only minimally before returning to a course close to the previous one.

CHRYSLER SWINGS INTO STRATEGIC ACTION

At their Chelsea proving grounds, Chrysler's engineers immediately swung into action. The recreated the Union's test procedure while a television crew filmed the entire demonstration and made quantities of tapes. Meanwhile, the Consumers Union's press conferences were about to begin in New York and Washington, D.C., the following day. That evening, some news networks had already begun to inform the public of Consumers Union's charges against Chrysler's Omni and Horizon cars.

But they balanced their coverage with a discussion of the excellent sales figures for the cars and their being awarded *Motor Trend's* "Car of the Year."

Wednesday, June 14, 1978; New York: Chrysler's executive was outside the Consumers Union's press conference, allowed admission only on the insistence of the media representatives who had learned of his presence. He was then allowed to share the podium with Consumers Union representatives.

Wednesday, June 14, 1978; Washington, D.C.: Chrysler's representative was denied admission to the press conference. He held his own sidewalk press conference after the Union's press conference.

In the meantime, the public relations staff was busy distributing tapes of the test demonstrations made the previous day to television news departments in New York and Washington, D.C., Chicago, and Detroit. The public relations staff had also been preparing for a barrage of questions, which came soon enough. Chrysler released statements forcefully denying the Union's charges, reminding readers that it had received praise from professionals and consumers alike. The statement was distributed to most U.S. news media. A radio actuality (sound bite) of the statement was also released to network radio news syndicates and key stations in the country.

There was more. An information kit on the complex subject of steering and handling was prepared for spokespersons staffing the telephones, so that they could respond intelligently and with One Clear Voice to general and technical media questions.

That same day, after the Consumers Union's press conferences, Chrysler held its own news conference at the Chelsea proving grounds. Detroit and network television and radio reporters, print journalists, and the long lead preview magazine writers were all present. Here again, the Union's test maneuvers were demonstrated. It was crucial to show that the Union's test was extreme and in no way related to real driving situations. In fact, one writer was overheard to say: "That's comparable to jumping out the second floor of your house, breaking a leg, and then accusing the house of being unsafe."

With its sound strategic planning and its immediate response (with proof) to refute the Consumers Union charges, Chrysler was able to garner some positive media reaction, demonstrated by these editorials:

Consumers Union, which issued its re-port with great public fanfare— simultaneous news conferences in New York and Washington—ought to be darn sure it knows what it's talking about. We're not at all sure it does.[3]

Anybody dumb enough to do this (the test) is probably certifiable, and anybody dumb enough to believe that it proves anything about a car's road ability or handling deserves to be working for Consumers Union. CU's motives may be squeaky clean, but we think they've soiled their treasured cloak of impartiality. The Omni/Horizon is as safe as the *Consumer Reports'* charges are irresponsible.[4]

The article in *Car and Driver* was given nationwide newspaper distribution through AP and UPI. Various network radio and television newscasts aired the editorial. Numerous national trade publications including *Automotive News and Advertising Age* published it.

Not only the national media were informed; public relations staff also made information available to the local media via video tapes and radio actualities distributed to Chrysler's 21 zone offices across the country. This information was also accessible to dealers.

Chrysler left no stone unturned. It petitioned the National Highway Traffic Safety Administration (NHTSA) and its Canadian counterpart, Transport Canada, to conduct their own tests of the Omni/Horizon cars.

Within a few weeks after the Consumers Union's charges, the two government agencies came forth with their own separate conclusions: Transport Canada, represented by a consultant and recognized automotive-handling expert from the International Standards Organization and the director of roads and motor vehicle safety in the Canadian Ministry of Transport, announced that "automotive specialists from Transport Canada had found that they

---

[3]"Unsafe or Unfair," *Washington Star.*
[4]"God Save Us from Our Protectors," *Car and Driver.*

handled in a normal and satisfactory manner in both obstacle avoidance maneuver tests and on the handling track."

NHTSA, after testings at both the Chelsea and Consumers Union proving grounds, concluded: "No evidence of a safety problem in the stability and handling characteristics of Chrysler's subcompact Dodge Omni and Plymouth Horizon."

Chrysler recorded both government agencies' endorsement on videotape and radio actuality statements with the corporation's chief engineer and sent them air express to New York, Chicago, and Los Angeles network offices. Radio actualities from interviews with the Canadian expert and the deputy administrator of NHTSA were sent to the *Voice of America*, *Armed Forces Radio*, and Canadian news outlets. These statements were also distributed over newswire throughout the United States. The statements were telegraphed to all 7,500 Chrysler dealers.

WHEN PUBLIC RELATIONS SAVES THE DAY

The News Analysis Institute analyzed the news coverage after the storm had blown over. In its finding, a negative story is one in which the greater part of the copy was devoted to criticism of the cars and a positive story has the Chrysler position dominating (See Figure 7-7). The Institute's report stated:

The results are unusual in two respects: Despite the negative nature of the event, Chrysler dominated the coverage in stories published, space, and circulation. Further, Chrysler's case was strongly stated in virtually all the unfavorable articles, and a Chrysler comment was usually introduced early in the article. Particularly effective in this respect was the executive's sidewalk

conference outside Consumers Union's Washington headquarters and the placements of Chrysler's formal rebuttal. Also notable in positive news were the coverage of Chrysler's press test of Omni/Horizon and its rallying of auto writers to support its claims.

In evaluating how public relations saved the day, Frank Wylie, Chrysler's public relations executive at the time, cited two key "life-savers":

Most of the writers in major cities had already experienced the Omni/Horizon from their preview rides and local test drives. This *firsthand experience* helped to nullify or dampen the negative effects of Consumers Union's charges. This is perhaps succinctly summarized by one free-lance writer who had attended one of Chrysler's previews: "I think your letting people drive the cars away was the smartest thing you folks have done in a long time." [Emphasis added.]

The other vital "life-saver" was the preparation made by the public relations staff to answer all queries with *One Clear Voice*:

We tried to anticipate every question that we could in connection with the breaking news elements of the story and be prepared to handle them quickly and efficiently. We didn't want anybody hanging with overnight or weekend stories with unanswered questions.

The best evaluation tool, however, still is the final results of the public relations strategy during this crisis. Although sales figures plummeted immediately after the Union's charges, Chrysler believes that they would have remained that way if they had not reacted immediately and forcefully to counter the charges.

The News Analysis Institute

955 LIBERTY AVENUE ● PITTSBURGH, PA. 15222 ● PHONE: (412) 471-9411

Analysis of
Consumers Union Report on
Omni / Horizon Handling Problems

	Stories Published	Space Secured Column Inches	Newspaper Pages	Circulation
Favorable	402	5,132	29.2	35,881,065
Unfavorable	342	4,815	27.4	22,928,866
Totals	744	9,947	56.6	58,809,931

	Pictures Published	Page-One Stories	Articles Running a Full-Page or Longer
Favorable	61	38	2
Unfavorable	68	17	–
Totals	129	55	2

	Chrysler or Product Name Used in Heading
Favorable	294
Unfavorable	224
Totals	518

FIGURE 7-7 Summary and analysis by the News Analysis Institute of the coverage of the Omni/Horizon, which helped Chrysler evaluate its counter-media activity.

(Courtesy of News Analysis Institute.)

What's truly revealing happened at the dealers. The total sales of the two cars broke all of Chrysler's previous new car records during their first year on the market. Dealers sold every Omni/Horizon they had and could have sold more, had they had any more to sell. In addition, the two cars were all-time Chrysler leaders in capturing owners of competitive cars by establishing a "conquest rate" of more than 67 percent. Two out of every three buyers traded in another make of car for the Omni or Horizon.

In the final analysis, Chrysler's open and honest rapport and relationship with the news media combined with positive anticipatory action to the charges helped save it from an otherwise major media crisis.

WHAT'S NEW FOR CHRYSLER

As the years have passed since this media crisis, Chrysler has experienced many changes. The company's ups and downs have included the glory years in the 1980s as Lee Iacocca became a living symbol of Chrysler and engineered an upswing in sales, followed by a downtrend in the company's profits and the exit of the legendary chairman in 1992. And, in 1998, the company became DaimlerChrysler with the merger of Chrysler with Daimler-Benz.

Since the merger, media coverage has primarily focused on the volatile financial state of the company. As of late 2000, the Chrysler division had lost $1.8 billion. Because of this, Dieter Zetsche, an executive from Daimler, was dispatched to the Chrysler headquarters in Michigan as the new president and CEO with the task of correcting the financial crisis. The merger itself created an image problem in that it was promoted as a "merger of equals" but many are now viewing it as a takeover of Chrysler by Daimler, and the cause of layoffs and plant closings.

DaimlerChrysler has future plans to manufacture cars using the technologies of both Chrysler and Mercedes-Benz, which could create promising results. However, in the meantime, the company is busy picking up the pieces of the 1998 merger, both internally and externally as the financial world watches. ■

QUESTIONS FOR DISCUSSION

1. During the Consumers Union flap, Chrysler dominated the news compared with its competitors. Though the reports contained some dangerous criticisms, is it possible all that this exposure actually helped the company? Explain why or why not.
2. Research has shown that the news media have limited effects on publics. How would you evaluate Chrysler's reaction to Consumers Union's charges in light of this statement?
3. What are some public relations or communications theories that you see in play in Chrysler's handling of the news media? Can you think of some other theories not used in this case that would have helped the sales figures for the Omni/Horizon cars to climb?
4. If you were in charge of managing this crisis, what are some strategic actions you would keep or abandon? Explain your answer in terms of public relations principles or communications theories, or both.
5. The News Analysis Institute found that the original introductory publicity for Omni/Horizon generated "the publication of 904 news stories . . . in newspapers with the combined total circulation of over 137 million people." How many potential customers read about these new cars?

PROBLEM 7-A Employer Interests and Media Interests in Conflict

Ted Square takes pride in his professional integrity. He has never deceived a news reporter, never offered a "pay off" for publicity, and never risked his own integrity for personal or employer gain.

Ted's boss is the owner of a multimillion dollar auto parts manufacturing firm whose foremost customer is a major auto maker. Ted's boss is a man of character. He has never pressed Ted for more publicity or more favorable press at whatever cost. He is a realist, taking and relishing whatever favorable publicity is generated by events, but not worrying about either the quantity, accuracy, or completeness of it. With his business strong and growing, the owner exhibits an attitude that is fully supportive of Ted.

One day, the owner is shocked when his vice president of operations confronts him and says it is time to make him a full partner. He claims that his efforts have made the business grow and prosper. The owner is in a quandary. He has been quietly preparing his son to run the business, figuring he could take over in about five years. Meantime, there is no denying that this vice president, acquired a few years ago from one of the Big Three auto makers, is of huge importance to the parts firm.

The owner refuses to be pressured by the vice president. He does assure him that in time to come he will earn more and more income, and ultimately, he says, a limited partnership might be available.

The vice president at this point reveals that he has received an offer from a prime auto parts competitor, including a partnership, and the presidency of the competing firm. He presents his resignation to the owner on the spot.

In the hour following this shocking meeting, several events with public relations overtones take place:

1. The managers of the product design, engineering, manufacturing, and marketing departments turn in their resignations. They are moving to the competing company with the vice president of operations.
2. All these executives have been promised a "much better deal" by the vice president of operations.
3. Gossip is going around the office and shop that the business may have to be closed down and all employees terminated or furloughed without pay.

The owner is busy on the telephone, lining up successors for all the "defectors," and trying to reach the buyer at the large auto company customer to make sure the contract is intact and unaffected. His financial vice president is busy calling other customers, brokers, and others to reassure them that the business is not threatened. In the meantime, Ted's department is working on statements the owner wants to make to employees, automotive trade press editors, the local media, and wire service stringers.

Midway into these efforts, word is passed to Ted Square by his secretary that the local bureau chief of a financial newspaper, a long-time friend, is on the telephone. Ted has to take the call, and he hopes that it concerns some other subject. But it does not. The conversation goes this way.

"Ted, this is George. I'm up against our deadline in 15 minutes, but we have a rumor down here that your vice president of operations has resigned."

"Yeah, George. I've been working on a release about it. Do you want the name of the man who will succeed him?"

"Sure."

"It's Lem Jones. He has been the vice president's righthand man for several years. Consequently, the business will go right along."

"Thanks, I'll get this into the works. Let me have more details as fast as you know them."

That was it. George, despite being a trained newsman, failed to ask Ted where the vice president was going, or the full circumstances of his resignation. Ted, for his part, was aware of more than he told. He simply answered specific questions and minimized the importance of the events, even though he knew the story would get financial front-page coverage if he added more details.

As it developed later on that day, the financial newspaper was scooped by a local newspaper whose reporter had called the vice president of operations personally, had gotten the name of the company he was joining, had called them, and had obtained quotable details. The local bureau chief, Ted's friend, was embarrassed. His boss in New York had chewed him out. He blamed Ted for holding back information that was newsworthy, and said, "I'll never be able to trust you again."

"I'm sorry you feel that way," Ted told him. "I had no information from the operations vice president, or the other guys who were resigning, and no one gave me authority to speculate, or to speak for them. What I had officially from the president, I gave you. You didn't ask for anything else. If you had, I could have referred you to the operations VP."

"OK," the bureau chief said, "that's what you say now. But every time you call me, remember, I've got a long memory."

Obviously, this was something for Ted to think about. He reasoned that his obligation was first and last to his employer. He had to release information of news value for which he was the authoritative source. But he did not have to go beyond that, and particularly not if it might be harmful to his employer. The damaged relationship with the major financial newspaper was seriously worrisome.

Who was right: Ted? The bureau chief? Both? Neither? If you had been Ted, how would you have handled the situation so that your employer's interests and your good media relationship with George were both protected? What would you have done differently?

If your company was publicly owned, would you have acted differently when George called?

PROBLEM 7-B Dealing with the Media in a Sticky Situation

You are the public relations director of Alger Tiberius Software Inc., an up-and-coming software development company. Things have been exciting in the last few days since the introduction of a new software program, Manufacturing Efficiency Revolution (MER). When integrated into the computer controls of manufacturing equipment, it will increase the efficiency of that equipment and cut production time in half. This program will revolutionize the manufacturing industry. Magazine previews of the product have been complimentary, and it looks as if the company has an instant best seller on its hands.

But bad news hits one day when your morning coffee is accompanied by a newspaper clipping from the *Local Yokel Times,* quoting Don T. Figgle, your president and CEO, who is particularly proud of the new product and has taken every opportunity to brag about its merits in the press. In an off-hand comment he makes to a reporter at a local restaurant, Figgle is quoted as saying that "this product will virtually replace about 15 percent of the American manufacturing workforce. It cuts out about half of the unnecessary actions done in factory production."

Figgle's quote is followed by the reaction of the AFL-CIO in response to this new information about the product. Ned T. Green, official spokesman of the organization, is quoted as saying, "This new product was not presented with this information to the labor and computer industries. Efficiency gains in manufacturing were discussed but not the elimination of a sector of our workforce. AT Software in effect lied to the public about the impact this software program will have on the American workforce."

Needless to say, this turn of media coverage is unexpected and unwanted. Figgle was correct in saying that the software would revolutionize the computer and manufacturing industries but his statistics were incorrect. The product would eliminate 10 percent of jobs for the manufacturing workforce but would create jobs in a different area for other workers. Those who would lose their jobs could be retrained for other areas. You arrange another press conference for Figgle to disseminate the correct statistics available to the press, but whether the jobs are cut by 15 percent or 10 percent, loss of employment is the real story for the media. They are already printing a tidal wave of stories with headlines like "Computer Cover-Up Leaves Workers High and Dry" and "AT Software Sends Workers Packing."

By the following morning, negative media coverage has not abated. Although the news media now have the right statistics, emphasis is on the 10 percent of workers allegedly to be put out of work by the software. To top it off, a newly formed activist group, WACS (Workers Against Computer Software), is picketing outside of the main offices of AT Software with signs proclaiming "AT Software Trades in People for Programs." The local TV stations are all present to cover the protest and give up-to-the-minute reports.

In addition the media is out in full force and has gone to the local congressman Bill Zealot for reaction. His last election campaign was focused on creating jobs for America. Zealot, up for reelection in the fall, pledges his loyalty to the hard-working American public and vows to fight "big business pushing aside the little guy and trying to make him obsolete in the name of progress." It looks as if there may be legislative reaction against MER.

Later that afternoon you receive a call from the Computer Software Programmers Association (CSPA). Initially, they were behind this program, but with all the bad press they're getting a bit nervous. They don't want to endorse a program that will cause so much flak. Without the backing of CSPA, the future of this product is going to be difficult.

It is now 9:00 P.M. and things look a bit bleak for MER and AT Software. Clearly what should have been a great announcement has become garbled by the gatekeepers. You are wondering how to get the real message out to those audiences that matter. You ask yourself:

- Who are those groups that are garbling my message?
- What other groups are likely to become involved?
- What are the likely behaviors of each group?
- How can I minimize their messages and maximize mine to the publics I would like to reach?
- Can I reach those publics without utilizing usual venues, in order to avoid media, political, and activist gatekeepers?

1. With those questions in mind, how would you go about creating a plan to reach key publics with one-on-one communication in order to stay some of the immediate damage caused by the negative reactions of those groups who have been most vocal?
2. Could AT Software have avoided this negative uproar to MER? What actions should have been taken before presenting this product to the public through the media?

PUBLIC ISSUE CAMPAIGNS AND DEBATES

The backbone of Jeffersonian democracy is an intelligent, well-informed public and electorate.

The handling of public issues makes evident the link between public relations and the idea of democracy. For the people to be able to participate in decisions that affect their lives, those decisions must be put before them in a thorough, forceful manner. The ramifications, pro and con, of potential decisions need to be debated fully. *In the Court of Public Opinion, public relations practitioners are the attorneys.*

In this setting, an *issue* is a subject on which there are (1) two or more strongly opposing arguments, (2) emotional involvement of a large number of people, and (3) concern that the decision will have an impact on people's lives or the smooth functioning of society. Gun control, abortion, smoking policies, and the other topics in this chapter clearly meet these criteria.

When issues get out of hand—that is, cannot be settled before they become huge and threatening—they move to the category of *crisis*. A crisis is a public or organizational issue that has grown to such proportions that its ultimate resolution appears to mark a turning point. Depending on the decision, things may not be the same afterward. Chapter 9 presents several crisis cases.

While businesses, schools, hospitals, and other established organizations with sophisticated public relations policies devote substantial effort to anticipating or avoiding issues that might have a negative effect, they will also raise issues when they believe that public discussion might be beneficial. In contrast, there are many special interest groups whose major activity is to raise issues—in the American democratic tradition in which the people ultimately decide. Because of the number of variables at play and the societal importance of public debate, dealing with issues is one of the most challenging segments of public relations.

TYPES OF ISSUES

Issues can be assigned to four categories:

- **Latent.** Just being formulated by far-thinking scholars or social activists but with sufficient apparent validity that it could become an issue sooner or later.

- **Emerging.** Starting to be written about in scholarly journals or specialty media; perhaps a special interest organization adopts the idea or a new group forms around it; early adopter opinion leaders begin to be aware; it starts to spill over to wider publics, but no coherent action plan or broad support is yet evident.
- **Hot.** A full-blown issue in current debate.
- **Fallout.** Leftover remnants from the settlement of hot issues, which can come back onto the public agenda because they have already attained visibility.

Elements of all four categories are evident in many of the cases.

TARGET AUDIENCES

Most of the time, practitioners work with specified target audiences such as employees, neighbors, stockholders, members, donors, and customers, who are perceived to have self-interest reasons to support the organization. These audiences make up the organization's constituency. Contacts with them seek to reinforce, broaden, or deepen the two-way commitment. (See Figure 8-1.)

THEN THERE'S THE GENERAL PUBLIC

When the term *general public* is used, it usually describes the uncommitted, often uninterested bystanders whose support or opposition might ultimately have a bearing on the outcome of a situation or issue. Because they are unaware or uninterested, members of the general public do not feel much of a stake or depth of conviction.

If a matter eventually will be on the ballot, or voted on by a legislative body, or decided in the marketplace, where people "vote with their dollars," involvement of the general public can be vital. If social policy is being set, it is the general public that will decide what it will be—with or without laws to enforce it. At other times, interest in an issue will be so specialized that the general public will forgo its right to participate and leave the decision to the special interests who do care about the subject.

Therefore, the first problem faced by practitioners is to get people interested. Sometimes individuals or organizations will seek to do this by attempting to speak for the general public. When consumer advocates began questioning the quality and price of various products or services, they took on a task that most people had often done themselves—so people were happy to have this leadership. But when religious fundamentalists claimed to speak for average citizens in demanding the removal of certain books and magazines from libraries and newsstands, the public rejected them. In both cases, these spokespersons were not elected or otherwise appointed by those for whom they undertook to speak. They were accepted or rejected by public consent. This principle is key to understanding issue debate.

Persons or organizations that take stands on issues, pro or con, or neglect to do so, exercise a privilege and a prerogative in the democratic process. It is fundamental to effective public relations that this freedom of expression prevail. Without it, the individual or the organization is totally subject to the point of view of the state or of the noisy and the militant. Given freedom of expression as a basic underpinning of public

STAKEHOLDERS

NCR

We believe in building mutually beneficial and enduring relationships with all of our stakeholders, based on conducting business activities with integrity and respect.

EMPLOYEES

NCR

We respect the individuality of each employee and foster an environment in which employees' creativity and productivity are encouraged, recognized, valued and rewarded.

SHAREHOLD

NCR

We are dedicated to creating value for our shareholders and financial communities by performing in a manner that will enhance returns on investments.

COMMUNITI

NCR

We are committed to being caring and supportive corporate citizens within the worldwide communities in which we operate.

NCR's Mission: Create Value for Our Stakehol

CUSTOMERS

NCR

We take customer satisfaction personally: we are committed to providing superior value in our products and services on a continuing basis.

NCR's Mission: Create Value for Our Stakeholders

FIGURE 8-1 A semantic twist to the concept of constituency is *stakeholders*, an umbrella identification denoting every group that has a stake in this issue.

(Courtesy of NCR Public Relations.)

relations practice, experience suggests that this concept is balanced and weighted by many adjustments. For example, the theoretical democratic process suggests that the majority rules. In reality, this does not always hold true. Quite often, a minority prevails. Less than half of eligible voters register to vote, and an even larger percentage of those who register do not vote. In almost all elections, it is a vocal, motivated, active minority who votes, and therefore rules. Within most organizations, to use another setting, there is almost always a relative few who hold the decision-making power for the whole body politic or membership.

Three cases in particular in this chapter illustrate the concept that a general public does exist, available to be influenced, but that the perceived will of that unorganized body is carried out through groups focusing on a particular issue or concern. One group took on the spotted owl as its concern. Another became an advocate for nonsmokers. Still another wanted stores to be open on Sundays.

In a slightly different context, Planned Parenthood claims to speak for the rights of women, and across the aisle the Right to Life movement offers its position on moral issues as one that has precedence over personal choice.

The uncommitted general public provides an arena (via public relations campaigns, the news media, and sometimes the courts) in which the motivations of special interest groups can be challenged by those who openly represent viewpoints or programs claiming to deserve a higher priority or to embody a higher moral purpose.

The general public and its elected representatives hold the key in the continuing controversy between the business sector and government agencies over how much regulation there should be, what kind, by whom, and with what reporting requirements and penalties.

PUBLIC SERVICE AS PREVENTIVE PUBLIC RELATIONS

Public service programs are expressions of an organization's concern for societal problems and needs. The public relations responsibility for organizations engaged in public service programs is normally that of creator and implementer. This role calls for the handling of:

- Strategy, planning, and research
- Program design
- Civic participation
- Government and educational liaison
- Meetings and events
- Media placement and relations
- Preparation of print, audio, and visual materials
- Interviews and news conferences

Some public service programs spring out of a crisis or an emergency, from criticism of an organization's doings, or from public clamor, as in the conservation of endangered species.

Increasingly, public service programs have not waited for problems to arise. They have been devised to head off the difficulties posed by protests, confrontations, or increased governmental regulations. Public service programs are seen as practical means of demonstrating socially responsible behavior, gaining trust for good deeds, building customer or clientele goodwill, or building working relationships with a constituency of public officials, investors, members, donors, or voters. For most successful enterprises and institutions, the attitude is that public service programs and expenditures are important to earn public approval. As a practical matter, management normally places two requisites on public service programs:

1. A program must fit logically into the mission, the objectives, the timetable, and the field of endeavor in which the organization has expertise.
2. There must be an identifiable, measurable benefit to the organization as well as to the public groups or noble purpose involved and affected.

Such strategic public service programs often call for cooperation between public relations or public affairs, human resources, marketing, and other departments.

SPECIAL INTERESTS

Citizens in a democratic society tend to band together in polarized common interest groups such as labor unions or manufacturers' associations, meat eaters or vegetarians, hunters or conservationists. People feel that collectively, on a given issue, their voices and their votes can get the attention needed to favorably influence decisions.

The United States, more than any other free nation, has become the world's prime example of what happens, both good and bad, when the democratic process is carried to an extreme. The nation has become factionalized to a point where the decision process is hobbled by a host of single-issue champions, protesters, and crusaders. On many public issues, factionalization has generated such a severe confrontation that reconciliation becomes impossible.

The practice of public relations, historically and now, is deeply involved in helping factions to have their voices heard and their influences felt on behalf of their particular special interests.

In representing competing or opposing factions, practitioners face off against each other much as lawyers do in lawsuits or courts. The justification, if any is needed, is simply that each faction, in the eyes of its sponsors and its beneficiaries, holds that its view or needs do, in fact, serve the best interest of all. This freewheeling debate in the court of public opinion, or the marketplace of ideas, is exactly what Jefferson and the Founding Fathers had in mind when they created the United States as the first true democracy.

IMPORTANCE OF COMPROMISE

Given factionalization and confrontation, it remains for elected government in a free society to assume the roles of *referee* among contestants and *interpreter* of the greater public good.

When powerful and determined factions or special interests meet head on, the outcome is generally a reconciliation, with both sides compromising a bit. For example, in the matter of environmental protection, the upper atmospheric layer, or ozone, high above the earth filters out some of the sun's ultraviolet rays, helping assure that humans can live above ground and expose themselves to the sun. Chlorofluorocarbons (as in spray deodorant, insecticide, and detergent cans) have been identified as damaging to the ozone layer. The government, acting in the public interest and spurred by environmentalists, considered a ban on certain chlorofluorocarbons. Makers of products using them said, in effect, "Give us some time to switch over without loss of the market." Granted time, manufacturers set about providing nonpressurized containers for their products and advertising and promoting the desirable features of roll-ons, pump-can devices, and wipe-ons.

There has been so much of this kind of compromise in areas of social concern, from integration to equal employment opportunity, from atmospheric pollution to metropolitan area blight and roadside litter, and even sexuality, that the phrase *an era of trade-offs* has come into popular use.

THE UNFORGIVING DECADE

On the other hand, there is a tendency today toward emphasizing those issues that have become so emotional, or are so deep-seated, as to evoke almost (or actual) religious fervor in their adherents. These divisive issues seem to tear at the social fabric and raise doubts about the future of the democratic process. Among them are abortion, assisted or legalized suicide, medical triage, sex education in schools, other items of educational curricula, gun control, smoking, homosexuality, and civil rights for animals.

Overzealous "believers" among activists have resorted to violence—the murder of physicians at feminine health clinics—and angry protest against organizations—picketing or boycotting companies that have, or don't have, medical coverage for homosexual "spouses." These zealots can swerve an organization far off course unless public relations practitioners are sufficiently knowledgeable and influential to prevent overreaction. Because a few zealots put you in the headlines is no reason to panic, or to pander to what are often their very undemocratic, minority-opinion demands.

One result of this social warfare is what public relations consultant Ann Barkelew terms "The Unforgiving Decade." She notes that no matter what actions you take or which policies you adopt, *someone* is going to be angry enough to denounce you—loudly and publicly.

Dayton Hudson Corporation (DHC) discovered this principle when pickets ringed a company department store unexpectedly one day—protesting an activity the company had taken for granted. The "pro-life" picketers were angry that DHC contributed (as it had for years) to Planned Parenthood, whom the picketers considered to be promoting abortion. (Planned Parenthood says this is not true; they counsel on abortion as well as all other choices available to pregnant women who seek their advice.)

Because the contributions had continued for years, a way out, thought one company official, seemed to be to discontinue them—with the rationale that under any circumstance contributions should shift among various causes. But when this "solution" was announced, an even *larger* number of pro-choice picketers surrounded the store.

No matter how the issue was to be resolved, the company was going to make enemies and probably lose some customers.

ISSUE ANTICIPATION TEAMS*

Issue anticipation (IA) teams are working well for many organizations that wish to identify issues before they become a problem. In many organizations, setting up IA teams both meets the need *and* deals with the middle management "wall." Teams usually involve managers from all ranks and departments. To keep interest high, teams report every so often to a formal "issues board" composed of senior officers. Some organizations have one team that looks at the realm of issues. Others have several teams concentrating on specific areas of concern. At its simplest, the team answers two questions: (1) What's happening out there and in here? (2) Could it affect us or become an issue for us?

BENEFITS OF TEAMS

- Serving on a team is an honor, which motivates the members.
- It forces them to read and observe things they previously didn't.
- Members interact with people they might not come in contact with otherwise.
- Consensus and teamwork are essential.
- Supervising managers start to think broadly about the implications of what the organization does and are sensitized to public relationships.
- Helps identify and train the rising stars.

pr reporter, April 27, 1987.

One resolution would be to count heads; which group has the most supporters, so could do the most damage? But what organization wants to be in such a losing situation? An alternative strategy is to work with the "side" that will be favored in order to gain pledges of extra business and support to make up for the lost customers. Neither is ideal, and both keep the organization on the hot seat of being identified with a divisive issue.

ISSUE ANTICIPATION

The way to avoid issues is to see them coming and to find ways to reach accommodation before they become public and "hot." (See box.) Some say, indeed, that the real value of public relations is what *doesn't* happen! Jim Grunig's paradigm (See also Chapter 2) is a superb issue anticipation and planning tool:

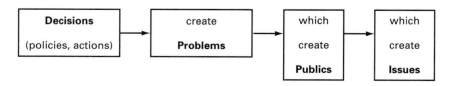

The most noticeable element of this paradigm is that publics are subsidiaries of stakeholder groups—not vice versa.

- Stakeholder groups are people who should care and be involved because the subject could or will affect them.
- Nevertheless they contain large contingents who don't get the message, can't be bothered, just plain don't care, or have such barriers that they won't do anything about the issue. *These segments together can be as high as 90 percent of the stakeholder group.*

The viable term for those who *do get excited* about the issue is therefore publics. He identifies three types who together are often limited to the 10 percent plus who will engage in the issue:

1. **Long haul**—those interested in the full ramifications of the topic
2. **Special interest**—those concerned only about certain elements of the topic
3. **Hot button**—those aroused only by emotionally debated elements

This is a useful way to manage issue anticipation by (1) focusing on which stakeholders are known to be skittish about which potential decisions, then (2) modeling how the three types of publics will fall out and what their response will likely be.

SCENARIO TECHNIQUE

The way to find foresight is by creating multi-scenario possibilities,[1] advocates Kerry Tucker, CEO of the San Diego pr firm Nuffer, Smith, Tucker. This means "creating stories of equally plausible futures," then planning for them. Highlights of the advantages:

- Putting trends in some kind of logical story form creates a fresh sense of understanding.
- Scenarios are "what if" stories, taking the most pressing forces on your organization and putting them together in a narrative.
- Once you know the alternative futures, you can plan for them; otherwise strategic planning is "scratching at the surface."

As you review the cases in this chapter, observe whether there were early warnings that might have enabled public relations practitioners to help their organizations take action to steer around the public debate that ensued.

References and Additional Readings

Alinsky, Saul. *Rules for Radicals: A Practical Primer for Realistic Radicals.* Vancouver, WA: Vintage Books, 1989.

Baskin, Otis. *Public Relations: The Profession and the Practice.* 4th ed. Columbus, OH: McGraw-Hill Higher Education, 1996.

---

[1]Kerry Tucker, "Scenario Planning," *Association Management*, April 1999.

Baus, Herbert. "Working with Influential Groups," in *Lesly's Handbook of Public Relations and Communications.* 5th ed. Chicago, IL: NTC Business Books, 1997, Ch. 32: 475–481.

Broide, Mace. "Having a Voice in Politics," in *Lesly's Handbook of Public Relations and Communications.* 5th ed. Chicago, IL: NTC Business Books, 1997. Chapter 7: 103–112.

Buchholz, Rogene. *Business Environment and Public Policy: Implications for Management and Strategy Formulation.* Upper Saddle River, NJ: Prentice Hall, 1989.

Coleman, Cynthia-Lou. "What Policy Makers Can Learn from Public Relations Practitioners." *Public Relations Quarterly* 34 (Winter 1989–90): 26–31.

Corporate Public Issues and Their Management offers a variety of information regarding public policy formation and issue management. For more information contact: Issue Action Publications, Inc., 207 Loudoun Street S.E., Leesburg, Virginia 22075, 703/777-8450, www.issuemanagement.org.

Cutlip, Scott, Allen Center, and Glen Broom. *Effective Public Relations*, 8th ed. Upper Saddle River, NJ: Prentice Hall, 1999.

Ewing, Raymond. *Managing the New Bottom Line; Issues Management for Senior Executives.* Homewood, IL: Business One Irwin, 1987.

Foundation for Public Affairs. *Public Interest Profiles 2001–2002.* Washington, DC: Congressional Quarterly, 2000.

Fox, J. F., "Communicating on Public Issues: A Changing Role for the CEO." *Public Relations Quarterly* 27 (Summer 1982).

Hammack, David. *Making the Nonprofit Sector in the United States: A Reader.* Bloomington, IN: Indiana University Press, 1998.

Heath, Robert. *Strategic Issues Management: Organizations and Public Policy Challenges.* Thousand Oaks, CA: Sage Publications, 1997.

Jones, Barrie, and Howard Chase. "Managing Public Policy Issues." *Public Relations Review*, Vol. 5, No. 2 (Summer 1979). A classic.

Kelley, Stanley, Jr. *Professional Public Relations and Public Power.* Baltimore, MD: Johns Hopkins University Press, 1966. Classic study of a perennial question.

Lesly, Philip. "Policy Issues, Crises, and Opportunities" in *Lesly's Handbook of Public Relations and Communications.* 5th ed. Chicago, IL: NTC Business Books, 1998. Chapter 2: 19–37.

Mathews, David. *Politics for the People: Finding a Responsible Public Voice.* 2nd ed. Champaign, IL: University of Illinois Press, 1999.

National Rifle Association. For pamphlets explaining the organization and its objectives and programs, 1600 Rhode Island Avenue, N.W., Washington, DC 20036, www.nra.org.

Newsom, Doug, Judy Van Slyke Turk, and Dean Kruckeberg. *This Is PR: The Realities of Public Relations.* 6th ed. Belmont, CA: Wadsworth Publishing Company, 1996. Chapter 9, "Laws Affecting PR Practice."

Olasky, Marvin, "Engineering Social Change: Triumphs of Abortion Public Relations from the Thirties through the Sixties." *Public Relations Quarterly* 33 (Winter 1988–89): 21.

pr reporter, Vol. 37, No. 14 (April 4, 1994). Lead article concerns the value of public relations in grassroots organizing and coalition building.

Public Relations Body of Knowledge. New York: PRSA. See abstracts dealing with "Ethics and Social Responsibility."

Scheel, Randall. *Maxims for the Issues Manager.* Stamford, CT: Issue Action Publications, 1991.

Sopow, Eli. *The Critical Issues Audit.* Leesburg, VA: Issue Action Publications, 1995.

Stoltz, V. "Conflict PR in the Formation of Public Opinion." *Public Relations Quarterly* 28 (Spring 1983).

The Futurist, six times yearly magazine on significant trends and where those trends are leading, from the World Future Society, 7910 Woodmont Ave, Suite 450, Bethesda, MD 20814, www.wfs.org.

Public service programs are regularly reported in the following periodicals:

pr reporter, PR Publishing Co., P.O. Box 600, Exeter, NH 03833.

PR News, 201 Seven Locks Road 300, Potomac, MD 20854.

Public Relations Quarterly, P.O. Box 311, Rhinebeck, NY 12572-0311.

CASES

CASE 8-1 VALUES ON A COLLISION COURSE

The process of obtaining lumber and wood pulp for domestic use, as well as for export, imposes a toll on the various environments in which wildlife can survive and flourish. Logging practices can threaten the existence of birds, fish, animals, and plant life. Single-minded timber practices are among the consequences of developing technologies that have resulted in the disappearance of 200 species of wildlife, and some 230 more are on endangered lists. Birds have made up a large part of the loss, as nearly 80 species have become extinct in 300 years in the United States.

The lumber industry plays a significant role in the fate of our forests and the wildlife that dwells within them. The U.S. Forest Service has been selling timber companies the rights to cut trees in old-growth forests at a rate of about 62,000 acres annually—under a directive from Congress to create jobs in timber regions. At this rate, most authorities estimate, the old-growth forests will be gone in 20 years.[1] Today, only 2.4 million acres of Pacific old-growth forests remain; a mere remnant of the 19 to 20 million acres of ancient forests that once existed in Washington and Oregon alone.[2] Old-growth forests consist not just of ancient standing trees, but of fallen trees, snags, massive decaying vegetation, and

numerous resident plant and animal species, many of which live nowhere else. More than 200 species of fish and wildlife flourish in ancient forest ecosystems, and more than 1,500 species of invertebrates can inhabit a single stand of ancient forest. One tree can be home to 100 separate plant species. These forests provide habitat for as many as two dozen threatened or endangered plant and animal species.[3]

Through most of our country's history there was little or no demand for logging in the national forests. Intensive logging began during World War II and increased over the years. After 30 years of extensive logging, the National Forest Management Act was adopted in 1976 in hopes of serving both environmentalist and industrial groups. But despite increasing concern over the environment, logging sales by the Forest Service continued, as authorized by Congress.

One endangered species that survives in Pacific Northwest ancient forests is the northern spotted owl (See Figure 8-2). Because of past habitat loss from logging and development, today's population of northern spotted owls represents a small fraction of the numbers that once existed. Studies show that the owl population continues to decline.

---

[1]Sy Montgomery, "Protective Legislation Filed," *Boston Globe*, July 6, 1992.
[2]Ibid. We thank the Wilderness Society for information provided for this case—though readers must realize this excellent public service organization does have a viewpoint on these issues.
[3]Taken from "Ancient Forests of the Pacific Northwest and the Northern Spotted Owl" provided by the Wilderness Society.

FIGURE 8-2 The northern spotted owl has been the centerpiece of extreme controversy in the Pacific Northwest.

(Courtesy of the Wilderness Society.)

Special interest groups that favor owl preservation, forest conservation, and timber production have found themselves head to head in the battle of "whose cause is most important." The thrust of this case study shows that *maintaining positive relationships through changing issues is difficult* and that *compromises don't necessarily result in a happy ending.* The best solution may be found in shifting the focus of the controversy to an activity that aims for a win-win resolution. It is a truism that we can't have the best of both worlds. There have to be choices and trade-offs.

The question is "Can one aspect of an issue oversimplify the issue in its entirety—therefore hindering the progress of achieving a positive resolution?"

In this particular study, the trade-off hinges on the disciplining of industrial practices. Specifically, how much restraint in normal timber logging operations is acceptable in order to help save the spotted owl, uphold the Endangered Species Act, conserve old-growth forest, and yet preserve timber industry jobs?

MORE THAN JUST OWL VERSUS LOGGING

The Wilderness Society and the lumber industry sought publicity to gain public awareness and support for their respective concerns and their solutions—both economic and environmental. These debates centered around the overruling of the Endangered Species Act that allowed logging on 13 tracts of land designated as spotted owl habitat in the Pacific Northwest.

In 1992 the Forest Service found itself the center of attention throughout the debates. Until this time, the Forest Service was rarely faced with the challenge of negotiating with two strongly opposed viewpoints. They had maintained a good reputation for their work with communities, but were now considered the bad guy by two significant parties. Environmental groups lobbied the Forest Service to protect the spotted owl and save the old forests, and the timber industry wanted it to preserve logging jobs. Naturally, the Forest Service aimed to accomplish both, but as it was to find out, a compromise doesn't always satisfy opposing parties.

ENDANGERED SPECIES ACT BECOMES ENDANGERED

In 1973, Congress passed the Endangered Species Act (ESA). The act prohibits anyone, with a few exceptions, from killing, capturing, or harming a listed endangered species. Federal agencies must ensure that any action they authorize, fund, or carry out will not jeopardize the continued existence of any endangered or threatened species. The act calls for the creation of "Recovery Plans" that help restore endangered species through conservation programs. The ESA, however, was first overruled in 1979 when Grayrock Dam was built in Wyoming—despite the threat to whooping cranes, a listed endangered species, on the Platte River in Nebraska. Environmental groups were outraged at the prospect of changing the law in order to satisfy ever-increasing human technologies.

In 1992, the Endangered Species Act was overruled a second time. The original Recovery Plan was designed to rescue the spotted owl from extinction by preserving 5.4 million acres of ancient forest but at the estimated cost of 32,000 logging jobs. The subsequent Preservation Plan, upheld by the Bush administration, allowed limited timber harvests in areas in Washington and Oregon populated by the northern spotted owl. This overruling aimed to preserve 17,000 logging jobs and maintain the economy in small towns dependent upon the timber industry; it would, however, result in the eventual extinction of the owl in those areas. The decision aimed to halt the dispute between the environmentalists and the logging industry by allowing limited timber harvests in certain old-growth forests while the government came up with a plan to protect the owl.[4]

The response to the Preservation Plan compromise was not favorable. Both parties felt cheated of their goals. The northern spotted owl would still reach extinction within decades, and the timber industry would still lose logging jobs. The one group

---

[4]"High Court Backs Some Logging in Spotted Owl Areas," *Boston Globe*, March 26, 1991.

that felt satisfied with the plan were those working in certain lumber companies. Some lumber companies profited from the spotted owl controversy because the curtailment of cutting raised the price of lumber and increased profits.[5]

OPPOSING PARTY STRATEGIES

To counteract opponents in these highly publicized debates, special interest groups initiated activities to gain awareness and public support for their causes.

The Wilderness Society

Founded in 1935, the Wilderness Society is the largest national conservation organization devoted primarily to the protection and management issues of public lands. The society employs a combination of advocacy, analysis, and public education in its campaigns to improve management of America's national parks, forests, wildlife refuges, and Bureau of Land Management lands.

One lobbying activity of the Wilderness Society during the debates included the unveiling of a series of computer-generated maps showing the heavy fragmentation of remaining ancient forest in 12 national forests of the Pacific Northwest. The maps were given to members of Congress in hopes of them using the data as the raw material to help forge a solution that would protect ancient forests and establish a sustainable regional economy. The maps showed that more than 75 percent of the remaining old growth found in the 12 national forests located in Oregon, Washington, and northern California is unprotected, and the remaining areas are in isolated and highly fragmented stands.[6]

Developing its thematic arguments, the Wilderness Society stated that lumber mill automation, improved labor productivity, and rising raw log exports—not the spotted owl—were the main contributors to the loss of 26,000 timber jobs since 1979. They also advised that a 25 percent reduction in raw log exports could provide the equivalent of between 4,500 and 5,000 U.S. timber jobs—jobs that would turn raw logs into finished products.

The Wilderness Society agreed that logging has a place, although diminished, in the future economy of the Pacific Northwest. The issue facing Congress was how to cushion an economic transition that would occur regardless of the fate of the spotted owl.

The Timber Industry

The timber industry argued that studies of old-growth forest measurements have been inconsistent. Environmental organizations and the Forest Service reported the existence of approximately 3,000 pairs of the spotted owl. The timber industry, however, reported that 4,018 owl pairs and 2,047 owl singles existed for a total population of over 10,000 northern spotted owls, well above the previously quoted figures. Research shows that owl population and reproduction are not correlated with the amount of suitable habitat within the study sites and that more environmental factors are likely involved.[7]

The timber industry argued that the loss of logging jobs in the timber industry in the 1980s was due to the economic recession and not to automation. They claimed that employment levels remained fairly constant since 1983.[8]

---

[5]Bill Richards, "Owl of All Things Help Weyerhauser Cash in on Timber," *The Wall Street Journal*, June 24, 1992.
[6]Taken from a news release distributed by the Wilderness Society, February 20, 1992.
[7]Ross Mickey, "The Northern Spotted Owl: The Rest of the Story," *Building Towards a Balanced Solution*, compiled by the Northwest Forest Resource Council, April 1993, p. 10.
[8]Charles Burley, "Employment and Mill Automation," Ibid, pp. 5–6.

Key arguments included that timber sales reductions would result in worker displacement, business closure, social service demands, and the many personal problems associated with unemployment.[9] Furthermore, restrictions on timber sales in the United States would only result in the logging of other forests worldwide.[10]

The U.S. Forest Service

The U.S. Forest Service is charged with maintaining national forests as a resource for the citizens of the United States. In the spotted owl controversy, it became clear that there was no longer any consensus or even tacit consent on which management programs could be developed.

To grasp the full implications of the spotted owl and timber industry debates, the Forest Service reviewed literature on the owl, heard presentations from scientists doing spotted owl research, considered the concerns of numerous interest groups, and conducted field trips in Washington, Oregon, and northern California to examine the owl's habitat. The Forest Service recognized that much of the attention directed toward the owl stems from a growing debate over managing old-growth forests on federal lands and from a concern about protecting biodiversity. They understood the larger issues, but kept to a mandate of developing a conservation strategy specifically for the spotted owl.

The U.S. Forest Task Force developed a conservation strategy. The outcome was a mapped network of Habitat Conservation Areas (HCAs) that would ensure a viable, well-distributed population of owls. Wherever possible, each HCA would contain a minimum of 20 pairs of owls with a maximum 12-mile distance between HCAs.

Logging and other forestry activities would cease within HCAs.

Though each interest group hoped that the Forest Service would support its cause, the Forest Service saw its role as an attempt to *maintain positive relationships* between the parties.

SEEKING CONSENSUS

On April 2, 1993, President Clinton held a Forest Conference in Portland, Oregon, to break the gridlock over federal forest management that had created confusion and controversy in the Pacific Northwest and northern California. The conference aimed to achieve economic diversification and new economic opportunities in the region.

The Forest Conference called for a plan that recognized both the importance of the timber industry to the economy of the Northwest and the need to preserve old-growth forests as an irreplaceable part of our national heritage.

Five principles gave guidelines to the three committees organized to put the plan together.

1. Remember the human and economic dimensions of the problem.
2. Protect the long-term health of our forests, wildlife, and waterways.
3. Make all efforts scientifically sound, ecologically credible, and legally responsible.
4. Produce predictable and sustainable levels of timber sales and nontimber resources that will not degrade or destroy the environment.
5. End the gridlock within all branches of the federal government and insist on collaboration, not confrontation.

---

[9]Robert Lee, "Effects of Federal Timber Sales Reductions on Workers, Families, Communities, and Social Service," Ibid., p. 1.
[10]Con Schallau, "Global Implications of Timber Supply Restrictions," Ibid, p. 8.

A NEW PLAN

The outcome of the conference, the Northwest Forest Protection Plan, calls for reducing timber harvests in the Pacific Northwest to an average of 1.2 billion board feet annually for 10 years. This value is approximately 75 percent less than the industry's harvest throughout the late 1980s. Restrictions would be placed on timber cutting around spotted owl nests on private lands. Logging would be limited in protected reserves established on federal lands.

Anticipating a loss of 6,000 timber industry jobs, a 5-year, $1.2 billion economic assistance package was designed to create 8,000 jobs and provide retraining opportunities. And finally, the plan asks Congress to encourage more domestic milling by eliminating a tax subsidy for timber companies that export raw logs.

The plan also calls for new methods of forestry. "New forestry" sets out to turn younger stands of trees into forests that look more like old growth in hopes of increasing habitat for old-growth species. Loggers practicing new forestry set out to reshape the woods, taking out the uniformity by randomly cutting trees to create meadows for wild grasses and leaving the downed trees to rot to promote ground vegetation.

CONTINUED OPPOSITION

Despite these efforts to appease the opposing parties, the Forest Protection Plan didn't receive favorable response. Environmental-

ists recognized the plan as a positive first step, but argued in favor of the creation of permanent reserves on 8.6 million acres in three states. Environmental scientists said that new forestry wouldn't work because forest systems contain complex details of biological, physical, and chemical processes that cannot be reproduced by humans.

The timber industry wanted the administration to permit higher harvests over a period of years. The target of 1.2 billion board feet would be a substantial loss, resulting in higher lumber prices, a slowdown in home purchases due to greater costs, and a stalled economic recovery. Those in the timber industry also disagreed with new forestry because it doesn't allow for logging. It is *no forestry*.

SHIFTING THE FOCUS

Despite the opposition, the Forest Protection Plan is attempting to solve the spotted owl controversy in the context of a broader strategy. It has *shifted the debate* from the protection of individual owls to the preservation of an ecosystem for various species. It recognizes that a long-term management plan for natural resources in the public domain can no longer be based on a single set of values but must take into account a broad diversity of national interests. ∎

QUESTIONS FOR DISCUSSION

1. The strategy of the Clinton administration was to shift the focus of the controversy from owl protection to the preservation of ecosystems for various species. Will this decision provide a long-term solution to the issue? Or will environmentalists and timber industry employees never reach a satisfying compromise? List the reasons either may result.

2. The Endangered Species Act appears to be easily overruled when economics takes a front seat on an issue. What would be the best way in terms of strategy and communications vehicles to go about revitalizing the act to deter future overrulings?

3. The introduction to this chapter offers four categories of public issues: latent, emerging, hot, and fallout. Where does wildlife preservation fit? How about endangered species? If not in the same category, why not?

4. Take the position of the environmental coalition, the timber industry, the Forest Service, or the Clinton administration and prepare a plan for communicating and gaining support for its messages and solutions.

CASE 8-2   REPRODUCTIVE RIGHTS AND THE ABORTION ISSUE

Abortion has ridden a high wave of debate and challenge ever since it was legalized in 1973 by the famous Supreme Court case *Roe v. Wade*. In the early 1990s the battle cries were heard once again as new laws were being proposed to restrict the *Roe v. Wade* ruling. In the summer of 1992, the nine justices on the Supreme Court were faced with a decision that could severely limit abortion rights and possibly overturn this precedential case, making abortion illegal again. So-called right-to-life groups and pro-choice groups stepped up their efforts to sway public opinion.

EXACTLY WHAT ARE THEY FIGHTING FOR?

With the legal decision of *Roe v. Wade* came a struggle in the Court of Public Opinion. Is there any hope for resolution of this issue? More than likely no. The two sides cannot even agree on what issue they are fighting over. On the pro-choice end of things women are fighting for the right of individual liberty and jurisdiction over their bodies. On the pro-life side are fetal life and the issue of murder. The division is great and possibly unbridgeable. Abortion has become a test of democratic decision making itself. Yet it is far from a new topic. It began eight decades ago with one woman's concerted efforts.

MARGARET SANGER'S CRUSADE

The 80-year effort of what we know today as Planned Parenthood International is an incredible story. Like many crusades, this movement started with one person of conviction and dedication: Margaret Sanger was born in 1883, the sixth child of 11 in a Corning, New York, family. Sanger, a frail, red-headed nurse, came to her rebellion at midlife, married, the mother of three, and taking the cure for tuberculosis (See Figure 8-3).

Working as a nurse on New York's Lower East Side, she was shocked at the circumstances of poverty and degradation surrounding countless attempts at self-induced abortion and the arrival of unwanted babies. Her actual decision to devote her life to changing these circumstances for the better came when she experienced the pleadings of a woman for help, and the death of a woman who had tried to abort her own pregnancy.

Sanger realized the immensity of the undertaking and the overpowering odds against her. To begin with, there was on the books the old Comstock Law of 1873 that made the distribution of contraceptive information a federal offense. Lurking in the wings was the sacred dogma of the Catholic Church. If these weren't enough, most people living in poverty, who needed help the most, had survival, not morality, or even education, as the highest priority in their lives.

Giving Birth to a Crusade

The launching of Margaret Sanger's personal crusade came in the form of several articles in *The Call*, then a leading radical paper, titled "What Every Woman Should Know" and "What Every Girl Should Know" with the theme of emancipating

FIGURE 8-3 Margaret Sanger, founder and crusader.

(Courtesy of The Sophia Smith Collection, Women's History Archive, Smith College, Northampton, MA 01063.)

women, via contraception, from sexual servitude.

That was in 1912. Sanger gave a name to her proposition: "birth control." Her philosophic approach was remarkably simple: *Every child born should be wanted by parents who are prepared to care for that child.* Otherwise, conception should be prevented. At the time, topics such as sexual relations and reproduction, or such personal matters as veneral disease, hernia, menstruation, or a spastic offspring, were not freely discussed. Margaret Sanger's initial problem was how to rally support for changing public attitudes on a matter that grown men would not discuss because the open discussion of it was regarded by most people as immoral. Worse, many influential people who might have helped her saw the birth control crusade as simply another aspect of the women's rights movement, which was itself very controversial.

Margaret Sanger could not wait for resolution of the unwanted-child problem as a rider on the political issue of suffrage for women. She decided to do her homework, and to that end, with her husband and three children, went to France, where family planning was an accepted part of life. There she queried doctors, midwives, druggists, and a great many women, collecting formulas, techniques, and devices.

On her return, she established a publication, *The Woman Rebel*, in which she attacked the Comstock Law. *Her strategy was to test the law by breaking it. The Woman Rebel* was promptly banned from the mails, and Sanger was threatened with a prison term and a $5,000 fine. She continued defiantly. The magazine became a best seller overnight.

The next move was the preparation of a pamphlet, *Family Limitation*, with undistributed quantities stored in various large cities for release *at the strategically right time.* When she was arraigned for *The Woman Rebel,* she fled to Canada and then to England; when she was 3 days out at sea, she wired her associates to distribute 100,000 copies of the pamphlet. Before long, that publication was translated into 13 languages.

Her flight to England was not to avoid the trial that would test the Comstock Law. Rather, the world events that were leading toward war made the timing seem wrong to Sanger.

This second tour of Europe, without her family, enabled her to study birth control practices in detail. She visited the world's first birth control clinic in Amsterdam and was coached in contraceptive techniques. (She personally thought that use of the diaphragm was the best practical approach.) During the sojourn abroad, she also came to perceive her own crusade more clearly and objectively in its relationship to a nation's overall health and economic well-being.

When she rejoined her children in New York, ready to face trial, she found that the public attitude had shifted noticeably in her favor. The term *birth control* had caught on. Her husband had become something of a hero for having served a 30-day jail term after being tricked into a violation of the Comstock Law. Comstock himself had died; the government had backed off, and now Sanger was free of the threat of imprisonment.

The Comstock Law, however, still had not had its courtroom test.

Sanger embarked on a lecture tour, then returned to establish, in a deprived section of Brooklyn, the first birth control clinic in this country. She found that, with the Comstock Law still on the books, no doctor wanted to run the clinic and expose his professional neck. So Sanger, with her sister and a friend, ran it. Within 10 days, they were arrested and carted off to jail. While free on bail, they reopened the clinic, were arrested again, and served 30 days in jail (See Figure 8-4).

When the case was subsequently brought to the court of appeals, the judge upheld the conviction but interpreted the law broadly to mean that a doctor could give contraceptive advice to a married woman if it was of benefit to her health.

Sanger took her courtroom triumph back on the road in a series of lectures and ran into some opposition that had previously been publicly silent—the Catholic Church. One zealous archbishop induced the New York police to close down one of her

FIGURE 8-4 Sanger and sister under arrest in 1916.

(Courtesy of Planned Parenthood Federation of America.)

meetings. This action proved to be a stroke of good fortune for Sanger, because the press interpreted the action as a breach of freedom of speech and came to her defense—despite prior descriptions of her by some papers as a "fanatic" and a "crackpot."

The headlines were largely favorable to the crusade. In the ensuing debate, according to accounts published later, the archbishop argued that birth control violated the laws of nature, and Sanger responded that celibacy for nuns and priests did the same.

This did not mean the end of opposition or any substantial long-term change in convictions about sexual relations and morality, for these had been deeply ingrained for centuries. Symptomatically, young men still hesitated to buy condoms, or "rubbers," as they were commonly called, from a female clerk in a drugstore. Purchases were made surreptitiously, in whispers, and the products carefully concealed from those, such as parents, who would disapprove because of the implication of prospective immoral conduct. Sexual relations involving the educated and affluent that resulted in venereal disease or in pregnancy among unmarried women, which might have been avoided by the use of condoms, were cause for the shaming of a whole family, even of a whole neighborhood.

Four years after she started, Margaret Sanger's campaign indisputably had the aura of a movement with the potential of a social revolution.

The Maturing of an International Movement

Important punctuations of the birth control crusade came at the structural and public affairs levels. The Voluntary Parenthood League had been organized while Sanger was in France, by a group interested mainly in the suffragette and feminist movement. Subsequently, birth control leagues were started in several cities and unified as the National Birth Control League—shortly

after, changed to the American Birth Control League—with Sanger as its president and with its own publication (See Figure 8-5). Then the Clinical Research Bureau opened. Scores of birth control clinics were opened. Distinguished doctors gave endorsement and counsel. Respected citizens of wealth and influence supported the activities openly and enthusiastically. Over the years, events gave increasing strength to the movement.

➤ 1935   Radio censorship of birth control was ended by NBC.

➤ 1936   The U.S. Circuit Court of Appeals ruled that physicians could distribute through the mails material "for the purpose of saving life or promoting the well-being of their patients."

➤ 1937   The American Medical Association endorsed birth control.

➤ 1942   The U.S. Public Health Service adopted a policy of giving requests from state health offices for financial support of birth control the same consideration and support given other state medical programs.

➤ 1950   President Eisenhower became honorary chairman of Planned Parenthood and the first of many presidents, including John Kennedy, a Catholic, to endorse and aid the program.

➤ 1960   The first contraceptive pill was introduced. One of its three developers is a Catholic, Dr. John Roch, showing how far professional and public attitudes had moved.

➤ 1966   The American Nurses Association recognized family planning education as part of

BIRTH CONTROL REVIEW

Edited by Margaret Sanger

NOVEMBER, 1923

UNWANTED BABIES

Official Organ of
THE AMERICAN BIRTH CONTROL LEAGUE, INC., 104 FIFTH AVENUE, NEW YORK CITY

FIGURE 8-5   The official house publication.

(Courtesy of Planned Parenthood Federation of America.)

the nurse's professional responsibility.

➤ 1967   Social Security amendments created a family planning project grants program and gave a mandate to state welfare departments for service to those of extremely low income.

➤ 1967   The United Nations Fund for Population Activities was established in response to resolutions in the General Assembly

and the Economics and Social Council.

➤ 1970   Congress adopted the Family Planning Services and Population Research Act.

➤ 1973   The Supreme Court ruled that abortion is a matter to be decided between a woman and her doctor in the well-publicized *Roe v. Wade* case.

➤ 1976   Congress enacted the Hyde Amendment, cutting off

federal (Medicaid) funds for abortions for poor women.

➤ 1981 President Reagan opposed abortion and asked that the 1973 ruling be overturned.

➤ 1992 President Bush comes under fire during the election for his endorsement of the global gag rule which prohibited staff (including doctors) in clinics receiving public funds from even discussing the abortion option. It is referred to as a global gag rule because it also prohibits any U.S. family planning funds from going to overseas groups that provide abortions or engage in abortion-related advocacy using their own privately raised, non-U.S. funds. Bill Clinton runs on a pro-choice platform and ascends to the presidency after 12 years of Republican politics.

➤ 1993 President Clinton overturns the global gag rule by executive order.

In 2000, however, the pro-choice atmosphere of the Clinton administration was replaced with a more moderate outlook with the election of President George W. Bush. One of his first acts as president was to issue an executive order in 2001 that reinstituted the global gag rule.

Along the way, the American Birth Control League had changed its name to the Planned Parenthood Federation of America (PPFA). In the meantime, world population trends had become an important concern to governments. Many argue that starvation and poverty can never be conquered so long as population is increasing so rapidly, particularly in Third World nations. Sharing

in this global concern the PPFA helped found the International Planned Parenthood Federation, under the dual leadership of Margaret Sanger and Lady Rama Rau of India.[1]

The Goals

Apart from contending with organized opposition, PPFA formulated a number of goals:

➤ Meet the unmet family planning needs among individuals who cannot afford them.

➤ Reduce unwanted pregnancies and births among teenagers.

➤ Preserve and ensure access to safe, legal abortion services and counseling for all women, regardless of age or ability to pay.

➤ Advance research in human reproduction.

➤ Reduce the unmet need for fertility regulations around the world.

Continuity and Leadership

Margaret Sanger, as rebel, missionary, and spokeswoman, did not let a false vanity get in the way of the crusade. When her efforts gained the momentum of a bandwagon, she was swept along in it. Over the years, she became almost eclipsed by the movement she had created. Whether this was good and wise is arguable. Some feel it would have been better if she had become the central dominant figure in the crusade, with a public image of heroic proportions comparable with that of Carrie Nation, Florence Nightingale, Gloria Steinem, Davy Crockett, Louis Pasteur, Martin Luther King, or Jonas Salk. We might in this study be dealing with the "Margaret Sanger Parenthood Plan," or

---

[1] A worthy subject for further study or a thesis is the effort and effectiveness of the United Nations Fund for Population Activities. Background material available 220 East 42nd St., New York, NY 10017.

perhaps "sangerization" (like pasteurization) or "the Sanger method" (like the Salk vaccine).

Never robust, Sanger worked tirelessly until her health dictated a move to Arizona, and rest. She died in 1965 at age 82.

ON THE OTHER SIDE OF THE ISSUE

The decision of the Supreme Court in 1973 guaranteed the right of a woman to end pregnancy up to the point at which the fetus was potentially able to live outside the womb. With this decision, the issue shifted. The posture of Catholic and other conservative religious dogma and the natural resistance of many poor and illiterate people had constituted a significant opposition and a political force to be reckoned with. After the court's decision, organized anti-abortion and pro-life groups joined importantly in the opposition.

Counterforces Gain Strength

The philosophy of pro-life groups has been that "all human life is precious and equally deserving of protection under the law. The philosophy embraces the human right of the preborn child to live at any time after conception."[2]

Initially, the pro-life groups sought to overturn the Supreme Court ruling, and then turned attention to the inhibiting of federal grants for abortions. There was some headway with Congress. An amendment to a Health, Education, and Welfare bill prohibited use of HEW funds except when the life of the mother would be endangered if the pregnancy continued.

Initially, the pro-life groups were not organized or marshaled into a dominant movement as Planned Parenthood was. As a result, several groups had to concentrate on "catch-up" efforts to identify a constituency. Publicity was the most readily available vehicle in the public arena. One of the impressive and unusual pieces of publicity was a special edition of the *National Right to Life News* reproducing an exhaustive series of articles in the *Chicago Sun Times* on "The Abortion Profiteers." One of the special events has been an annual March for Life in Washington, duplicated in several major cities. Another event has been the convention of the National Right to Life movement.

Among the vehicles in pro-life programs are:

➤ Counseling hotlines

➤ Speakers bureaus

➤ Informational videotapes

➤ Slide shows

➤ Annual banquets

➤ Volunteers trained in communications

➤ Pamphlets and brochures

➤ Espousal of Billings (rhythm) method of birth control

➤ Organized protests at abortion clinics

The latter, tragically, have often become violent under the influence of zealots.

The murder of Dr. David Gunn outside of a Pensacola, Florida, clinic in 1993 introduced an escalation of the violence and harassment directed at abortion clinics. Michael Griffin was convicted and sentenced to life in prison for the murder of Dr. Gunn. Since 1993, six other people with a connection to an abortion clinic have been murdered and hundreds of other crimes

---

[2]See Robert M. Byrn, "An American Tragedy: The Supreme Court on Abortion," *Fordham Law Review*, May 1973. See also John Lippis, *The Challenge to Be Pro-Life*, a booklet, National Right to Life Committee, 419 7th Street, N.W., Suite 500, Washington, DC 20004.

Incidents of Violence & Disruption Against Abortion Providers in the United States and Canada

Violence	1977–85	1986	1987	1988	1989	1990	1991	1992	1993	1994	1995	1996	1997	1998	1999	2000	2001	TOTAL
Murder[1]	0	0	0	0	0	0	0	0	1	4	0	0	0	2	0	0	0	7
Attempted Murder	0	0	0	0	0	0	2	0	1	8	1	1	2	1	0	1	0	17
Bombing[1]	21	3	0	0	1	1	1	0	1	1	1	2	6	1	1	0	0	40
Arson[1]	36	7	8	5	8	10	8	19	12	11	14	3	8	4	8	2	0	163
Attempted Bomb/Arson[1]	21	4	7	3	2	3	1	13	7	3	1	4	2	5	1	3	2	82
Invasion	149	53	14	6	25	19	29	26	24	2	4	0	7	5	3	4	0	370
Vandalism	119	43	29	29	24	26	44	116	113	42	31	29	105	46	63	56	11	926
Trespassing	0	0	0	0	0	0	0	0	0	0	0	0	0	0	193	81	12	286
Butyric Acid Attacks	0	0	0	0	0	0	0	57	15	8	0	1	0	19	0	0	0	100
Anthrax Threats	0	0	0	0	0	0	0	0	0	0	0	0	0	12	35	30	0	77
Assault & Battery	25	11	5	5	12	6	6	9	9	7	2	1	9	4	2	7	2	122
Death Threats	49	7	5	4	5	7	3	8	78	59	41	13	11	25	13	9	1	338
Kidnapping	2	0	0	0	0	0	0	0	0	0	0	0	0	1	0	0	0	3
Burglary	7	5	7	1	0	2	1	5	3	3	3	6	6	6	4	5	2	66
Stalking[2]	0	0	0	0	0	0	0	0	188	22	61	52	67	13	13	17	1	434
TOTAL	429	133	75	53	77	74	95	253	452	170	159	112	223	144	336	215	31	3031
Disruption																		
Hate Mail/Harassing Calls	58	53	32	19	30	21	142	469	628	381	255	605	2829	915	1646	1011	43	9137
Bomb Threats	116	51	28	21	21	11	15	12	22	14	41	13	79	31	39	20	8	542
Picketing	406	141	77	151	72	45	292	2898	2279	1407	1356	3932	7518	8402	8727	8478	1336	47517
TOTAL	580	245	137	191	123	77	449	3379	2929	1802	1652	4550	10426	9348	10412	9509	1387	57196
Clinic Blockades																		
Number of Incidents	0	0	2	182	201	34	41	83	66	25	5	7	25	2	3	4	0	680
Number of Arrests[3]	0	0	290	11732	12358	1363	3885	2580	1236	217	54	65	29	16	5	0	0	33830

All numbers represent incidents reported to or obtained by NAF. Actual incidents are likely much higher. Tabulation of trespassing incidents began in 1999.
1. Incidents recorded are those classified as such by the appropriate law enforcement agency. Incidents that were ruled inconclusive or accidental are not included.
2. Stalking is defined as the persistent following, threatening, and harassing of an abortion provider, staff member, or patient *away from* the clinic. Tabulation of stalking incidents began in 1993.
3. The "number of arrests" represents the total number of arrests, not the total number of *persons* arrested. Many blockaders are arrested multiple times.

FIGURE 8-6 NAF Violence and Disruption Statistics

Source: National Abortion Federation Web site, www.prochoice.org (April 2001).

(including arson, vandalism, and death threats) have been perpetrated against numerous clinics, and their employees and patients (See Figure 8-6). However, the use of blockades employed by many antiabortion groups has been greatly reduced by the passage of the Freedom of Access to Clinic Entrances Act in 1994.

Like every other subject connected to the abortion issue, there is disagreement over who is behind the acts of violence. Many pro-choice supporters blame these criminal acts on the pro-life movements directly or on individuals who are motivated by pro-life rhetoric. Pro-life groups maintain they are not connected to these violent acts because the perpetrators have no regard for human life.

AN AREA FOR COMPROMISE?

Intermediaries for pro-life and pro-choice groups have sought a basis for compromise and understanding, if not total reconciliation. In the main notable occasion, the National Organization for Women (NOW) issued invitations to 20 pro-life and 20 pro-choice organizations to a joint conference on abortion. In response, the president of the National Right to Life Committee called publicly for a moratorium on abortions prior to the meeting.

When the conference convened, most of the pro-choice groups had sent representatives. About half of the pro-life groups had. Others, including National Right to Life, had sent observers. Hope for meaningful dialogue on this occasion was destroyed, however, when the conference was disrupted by the dramatic and unexpected display of a 5-month-old aborted fetus.

One trained observer of the conference, speculating on the future prospects, said that both sides had been friendly, conciliatory, and respectful to each other, but after the disruption, "distrust had crept in."

THE MAKINGS OF A STAND-OFF

The issue between pro-life and pro-choice groups has been increasingly narrowed to the matter of abortions. Inevitably it has taken on major legal aspects. Along with the question of prayer in schools and the separation of church and state, it has fueled political rhetoric.[3] The issue is growing more and more political—one of the first things candidates are asked about is where they stand on abortion.

There was a flurry of activity in 1983–1984, kicked off by the tenth anniversary of the Supreme Court ruling. Officials in the Department of Health and Human Services (formerly HEW) proposed that parents be notified when their daughters sought birth control devices from government-aided clinics. This proposal, dubbed the "squeal rule," was headed off or put in limbo by a federal judge. It was subsequently challenged by the American Civil Liberties Union. An amendment to the Constitution, sponsored by Sen. Orin Hatch, was defeated. Some effort was made to make the issue an aspect of the Equal Rights Amendment movement. With states and localities involved, and a national election pending in 1984, politicians were loath to come down decisively on the issue.

Meanwhile, Planned Parenthood added more and more counseling clinics, some providing referrals or abortion services. Pro-life groups, principally the Christian Action

---

[3]For added background on the issue, see such early articles as "Ecumenical War Over Abortion," *Time*, January 29, 1979; *A Larger Mission*, Planned Parenthood Federation, 810 Seventh Avenue, New York, NY 10019; *The Right to Choose*, a reprint, Zero Population Growth, 1400 16th Street, N.W., Suite 320, Washington, DC 20036; "The Battle over Abortion," *Time*, April 6, 1981, a cover story, and "Holding Firm on Abortion," *Time*, June 27, 1983.

Council (Birthright) and Pearson Institute, sought to break the deadlock by a combination of violent and peaceful campaigns. There were incidents of clinic bombing and arson. Radical groups such as Operation Rescue orchestrated violent protests outside abortion clinics. As mentioned, a pro-life zealot killed a Florida abortionist on his way into the clinic where he worked. These extreme acts have backfired in public opinion. On the peaceful side, there was the establishment of counseling centers for pregnant women. Presumably, the help given would discourage women from having abortions as the only or preferable alternative. Pro-life groups responded with picketing and labeling the counseling as deceptive (see Figure 8-7).

Planned Parenthood increasingly has gone to Congress or court to defend its gains. It vehemently opposed the nomination of Judge Bork to the Supreme Court, challenged the Agency for International Development for imposing conditions on the receipt of family planning funds, and brought suit against the Secretary of Health and Human Services over its eligibility for federal funds. Other challenges have been addressing state restrictions on abortion in the Supreme Court. In 1992, Pennsylvania passed a law that required women to wait 24 hours after requesting an abortion to have the procedure. Mississippi passed a consent law that required girls under the age of 18 to acquire parental permission for abortions or prove to a judge that it is not in their best interest to notify their parents.

By the end of the 1980s, Planned Parenthood had 190 affiliates in the United States, serving some 2.5 million clients who made a total of nearly 4 million visits to the 816 clinic centers. Some 100,000 abortions and vasectomies were performed, but the majority received laboratory tests, diagnosis for pregnancy, and whatever counsel seemed in order for each person. Planned Parenthood operated on a budget approaching $500 million, making it the third largest international service organization after the United Nations and the Red Cross. Public relations activities were headed by a vice president for communications.

WE'RE BACK WHERE THE CASE STARTED

Abortion has retained its label as a "hot" issue because it continues to be a subject of current debate and has become a politicized issue. When George W. Bush was inaugurated as president in 2001, interest groups on both sides of the abortion issue put their supporters on alert because of the likelihood that President Bush will have the opportunity to nominate two or three appointees to the Supreme Court. Since the president is viewed as a conservative and is anti-choice, each side has a great interest in who will fill a vacancy on the Supreme Court and how that new justice will aid in either overturning or retaining the *Roe v. Wade* decision.[4]

As of early 2002, three of the current Supreme Court justices were over 70 years of age, so it is likely there will be new appointees during the Bush administration when one or more justices retire. For the pro-choice supporters, the fear is that two or three new conservative justices could result in *Roe* being overturned and the fight for

---

[4]Throughout the 1990s, the Supreme Court handed down numerous decisions concerning issues that affect reproductive rights. The Court upheld the 1992 Pennsylvania statute noted on this page after a challenge brought by Planned Parenthood of Southeastern Pennsylvania. Most of the other decisions handed down by the Court concerned "buffer zones" created around health clinics that provide abortions. The Court ruled that these zones do not infringe on the First Amendment rights of anti-abortion protesters as the creation of the zones do not regulate their speech in any way.

FIGURE 8-7 Pro-life groups use emotion-based techniques to make a point and to attract media attention.

(Courtesy of San Diego Union-Tribune Publishing Co. Photo by John Gibbons and Joe Holly.)

reproductive rights would be pushed back decades. In March 2001, President Bush greatly limited the role the American Bar Association (ABA) plays in the review of judicial nominees. Since the Eisenhower administration, the ABA had reviewed the professional qualifications of nominees before any candidates were announced and provided the White House with recommendations. Conservatives have frequently disagreed with the ABA's recommendations, most recently during the unsuccessful nomination of Robert Bork in 1987. Now, the Bush administration will not provide the

ABA with the names of candidates prior to their nomination. This change in the judicial review process also has pro-choice proponents concerned.

In preparation for a future struggle over the appointment of new Supreme Court justices, pro-life and pro-choice interest groups are organizing and developing strategies to promote their viewpoints. While a mass mailing seeking funding and support is still a tried and true method of reaching people, most organizations are now posting their positions on their Web sites. For example, both the National Right to Life Committee and the National Abortion and Reproduc-

tive Rights Action League (NARAL) have addressed the future of *Roe* under the Bush administration on their Web sites. Planned Parenthood has a special section on their Web site entitled "Roe v. Bush.com."

Pro-choice and pro-life groups are also sending a message to the president as well as to their supporters. Each group hopes that *its* voice will influence the president's selection for a new justice. However, since the abortion issue continues to be so volatile, it is likely that a lengthy battle over any nominee will keep a new vacancy open for some time. ■

QUESTIONS FOR DISCUSSION

1. In getting her crusade started, Margaret Sanger had to rely on the printed word and limited personal contacts. There was no radio or television. Her strategy was to educate, to test laws by breaking them, and to arouse sympathy by being the underdog. If she started out today, and you were her adviser, what would you recommend as strategy, message, and communication vehicles?

2. The Right to Life movement has concentrated heavily on the rights of an unborn fetus and the question of abortion. In the process, that emphasis may tend to put the two main divisions of Christianity, Catholics and Protestants, in more of a head-to-head antagonism than is comfortable for most followers of both segments. Can you envision some points of common interest where combined effort might foster increased adjustment and reconciliation without abridging the laws or sacraments of either church? Apparently, little kids

sharing a neighborhood can attain this goal, so why not adults? Consider such common interests as poverty in America amidst plenty, and the inability of 60 million Americans to read well enough to understand an explanation of the rhythm method, or to understand a map giving the location of a counseling center, or to write well enough to fill out a driver's license application. How might some avenues of common effort be tested using communications staff and volunteers?

3. Fear of contracting AIDS has been credited with the increased use of condoms, with less sexual promiscuity among single people, and with greater fidelity among married couples. Does this trend suggest that in almost all matters a threat to our physical well-being is more persuasive than an appeal to our conscience, intelligence, or character? If that is not safe ground for a generalization, what are some exceptions?

CASE 8-3 TAKE YOUR CHOICE—TOBACCO OR HEALTH

Health issues have gone public the past several decades. Anything that may jeopardize health has come under fire. One issue that has ridden a high wave of interest and debate is the question of whether smoking endangers health—of the smoker and of those around that smoker. The extent of the role that the government plays in the tobacco industry by enacting laws and regulation has also created controversy. When does governmental regulation become an infringement on personal rights? This is not a phenomenon unique to tobacco products. Any product or service linked to a potential cause of cancer, heart disease, or any other ailment has faced increasing challenges. Ask the people who made asbestos or cyclamate sugar substitute or who operate tanning studios.

HISTORICAL BACKGROUND

The smoking of tobacco occurred long before Christopher Columbus arrived in the New World and brought it back to Europe. Native Americans had been smoking the plant for centuries. Not until the development of the cigarette-rolling machine in 1881, however, did smoking gain widespread usage.

From the 1870s until the 1900s, smoking and the use of tobacco in other forms were frowned on socially as objectionable masculine habits, particularly in the presence of ladies. Although this habit was merely looked down upon for men it was totally unacceptable for women. Nevertheless, around the turn of the century some women began smoking, although many were deterred from beginning the habit by anti-cigarette crusades and bans. Railroad companies forbade women to smoke on trains. Several cities, including New York, had ordinances that prohibited women from smoking in public places.

By the 1920s, the number of women smoking had increased noticeably, and advertisers clamored to claim a share of this potentially massive market. The first advertisement showing a woman smoking appeared in 1919, but it was not until 1927 that advertising was aimed on a large scale toward women (See Figure 8-8).

In 1927, George Washington Hill, colorful and hard-driving head of the American Tobacco Company, began using the slogan "Reach for a Lucky Instead of a Sweet" to promote his Lucky Strike cigarettes. This advertisement appealed to women by indicating that they could find some sort of oral gratification and still keep their figure.

The canny Hill saw that change of societal acceptance of smoking for women needed special efforts from others to reinforce his advertising. He called in public relations counsel Edward L. Bernays for his ideas on how to increase sales among women. He also hired publicists Ivy Lee and Harry Bruno for their ideas on other problems. And he selected advertising pioneer Albert Lasker to handle his Lucky Strike advertising. Asked later why he had hired so many public relations experts, he was reported to have said "to keep my competitors from hiring them."

Bernays sought the opinion of a psychoanalyst to learn what rewards women might see in cigarettes. This was quick, inexpensive fact-finding. Dr. A. A. Brill said women most likely regarded cigarettes as symbols of freedom. Cigarettes could be perceived as torches of freedom, symbols protesting man's inhumanity toward women, symbols of determination to be emancipated. Moreover, he told Bernays, "Smoking is a sublimation of oral eroticism; holding a cigarette in the mouth excites the oral zones."

DRAMATIZING THE SYMBOLS

One of Bernay's projects to erode the social taboo against women smoking in public was to arrange for 10 debutantes of social prominence to join the annual parade of Easter Sunday fashion finery down New York's Fifth Avenue. As they strolled, they "lighted the torches of freedom" and proceeded to walk along with cigarettes in hand. They puffed and posed for the New York newspaper photographers and reporters who had been alerted by Bernays and seized the event for front-page coverage. This one symbolic event echoed across the media nationally, breaking the ice for general acceptance of smoking in public by women.

Fifty years later, Bernays was frequently asked about his efforts to get women smoking. He would respond that in the 1920s he had no knowledge of any link between smoking and lung cancer. Had he been aware, he said, he would have refused to work for Hill.

SURGEON GENERAL GETS INTO THE ACT

As government and private research agencies learned more about carcinogenic agents, and their findings were passed on to the public by the media, opposition to smoking, regardless of sex, grew and took on organized forms under the aegis of the American Cancer Society and other groups. The lines were drawn, and the battle for public support began. On one side was the tobacco industry and those dependent on it economically. On the other were all those engaged in public health and life extension services, specifically those involved in the prevention and control of cancer.

A major event came in 1964 when the U.S. Surgeon General announced that cigarette smoking was definitely linked to cancer, and subsequently a warning message was required on any cigarette package or advertisement.

A PROGRAM FOR OPPONENTS

Even as tobacco growers were granted governmental subsidies, the Department of Health and Human Services (HHS)[1] was distributing information about the hazards of smoking and lobbying for laws restricting the use and the advertising of cigarettes. In conjunction with the American Cancer Society, American Heart Association, and American Lung Association, the department has taken a proactive stance involving public education, regulation, and research backed by higher budgets, more aggressive efforts (advocacy), and a renewed commitment by all. The main elements in the antismoking program have been:

➤ Asking major broadcasting networks to increase antismoking public service announcements.

➤ Development of education programs in schools, aimed at preventing teenagers from starting to smoke.

➤ Banning smoking originally in HHS buildings and then extending the ban to the 10,000 or more other federal buildings, local governmental structures, and eventually to most public buildings.

➤ Examining the federal policy on cigarette taxes (the tax, unchanged from 1951, was doubled in 1982 and is now the target of revenue raisers every time funds are needed).

➤ Asking insurance companies to offer premium discounts to nonsmokers.

➤ Ordering the Food and Drug Administration (FDA) to have drug manufacturers label products indicated by research to have higher risks for smokers, especially birth control pills.

ON THE OTHER SIDE

The natural coalition of forces for opposing efforts to control and restrict the smoking of tobacco starts with those whose livelihoods and economic well-being are tied to the raw product. This group includes growers and their employees, communities dependent on tobacco as an agricultural commodity, processors of it, and maufacturers of cigarettes and cigars. In addition, those endeavors that supply the various substances, tools, and vehicles needed—from planting and movement of goods to market to sales promotion—all have a vested interest. This large array of interests has the funding to mount effective communications programs and to lobby government officials. And of course, there also are the millions who smoke and want to continue to do so.

---

[1]See the Department of Health and Human Services Fact Sheet on preventing disease and death from smoking on its Web site (www.hhs.gov).

Organized opposition has come mainly from the Tobacco Institute, a nonprofit, noncommercial wing established by the 11 major tobacco companies in the United States in 1958. For quite a few years, the Tobacco Institute[2] took a defensive, circle-the-wagons, reactive stance. In more recent times, the stance has become more proactive, with the core claim being that smoking is a civil liberty, a matter of free choice, a right that the government is trying to infringe upon. Its slogan has been "Freedom of choice is the best choice." Early in the 1980s, advertisements with that message appeared in national magazines with two short essays that smokers and nonsmokers can live together without need for govern-

ment intervention (See Figure 8-9). This has been a continuing theme in defense of smoking.

The Institute has stated its case in the past as:

➤ Tobacco smoke is not a major source of air pollution.

➤ People are not allergic to tobacco smoke.

➤ Nonsmokers in a smoke-filled room do not inhale significant amounts of smoke.

➤ A report by the Surgeon General states that carbon monoxide in a smoke-filled room exceeds permissible levels, but such condi-

FIGURE 8-9   Example of Tobacco Institute approaches to creation of opportunities to tell the industry's side of the story.

(Courtesy of the Tobacco Institute.)

---

[2]The Tobacco Institute was closed down as part of the Master Settlement Agreement reached in 1998 between tobacco companies and 46 state attorneys general.

tions would rarely be found in real life.

➤ Antismoking efforts have increased lately, but the evidence against smoking is not increasing.

➤ Thorough review of the world's scientific literature indicates that smoke is not a significant health hazard to the nonsmoker.

➤ Common courtesy, rather than laws, should determine non-smokers' rights.

BATTLE AND TESTING GROUNDS

The right of each individual to decide for himself or herself has been the platform on which the tobacco interests have taken their stand against state or local propositions to control or restrict smoking. Today many cities have ordinances that prohibit smoking in certain public areas. Perhaps the most notable early example was the passage of an ordinance by the city of San Francisco in 1983 requiring employers to provide separate areas for workers who smoke. The tobacco industry gathered 30,000 signatures on a petition, forcing the issue onto a major election ballot. The antismoking groups prevailed in the election, although the tobacco industry spent nearly 10 times more on its campaign.

The battle against smoking has not only been waged by the government in passing public ordinances. Now it is also an important factor in the workplace. Some recent statistics provided by the American Lung Association Web site (www.lungusa.org) reveal how attitudes about smoking in the workplace, and in public, have changed:

➤ 95 percent of Americans, both smokers and nonsmokers, believe companies should either ban smoking totally or restrict it to separately ventilated areas.

➤ As of the late 1990s, more than 1,238 states laws had been enacted to address tobacco-control issues. Forty-six states and the District of Columbia have some restriction on smoking in public places. Of these states, 46 restrict smoking in government workplaces and 21 have extended those limitations to private sector workplaces.

➤ In August 1997, President Clinton signed an executive order requiring federal buildings to become smoke-free.

Many employers will not hire smokers because of their higher health risk and greater amount of days lost from work. Some companies have mandated that their employees smoke neither at work nor at home. Turner Broadcasting in Atlanta has declined to hire smokers since 1988. Controversy has arisen over what control an employer can have over an employee's private life. Where does smart hiring decisions end and workplace discrimination begin? Does the right to privacy become blurred if employees participate in an activity that will raise their health costs in the future? Statistics have indicated that smoking costs the nation $97 billion per year in healthcare costs and lost productivity. These issues and many more difficult questions will have to be addressed in the coming years.

ISSUES THAT JUST WON'T DIE

Beginning in 1981, the effect of passive smoke was magnified by research findings that indicated increased risk of lung cancer in nonsmokers exposed to it, which spurred others to join in the antismoking fight. The Environmental Protection Agency has also substantiated that secondhand smoke causes cancer. These pronouncements substantially enlarged the potential constituency for organized opposition to smoking. Antismoking groups gained momentum and pushed further for legislation in regulating and restricting smoking. Then in 1992, the EPA issued its warning against secondhand smoke and its dangers to nonsmokers. Since that time many major cities such as Los Angeles and Denver have passed public antismoking laws.

Late in 1984, Congress passed a bill requiring stronger warnings of health hazards on cigarette packages. Also in the legislative arena during the mid-1980s were bills introduced by antismoking groups that prohibited advertising of tobacco products on the grounds that advertisements lure nonsmokers, especially youngsters, into tobacco use. The industry, allied with civil rights and media organizations, countered with Constitutional arguments about free speech and evidence that advertising affects brand choices among smokers but does not increase the total volume. Although the bills that required a total ban on tobacco advertising failed, new issues continue to emerge that push tobacco advertising regulation back into the legislative arena. Recent controversy about Joe Camel, the cartoon character used to advertise Camel cigarettes, and its possible appeal to adolescents and even preschoolers, has caused the industry to reexamine its position.

In the media coverage, when the American Medical Association got ready to call for a ban on all cigarette advertising, a major metropolitan daily newspaper editorialized that it was understandable to ban broadcast tobacco advertising in 1971 on the grounds that the airwaves are considered part of the public domain. However, the editorial contended, newsprint media are privately owned and the ban would clearly abrogate First Amendment rights. Its point:

If a product is legal to sell, it should be legal to advertise. However, that editorial failed to mention that if advertising were banned from the electronic media and not newsprint media, they would stand to gain *all* the advertising dollars of the tobacco industry. The fact remains that cigarettes are the most heavily advertised products in all of the United States. Every minute, tobacco companies spend over $5,000 on advertising and promotion of their products.[3]

The levy of excise tax is another difficult issue. Antismoking groups favor increases to a point that smoking simply wouldn't be worth the dollar cost and might not be affordable to youngsters. The tobacco industry, with strong support from labor and some minority organizations, holds that excise taxes are regressive, taking a greater proportion from low-income families than from those in higher brackets.

The tobacco industry has conducted campaigns in states that propose tax hikes on cigarettes. In 1992, a Massachusetts health coalition initiated a petition that would put a proposal on the ballot to increase the tax by 25 cents. The petition also included that the increased revenue from the excise tax, a proposed $130 million, would be earmarked for health education and the creation of smoking cessation programs for adults.

The Committee Against Unfair Taxes, a tobacco-industry-financed group, issued a legal challenge to the petition drive, stating that this increase in tax pinpointed only one part of the public in order to pay for these programs. Furthermore, they protested that there was no legal restriction stated in the petition that indicated exactly how the state would spend the extra revenue.

While this controversy rages on, some of the major tobacco companies have taken

---

[3]Cited from a brochure from the American Lung Association, "Facts About . . . Cigarette Smoking," dated November 1990.

CARTOONS AND CIGARETTES: WHO'S THE AUDIENCE?

The controversy about using cartoon characters to sell a potentially harmful product such as cigarettes became a hotly debated issue in late 1991. The *Journal of the American Medical Association* devoted an issue to studies that researched the impact of smoking and its products on society. Of interest to many antismoking groups was one study that indicated that children as young as 3 or 4 years old could recognize the character Joe Camel (See Figure 8-10), the cartoon logo for Camel cigarettes. In this study of brand recognition, the kids identified Joe Camel more than any other popular logo, such as those for NBC, Apple, and Cheerios.

From this study the researchers concluded that this type of advertising lures children to smoke by utilizing pleasing images to entice them and demanded the immediate discontinuation of the ad campaign. RJR Nabisco, the manufacturer of Camel cigarettes, countered this accusation by stating that brand recognition does not necessarily mean that the children will begin smoking and cited its own research statistics that indicate that the average age of a Camel smoker is 18 to 24. In addition, RJR Nabisco was effective in discrediting the study's main researcher, Dr. Joseph DiFranza. In court, RJR Nabisco produced evidence that indicated that DiFranza had decided he wanted to prove the detrimental effect cigarette advertising has on children *before* he conducted the study.

This controversy has further illuminated the issue of whether allowing cigarette companies to advertise their products is really a freedom of speech issue — or an opportunity to entice children to begin a harmful habit.

FIGURE 8-10   In 1999, the use of the Joe Camel image was discontinued as part of the Master Settlement Agreement.

(Courtesy of RJR Nabisco.)

steps to protect their shareholders, and perhaps other stakeholders, by diversifying their product mix. As examples, Phillip Morris acquired General Foods, a $5.6 billion transaction. R.J. Reynolds put up $5 billion for Nabisco. Then in 1988 RJR Nabisco was taken over for a whopping $25 billion by Kohlberg, Kravis, Roberts Co., corporate buyout specialists, proving, if nothing else, that there was still money to be made one way or another in tobacco.

Incongruously to some analysts of the tobacco industry, the tone of its promotional literature the past few years has been aggressive. However, many times it is seen working behind the scenes in promoting scientific research that casts doubt on the effects of smoking and championing individual rights causes to question the effectiveness of smoking laws. Then, on occasion, public statements by spokespersons have been moderate if not conciliatory. One observer of the industry has suggested that the moderated tone reflects the vulnerability of the industry in the liability suits being brought against it.

On the antismoking side, the Coalition on Smoking OR Health (an alliance of the American Heart Association, American Lung Association, and the American Cancer Society) has increased its efforts, encouraged, no doubt, when Congress passed a law banning smoking on any domestic commercial airline flight. It didn't hurt matters for them, either, when the EPA issued its warning against secondhand smoke. They have taken this new evidence and used it to emphasize that smoking is not just an event that affects the smoker. Assistant Surgeon General John Duffy has stated that "there is no such thing as a nonsmoker in America today. As long as we have to live and work around smokers, we must accept some of the risks of smoking."[4]

The prime source of programmed antismoking activity continues to be the American Cancer Society. It directs the annual Great American Smokeout, a national event in which smokers all quit on the same day (See Problem 8-A). The Society offers a promotion guide for that event. It also has available a news media handbook, *Smoke Signals*, with a variety of ideas and instructions for groups wanting to tell the story in news outlets (See Figure 8-11).

TOBACCO DEBATE UPDATE

Since the 1992 Supreme Court ruling for Rose Cipollone's family (Ms. Cipollone died in 1984), it has been an uphill battle for the tobacco industry. Health issues, legal comments, and public opinion have all turned against the industry. The war is just about over, and the health forces are prevailing. Tobacco companies are left to fight over 22 percent of the American public still smoking while pushing diversification and overseas expansion. The following is a summary of the principal disputes faced by the major tobacco companies in recent years.

In the courts, there have been huge monetary judgments against the major tobacco companies. Additionally, they are facing a lawsuit filed against them in 1999 by the United States Department of Justice.

➤ In June 2001, a Los Angeles jury found the Philip Morris Company liable for the lung cancer killing the plaintiff (*Richard Boeken v. Philip Morris, Inc.*) in the case and ordered the company to pay $3 billion in punitive damages. As

---

[4]The Need for a Safe, Healthy, and Smoke-Free Workplace, *World Smoking and Health*, American Cancer Society, Summer 1990, p. 3.

In one of the most famous liability suits, Rose Cipollone brought suit against three different cigarette companies, citing them as liable for her smoking-related illness. This suit paved the way for many more cigarette maker liability lawsuits when her case was brought before the Supreme Court in 1992. Their ruling stated that cigarette manufacturers may be sued if they have allegedly deceived the public about the dangers of smoking. The industry was claiming that the warning labels on the packages were enough to shield them against any personal injury suits.

The ruling, however, does not make it easy for a smoker to prove the liability of the cigarette manufacturer. The plaintiff must "convince juries that smokers were not primarily at fault for starting and continuing their habit because they relied on industry misrepresentations."[5] The depiction of healthy people in cigarette advertisements is not enough to prove that the industry has been deceptive.

[5]James H. Rubin, "Cigarette Makers Can be Sued," *Boston Globe*, June 25, 1992, pp. 1–4.

FIGURE 8-11 Illustration in *Smoke Signals* booklet dramatizes smoking as the major killer among dreaded causes of death.

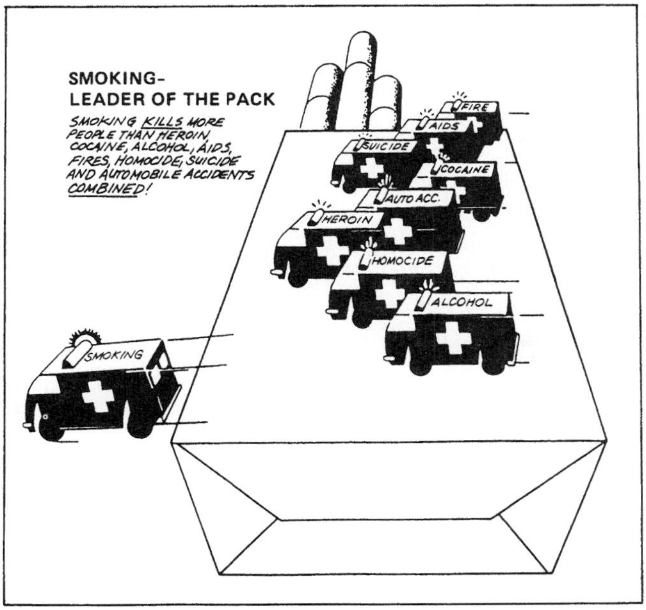

(Courtesy of the American Cancer Society.)

in most cases the industry loses, it will be appealed. According to the Tobacco Control Resource Center, Inc. and The Tobacco Products Liability Project of Northeastern University School of Law Web site (www.tobacco.neu.edu), this verdict was the seventh defeat for the tobacco industry over the last 23 jury verdicts on individual claims dating back to February 1999.

➤ In July 2000, in the first class action suit brought on behalf of smokers, the five major cigarette makers—Philip Morris, Lorillard, the Liggett Group, R.J. Reynolds Tobacco Company, and Brown & Williamson Tobacco Corporation—were ordered by a Florida jury to pay a record $145 billion in compensatory and punitive damages. This is known as the Engle case.

➤ The lawsuit filed by the Justice Department in 1999 "alleges that tobacco companies engaged in a 45-year pattern of false and misleading statements about the health effects of their products and tried to cover up information that contradicted their marketing."[6] The suit seeks more than $100 billion in damages and is expected to go to court in 2003.

The Master Settlement Agreement (MSA), reached in November 1998 between the tobacco companies and the state attorneys general of 46 states, puts numerous restrictions on the tobacco industry. Some the regulations in the MSA include:

➤ Restrictions on outdoor advertising, including billboards

➤ Beginning in May 1999, there are restrictions on the types of cartoons that can be used in the marketing of tobacco; as a result, the use of the Joe Camel image was discontinued

➤ The tobacco industry is prohibited from directing its advertising at the youth market

➤ The dissolution of the Tobacco Institute and the Council on Tobacco Research

The apparent cooperation of the tobacco industry in the Master Settlement Agreement was actually part of a resolution to a lawsuit brought by the state of Minnesota against the cigarette producers. However, according to an article in *Advertising Age* magazine, the tobacco industry has already violated the Agreement by continuing to spend millions of dollars targeting the youth market.[7]

In July 1998, President Clinton issued an executive memorandum that the tobacco industry release documents that had historically been concealed from the public. There are now numerous Web sites providing tobacco industry documents. The increase of governmental intervention in the operations of tobacco companies is likely a result, in part, of the release of information about the industry's practices to the public.

One of the few places the tobacco companies can still present their explanation of the issues—outside of the courtroom—is on their corporate Web sites. Some of the points that are advocated on most of the company Web sites are:

---

[6]*Washington Post*, April 26, 2001, p. A2.
[7]*Advertising Age*, February 5, 2001, p. 18.

➤ Smoking is a matter of choice.

➤ Cigarettes are a legal product.

➤ Through continued production and research, a safer cigarette may be created.

➤ Stopping the production of tobacco products would have a great economic impact on the industry's employees and their families and others in tobacco-related jobs.

The corporate Web sites also include tips for quitting smoking, descriptions of their youth smoking prevention programs, and information on their social responsibility programs. With continued governmental regulation, court-ordered damage payments, and general bad press, the tobacco companies are most likely grateful they have this one outlet for presenting their side of the story and their image as responsible corporate citizens. ■

QUESTIONS FOR DISCUSSION

1. On the basis of the information in this case, your personal knowledge, and a professional, objective mind-set, which, if any, of the following conclusions might be supported by maxims of persuasion or by the strategy and tactics used on either side?

   a. The antismoking coalition and the tobacco interests have been equally effective in their communication programs.

   b. One side (which one?) has focused more on influencing behavior than opinion.

   c. The aims and actions of both sides, one side, or neither, reflect a genuine concern for public opinion and behavior over the long haul.

   d. The tobacco interests give more evidence of "issue anticipation" than the antismoking coalition.

   e. The public relations thinking and actions on both sides can be decisive factors in attaining a reasonable solution.

2. On the smoking side of the debate, there is the personal freedom to make choices in life. On the antismoking side, there is personal health. Both are strong appeals to self-interest. Are there other appeals you find significant in the contest?

3. The chapter introduction talks about stakeholders. Among the tobacco interests, stakeholders would be vehicles that carry tobacco advertising. Can you think of any others? Among the no-smoking stakeholders would be insurance companies. Are there others? Does that leave anyone or any group in the middle, the neutral, or "don't care" category?

4. Are there moral and ethical considerations a practitioner should take into account before serving an employer or client involved in the tobacco, liquor, pornography, or handgun industries? Put another way, should the moral and ethical standards of a professional be essentially the same as those of his or her employer or client? Whether yes or no, can you think of a situation in which you would make an exception?

5. The issue of whether a company has the right to mandate what an employee can do in his or her spare time has been hotly debated in recent years. From the employer's viewpoint, what would be acceptable to make restrictions on and why? From the employee's viewpoint?

CASE 8-4   GUNS—FOR WHOM? FOR WHAT?

An emotionally charged controversy has long swirled around the availability, ownership, and use of rifles and handguns. On one side are those who are shocked by crime rates and feel that violent behavior is encouraged by gun ownership. On the opposing side are the constitutional rights to keep arms and to be secure in one's home. There are legal provisions for game hunting and target shooting as sport, recreation, and employment. Somewhere in between are the wildlife conservationists, the millions who must walk dark streets at night, and the millions who, by nature, abhor violence and killing in any form.

FACT FINDING

The Second Amendment to the Constitution of the United States (Article 2 of the Bill of Rights) stipulates "a well-regulated militia, being necessary to the security of a free State, the right of the people to keep and bear arms shall not be infringed." The interpretation and the ongoing applicability of this amendment constitute the basis for the controversy involving the personal and private ownership of guns.

Key words in the constitutional amendment appear to be *militia* and *keep and bear arms*. One dictionary defines *militia* as "all able-bodied male citizens from eighteen to forty-five, not members of the regular military forces, and legally subject to call for military duty." That is clear enough as applied to Colonial times. But what is a "militia" in modern times when the United States has a trained standing army, large

Reserve and National Guard units, a Pentagon brain center, and a worldwide intelligence network, all of which are backed by an enormous nuclear capability that could be unleashed by a word of command and the pressing of a few buttons?

As for the right to bear arms, did our nation's founders intend that one needed to be a *member* of the "militia," or might he be *any able-bodied man or woman*? And do "arms" apply only to flintlock weapons of 1776, or should they include the automatic pistols, AK-47s, and other weapons of today? Such questions of definition make up only one small part of a long and many-sided debate.

Meantime, since those pioneer days, the conversion of gun usage to criminal ends has unfortunately attained disturbing proportions. In 1996, handguns were used to murder two people in New Zealand, 15 in Japan, 30 in Great Britain, 106 in Canada, 213 in Germany, and 9,390 in the United States, according to the Brady Campaign to Prevent Gun Violence. The good news is that these statistics are declining in the United States. According to the FBI Uniform Crime Reports for 1999, there were 8,259 murders using firearms—65 percent of the total murders committed that year (12,658). Of the total, about 50 percent involved the use of a handgun, 4 percent a shotgun, and 3 percent a rifle. Firearm injuries are now the second leading cause of injury or death nationwide, surpassed only by those involving motor vehicles, according to the Centers for Disease Control and Prevention.

THE LEGAL CONTROLS

The old cliché "There ought to be a law against it," seems appropriate. There have been four significant federal laws. The first one, the National Firearms Act of 1934, aimed at control of special weapons. This statute covers such firearms as sawed-off shotguns, but does not involve the pistols, revolvers, regular shotguns, and rifles commonly displayed in gun shops.

The second federal statute—The Federal Firearms Act—came 4 years later, in 1938. It prohibited the interstate shipment of all firearms to or by convicted felons, persons under criminal indictment, and fugitives from justice. In addition, it required manufacturers, dealers, and importers doing firearms business across state lines to have a federally issued license.

Twenty-five years later, in 1963, just a few months before President John F. Kennedy was assassinated, a third federal statute was introduced in the Senate (S.B. 1975). It was known as the Gun Control Act. Its purposes were to ban mail order and interstate shipment of firearms to individuals, to stop over-the-counter sales of guns to minors, to prohibit possession of guns by convicted criminals, and to bar the importation of concealable foreign handguns. This act, with some modifications from the form in which it was initially offered, was passed in 1968.

Then, after years of often acrimonious debate, the Brady Bill was enacted in 1993. The Brady Handgun Violence Prevention Act established a national system of background checks and waiting periods for people buying handguns from federally licensed firearms dealers. The Act is named after James Brady, a former press secretary who was wounded in the 1981 assassination attempt on President Ronald Reagan.

Local governments, meanwhile, have been free to establish certain controls of their own. All of the states and hundreds of cities and townships have done so. Localized restrictions are noted in a publication from the Bureau of Alcohol, Tobacco, and Firearms.[1]

This whole matter is complex and emotional. There are strong personal convictions and frequent flare-ups of public controversy. Hunters, hobbyists, competitive range shooters, law enforcement personnel, wildlife conservationists, gun and ammunition makers, and frightened nightshift workers, among others, hold strong convictions. The victims of armed robbery, rape at gunpoint, kidnapping, and hijacking, and the families and friends of those killed or maimed by gunshot, harbor deep emotional feelings. At times, a whole nation has been shocked with guilt.

Numerous school shootings—from Littleton, Colorado, to Bethel, Alaska, from Conyers, Georgia, to Johnston, Rhode Island—have brought national focus on the horrors wrought by guns and emotional outcries for more gun control, longer waiting periods, mandated gun locks, stricter licensing, and restricted sales. On the flip side, NRA advocates point their fingers at people, not guns, and ask "how do you legislate sanity?" In the court of public opinion, both sides are strong participants.

REPRESENTING GUN OWNERS

The National Rifle Association (NRA), founded in 1871, boasts more than 4.3 million members. It marshals and sustains

---

[1]The particulars are available in *State Laws and Published Ordinances: Firearms*, from the Department of the Treasury, Bureau of Alcohol, Tobacco and Firearms, Superintendent of Documents, N. Capitol and H Streets, Washington, D.C. 20401; or on the Web at www.atf.treas.gov/firearms/statelaws/.

resistance to restrictive firearms measures that its members feel might infringe on the Second Amendment. At the same time, it supports mandatory sentences for the misuse of a firearm in the commission of a crime (See Figure 8-12).

The objectives of the NRA extend to the use of firearms for pleasure and for protection by law-abiding citizens. The NRA describes itself as an independent, nonprofit organization. In its literature, the NRA asserts that law-abiding Americans are constitutionally entitled to the ownership and legal use of firearms. Some programs of the NRA, as it has described them, include:

➤ Guardianship of the Second Amendment right. Through its Institute for Legislative Action and Political Victory Fund, the NRA continually monitors, tracks, and systematically combats all threats to the right to keep and bear arms at the federal, state, and local level, and supports lawmakers who uphold that constitutional duty.

➤ Sponsorship of various shooting clubs and marksmanship programs. Initiation of civilian marksmanship programs more than 100 years ago and youth training more than 70 years ago.

➤ Participation on a national board to promote rifle practice and to operate national rifle and pistol matches.

➤ Assignment by the U.S. Olympic Committee as the national governing body for competitive shooting in the United States and membership in the International Shooting Union.

➤ Creation of a code of ethics for hunters and the nationwide "Sighting-In Day."

➤ Donation source for various trophy awards.

➤ Origination of safety training for hunters and safety courses for firearms in the home.

➤ Functioning as a certifying agency for instructors, counselors, and referees.

➤ Total financial support for all expenses of U.S. shooting teams in international competition.

How the NRA Is Financed

The NRA has three affiliated organizations that qualify as 501 (c) (3) tax exempt, nonprofit charitable organizations, for which donations are tax-deductible for Federal income tax purposes. These are (1) The NRA Special Contribution Fund (Whittington Center), (2) the Firearms Civil Rights Legal Defense Fund, and (3) The NRA Foundation. Through membership dues, contributions, and the sale of items related to membership or gun ownership, the NRA has an annual budget of about $80 million.

The NRA publishes *American Rifleman*, *American Hunter*, and *America's First Freedom* magazines for members. *Shooting Sports USA* is available to members and nonmembers by subscription only. Advertising in these publications is another source of income. The NRA also has a publication called *InSights* for its junior members, publishes range plans and instructions, handbooks, instruction manuals, and a wide variety of pamphlets (See Figure 8-13).

Ancillary sources of revenue include the sale of jewelry, books, brochures, clothing, collector coins, competition aids, decals, pins, patches, glassware, handbooks, hats, videos, targets, charts, and many other items.

An Active Constituency

Despite a strong public support among Americans for federal gun legislation, the NRA claimed, as far back as the 1960s, the

FIGURE 8-12 NRA poster urging greater jail sentences for crimes.

(Courtesy of the National Rifle Association.)

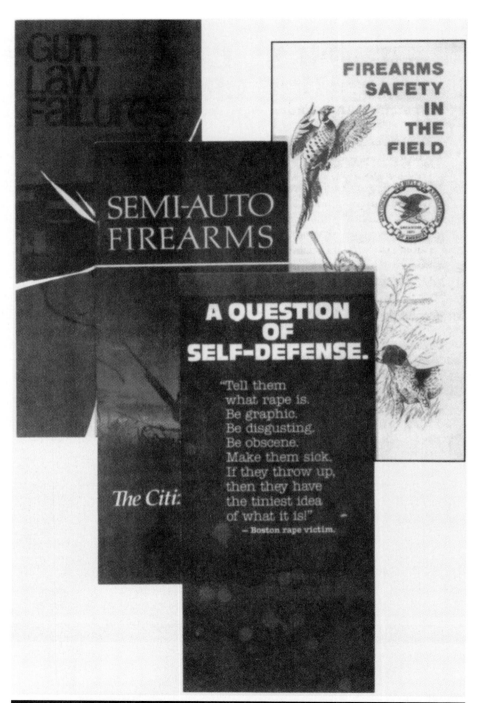

FIGURE 8-13 Example of the many brochures and manuals available from the NRA.

(Courtesy of the National Rifle Association.)

ability to produce "within seventy-two hours more than half a million letters, postcards and telegrams to members of Congress on any gun bill issue."[2] Its target constituency includes 80 million gun owners, veterans of all wars, licensed hunters, gun club members, gun collectors, gun dealers, and manufacturers of equipment for hunting and target shooting.

The NRA Strategy and Tactics at Points of Controversy

When shocking incidents such as assassinations, school shootings, and gang-related violence seize the front page, public opinion swings suddenly and widely. The public often sympathizes with the families and friends of the victims, deploring the senselessness of violence and demanding the apprehension of the perpetrator, swift and stern justice, and stricter controls of firearm ownership. Concerned citizens write letters to editors. Law enforcement officials speak up for gun registration, regulation, and other controls.

> ➤ In the immediate aftermath of tragic episodes and public outrage, the NRA has not often taken a stance of overt rebuttal. Its strategy seems to be to lie low, knowing that the pendulum of opinion will in time return to positions held before the shocking event.

In its dealings at the political or legislative level, however, the NRA has not wavered or gone silent. Its lobbying strategy for many years has emphasized that "Guns don't kill people: people kill people," implying that people rather than guns require more control—sterner penalties for criminal use of a gun are what is really needed. Its

lobbying tactics, with an amazing track record of successful opposition to restrictive legislation, have been assertive, not defensive. Its opposition to the Brady Bill, first proposed in 1985, helped to delay the passage of this bill for 7 years.

In its public information and education, the NRA has emphasized these points:

1. Firearms legislation would disarm the law-abiding citizen without affecting the criminal, who would ignore the legislation.
2. If firearms were not available, some other weapon would be used by the criminal.
3. Most weapons found in criminal hands have been stolen.
4. Registration of arms might leave law-abiding citizens at the mercy of criminals, of a subversive power if it infiltrated, or of the nation's enemies if they occupied the country.

The Role of Public Relations

Within the structure of NRA, its Institute for Legislative Action includes governmental affairs, field services, information services, member services, and fiscal services. This is the organization's area of expertise. Since 1997, NRA has been steadily ascending *Fortune* magazine's "Power 25"—the magazine's listing of the most influential lobbying groups in America. In 1997, NRA ranked sixth. In 1998, it moved to fourth. In 1999, it made second place. *Fortune* did not do the rankings in 2000. In 2001, NRA reached the number one spot, displacing AARP, which held the spot for years.[3]

Since 1981, public relations and advertising have been handled by the Mercury Group, the Washington affiliate of advertising giant Ackerman-McQueen. Ginny

---

[2]Richard Harris, "Annals of Legislation: If You Love Your Guns," *New Yorker*, April 20, 1968.
[3]"The NRA Goes Global" by Jason Vest in *Salon Politics 2000*, April 3, 2000.

Simone, an ex-local newscaster, is a public face for the NRA. Visit the "live news" section of the NRA's Web site and you'll see her presenting "news" gun lovers can use. NRA's president Charlton Heston is another public face—not only Hollywood's most visible reactionary, but its most effective activist, according to author Ed Leibowitz who shadowed Heston for weeks to write "Charlton Heston's Last Stand."[4] Heston stood out front as the NRA fought during the 2000 presidential election, attempting to turn it into a national referendum on gun rights. George W. Bush's win was a victory for the NRA.

ON THE OTHER SIDE OF THE ISSUE

The persuasive power of the NRA has given the impression in the past that those on the other side, the gun control advocates, are invisible and silent, perhaps overwhelmed or intimidated. To many neutrals or fence sitters, it might seem that the success of the NRA reflects popular public sentiment. Neither impression is complete or valid. Polls of the general public have shown that a majority of people of all ages, both men and women, in all geographic regions of the United States, favor federal legislation for control of guns, and particularly handguns—the "Saturday night specials"—called junk guns because they are small, cheap, and flimsily made.[5]

Gun control advocates have made these points:

1. There are as many firearms in the United States as there are people.
2. In most states, no license is required to purchase a handgun.
3. The United States is the only civilized nation in the world that does not regulate the ownership of firearms.

4. During 1 year there were more Americans killed by handguns in a 2-day period than were killed in all of England (a country that does not allow ownership of handguns) that whole year.
5. Guns should be treated like cars— they should be registered, and the people who use them should be licensed.

One legislator echoed those sentiments in urging a complete ban on the manufacture and sale of handguns. He cited a combination of congressional fear of the NRA and big business interests behind guns for the lack of tough federal legislation.

Statistical information backing up the gun control advocates is impressive. The U.S. General Accounting Office (GAO), in a survey of crime for 1 full year, found that 63.8 percent of all murders, 24.6 percent of all aggravated assaults, and 42.7 percent of all robberies were committed by persons using guns. The GAO asked Congress to consider specifically the denial of a gun to a person with a criminal record and the regulation of transfers of guns from one person to another.

In the past, attempts at federal legislation have failed repeatedly. Out of frustration, many states and communities have exercised local options. California, as one example among hundreds, enacted a "use a gun, go to jail" mandatory prison sentence for crimes involving use of a gun—as well as mandating a 15-day waiting period to purchase a handgun. The city of Oakland, California, has passed a local ban on junk guns, and Illinois has passed a state ban on junk guns. In 1989, a law banning semiautomatic assault weapons was passed by the California legislature. And in the wake of brutal shooting sprees, many

---

[4] *Los Angeles Magazine*, February 2001.
[5] A federal junk gun bill has been introduced, which, if passed, would require American-made handguns to meet the standards that apply to imported handguns.

state legislatures have banned the use of semiautomatic guns.

Not all local efforts at control gained popular support. In Massachusetts, voters had the opportunity of deciding whether to restrict handguns. On one side were police officials and citizens. On the other were state and national organizations and the arms industry, including a Massachusetts manufacturer of handguns. People versus Handguns got 31 percent of the vote. They had to settle for raising the level of public consciousness.

There Are Grassroots Citizens' Groups

In recent years, the most vocal national citizens' lobby has been Handgun Control Inc. James and Sarah Brady joined this group, as well as its sister organization, The Center to Prevent Handgun Violence (CPHV), after the attack on President Ronald Reagan where James Brady was wounded. Sarah Brady became the chair of CPHV in 1991. In 2001, Handgun Control was renamed the Brady Campaign To Prevent Gun Violence and CPHV became the Brady Center to Prevent Handgun Violence. Later that same year, these sister organizations merged with the Million Mom March—another gun control group with 230 chapters across the country. The three combined are the largest national, nonpartisan, grassroots organization leading the fight to prevent gun violence.

"This alliance sends a clear message that the gun control movement is uniting and targeted. For many years, we have been successful in passing effective legislation, while increasing public awareness of the scourge of gun violence. Today's announcement is an exciting next step in further raising an army of supporters that will enable us to continue to effect change in Congress and in state Legislatures," reads the Brady Campaign's announcement of the merger.

This merged organization seeks to attract enough contributing members to face off with the NRA in lobbying Congress for legislation, to alert its constituents to those candidates up for election who favor gun controls, to report the voting records of congresswomen and men on gun issues and the amount of financial support each gets from the NRA, and otherwise to provide a continuous rallying point.

BRINGING THINGS UP TO DATE

In legislative confrontations, the NRA is a single-issue organization. Its strategy is to take an inflexible posture. Officials are convinced that to make one concession would establish a precedent and invite a nibbling away at the Second Amendment right. A new advertising approach was quite dramatic (See Figure 8-14).

However, this ironclad stance received many blows in the 1990s because of the turning tide of public opinion and the lobbying efforts of the Brady Campaign and other gun control advocates, including police organizations. Specifically:

➤ *1994:* President Clinton signed into law the Violent Crime and Control Act, which includes the first-ever federal Assault Weapons Ban, banning the future manufacture and importation of military-style assault weapons.

➤ *1995:* In the wake of the Oklahoma City bombing, the NRA faced intense public scrutiny and widespread criticism for its views. NRA membership dropped and President George Bush resigned his life membership after it was revealed that the NRA called Bureau of Alcohol, Tobacco and Firearms agents "jack-booted thugs" in a fundraising letter.

➤ *1996:* Congress passed legislation to prohibit anyone convicted of a misdemeanor domestic violence

FIGURE 8-14 Bold NRA ads make the point that crime is rampant.

(Courtesy of the National Rifle Association.)

offense from buying or owning a gun.

➤ *1997:* Supreme Court struck down the background check requirement of the Brady Law. Still the waiting period and other provisions of Brady survived an NRA-financed challenge. Law enforcement continued to conduct background checks voluntarily until the National Instant Check System went into effect in 1998.

➤ *1998:* New Orleans became the first public entity to sue the gun industry.

➤ *1999:* In the wake of Columbine High School shooting, the U.S. Senate passed legislation to close the gun show loophole, which allows unregulated private sales. Unfortunately, similar legislation in the House was defeated and the Senate bill stalled in conference committee.

➤ *1999: Merrill v. Navegar* achieved the first appeals court ruling that a gun maker can be held liable for negligence leading to the criminal use of a gun.

➤ *2000:* District of Columbia became the 30th jurisdiction to sue the gun industry.

➤ *2000:* Smith & Wesson became the first gun manufacturer to settle with cities and counties suing the gun industry, agreeing to make sweeping changes to its manufacturing and distribution practices.

➤ *2000:* After 2 years of court battles, the Attorney General of Massachusetts became the first in the nation to use consumer protection powers to regulate guns.

Yet gun violence remains a major problem in the United States—although not in other First World nations. It remains to be seen what effect President George W. Bush will have on this public debate as both sides educate the public and do arduous battle through the U.S. Congress and the Supreme Court, as well as in the court of public opinion. ■

QUESTIONS FOR DISCUSSION

1. The strategy of the NRA has been to oppose any legal measures that might tighten controls. The grounds are that any of these would be a foot in the door leading to demands for more such laws. As an objective communications professional, how do you feel about this "no exceptions," "no compromise," "not one inch" attitude? Has your attitude changed at all by your studies of the ultimate purpose of public relations? If so, how and why?

2. For those who hold to a hard line on the gun issue (on either side) and those who hold to a hard line on birth control (either way), what similarities and differences do you find in the basis of their convictions? In their strategies and tactics?

3. Using the definitions of a public issue and a crisis given in the introduction to this chapter, which of the following would you consider issues, which crises, and which are neither?
   a. Birth control
   b. Gun control
   c. Integrity in public office
   d. Insurance rates
   e. Crime rates
   f. Drug usage

4. Can you think of a strategy that the NRA could take in order to influence

the public along its line of thinking? What strategies are they using that soften their position? That strengthen it?

5. Was this case presented in a biased manner? Give evidence for your position. This type of analysis is a regular task of public relations practitioners preparing plans and strategies.

6. How can a group with only 10 to 15 percent of the public supporting its views—which has historically been the case with the NRA—be so powerful? Why would officeholders listen to its views? What strategies do you feel enable such a minority view to prevail for so long? What must the Brady Campaign and others opposed to unregulated gun ownership do to successfully make their case?

CASE 8-5 ONE TOWN'S FIGHT TO AVOID SUPERFUND STATUS

The Berkshires region of Massachusetts is one of the most beautiful areas of New England. With the Housatonic River running through it, the quaint town of Pittsfield sits in the heart of Berkshire country. However, the area is not as pure as it appears. Pittsfield was the battleground for one of the most unpleasant environmental battles in the country. It was between General Electric (GE) and the Environmental Protection Agency (EPA).

Imagine if you learned that the town you live in has for years contained a chemical classified by EPA as a potential carcinogen, and that a major *Fortune* 50 company was responsible for the presence of that chemical. How would you feel about that company? You'd most likely expect them to take responsibility for cleaning up the contamination. But would you want them to be allowed to continue doing business in your area? This case examines why one town fought not only for the cleanup of its land, but also to maintain a relationship with the company responsible for the presence of the chemical.

GE'S HISTORY IN PITTSFIELD

In 1931, unaware of any environmental dangers present, GE began using PCBs (polychlorinated biphenyls) in the production of electric transformers and other products at its factory in Pittsfield, Massachusetts. PCBs were used as insulators and flame retardants and at the time were considered state of the art for this type of equipment. In the 1940s and 1950s, some landowners in the town obtained soil from the GE plant for use as fill at their properties. This soil was much later found to contain PCBs. GE continued to use PCBs in its manufacturing operations until just before Congress outlawed PCB use in 1977, when studies confirmed that the chemical causes liver cancer and reproductive problems in animals.

In 1981, Congress passed the Comprehensive Environmental Response, Compensation, and Liability Act, known as the Superfund hazardous waste cleanup program. Properties with a Superfund designation are eligible for federal cleanup under the EPA, which can sue responsible parties for up to three times the cost of the cleanup if the parties refuse to conduct the cleanup themselves.

By the time GE shut down its transformer and defense businesses in Pittsfield over a period of years in the late 1980s and early 1990s, 12 miles of the Housatonic River adjacent to and downstream of the plant had been directly contaminated and a 55-mile stretch of the river showed some effects of the chemical leakage. As a result of GE's use of PCBs, its 250-acre plant in Pittsfield was severely contaminated in several locations. Years later, traces of PCB were found in fish as far away as sections of the Housatonic River in Connecticut, and fish in the Massachusetts portion of the Housatonic registered some of the highest PCB levels in the United States.

Pittsfield had once been a thriving community. GE was a driving force behind the region's economy, employing over 14,000 people. Like many small- and mid-sized towns with a single major employer, Pittsfield relied heavily on GE for its economic life. But the closing of the majority of GE's property contributed to years of economic decline in Pittsfield. For decades the area struggled to diversify its economy, and to cope with the loss of defense and manufacturing jobs.

For almost two decades (from 1960 to 1979), GE's recently retired CEO John "Jack" Welch lived in Pittsfield and worked for GE in the company's plastics division. Under his leadership, it grew from a small niche business to one of the company's most profitable units. In 1981, Welch became CEO. When GE began to downsize its presence in Pittsfield in the mid- to late-1980s by exiting the power transformer and defense businesses, many residents felt GE—including Welch—was turning its back on them. However, the plastics operations remained; they are currently located on 75 acres in Pittsfield and employ 600 people.

ENVIRONMENTALISTS URGE HOUSATONIC CLEANUP

In 1992, the Housatonic River Initiative was founded by State Representative Christopher J. Hodgkins, one of the first people to urge the cleanup of the river, and George Wislocki, president of the Berkshire National Resources Council. The organization's grassroots mission was to remove PCBs from the Housatonic River to make the river fishable and swimmable.

For years, federal regulators worked with GE and interested parties to determine the appropriate cleanup plan. Although GE vehemently fought the designation as a Superfund site, it spent $130 million on cleanup and testing of potentially contaminated sites over more than a 10-year period.

In 1997, several important events sped the cleanup efforts. First, GE received negative publicity after a major testing of resi-

dential soil revealed substantial PCB contamination. Pittsfield residents learned that the soil they had received free from the GE plant years before for use in landscaping and construction of homes contained PCBs. Consequently, land on which more than 100 homes were built was contaminated. GE denied having any knowledge that the soil was contaminated.

In addition, records revealed that a retired GE engineer had warned the company about the potential problem in 1981. These findings prompted the EPA to request all company-related records regarding waste removal in Pittsfield. The State Attorney General's office ordered a grand jury investigation into the situation. Simultaneously, comprehensive cleanup negotiations began among GE, the EPA, the state, and the city of Pittsfield.

NATIONAL PRESS EYES PITTSFIELD

In August 1997, John Devillars, EPA Regional Administrator, proposed the GE/Housatonic River site as a candidate for the Superfund National Priority List. He promised to remove the nomination if GE agreed to a fuller and faster settlement than Superfund could provide. By this point, local, regional, and national news media had picked up the story and were offering readers regular coverage of the situation. *The New York Times*, *The Wall Street Journal*, *The Boston Globe*, and other papers were carrying stories with each new development.

In response to the national media attention, General Electric took out more than $100,000 worth of advertising in the local paper to try and ease homeowners' concerns, providing details of its cleanup efforts and denying that PCBs caused health risks as extensive as environmental groups claimed.

Around this time, Mayor Gerald Doyle Jr. publicly opposed support of Superfund, claiming such a designation would trigger "economic disaster" for the region, as companies would be hesitant to bring operations to the area. The mayor's comments initiated a deep public debate over the pros and cons of Superfund status. Environmentalists claimed Superfund status was the only sure way to guarantee the cleanup of the area, since Superfund status would allow EPA to clean up the sites and sue GE for up to three times the costs.

But those opposed to Superfund status pointed out that for years Pittsfield had been a thriving community, and that even with a reduced workforce, GE was still a driving force behind the region's economy. They claimed designation of Superfund would stigmatize the city and cost it money over the long run.

STALL IN TALKS BRINGS THREAT OF SUPERFUND STATUS

On April 2, 1998, the EPA talks reached an impasse. John Devillars, the EPA regional administrator, ordered the process for Superfund designation to begin. He said the property was one of New England's five most hazardous waste sites. He claimed Superfund status would give the federal government the resources and power to clean up the contaminated sites. GE said this move could set the stage for years of legal battles.

Less than a week later, Stephen Ramsey, vice president of corporate environmental programs at GE, wrote in a letter to EPA that there was no scientific link between PCBs and cancer or birth defects.

Later that month at the company's stockholder meeting, CEO John Welch debated Sister Pat Daley, who compared GE to the tobacco companies. The national media picked up the story reporting that Welch told Daley she "owed it to God to be on the side of truth."

MAYOR URGES PITTSFIELD TO AVOID SUPERFUND

Talks continued through the summer of 1998, with GE offering cleanup proposals and EPA presenting counterproposals. On June 12, 1998, Mayor Doyle wrote to Pittsfield residents to provide them with more information on the GE proposals, saying, "There is much to lose if we do not achieve a settlement." He said the EPA should negotiate a cleanup plan and avoid Superfund status. In addition, the local Chamber of Commerce sent memos to members asking them to lobby politicians to support Mayor Doyle's plan.

Business leaders praised Doyle's stance. But some environmentalists and residents felt the mayor pressured the EPA to make a deal. By late August, there was still a substantial divide on the key issues. An advisory board was set up and appointed by the mayor to advise the mayor on the issue. Four members of this board resigned because they disagreed with the way he was handling the negotiations.

AN UNPRECEDENTED AGREEMENT TO WORK TOGETHER

On September 25, 1998, the dispute was ended when GE and the EPA agreed to work together to clean up the contamination and avoid Superfund status. General Electric agreed to clean up PCBs on its land and in the surrounding affected areas. It would do so under standards, specified in the agreement, that EPA agreed were fully protective of health and the environment. GE agreed to clean up its factory site, the upper half-mile of the Housatonic River, and surrounding areas—including a school and several residential and commercial properties. The EPA agreed to clean up the next 1½ miles of the river under a cost-sharing agreement with GE. The agreement also set up a process for the continued study and ultimately the selection of a cleanup plan for the remainder of the river, which GE would have to carry out after any court challenges.

In addition, a new economic development authority was created, called the Pittsfield Economic Development Authority (PEDA), which was charged with encouraging and overseeing economic redevelopment within the city, including the GE plant. GE agreed to demolish approximately 2.1 million square feet of buildings at its 250-acre plant, and turn over 52 acres of land within that plant in an area that was once the heart of the Berkshire's economy, to PEDA. General Electric committed $10 million in cash over 10 years to the city to offset lost property taxes, $15 million in a rebuilding budget to assist PEDA with redevelopment efforts, and $3 million to a landscape budget, and agreed to pay for marketing studies to help attract new businesses to the site.

After the agreement had been made, several government officials—including Senator Edward Kennedy, EPA regional administrator John DeVillars, and Pittsfield Mayor Gerald Doyle—said elements of the process would serve as a national model for other communities facing similar challenges. Carol M. Browner, EPA administrator, said, "GE's agreement to help fund an economic redevelopment package to benefit the community is a significant part of the agreement. It ensures that public health and the environment will be protected and the local economy will prosper."

The settlement was finalized in a lengthy document that was filed in court in October 1999 and approved by the court in October 2000. In addition, the State Attorney General's office and GE reached an agreement to settle the grand jury investigation. ■

QUESTIONS FOR DISCUSSION

1. You are hired as a public relations consultant by General Electric in the fall of 1997. What strategic counsel do you provide to the company for responding to the developing media attention?

2. As Vice President of Corporate Affairs for General Electric in 1998, just before the final agreement is made with the EPA, you are charged with managing all media relations for the company. What is your official statement to the media regarding the outcome of the case?

3. What relationships should General Electric have focused on building—or rebuilding—after the agreement was reached on September 25, 1998?

4. What are the (a) legal and (b) ethical responsibilities of a company like GE to remediate conditions that occurred openly, legally, and honestly in an earlier era?

CASE 8-6   A CLASSIC: FREE THE TEXAS SHOPPER!

Some behavioral scientists say that the "silent majority" can be riled up only once a decade, after prolonged and careful focus on the subject of controversy. However, this tenet may be altered when it comes to issues that hit the general public close to home. For example, shopping.

BACKGROUND

Before 1985, the state of Texas had legislation on its books called "blue laws." These blue laws were based in the Christian ideal that everyone goes to church on Sunday—or ought to—and were responsible for keeping most retail stores closed that day. Most states once had such laws, but nearly all had been repealed. Not in the Bible Belt state of Texas, however.

A coalition was formed of like-minded retailers, including Target Stores, Kmart, and Zales, who believed it was time to do away with the blue laws. Organizations against repeal of the law were nonchain retailers, large department stores, car dealers, and especially churches.

The coalition was caught in a bind, because they knew Sunday shopping would mean greater sales but were concerned they would lose customers angered by the campaign. There was a long-standing assumption that fundamentalists, other church groups, and people living in rural areas would be against repeal, but no one knew for sure.

TIME FOR RESEARCH

The coalition decided to arm itself with data in order to know where the people of Texas really stood. A massive survey uncovered data that told them that:

➤ Two out of three Texans wanted the law repealed.
➤ Support for repeal was broad-based, including substantial support in rural areas and among fundamentalist groups.

Research was specific enough to determine *how each legislative district felt.* These data were subsequently made available to the legislators, who had to vote on repeal. Coalition representatives felt this was a very important part of their effort. When a legislator opposed the bill, evidence of support by his or her constituents was available.

CAMPAIGN PHILOSOPHY

The coalition decided to run a straightforward, honest, open, objective campaign so nobody could criticize them on those grounds. Retailers stressed their solid reputations in the communities, their support of local nonprofit agencies, their substantial business operations (representing a large share of total retail business in the state), and the large number of people employed.

Members of the coalition were accused by the opposition of being out-of-state companies, trying to change the Texas lifestyle and overturn local values.

But Target Stores' programs of social responsibility and community participation paid off. "After 16 years," they said, "we feel as much a part of the state as others do."

MOVING THOUSANDS TO ACTION

After gathering the research and deciding on a campaign philosophy, the coalition's next task was to convert expressed support to active support. This is how it was done:

1. Newspaper ads were run that strongly advocated action (See Figure 8-15) The bold copy and strong illustration generated substantial media coverage and word-of-mouth publicity.
2. The same ad was used as a bag stuffer in coalition members' stores.
3. An 800 number was set up for people to call to obtain information. Operators gathered personal information from callers, especially their shopping habits and location. They also read a prepared statement and requested permission to send it to each caller's legislator over that person's name. The 800 number was prominently carried in the newspaper ads and bag stuffers.

This strategy gathered 80,000 names in the coalition's databank. When the vote was being taken, if a legislator wavered, the coalition called these registered supporters and suggested they contact the legislator.

DEFUSING THE OPPOSITION

The Texas Authority Dealers Association—effective lobbyists with a long track record of political support for candidates—was a powerful force to be up against. They did not want to open their showrooms on Sunday. The coalition needed to devise a strategy that would remove them from the equation. The bill, as it was finally adopted, excluded them. They would remain closed on Sundays. They were then standing on the sidelines, no longer in the battle.

FINAL DECISION

The Texas Senate required a two-thirds majority to have the matter put on the docket for vote. Once on the docket, it needed only a simple majority to pass. Documented research and personal contacts from people in their districts spoke loudly to legislators. The coalition expected the bill to take at least two legislative sessions to pass—but it took only one.

TESTIMONIAL TO RESEARCH AND PLANNING

The campaign lasted 6 months and showed how effectively public relations can influence public policy. It also showed how important public relations is to the bottom financial line; retail sales subsequently increased because of Sunday shopping. The key was fact finding, discovering that the people of Texas support Sunday openings. This knowledge put the coalition in the position of representing the will of the people. Without the research, or with different findings, an entirely different approach would have been required—with, very possibly, a different result.

BLUE LAWS UPDATE

In recent years, blue laws have faded as an issue of public concern. However, they are still debated in some states. Beer and liquor sales are limited in Massachusetts, but not in the competing neighbor states of New Hampshire and Vermont, which is a controversial issue for some merchants and customers. Counties and municipalities in Bible

BLUE LAWS ADDRESS MORE THAN JUST SHOPPING

In addition to blue laws that keep stores closed on Sundays, there are other blue laws on the books. Some states still have antiadultery laws, for instance. Though ignored as archaic by law enforcement agencies, these laws have been used by some people to keep spouses in control, especially in divorce proceedings, and some people have attempted to have their spouses arrested if caught in the act of adultery.

Questions of violations of rights to privacy have arisen. But this is a relatively new "right," formulated by Supreme Court Justice Brandeis in the early years of the century. To many, the repeal of blue laws is imperative. Others would welcome more laws regulating personal conduct according to what they believe is "proper" conduct. When any specific action is taken by specific groups in either direction, emotional debate usually ensues—and you can be sure public relations counsel will be in the thick of it, ideally representing both sides so each gets its point across and the public can make an informed decision.

Belt states are often "dry" by local ordinance even though state statutes allow the sale of liquor. On the opposite side, in 1991, Kansas car dealers proposed a new blue law to prohibit automobile sales on Sundays. This proposal caused great conflict and debate, and the bill did not pass. ■

QUESTIONS FOR DISCUSSION

1. Suppose research showed that about half of the key Texas population opposed Sunday sales, while half supported them. What counsel would you have given the retail group? How would you have dealt with opposing groups?
2. If you were counsel to the opposing group, what would you have suggested they do to defeat the repeal proposal?
3. Assume that your employer is moving into a new state and wants to build the type of consumer support that Target and its allies created. What types of activities would you pursue? Draw up a plan.
4. In light of Chapter 2, what are some of the considerations that go into strategic thinking leading to a plan and a program? What are some of the elements beyond media and messages? Is your response to this question reflected in your response to questions 1, 2, and 3?

CASE 8-7   MOTHERS AGAINST DRUNK DRIVING—MADD

In response to tragedy, people often reach out to others for support. Many find comfort in doing what they can to right a terrible wrong or prevent others from going through what they have gone through. Often these support groups can become a powerful and compelling voice for social change. One of the most successful and accomplished of these coalitions is Mothers Against Drunk Driving (MADD). MADD's mission is twofold: (1) to provide support for those who have experienced the tragedy of a drunk driving accident and (2) to advocate, both socially and legislatively, against the act of operating a vehicle under the influence of drugs and alcohol.

MADD was established by Candy Lightner in 1980 in response to the loss of her daughter in a drunk driving accident. The organization currently has over 400 chapters across the United States. Between 1984 and 1989, MADD increased its membership of supporters and volunteers by over 500 percent. That trend continues today as drunk driving increasingly is recognized as a debilitating social illness. Funding raised and spent in support of education, public awareness, victims' assistance, and other programs has increased four times over (See Figure 8-16). Donations to MADD total nearly $43 million annually.

Although the incidence of fatalities in alcohol-related accidents decreased by 7.7 percent in the period between 1982 and 1990, the numbers are still staggering. In 1990, 17,366 people were killed in alcohol-related vehicle accidents.[1] Despite MADD's positive influence, there is still much to be done to change people's behavior relative to drinking and driving.

THE PUBLICS

MADD targets several audiences, all on different sides of a drunk driving accident.

➤ Along with its sister organization, Students Against Drunk Driving (SADD), MADD educates *teens* (a group with a high incidence of alcohol-related accidents) against the dangers of drunk driving.

➤ Another focus is the *adult driver* who may become impaired after a social night out (See Figure 8-17).

➤ The *repeat and reckless drunk driver*—the cause of many alcohol-related deaths—is targeted in MADD's legislative efforts for harsher penalties

➤ MADD also supports *public service professionals,* such as police, paramedics, and physicians, who must deal with the daily consequences of one person's carelessness.

➤ Finally, MADD maintains programs aiding family and friends who have experienced the trauma of a drunk driving accident.

---

[1]*Fatal Accident Reporting System*, U.S. Department of Transportation, National Highway Traffic Safety Administration, 1990, p. 22.

HELP
KEEP
FAMILIES
TOGETHER

This family was on their way to have a picture taken
for Christmas in 1988. They were torn apart when a driver,
with a blood alcohol content of .26 according to police
reports, crashed into their car, killing the parents—
Roy Lee and Lou Verla Adams. Their surviving
children—Ronald, Daniel, Joseph, Jason and
Roy, along with grandmother, Katherine,
went ahead with their mother's wishes
and later had this group picture
taken holding a photograph
of their departed
parents.

Mothers Against Drunk Driving

It's the little things that make us MADD.

Kristin Metayer, 1983-1986

MOTHERS

AGAINST

DRUNK

DRIVING

FIGURE 8-16 One way that MADD has raised public awareness is by distributing brochures that tell the personal story of families or children who have been affected by drunk driving accidents.

(Courtesy of MADD.)

TIPS FOR RESPONSIBLE HOSTING FROM MADD™ Mothers Against Drunk Driving

The decision to serve alcoholic beverages in your home carries with it a responsibility for the welfare of your guests. Responsible attitudes toward drinking should make us behave in such a way that we will never have to feel sorry for what happened. Remember, people don't like to admit they've had too much to drink, and may argue with you that they are sober enough to drive. Following is a list of arguments you might hear, and ways for you to respond:

"HEY, I'M NOT DRUNK!"

Share with them the penalties they'll face if arrested for drunk driving.

"I'LL JUST HAVE SOME COFFEE TO SOBER UP."

Only time sobers you up. Alcohol oxidizes at a rate of approximately one drink per hour.

"I ONLY DRANK BEER AND DIDN'T MIX DRINKS."

It doesn't matter. One 12-ounce beer, one 5-ounce glass of wine or an ounce-and-a-half of liquor contain the same amount of alcohol with the same intoxication potential.

"I LIVE REAL CLOSE, I CAN MAKE IT"

Statistics show that three out of four crashes occur within 25 miles of a person's home.

"I'VE DONE THIS A HUNDRED TIMES. I NEVER GET CAUGHT."

First, ask yourself "How did this person get invited to your party?"

Next, remind him/her there were over one million drunk driving arrests last year, over 22,000 alcohol-related crash deaths, and over 400 new tough-alcohol countermeasures passed at the state and national level.

"I NEED MY CAR."

Suggest to your guest that he/she spend the night, or call a taxi to drive him/her home. Or ask another, sober, guest to drive the intoxicated person home and have another sober guest follow with his/her car.

NEVER LET A PERSON DRIVE AWAY FROM YOUR PARTY DRUNK!

HERE ARE MORE TIPS:

If serving alcohol, always serve food. Provide seats for everyone, along with the table space to allow guests to set drinks down.

Have several jiggers at the bar so mixed drinks can be measured.

Choose a bartender of known discretion. Control the flow of alcohol – it's your home, you set the limit.

Have non-alcoholic beverages available for your guests.

If you serve an alcoholic punch, make it with a non-carbonated base.

Don't push drinks; push snacks.

Stop serving alcohol at least an hour before the party is to end.

FRIENDS DO NOT LET FRIENDS DRIVE DRUNK!

MADD
Mothers Against Drunk Driving

FIGURE 8-17 One way that MADD has targeted adults is by offering tip sheets for hosts of parties to facilitate a fun and safe party.

(Courtesy of MADD.)

GOALS AND OBJECTIVES

MADD works at the grassroots level to end the senseless deaths and crippling physical and emotional injuries caused by drunk drivers. MADD supports programs that:

1. Achieve *voluntary* liquor and beer industry support to curb alcohol advertising when television or live audiences have large percentages of those under age 21. One goal is to find alternate advertisers.
2. Encourage sponsors of sporting events to limit alcohol sales too late in the event, thereby increasing the probability that fans will arrive home safely.

3. Convince Congress to add a victim's rights amendment to the U.S. Constitution—similar to the Victim's Bill of Rights in the Michigan, Florida, and Rhode Island state constitutions.

ACTIVITIES AND TACTICS

Project Red Ribbon has become one of MADD's most successful campaigns. During the holiday season, red ribbons are distributed to drivers to be tied on car antennas and mirrors (See Figure 8-18).[2] The ribbon acts as a *reminder* not to drive if they become impaired, and as a *sign of solidarity*

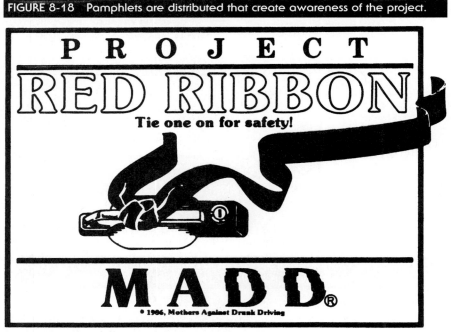

FIGURE 8-18   Pamphlets are distributed that create awareness of the project.

(Courtesy of MADD.)

---

[2]Originally, they were tied on door handles to keep drunks from getting into their cars—but most present-day handles have no place to attach them.

against drunk driving. The act of tying the ribbon also reminds the individuals of other preventive behaviors as well, such as calling a cab for a friend or holding his or her car keys to prevent drunk driving. The program is successful because it links a specific behavior (tying the ribbon) to a commitment against drunk driving *before* the first toast is raised, and it does this at the *point of behavior.*

- Alcohol-related deaths decreased from 76 per day in 1980 to 64 in 1989.
- According to the National Parents Resource Institute for Drug Education, beer, which is the number one drug of choice for teens, is most often consumed in vehicles.
- An independent research group found that television programs with a large percentage of under-21 viewers feature a high incidence of alcohol advertisements.

More than 30 million red ribbons are distributed each year by volunteers, MADD chapters, and supporting organizations, such as 7-11 stores, across the country (See Figure 8-19). In addition to grassroots support, several companies have tied marketing efforts to the program. Welch's promoted its nonalcoholic cider in conjunction with the program. This action may or may not have boosted Welch's sales, but it did give more exposure to the MADD program—and the antidrunk driving ideal.

Since 1990 Consolidated Freightways Motorfreight, a national trucking company based in California, has been a sponsor for MADD's Project Red Ribbon. From November to January, the company ties red ribbons to its fleet of 12,000 trucks. In addition, several Project Red Ribbon kick-off events are organized by Consolidated Freightways Motorfreight employees and held at their terminals. Some companies have found that supporting a social cause boosts employee morale by adding meaning to job performance, as well as creating public goodwill.

MADD's ultimate goal is to get year-long commitment against drunk driving, not just during the holidays. There is evidence that Project Red Ribbon helps reach this goal—MADD receives requests throughout the year for replacements for worn-out ribbons.

THE OUTCOME

Coalition efforts are paying off. In addition to the 7.7 percent decrease in fatalities over 10 years, the Omnibus Anti-Drug Act was passed in 1988. It is a significant victory in federal anti-DWI legislation. The enactment of the federally sponsored national minimum drinking age of 21 is another significant gain.

LEGISLATION: ANOTHER FORM OF PERSUASION

Years of scholarly research of public relations programming have combined to establish a four-point method for effecting mass behavior change—which is MADD's goal,

ONE-WAY AND TWO-WAY COMMUNICATION TOOLS THAT HELP MADD CARRY OUT ITS MISSION

1. *Support for the MADD message in television programming.* In 1988–1989, millions of Americans tuned in to their favorite television show and got a clear warning about drinking and driving— "The two don't mix." A portion of the credit goes to the Harvard School of Medicine Alcohol Project campaign, which encourages producers and writers to promote responsible drinking and designated-driver programs. MADD's national office served as script advisers.

2. *National poster contest.* More than 45,000 young people participated in the Third Annual Nationwide Poster/Essay contest aimed at preventing drunk driving. Cultural barriers were breached by including Spanish-language entries.

3. *Toll-free Victim's Assistance Crisis hotline* was established by MADD to provide support to those affected by a drunk driver's actions.

4. *Formation of Victim Impact Panels.* One hundred Victim Impact Panels were formed to serve as a forum for voicing grief, pain, and frustration associated with drunk driving accidents. These can send a powerful *emotion-laden* message to the public. Convicted drunk drivers are occasionally required to attend one of these panels as part of their sentence.

5. *Candlelight Vigils* are held to honor drunk driving victims and serve as a reminder.

6. *Crisis Response Teams* have been formed to assist families and friends of victims.

7. MADD is a strong *lobbyist for legislation for stiffer penalties* to keep the drunk driver off the road and to curb underage drinking.

8. MADD publishes *MADDvocate*, a magazine for victims and advocates.

---

of course (See box). Step 2 is enforcement, and this is where restrictive and punitive laws play their part. Thus, MADD"s program must include enforcement (including punishment) to preserve the whole agenda of behavior change.

Here are some of the laws that MADD—along with a host of coalition partners, often brought together by MADD—has been sucessful in having enacted. MADD deserves much of the credit for one of the most remarkable behavior change efforts in recent times. Only a decade ago it was still acceptable to talk about the "drunken party" you went to over the weekend. Today, in most circles, anyone who mentioned such behavior would be scolded and possibly shunned. In large measure, this change can be traced to the catalytic leadership of Mothers Against Drunk Driving.

1. *Drunk Driving Prevention Act of 1988.* States were offered incentives in the form of highway safety fund grants for passing legislation aimed at reducing alcohol-related offenses and deaths, including a minimum 21 drinking age—up from 18 in most states. The act was controversial, but eventually most states adopted the age to avoid losing federal funds.

2. *Victim's Crime Act of 1984.* This act provides compensation rights and

FOUR STEPS TO PUBLIC BEHAVIOR CHANGE THROUGH PR CAMPAIGNS

The work of Jim Grunig, Harold Mendelsohn, Brenda Darvin, Maxwell McCombs, and many others suggests this approach.

1. **Coalition campaign,** so that the target audience gets the feeling that everyone who counts is trying to persuade them, that it is obviously the thing to do socially. Appeals in such a campaign must follow three phases:

   • *Problem (or opportunity) recognition.* Gaining widespread understanding that the issue is an opportunity or a problem.

   • *Problem (or opportunity) personalization.* Making target audience realize it involves them, they could be affected.

   • *Constraint removal.* Letting them know they can do something about it.

2. **Enforcement.** Establishing rules and laws mandating or outlawing the behavior.

3. **Engineering.** Enacting a structural change to work around the situation, for example, raising the drinking age to reduce drunk driving accidents by young drivers.

4. **Social reinforcement.** When the behavior becomes the societally accepted norm and social rewards and punishments take over the job of enforcing it.

grants for the survivors of drunk driving accidents.

3. *Alcoholic Beverage Labeling Act of 1988.* This act states that all alcoholic beverage containers bear a warning about the dangers of driving after drinking. ■

QUESTIONS FOR DISCUSSION

1. MADD was an organization established by one who had suffered a great tragedy because of the carelessness of a drunk driver. Today the organization has been extremely successful in exacting changes in societal attitudes against drunk driving. What does their success indicate about relationships formed when people who have suffered the same tragedy band together?

2. Can you think of another organization that was formed because of an emotion-laden circumstance? Has it been as successful as MADD? Explain your answer.

3. What other communication vehicles could MADD utilize to spread its message?

PROBLEM 8-A Smokeout Can Be a Hot Potato

You are a first-year employee at W. L. Fixit Associates, a public relations firm in Piedmont, North Carolina, a city of 40,000 people that has long thrived on tobacco growing and manufacturing. Mr. Fixit started the agency 10 years earlier after handling communications for the local Chamber of Commerce. He is well known and knows everybody important in the region.

You're doing well. You've just been advanced to Associate Account Executive and assigned the Piedmont General Hospital as your very own client. Among other clients of the agency are a nearby college, a large resort hotel, a new downtown shopping mall, and the United Way.

At the hospital, you're helping them deal with complaints about the high costs of health care, as well as promoting greater use of a new day-care adjunct, annual fund-raising campaign, and employee morale.

One day in August, the Fixit senior account executive comes into your office and says, "You're about to get your first sticky wicket to handle." He tells you that the United Way has committed to implement the "Great American Smokeout" annual event of the American Cancer Society and has asked the Fixit agency to implement it with all their clients. Mr. Fixit feels that the agency could duck out by pleading a conflict of interest, but with a public health issue like this that would do the agency more harm than coming up with a plan that has a chance of keeping everybody happy.

Your supervisor tells you: "It will be your job to come up with a catchy, contagious 1-day event at Piedmont General." He hands you a packet that explains the Smokeout concept of affecting smokers' behavior, suggests ways to get the cooperation of various organizations, tie in local public health officials and other community leaders, attract the media, instruct those in the facilities how to prepare, make it a fun event, recognize and reward those who abstain for a day, and measure the success. The packet includes examples such as the organization that gave out survival kits including chewing gum and candy, another that put baskets of apples all around, another that set up smokeaters in designated smoke areas, another that removed cigarette vending machines on Smokeout Day, and another that sent a congratulatory letter from the president to each smoker employee who reported successfully abstaining on Smokeout Day. Then the account supervisor threw the curve.

"This is no piece of cake," he said. "Your hospital's largest contributor is the tobacco company over in Winston. There's a wing named for their founder, Colonel Piedmont. Also, have you noticed that the Piedmont's administrator is a chain smoker? That's why all the major committee meetings are held out on the penthouse roof in good weather. You've got to come up with an event that makes us look good enough to nonsmokers and the United Way without doing damage to our relationship with the hospital administration. Maybe you can persuade them there is a trade-off for them. As for smokers and the tobacco industry around here, don't do anything that could cause permanent alienation. Mr. Fixit wouldn't mind landing a tobacco account someday, and tobacco companies are branching out more and more into food products."

He added, "Mull it over. If you can't involve both sides working with each other, at least figure out a project in which neither's ox is gored so badly they have to fight back.

Put your ideas down on paper with a reasonable objective; keep in mind that United Way isn't a big-spending account; list what's new and newsworthy about your event, and explain what you have built into the plan to protect against seriously riling the tobacco people, including Colonel Piedmont's family, who made their millions on tobacco. Give me a call in 10 days and we'll take a look together at what you've come up with."

As you start thinking about a solution to this situation, you remember that the basis of a successful message strategy

- Emphasizes the benefit statement
- Avoids stiffening the resistance
- Asks for a willing suspension of disbelief

With this in mind, what further background research will you do before you start defining the objectives and activities of your program? Who will you talk to, what concerns do you anticipate, and how will you deal with them?

Using the feedback from this research, define the objectives of your program and describe and explain how the proposed activities will support your communications strategy; include some means of measuring the success in obtaining your objectives.

Do you see any ethical issues that might arise in handling this situation? If you do, how would you deal with them?

PROBLEM 8-B Refereeing a New Kind of Game

After earning three letters for sports at Louisiana State University, you were sidelined by a knee injury that kept you out of the professional draft. Fortunately, your journalism/public relations major helped you land a good job with Dorino, Marion public relations agency. The firm does some work for professional sports teams and suppliers and has good connections in the state capital. They also have a reputation for public service assistance to nonprofit organizations. You like it at Dorino, Marion. They like you.

The main account you personally handle is the subcommittee of the Mardi Gras, which brings in celebrities for the annual event. Your work tends to be seasonal except for periodic planning meetings, some out-of-town contacts, and some correspondence. Thus you have considerable spare time.

That situation changed suddenly one day, when the agency was approached to take on the public relations problems arising from the actions of Brother Omans, the charismatic, activist minister of the local Bible-for-Everybody Church. It seems that Omans, with the active support of a doctor who wrote an antiabortion book, has challenged the activities of the local Birth Control Institute Inc., an affiliate of Planned Parenthood International. They are known to perform and arrange abortions.

Brother Omans has notified the institute by mail that they are "committing murders" and that they risk "harsh judgment" in which "proper penalties can be imposed." He has led a picketing group, some of whose members went beyond passing out pamphlets to shouting at clients heading into the institute.

Mrs. Safeway, head of the institute, has gone to the police for protection. The police say that the pickets do not trespass as long as they stay on the sidewalk, that they have rights of assembly, and freedom of speech. If and when Brother Omans or his constituents break any law, they will be apprehended.

Mrs. Safeway is concerned that this reactive attitude may allow further escalation of potential violence. She therefore approaches Dorino, Marion to ask for advice in seeking a more proactive approach to the situation.

You are assigned the task of analyzing the situation and coming up with a proactive approach as a public service of your agency. You know that Louisiana favors restricting abortion rights and probably would, if it were legal, forbid any abortions except in very narrow circumstances.

To get your facts straight, even before you go to see Mrs. Safeway, you talk to a member of the local media with whom you went to school. He tells you that Brother Omans set up shop locally about 8 years ago. A profile the newspaper did on him shows that he has had quite a career. At one time he was a circus barker hailing originally from San Antonio, Texas, traveled through the southern Bible Belt, became a minister, and then moved to New Orleans. If he had anything in his background of moral turpitude, or arrests, there is nothing about it in the newspaper morgue.

From other sources, you find that in the past 8 years, Brother Omans, from the pulpit, has taken on or opposed witches, homosexuals, pornography, X-rated movies, the "mercy death" of a 93-year old comatose man, Mormon missionaries in general, and any woman who goes into politics specifically.

Armed with this information, you go to see Mrs. Safeway at the Birth Control Institute. She's scared. There have been so many instances of bombing or arson at Planned Parenthood clinics, she can envision some of Brother Omans's constituents making her place a target. She has notified the Planned Parenthood national office. She has read their Clinic Defense Manual and notified the appropriate offices in New Orleans of her concern. She hopes you can do something to calm the situation down, not antagonize Brother Omans, his doctor supporter, or his followers. She appreciates that your agency has agreed to take on this project as a public service. You respect her professionalism but recognize that some of her actions have themselves been adversarial.

Time to Fish or Cut Bait

Back at your office, you talk it over with your boss. You agree that there are such strong feelings on both sides that it would be tough to marshal enough neutral public opinion to induce a reconciliation without at the same time rousing special interests with strong bias toward a confrontation or worse.

"This looks like one of those situations calling for a brainstorming session at the agency, bringing together representatives of groups with a stake in peaceful coexistence, and no ax to grind, on abortion," your boss says. "Maybe we can get a strategic plan out of the session. If not, it will put Brother Omans on notice that some important people are watching him, and it may reassure Mrs. Safeway she isn't about to be bombed."

Your boss instructs you to make up an invitation list of about 15 organizations, starting with city hall, the police department, and the county medical society; a brief statement of the meeting's purpose; and a tentative agenda for the meeting. "When you get those done, let me have a look," your boss says.

1. Before you start on this project, what issues affecting other members of the firm and the firm's reputation in the community might you want to discuss with your supervisor? How would you suggest dealing with them?
2. Do you agree with the suggestion that the invitations list should include city hall and the police department? If so, why? If not, on what basis would you suggest omitting them?
3. Would you include Mrs. Safeway or Brother Omans or both in this initial meeting? What could be the positive and negative results of having them there?
4. What would be your list, the statement to invitees, and the agenda?
5. What would be your recommendation in alerting or not alerting the media and dealing with the possibility of a premature leak?

PROBLEM 8-C Anticipating Emerging Issues

You are in a one-person pr department for a large public school in the Midwest. You've done everything from writing newsletters to campaigning to passing a referendum for a school addition. The school is doing well, no big problems to contend with, just the day-to-day communications. But your antenna is always up, listening to your publics — students, teachers, administrators, community members, parent-teacher organization, elected officials, etc.

Last week you had a call from a parent complaining about the name of the school's mascot — The Braves. You also noticed an article in the local paper about a group called Find Another Name dealing with this issue of using American Indian names and mascots. An emerging issue? Or just a coincidence? A staff meeting with the principal is coming up on Friday. You decide to look into the issue and make a recommendation.

There currently is no issue anticipation team within the school and it crosses your mind that it would be beneficial for the school to have one, but everyone is so overworked you wonder how it could happen. Even so, you decide to recommend an issue anticipation team be formed and the subject of the school's mascot be considered.

For the upcoming meeting, put together a report regarding the school's mascot and make a recommendation for the school. Consider the ramifications of changing and of not changing the name. Also make recommendations for forming an issue anticipation team, where members would come from (school, parents, community, etc.), how often they would meet, what work they need to do between meetings, and how this would help the school and the community.

9 | CRISIS MANAGEMENT

Because a true crisis is a turning point, after which things may change drastically, an organization not prepared to deal with crisis is constantly at risk. Even sudden emergencies of crisis proportion can be anticipated—if not avoided—so risk management, issue anticipation, and crisis communication programs have become an important part of public relations technology.

Despite this sophistication in the work, the term *crisis management* does not imply that an organization or its public relations staff can *manage* external influences. What can—and must—be managed is the *response*. This depends on the practitioner's thorough understanding of three things:

1. The **public and political environment** in which the crisis is occurring.
2. The **culture and inner workings of the organization** facing the crisis.
3. **Human nature**—how will the persons and groups involved most likely react to the crisis itself, to attempts to alleviate it, and to various communications, events, or activities?

UNDERSTAND HOW PEOPLE TYPICALLY RESPOND TO ISSUES

Philip Lesly, a veteran public relations counselor and philosopher/critic of the field, developed the following model. On any given issue dividing public opinion, people will fall into these groups:

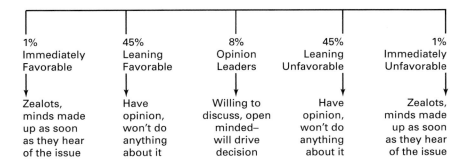

1% Immediately Favorable	45% Leaning Favorable	8% Opinion Leaders	45% Leaning Unfavorable	1% Immediately Unfavorable
Zealots, minds made up as soon as they hear of the issue	Have opinion, won't do anything about it	Willing to discuss, open minded– will drive decision	Have opinion, won't do anything about it	Zealots, minds made up as soon as they hear of the issue

Zealots will be the first to take firm stands on the issue—for and against. The majority, however, will watch to see which way the opinion leaders go before they are firm enough in their views to speak or act.

Public relations efforts must focus on the opinion leaders—the 8 percent who can influence the 90 percent. Resist the temptation to capitalize on the zealots who support your view. They anger people on both sides of the issue, including those inclined to agree with them.

Keep in mind that opinion leaders are rarely the visible leaders (elected officials or organization officers). Look for them at all levels and in all segments of society. The opinion leaders are not necessarily the educated and articulate, but are always the familiar and trustworthy. Most of us are inclined to seek reinforcement for our choices from people who are in the same situation we are, not from people who are "different."

HUMAN NATURE

When people are subjected to great emotional stress, their normally self-controlled behavior tends to become irrational and unpredictable. Their reactions turn down the steps of Maslow's hierarchy of human needs. At the bottom, of course, are a person's physical needs. One step above are a person's safety needs. When people feel that physical needs and safety needs are threatened, they are prone to panic. In panic, people's baser instincts for survival take command. This "survival" might be physical, financial, social, or some other component vital to a person's life, but you can count on self-interest or self-preservation to take command of a person's emotions and actions.

These phenomena become immediately apparent in such catastrophic circumstances as fires, floods, explosions, and tornadoes. The same pattern emerges, with less severity, in noncatastrophic situations such as a scarcity of gasoline or coffee, a spate of crime in a community, or even a standing-room-only crowd at a public event. The symptoms of potential panic and the concern for self are there. Similarly, sensations approaching panic may invade us when it appears that we may miss a departing airflight, lose a dear friend, find ourselves unexpectedly deprived of light in our home at night, or walk a dark street to our parked car.

THE ROLE OF COMMUNICATIONS

People tend to get reassurance concerning their physical well-being and safety largely from believable information that pierces through the uncertainty, rumors, and gossip. Human nature, fortunately, has a toughness about it, enabling most people to handle substantial bad news or physical danger by making adjustments. Knowing the alternatives, we make the best of even a bad deal. But we find it very difficult to cope for long periods with the uncertainties that come from not being informed or not trusting the information, whether the threat to us is as vital and near as a local rumor of a toxic chemical leak or as remote and impersonal as a drop in the Dow Jones stock market average.

Not every crisis is of the "instant" variety. Some crises develop over a period of time—days, weeks, or even months. Nevertheless, these events are just as much a crisis as those that are fast-breaking. But the consequences for managing a crisis, for keeping credible communication flowing, are intensified when the situation drags out. In any case, the public expects the leaders of trusted organizations to act with total honesty and sensitivity during and after a crisis.

TYPES OF CRISES

Institute for Crisis Management (ICM) defines a crisis as "a significant business disruption that stimulates extensive news media coverage. The resulting public scrutiny will affect the organization's normal operations and also could have a political, legal, financial, and governmental impact on its business." ICM identifies four basic *causes* of a crisis:

1. **Acts of God** (storms, earthquakes, volcanic action, etc.)
2. **Mechanical problems** (ruptured pipes, metal fatigue, etc.)
3. **Human error** (the wrong valve was opened, miscommunication about what to do, etc.)
4. **Management decisions, actions, or inaction** (the problem is not serious, nobody will find out)

Most fall in the last category and are the result of management not taking action when they were informed about a problem that eventually would grow into a crisis.

There are two basic types of crises, depending on the amount of warning time: (1) a **sudden crisis**, which comes without warning (employee injury, death of a key executive, oil spills, product tampering, etc.) and (2) a **smoldering crisis**, which is generally not known internally or externally until it goes public and generates negative news coverage. These problems are operational or organizational weaknesses, bad practices, and other discoverable or predictable bombs waiting to explode. Issue anticipation teams (See Chapter 8) can expose and eliminate these crises. ICM's analysis of business crises since 1990 indicates that the sudden crises are the minority. The majority are smoldering crises.

NEWS MEDIA INFLUENCE

The interpretation of public events affecting our lives falls heavily on the news media. News prerogatives and privileges are legally assured by the First Amendment to the U.S. Constitution. Abuses of these rights surface most often when fierce competition among the media makes a competitive advantage more important or urgent than simple truth and accuracy in protecting the public interest.

In recent years, few would argue that news media have been responsible carriers of information needed by citizens; most would say they have concentrated on scandals and titillating trivialities that provided public entertainment. This perception must be taken clearly into account when planning crisis strategy.

Similarly, the obligation of public relations toward the public interest is sometimes submerged or subverted by the desire to attain the special competitive interests of employers or clients.

A classic example of news media importance in alleviating uncertainty and preventing panic, or fostering the causes of panic, was the Three Mile Island nuclear plant accident in 1979. The onslaught of newspeople from literally all over the world was a new experience for the few thousand residents of the area. They were accustomed to the presence of the nuclear plant but not to the swarm of reporters and photographers seeking to outdo each other in shock-inducing coverage under the pressure of news deadlines. Some news media, in spite of the temptations, did not yield to the competitive advantage that might have come from purveying rumors and gossip of dire predictions. Others clearly did.

For the power company and the Nuclear Regulatory Commission, this was an experience for which there were no precise precedential guidelines, no rules. Their early silence was lamentable. However, an admission that they did not know what was happening might have been even worse.[1]

Under the circumstances, local panic was averted more by what President Carter's visit communicated *symbolically* than by any *information* issued by the company or nuclear authorities or by any suggestions, analyses, or complaints on the part of news media.

After the problem had been brought under control and an evaluation was conducted in an unemotional environment, testimony brought out that it was the lack of information that distressed neighbors and local officials most of all. Lacking trustworthy information, humans tend to assume the worst. Trust must precede information.

The ability to communicate trustworthy information, whether directly or via news media, is a measure of a practitioner's effectiveness or ineffectiveness. In unexpected situations of disaster, crisis, or emergency, the news media and the practice of public relations have had their finest examples of public service and their most severe episodes of failure and ineptitude. The cases in this chapter illustrate this point.

FUNDAMENTAL GUIDELINES

There are some guidelines that continue to help organizations handle crisis communication situations. Among them are:

1. **Anticipate the unexpected.** There are few events that cannot be anticipated. You might not know when they will happen, but an organization can anticipate a fire, a flood, a strike, a fatal accident on the job, a robbery, and many other unexpected events. Unfortunately, *the greatest single obstacle to effective crisis preparation is management denial that one will occur,* notes ICM.
2. **Institute and practice a crisis communications plan** for those events that may happen to your organization.
3. **Train employees** in what to do in these circumstances.

---

[1]Rear Admiral David M. Cooney, former Chief of Information, Department of the Navy, makes the point that "in the early stages of a crisis situation, you don't tell people things you don't know or aren't sure of. . . . You never involve yourself in conjecture . . . because the chances are that you are going to be wrong. A crisis situation breaks down to certain questions. What happened? Why did it happen? What are you going to do to keep it from happening again? What is the overall impact on the people who are involved and their dependents?" He recommends, "Be organized always to handle a crisis in the next 15 minutes."

4. Have **one spokesperson** communicating to the public and media during the crisis.
5. If it is a crisis affecting the public, rather than just the organization, **another spokesperson** or persons will also be required to keep elected officials and opinion leaders directly advised.
6. **Do not speculate** on the cause, the cost, or anything else. Provide information about only what is known.

References and Additional Readings

Armbruster, Timothy. "Crisis in Cleveland." *Public Relations Journal* (August 1968). Classic community crisis.

Barton, Laurence. *Crisis in Organizations II.* Cincinnati, OH: South-Western Publishing Company, 2000.

Fink, Steven. *Crisis Management: Planning for the Inevitable.* London, England: Kogan Page Ltd., 2000.

Gorski, Thomas. "A Blueprint for Crisis Management." *Association Management* 50, 1 (January 1998): 78–79.

Hudson, Howard Penn. "Crisis Communications." *Public Relations Quarterly* 42, 3 (Fall 1997).

Institute for Crisis Management, P.O. Box 219, Louisville, KY 40201-0219, 812/284-8351, www.crisisexperts.com (has a crisis bibliography online).

Irvine, Robert. *When You Are the Headline.* Louisville, KY: ICM, 1987.

Jackson, Debbie. "Bayer Mobilizes Resources to Counter Crisis at Home." *Chemical Week* 152 (April 21, 1993): 24–31.

Johnson, Daniel. "Crisis Management: Forewarned Is Forearmed." *Journal of Business Strategy* 14 (March/April 1993): 58–64.

Lerbinger, Otto. *The Crisis Manager: Facing Risk and Responsibility*. Mahwah, NJ: Lawrence Erlbaum Assocs., 1996.

Lerbinger, Otto. *Managing Corporate Crises.* Boston: Barrington Press, 1986.

Lerbinger, Otto. "Beyond Crisis Management—Issues Raised by Three Mile Island." *purview* (supplement of *pr reporter*, September 10, 1979). Discusses three articles in *Public Opinion* (June/July 1979).

Lerbinger, Otto, and Nathaniel Sperber. *Managers Public Relations Handbook.* Reading, MA: Addison-Wesley, 1982. See chapters 1 and 2.

Lesly, Philip. *Overcoming Opposition.* Upper Saddle River, NJ: Prentice Hall, 1984.

Lukaszewski, James. *Crisis Communication Planning Strategies: A Crisis Communication Management Workbook.* White Plains, NY: Lukaszewski Group, 2000.

Maggart, Lisa. "Bowater Incorporated—A Lesson in Crisis Communication." *Public Relations Quarterly* 39, 3 (Fall 1994): 29–31.

Marra, Francis. "Crisis Communication Plans: Poor Predictors of Excellent Public Relations." *Public Relations Review* 24, 4 (Winter 1998): 461–474.

Mindszenthy, Bart, T. A. G. Watson, and William Koch. *No Surprises: The Crisis Management System.* Toronto: Bedford House Communication, 1988.

Nagelschmidt, Joseph, ed. The *Public Affairs Handbook.* New York: Amacom, 1982. Several leading public relations practitioners and corporate executives share their experiences on all aspects of issues and crises.

pr reporter Vol. 43 No. 33 (August 21, 2000). "Lessons from Firestone—and Ford—in Massive Recall. First Rule Violated: Always Begin by Saying You're Sorry."

pr reporter Vol. 36 No. 19 (May 10, 1993). "United Way Case: Answer to Crisis Is Prior Work on Basics."

pr reporter Vol. 31 No. 26 (June 27, 1988). Lead article emphasizes challenge to influence behavior and induce action by supertargeting, focused appeals, rather than broadsides to shape attitude or opinion. Cites Dayton Hudson's thwarting of a takeover attempt covered by Case 9-5 in this chapter.

pr reporter Vol. 22 No. 38 (October 8, 1979). "Investigative Reporter Says Candor and Immediate Answers Not Always Necessary, Even in Crisis Communications." Cites views of Les Whitten, senior reporter on Jack Anderson's staff.

Public Relations Body of Knowledge. New York: PRSA. See abstracts dealing with "Media Relations, Including Crisis Management."

Rosnow, Ralph. "Rumor as Communication: A Contextualist Approach." *Journal of Communication* 38 (Winter 1988): 12–28.

Schoeny, Heather. "Koala Springs International's Product Recall." *Public Relations Quarterly* 36 (Winter 1991–92): 25–26.

Shell, Adam, ed., "Communicating Foreign Crises; Panel Debates Best Approach," *Public Relations Journal* 50 (February, 1994): 4.

Shell, Adam. "At City Hall, Every Day's a Crisis." *Public Relations Journal* 48 (February 1992): 7.

Snyder, Leonard. "An Anniversary Review and Critique: The Tylenol Crisis." *Public Relations Review* 9 (Fall 1983): 24–34.

Tiller, Michael. "Is Your Disaster Plan Effective?" *Management Review* 83 (April 1994): 57.

Wylie, Frank. "Anticipation: Key to Crisis Management." *Communication World* 14, 7 (July 1997): 34–35.

Four classic programs worthy of investigation:

(1) The handling of employee news when a company president and four employees were killed in an air crash, Southern Company Services, P.O. Box 720071, Atlanta, GA 30346;

(2) A disaster plan by Johns-Manville, in *pr reporter*, June 18, 1979;

(3) Closing an oil refinery in a small town, Amoco Company, P.O. Box 5077, Atlanta, GA. 30302, ask for PR manual *Communications During an Emergency*; and

(4) Oil spill off Santa Barbara, California in "Effects of the Santa Barbara Blowout," *US News and World Report*, February 8, 1971.

CASES

CASE 9-1   THERE'S A SYRINGE IN MY PEPSI CAN!

Large corporations are always potential targets for those who seek fame or fortune at the expense of those companies. In the summer of 1993, PepsiCo, makers of Pepsi-Cola and Diet Pepsi, among other beverages, found itself an unwilling subject in one of the most widespread news stories of the day, a story in which the PepsiCo was implicated in multiple claims of foreign objects being found in unopened cans of Diet Pepsi.[1]

This confidence crisis put the international soft drink company before the public in a way no company wants to be viewed. But the ensuing activities of the Pepsi response team, and the U.S. Food and Drug Administration, calmed the crisis and won for the company the coveted "Best of Silver Anvils" in the 1994 Public Relations Society of America competition.

THE SITUATION

On June 9, 1993, Tacoma, Washington residents Earl (Tex) and Mary Triplett reported finding a used syringe in a half-empty Diet Pepsi can. They turned the can over to their lawyer who contacted the county health department.

The next day, local television station KIRO aired a report of this incident, citing a Sudafed tampering just 2 years previously, and the fact that needles aroused concerns about AIDS. No other news medium covered the story that day.

The following day, June 11, a second needle claim was made in Washington, and the *Seattle Times* and other local media picked up the story, adding that in neither case had there been reports of injury resulting from the incidents.

On June 12, the Food and Drug Administration (FDA) did not recommend a recall, but did issue a five-state consumer alert, asking consumers to pour soft drinks, particularly Diet Pepsi, into a glass or cup before drinking it. The next day, a New Orleans man claimed to have found a syringe in a can of Diet Pepsi, and by June 14, 10 more claims were reported.

Wire services and national broadcast media picked up the story as more reports came in. The coverage was second only to the Supreme Court nomination of Ruth Bader Ginsburg, as people reported finding syringes, sewing needles, pins, screws, a crack cocaine vial, and even a bullet in Diet Pepsi cans.

By June 16, claims had been reported in 24 states, including one from a reporter for the *Milwaukee Journal* who said she had no plans to sue Pepsi after finding a needle in a can of Diet Pepsi. Meanwhile, the *Los Angeles Times* and CBS reported the needle found by the Tripletts may have belonged to

---

[1]This case was prepared by University of Central Florida students Aimee Brownell and Troy Jewell under the supervision of instructor Frank R. Stansberry, APR, Fellow PRSA.

a diabetic relative. In one week's time, more than 50 incidents had been reported to the police, the FDA or the media. None, however, reported any illness or injury associated with the incidents.

THE FACTS

Throughout this 7-day nightmare, neither Pepsi nor the FDA could see any rational reason for the alleged incidents being reported. Soft-drink filling lines are high-speed, high-tech production lines in which empty, open aluminum cans are fed (upside down) down a conveyer at high speeds (1,200 a minute) to be filled. During this roller-coaster ride, the cans are cleaned with heat, water, and air before being inverted, passing through a closed filling filter/screen, and emerging filled and capped at the end. At no time is there an opportunity for foreign objects to find their way into the container, except during the brief time in the filling chamber. Further, the objects being reported are not those commonly found in a soft-drink plant or any other workplace.

The geographic spread of the reports was also difficult to understand. Canning plants are regional operations. The plant in Washington serves only five western states. Yet contaminants were being reported all across the county. These products were being produced by numerous canning operations so there was no direct link among them except for the brand of the product being produced, and the production process. Unless there was a concerted effort to tamper with Diet Pepsi, there was no reason to link the widespread reports to a single production problem. The FDA said continually it could find no connection from a production standpoint among the growing number of complaints.

PepsiCo, convinced its production operations were not at fault, decided against any recall of the products involved. PepsiCo

President Craig Weatherup, taking the "point guard" position on the response team, said repeatedly in interviews that "there is no health issue" around the reports, citing the lack of any illness or injuries associated with the reports.

In a *Wall Street Journal* interview, Weatherup said, "We've gone through every can line, every plant, numerous records. All the evidence points to syringes going into the cans after they were opened."

THE PERCEPTIONS

"All the evidence" was lost on the news media and the consuming public, however. "When the national media juggernaut gets hold of something, and you're it," PepsiCo Vice President of Public Affairs Becky Madeira told a PRSA workshop a year later, "it's a public trial, and it's not much fun. This was a crisis without precedent."

Fueling the controversy were the continued reports of new contaminants found in Diet Pepsi. In city after city, residents came forth to press their claims of having found foreign objects in their cans of Diet Pepsi. Time after time, the familiar Diet Pepsi logo (being advertised at the time with the popular Ray Charles jingle punctuated by "Uh Huh") was being seen in the media with either an alleged contaminant object or a facsimile.

Weatherup continued the counter-attack, saying he was "99.99 percent sure" the incidents were not related to anything under Pepsi's control. But sales slipped. Weatherup, in a follow-up report after the crisis had been put to rest, said, "The week of the hoax, sales dipped only 3 to 4 percent . . ." but 3 percent of Diet Pepsi's sales still represents millions of dollars. The perception crisis was real, indeed.

Adding to the difficulty in containing the spreading number of incidents was a 10-year pattern of substantiated and unsubstantiated product tamperings—some with fatal consequences. In 1982 (and later in 1986) deaths were reported from Tylenol capsules laced with poison (See Case 6-3). In 1986, rat poison was found in Contac (and other) products; glass fragments were discovered in Gerber baby food; and two people died in Washington after taking cyanide-laced Extra-Strength Excedrin. And there were the deaths of two people in Washington from ingesting Sudafed. The consuming public had reason to be concerned, as did Pepsi. With the number of soft-drink alternatives available, some consumers were opting for the competition.

THE PROBLEM

The problem for Pepsi was how to stem the reports, show the safety of its products, and win back the customer loyalty, which had made Diet Pepsi the number two diet drink in the country.

Timing was important because the reports were mounting before the wildfire of news reports. "Speed is essential," said Madeira, "but so is accuracy. It is very dangerous to attempt to explain the cause of the crisis without facts that are corroborated from outside experts. In our case, the expert was the FDA."

The most important question was "Is there a health risk?" The FDA took the lead in answering this question, and almost immediately determined that, in the two Seattle-area reports, there was no health hazard or risk.

A second question involved the presence of syringes and needles in or around the filling process. Again, the FDA became the intervening public and determined, after an exhaustive examination of Pepsi's procedures and facilities, that the high speed and integrity of the filling lines made it impossible for any such object to find its way into the canning process. There was no internal

tampering. Whatever was turning up in the cans had been placed there after the cans were opened. FDA Commissioner David Kessler agreed that there was no health risk from the tamperings and, most probably, no relationship between the alleged tampering reports popping up coast to coast.

The facts obviously weighed heavily in Pepsi's favor—the randomness of the reports, the security of the filling line process, the dubious nature of all the claims, the variety of objects being reported, and the fact that needles and syringes are never found in production-line situations under normal conditions. No one said there were any health issues resulting from the tamperings. There was no reason to think any of the reports had merit.

Perceptions, fueled by media reports, however, were just the opposite. Consumers in nearly two dozen states were lining up to claim contaminants were found in Diet Pepsi cans. Diet Pepsi cans were on television as much as Jay Leno—nightly. In fact, Leno and his peers were having a field day with the issue, poking fun at the difficult situation in nightly monologues. Editorial cartoonists also joined the spoofing by suggesting that everything from a power drill to the famous "missing sock" was turning up in Diet Pepsi cans. For a seemingly endless 96 hours, the Diet Pepsi scare was the nation's top news story. Something had to be done, and the Pepsi team mobilized and swung to the offensive.

THE PUBLIC RELATIONS IMPACT

When the story first broke on June 9, Pepsi let the local bottler, Alpac Corporation, handle the media inquiry. Operating under the premise that the plant was secure, Alpac also had to investigate any possible way an object *could* have been introduced during the filling process. Working with local health officials and the FDA, Alpac assisted in the investigation and found nothing that would implicate the filling line.

The plant was opened to the media and the plant owner, manager, and quality assurance manager were made available to the press. All they were able to say at the time, however, was that the situation was unusual and that they would do everything they could to cooperate with local authorities to find the cause of the crisis.

But even these findings did not stem the tide of complaints filtering in or the growing media interest in the problem. Pepsi was going to have to get involved at the national level; the problem was more than Alpac's to solve.

Crisis coordinator Madeira identified four primary publics to be addressed:

➤ The news media
➤ Customers (those who purchased the product for retail sale)
➤ Consumers
➤ Employees and local Pepsi-Cola bottlers

The **public affairs department**, which Madeira directed, had a team of six media relations specialists prepared to respond to media inquiries and to provide regular updates of facts and developments. *One Clear Voice* was the key approach. A second team wrote and produced video news releases, audiotapes, press releases, charts, and diagrams of the production process and photos for external and internal distribution.

Consumer Relations had 24 people manning the 24-hour toll-free hotlines, taking calls from consumers, hearing reports and comments, and monitoring public opinion as it developed.

Scientific and Regulatory Affairs assigned technical and quality assur-

ance specialists to work with the FDA and local health departments to evaluate and track each complaint.

Sales and marketing personnel were responsible for maintaining relationships with its customers—supermarkets, restaurants, convenience stores, and others who sold Pepsi products to the consumer.

Manufacturing experts assisted the FDA and developed simple, easy to understand explanations of the filling line process for the news media and the public.

The **legal department** was involved at all stages of the reporting and communication process.

The entire effort was kept in-house as opposed to bringing in an outside crisis communication consultant.

Pepsi's response centered on four principles:

➤ **Put public safety first.** Look at the problem through the perspective of the public and address their concerns.

➤ **Find the problem and fix it.** Pepsi was convinced the problem was not within its production facilities, so it worked with the regulatory authorities to demonstrate the security of their plants, and to investigate and respond to all complaints.

➤ **Communicate frequently, quickly, and regularly.** Use both broadcast and print communication tools. Be honest, available, and informed about what the media needs and be prepared to meet those needs.

➤ **Take full responsibility for resolving the crisis.** Pepsi realized quickly that this was a problem that the public expected it to help resolve. Pointing fingers at consumers or ducking responsibility was never an option even though most on the crisis response team felt the reports of foreign objects were hoaxes.

The chief weapon in the defusing of the crisis would be a compelling video news release showing exactly what happens on a can filling line and how difficult it would be to introduce any foreign element into a can during this process.

Television had brought the crisis into 100 million American homes and television would be Pepsi's best opportunity to expose the folly of the reports. On June 15, 6 days after the Tripletts said they found the syringe, Pepsi presented a dramatic look at an ordinary can filling line. The same consumers who had seen the Diet Pepsi cans with syringes now saw millions of the blue and red cans whirring by at the rate of 1,200 per minute. Image confronted image—and news programs picked up the video news release (VNR) in such numbers that soon nearly 300 million viewers had seen the footage.

That initial VNR and three subsequent ones presented the company's position that its production lines were safe and secure. Diet Pepsi was safe when it left the plant. Weatherup, continuing his role of spokesperson, appeared on a dozen major TV shows and the Pepsi public affairs team had conducted nearly 2,000 interviews within the week.

"Our strategy was to reassure the public that this was not a manufacturing crisis," said Madeira. "What was happening was not occurring inside our plants."

The strategy worked, assisted by some excellent support from the FDA and some good luck. A third Pepsi-Cola VNR contained images from an in-store surveillance camera that showed a woman trying to stick a syringe into a Diet Pepsi can while the cashier was not looking. Tampering with the food supply is a felony and the woman was arrested. When the arrest was made, the VNR was released and the hoax began to crumble.

Many who had made claims against Pepsi began to recant their stories for fear of prosecution. In states across the country, arrest after arrest was made and reported by the media. Those who tried to profit at the expense of "big business" were located and apprehended. The media had gotten the message and were eager to highlight the consequences faced by the perpetrators. Weatherup continued his offensive and, as the number of arrests increased, claimed vindication for the Pepsi products.

By June 21, Pepsi was being defended and applauded in editorials and columns around the country and the FDA announced happily that "the hoax is over." A year later, 54 people had been prosecuted by the states in which they resided for their roles in the hoax, and all had been convicted. The *Milwaukee Journal* reporter had also recanted her claim but lost her job.

In newspapers across the country, Pepsi ran a clever ad stating "Pepsi is pleased to announce . . . nothing." The crisis was over.

SECOND GUESSES

Monday morning quarterbacks had a field day with the hoax and its many elements. Most of the second-guessing involved the timing of Pepsi's rebuttal. "I don't understand why Pepsi didn't explain everything on the first day," said Don Smith, the city editor of the *Seattle Post Intelligencer*, who was skeptical about the reports from the beginning. In spite of his misgivings on timing, Smith's evaluation of the Pepsi response was "they did fine."

Steven Fink, a Los Angeles-based crisis communication consultant, told the *Toronto*

Globe and Mail that Pepsi had two crises—one of reality and one of perception. "The crisis of perception is that the company is not protecting the safety of their consumers . . . If the public has the perception that the company was playing fast and loose with their safety, this will hurt the company in the long run."

The lack of a recall spurred some critics, too. Tylenol's swift (and expensive) recall of its products in 1982 left the impression that a recall was the linchpin of any product safety issue. Pepsi, however, saw no health or safety concerns resulting from its problems and opted against a product recall.

"The cost of a recall is a valid corporate concern," said Mayer Nudell, a crisis management consultant, "but they [Pepsi] have to weigh the short-term implications for the bottom line against the long-term corporate image and therefore market share and public receptivity and everything else. Very often, it's that long-term image that corporations sometimes lose sight of."

While Pepsi eschewed the recall, several retailers grew uneasy with the escalating furor and pulled the product from their shelves. Sheetz, a convenience store company with 250 stores in four mid-Atlantic states, pulled 16-ounce bottles of Diet Pepsi off its shelves after a West Virginia man reported finding a syringe. Other grocers and convenience stores from Iowa to Oklahoma followed suit. Kroger, the nation's largest food chain, offered customers a full refund on Pepsi products if they were uneasy after hearing the news reports.

Madeira concedes things might have been handled better, but points out "time was the enemy. It took us time to conduct the investigation in the plants, await FDA conclusions, and then get the information together to answer all the questions. The dynamics changed every hour. There is no standard crisis communication formula where you pull out your crisis readiness plan and implement it. You have to adapt your plan and process to the circumstances. In this case, this wasn't a product or public health crisis, it was a media problem. The more you saw that visual of the can and the syringe, the greater the concern became."

Looking back, she admits Pepsi did not expect that this would be a national story. "We have things that happen locally, and you do your job locally, and it's over and done with," said Madeira.

While that wasn't the case, few will argue with the success of the response. Sales dipped but soon recovered. Pepsi's positive relationships within the FDA paid huge dividends. In addition to using the FDA experts as counselors during the crisis, Pepsi was able to benefit from those same experts being powerful opinion leaders by speaking as third-party endorsers of the company's lack of culpability.

Pepsi's strong understanding of the news media and the experience built up over the years also contributed to the success. Even though Pepsi was the victim of a week-long media feeding frenzy at its expense, Madeira and her staff worked with reporters in getting the situation turned around. "Your only defense when your company is on trial in the media," she said, "is to be a participant in that trial." ■

QUESTIONS FOR DISCUSSION

1. Discuss the implications of Pepsi's strategy, specifically
   a. Putting public safety first
   b. Taking full responsibility for solving the problem
   c. Using the media to present its case
2. Differentiate between "solving the problem" and "solving the situation."
3. Evaluate Pepsi's decision not to order a product recall. What are the plusses and minuses of such a decision?
4. What options did Pepsi have on June 10, 1993? Did the company select the correct course of action? Why or why not? What other choices could the company officials have made?
5. Discuss the role of the FDA in addressing/solving the situation. Was Pepsi's use of the FDA beneficial? Why? How?
6. Could this "crisis" have been avoided? How? Shortened? How?
7. Did the news media behave responsibly in reporting this story? Cite examples to support your answer.
8. Discuss the communication tools employed by Pepsi in solving the problem. Specifically evaluate the role of VNRs.
9. What was the "turning point" in Pepsi's resolution of this problem? Cite examples to support your answer.
10. When "perception is reality, facts notwithstanding," how can a company such as PepsiCo create new perceptions? Did the company succeed? Cite examples from the case to support your answer.

CASE 9-2   A CLASSIC: BHOPAL—A NIGHTMARE FOR UNION CARBIDE

In effective handling of a critical issue, preparation and anticipation are key considerations. Managing issues means intercepting the ninety percent that are self-inflicted. Critical issues may be created in any of the following manners:

➤ Maintaining irresponsible policies

➤ Failing to monitor internal activities

➤ Not applying sound response strategies when faced with criticism

➤ Failing to allocate adequate resources and priority to anticipating issues

And, of course, sometimes crises will occur even when all possible preparations have been made.

When an issue escalates, it may become a crisis. A crisis is defined as a highly stressful struggle or conflict within an adversarial environment. It is marked by a potentially damaging turning point that could result in financial or mortal disaster—after which things will never be the same.

Effective communication is an essential part of trying to control any crisis situation. It is the responsibility of the company or organization to provide information about what is happening, the effects it will have on numerous publics, and what the company plans to do to resolve the situation. The questions most asked by the publics involved are:

1. What exactly has happened?
2. Why was information about the crisis not released sooner?
3. What could have been done to prevent it from happening?

When a crisis hits, its effects are felt throughout an organization. The atmosphere is emotionally unstable and forces those involved to react quickly and sometimes without thinking of long-term ramifications, even if there is some sort of anticipatory plan in place.

The focus of this case (as well as Case 9-3) is the analysis of a major industrial corporation and how it anticipated and managed its crisis—or, you be the judge, how it failed to do so.

HISTORY

In December of 1984, Union Carbide Corporation (UCC), a chemical manufacturer, was the 37th-largest industrial organization in the United States.[1] The chain of events that occurred on December 2 and 3 in Bhopal at Union Carbide India, Ltd. (UCIL), changed the face of UCC forever.

---

[1]Our thanks to Bob Berzok, Director, Corporate Communications, at Union Carbide for providing us with a wealth of information for this case.

UCC had formed UCIL in the 1920s for manufacturing its products there. After India gained its independence from Britain in 1947, the government began to push for greater ownership in the country's businesses.

According to J. J. Kenney, the director of federal government affairs (now retired), construction of the Bhopal plant in 1977 was controlled by the regulations of the Indian government. After UCC gave the preliminary plant designs to the government, government agencies took over the final design and construction of the Bhopal facility.[2] It was the government that approved the plant design when the facility was built.

The government wanted the plant to be as labor-intensive as possible—in order to provide needed employment—so it had not installed the computer systems in use at UCC plants in the United States to monitor operations.

By the time of the Bhopal tragedy, UCC had reduced its share of ownership to 50.9 percent, while the Indian government and private citizens owned the other 49.1 percent. Plant operations were managed solely by Indians.

THE CRISIS HITS

At about 11:30 P.M. on December 2, a leak in one of the valves was discovered by employees at the plant. The leak was detected after a report that the eyes of some employees were tearing from irritation. At approximately 12:15 A.M. a control room operator reported an increase in tank pressure. The tank contained liquefied methyl isocyanate (MIC), a lethal pesticide. A safety valve ruptured and released excess liquid into an adjacent tank, where a caustic soda solution should have neutralized the chemical. This neutralization did not occur.

In the case of an emergency, the safety system was supposed to flash (instantaneously light and burn) any escaping gas to prevent it from entering the outside atmosphere. This system was not operating, and 40 tons of deadly gas poured into the neighboring community.

Theories as to how the leak had occurred were many and widespread. One popular theory reported extensively in the newspapers was that an employee had failed to follow correct procedures and thus started the reaction that released the MIC gas: It wasn't until 1½ years later that investigators found that an employee had sabotaged the tanks by deliberately connecting a water hose to the MIC tanks (See Figure 9-1).

DEATH IN THE COMMUNITY

Many residents in the area thought UCIL manufactured *kheti ki dawai,* a harmless medicine for the crops. In reality, the chemical-turned-gas was lethal to humans because it formed liquid in the lungs of its victims. While some died in their sleep, others drowned from the liquid in their lungs while running through the streets looking for help.

Official estimates stated that 1,700 residents were killed. In addition, 3,500 were hospitalized and 75,000 were treated for injuries sustained from exposure to the gas. Death figures range from anywhere between 1,700 to 4,000. It was also estimated that 60,000 people will require long-term respiratory care. These figures earned it the designation as "the worst industrial disaster ever."[3]

Many of those killed were living in shantytowns constructed illegally near the plant. UCC had repeatedly requested that these be moved from the area. Instead of

---

[2]Lee W. Baker, *The Credibility Factor*, Homewood, IL: Business One Irwin, 1993, p. 48.
[3]Ibid, p. 45.

Union Carbide and Bhopal

Setting the Record Straight on Employee Sabotage and Efforts to Provide Relief

WHAT REALLY HAPPENED AT BHOPAL? Since the tragedy in December 1984, Union Carbide Corporation's primary concern has been with providing relief and assistance to the victims, and determining how the incident happened. Generally, initial details and subsequent news reports and books have contained a great deal of erroneous information. New information uncovered during an on-going investigation has led UCC to the conclusion that the tragedy was caused by employee sabotage and that there was a cover-up afterwards by certain operators on duty that night.

FIGURE 9-1 Union Carbide published a brochure that illustrated its hypothesis as to how the tragedy in Bhopal happened. Shown here is "Setting the Record Straight on Employee Sabotage and Efforts to Provide Relief."

(Courtesy of Union Carbide.)

requiring the people in these illegal shanty-towns to move, the Indian government changed the law to make it legal for them to be so close to the plant.

UCC POLICIES BROKEN

The magnitude of disaster at the Bhopal facility was partly attributed to the many breakdowns in its safety equipment (See Figure 9-2). The plant would poorly repair or simply shut off malfunctioning equipment. Both of these actions are serious violations of UCC policy. The following inconsistencies contributed to the conditions during the emerging crisis:

➤ A cooling unit was shut down months before the incident. Policy stated that this unit must remain functioning to prevent overheating.

➤ A flare tower, designed to flash escaping gases, had been out of service for 6 days.

➤ A scrubber (an apparatus used for removing impurities from gases), which was to be continuously running, had been down for 2 months.

➤ The warning system was inadequate for the tasks that the plant was performing. There were no alarms, no employee drills, no public education, and so on.

COMMUNICATIONS DIFFICULTIES

From the beginning, UCC encountered problems in addressing public concerns because of the physical communication difficulties it encountered.

FIGURE 9-2   A diagram of the system setup at the UCIL plant in Bhopal.

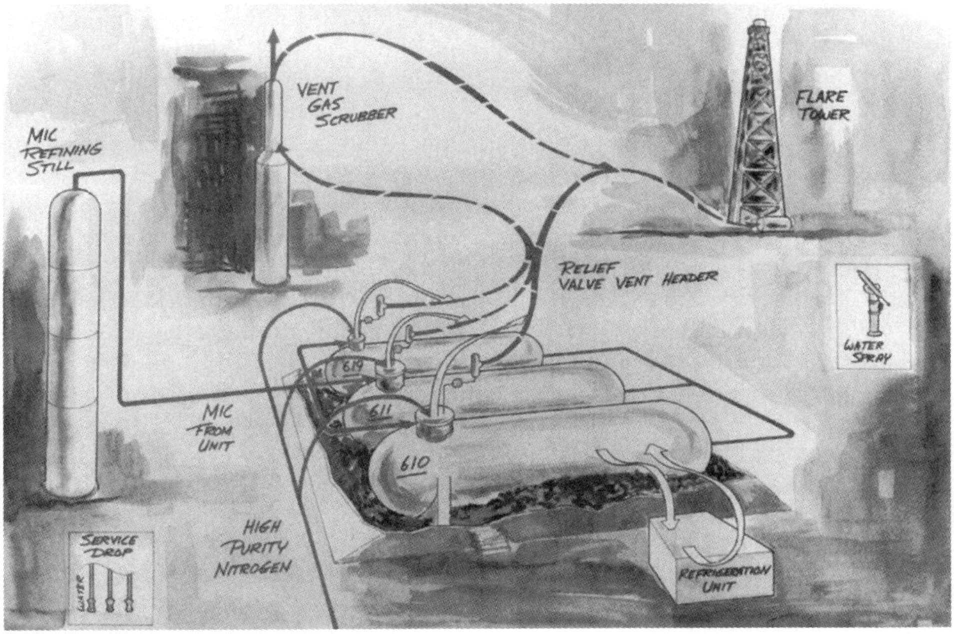

(Courtesy of Union Carbide.)

➤ *In an international incident such as Bhopal, communication difficulties can be caused not only by physical boundaries but also by cultural ones.* UCC communicators in the United States from the beginning tried to be open and candid. However, UCIL officials in India were advised by legal counsel not to communicate.

➤ *Bhopal, a city of 750,000, had only two international telephone lines serving the city. This situation hampered any communications that were necessary.* Because of this obstacle, UCC was receiving the bulk of its information from media reports.

➤ *The company's communication specialists who were put on this case found it extremely difficult to obtain reliable information from India.*

➤ *The Bhopal facility failed to educate the community.* Death could have been avoided if the citizens had been instructed to place a wet cloth over the face. Most of the deaths that occurred were the old and the young because their lungs could not withstand the poison.

➤ *Communications management for UCC in the United States was among the last to know about the incident.* Hours after the incident, Edward Van Den Ameele, UCC press relations manager and officer on duty, received a call at 4:30 A.M. at his home from a reporter from CBS radio. The reporter was calling for a reaction to the pesticide leak. This was the first that Van Den Ameele had heard of it.

➤ *The plant manager of the Indian subsidiary had no background in communication, let alone crisis management.* He told a local official that "this will probably have no ill effect."

UCC ACCEPTS MORAL RESPONSIBILITY

UCC did have a domestic crisis plan, but what happened in Bhopal was unimaginable for all. The initial reactions of UCC executives in the United States were humanitarian ones. Within hours of hearing the news of the chemical leak and what limited information was available, CEO Warren Anderson declared he was traveling to India to serve as the immediate supervisor of the situation and offer any assistance that the company could contribute. UCC also announced it would cease producing MIC until the cause of the explosion was known. Anderson announced that UCC would be open with the public and the media.

Unfortunately, communication was poor *in* Bhopal as well. While the Indian government had assured Anderson that he could travel safely there, when he arrived he was placed under "house" arrest for charges of "culpable homicide." In addition, he was faced with the challenge of conducting communications in an area that displayed an emotionally gripping scene.

UCC declared that it accepted moral responsibility for the tragedy. One week later, UCC offered $1 million to the Prime Minister's Relief Fund, which was accepted. Four months later it offered another $5 million in humanitarian aid to the Indian government. In this instance it was refused. UCC then offered the money to the Red Cross to disburse to those who needed it in India—and that was turned down for more than a year.

LESSONS LEARNED FROM BHOPAL

According to Bob Berzok, director of communications at Union Carbide headquarters in Danbury, Connecticut, UCC learned four very important lessons from the Bhopal incident.*

1. It is important to be *open and candid* in every message prepared to deal with a situation. Attempts to shield information are immediately picked up by the public.

2. In the event of a huge crisis, *make immediate use of existing programs that are*

identified with the organization and accentuate their strengths.

3. Don't forget *secondary publics*, "When you have a sudden crisis like Bhopal, two audiences people think of communicating with are press and employees. It's important to consider shareholders, government officials, and customers," advise Berzok.

4. Each crisis is different—*there is no formula for dealing with them.*

*pr reporter, April 23, 1990.

THE AFTERMATH OF BHOPAL

After the Bhopal incident and the intense scrutiny and criticisms UCC received from the public and the media, the company grew cautious. Many of the company's lucrative divisions were sold off, and by 1991 the company was half the size it was before Bhopal.

UCC poured money into its safety systems and supervisory procedures, some analysts say too much, according to *The Wall Street Journal.*[4] Maintenance practices that should have taken 30 minutes began to take 3 or 4 hours to complete. Even CEO Robert D. Kennedy (replacing Anderson in 1986) concedes that the same safety levels were achieved at some of his rivals' plants, while spending a fraction of the cost incurred by UCC.

As for the legal outcome of the Bhopal tragedy, UCC settled Indian civil suits in

1989 for $470 million. The Indian courts have recommended that former CEO Anderson be extradited to India to face charges for culpable homicide. To date, the Indian government has not requested Anderson's extradition from the U.S. government.

As indicated earlier, the principle that 90 percent of all crises are self-inflicted seems evident in this case. After receiving reports from the Bhopal facility that everything was in order, UCC could have conducted regular inspections to confirm the statements presented. Simply relying on reports received from the plant obviously was not enough. If those inspections had been done, the company may have avoided the serious magnitude of the incident, prevented some of the deaths and injuries, saved legal fees and fines, and maintained a positive reputation. A proactive plan focusing on safety measures and policies covering

---

[4]"Wounded Giant: Union Carbide Offers Some Sober Lessons in Crisis Management," *The Wall Street Journal*, January 28, 1992.

topics such as community relations, internal responsibility, and inspection requirements could have saved UCC from its own near demise and lost reputation. The public relations staff therefore has a stake and a role in monitoring operations. ∎

QUESTIONS FOR DISCUSSION

1. As indicated from the Bhopal disaster, Union Carbide India, Ltd., did nothing to prepare the community for any potential hazard that could have and did occur. What are some proactive actions or programs that UCC could have implemented in order to avoid the fatal tragedy that occurred? What is the public relations role in them, if any?

2. Compare Bhopal with the Responsible Care program (Case 4-1). What part do you think the differing cultures and governments in the United States and India played in the Bhopal tragedy?

3. From all appearances, it seems that UCC was innocent of any direct causes of the Bhopal tragedy. Yet the company was all but destroyed by it. Did public opinion actually cause this near destruction? Might it have been caused by company overreaction or feelings of guilt? If not these, then what were the causes?

CASE 9-3   A CLASSIC: WHEN POSITIVE ACTIONS DON'T RESULT IN POSITIVE PERCEPTIONS[1]

On March 24, 1989, the *Exxon Valdez* struck Bligh Reef in Prince William Sound, releasing 11 million gallons of crude oil (one-fifth of its cargo) into the sea.[2] This incident created a crisis of epic proportions for Exxon. The mission was to clean 1,300 miles of shoreline, approximately 15 percent of the area's 9,000 miles of shoreline, and restore the area to its original condition. In 1992, after the completion of successful and extensive cleanup efforts, a federal on-scene coordinator (the U.S. Coast Guard) declared the cleanup complete saying, "Further shoreline treatment would provide no net benefit to the environment." The State of Alaska confirmed these findings. However, the damage for Exxon did not end

with the termination of cleanup efforts. What was the real problem?

PERCEPTIONS, NOT FACTS; ACTIONS, NOT WORDS

While it was only the 34th largest oil spill at that time, it goes on record as one that people will remember the most. In one study, the *Exxon Valdez* remains one of the most remembered corporate crises.[3] Environmentalists have perceived it as limitless in damage even though there are few remaining signs of the spill. Many have characterized the accident as civilization once again trouncing on nature in order to reap the benefits of its limited resources and

---

FACTORS TO CONSIDER WHEN DEVELOPING A CRISIS COMMUNICATION PLAN

- Develop a crisis communication plan in advance to handle any situation; determine exactly how and what key publics will be instructed to do in case of an emergency.

- Conduct research to discover information that is not readily available.

- Insist that all company operations be monitored regularly. A crisis that results because of operational failure without these preparations will surely cause the company to lose credibility.

---

[1]This case was developed from a case study authored by two University of Florida students, Fred Forlano and Greg Lorenz, under the direction of Frank Stansberry, Manager of Guest Affairs for Coca-Cola U.S.A. at Epcot Center.
[2]Lee W. Baker, *The Credibility Factor*, Homewood, IL: Business One Irwin, 1993, p. 38.
[3]*pr reporter*, July 12, 1993.

associate it with the deaths of many birds, otters, and other aquatic life.

In reality, the Alaskan food chain has survived (See Figure 9-3). Pink salmon harvests set records in 1990 and 1991. Tourism has rebounded strongly and so have Exxon's profits. It appears that the only thing severely damaged was the company's reputation. Those who remember it perceive it as a disaster that was poorly handled by Exxon.

HOW DID THESE PERCEPTIONS DEVELOP?

Today, the spill has been cleaned up and Exxon is thriving as it was previously, but the residual effects of the ordeal linger.

From the beginning, Exxon concentrated on emphasizing cleanup efforts rather than addressing the public perception that it didn't do enough, soon enough (See Figure 9-4). This emphasis was apparent from the moment that CEO Lawrence G. Rawl entered the picture. Unfavorable media comparisons were made of Rawl with the positive images of James Burke of Johnson & Johnson and his handling of the Tylenol incident (See Case 6-3). He was characterized as opposed to serving as a spokesperson, or even publicly showing interest, because he remained in New York until 2 days after the spill. When he finally entered the scene, he presented himself as rigid and aggressive, not bowing to the

FIGURE 9-3   Exxon published a series of reports about the aftermath of the *Valdez* oil spill and its effect on Prince William Sound and the Gulf of Alaska. Shown here is a report entitled "Three Years After" from October 1992.

(Courtesy of Exxon Company, U.S.A.)

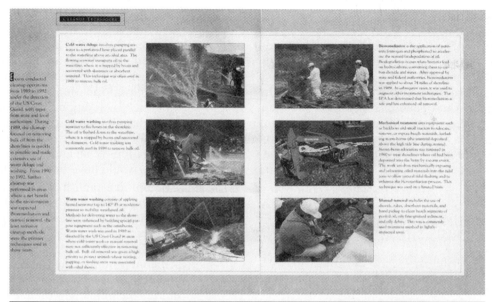

FIGURE 9-4 Exxon used many techniques in order to clean up the shoreline along Prince William Sound in Alaska.

(Courtesy of Exxon Company, U.S.A.)

groups that opposed him or to the media. His inflexibility may have cost him opportunities to seek positive relationships with the various publics.[4]

When Exxon designated a location for a crisis center, the company created another situation that conflicted with its goals. It staffed the media center in Port of Valdez. Information was often slow in coming, and communication lines to Port of Valdez became jammed with information inquiries from media. It was also hard for management in New York to get information.

Another problem hampering Exxon's credibility was that it did not address how the public was perceiving the spill and its effects. It focused primarily on the *facts* concerning cleanup efforts and let *impressions* about long-term effects on the region form on their own. These facts consisted of dollar amounts, size of work force, and stories about the confusion they had to overcome to begin the process. The public, knee deep in "green issues," found no reassurance that Alaska's vast natural regions would recover.

For legal reasons, it was difficult for Exxon to show remorse or even admit to the environmental ramifications of the crisis. It did not realize the significance of visual images and the emotional response they evoked. Media images of animals in distress were displayed often and increased negative percpetions of the company. Exxon's credibility and reputation were being strongly questioned at this time.

---

[4]When Rawl was asked later why he did not become more of a force in the crisis communications, Rawl replied that "his first instinct was to head to Alaska . . . but he was swayed by his colleagues' arguments that he would 'just get in the way'." From Lee Baker, *The Credibility Factor*, Homewood, IL: Business One Irwin, 1992, p. 41.

Exxon's full-page apology ads on April 3, 1989, were badly timed and plagued with conflicting messages. They claimed that, "Exxon has moved swiftly and competently to minimize" the damage. In the *same* papers, front pages reported how slowly the company had been in starting the cleanup, with a specific list of unflattering reasons why. The actual "we're sorry statement" appeared in the last paragraph, vastly minimizing readership in today's sound-bite world.[5]

COMMUNICATIONS IS THE HUB OF A CRISIS SITUATION

Exxon became the scapegoat for all environmental causes. CEO Rawl served as a prime example of stereotypical negative perceptions of the corporate executive. Topics discussed in the media portrayed Exxon as being money-focused and inhuman. How could a company so vast have such poor crisis communication planning? Hadn't they learned by other companies' examples what they should do and how they should act during a crisis? Remembering that hindsight is 20/20, here are some basic communication principles that Exxon should have kept in mind before and after the *Valdez* ran aground.

➤ Develop a plan that will construct a positive image. Or at least try not to create a situation that will put you two steps back.

➤ Exxon could have spent more time emphasizing the personal commitment being made, rather than the processes involved and the $2.5 billion spent on cleanup.

➤ Conduct media research to discover the realities of opinions conveyed to the public. Are the messages strong, or do they have gaps that you can fill with your own information? Whose side is the media on? What are they saying to whom? Where are they getting their information, and is it accurate? In addition, conducting gap research (gap research measures the gap between reality and expectations of an audience) with publics would have been fruitful.

➤ Attempt to establish credibility by being honest and personable with the public. If Rawl was not an effective spokesperson, he could have been replaced with someone who had the training and experience. The faces and images the public saw on television were the ones that are associated with Exxon.

Much like UCC in the Bhopal case (Case 9-2), Exxon needed to make certain that all information was accurate, consistent, and complete. Cases like this illustrate why candor is the best policy. Reveal what is being done and why. Convey what is known and when it became known. Don't let the media find out for themselves. Exxon did not follow these basic guidelines when cleanup efforts halted for the winter in September of 1989. Rather than telling the public that because of weather limitations, cleanup would prove fruitless, Exxon simply discontinued efforts for the season. Cleanup continued until the federal on-scene coordinator and state declared it complete in 1992, but the public did not completely understand the cleanup process. They needed someone to explain it to them, and *it could have been Exxon.*

When it comes to the source of communication, make certain that the spokes-

---
[5]*pr reporter*, April 17, 1989.

person is qualified, with proper crisis communication training. Shooting from the hip should be avoided, and a clear message should be sent at all times. Providing the image of sympathy and remorse, complemented with sincerity, may have saved Exxon's reputation and, in turn, made the future seem brighter for all the parties involved.

A plan that defines all necessary contacts and a proposed sequence of events could have been developed. A spill of any variety would involve the media, state and local governments, environmental groups, and internal and external publics. The support of employees is crucial. At a time when it is difficult to reach the spokesperson, the media often will create its own in a security guard or a technician.

The cleanup effort was not effectively coordinated with the efforts of all groups involved. No one knew what each group should do or when. Observers felt that both of these aspects should have been considered and put into the crisis plan as well. Even if a plan was not in place, as soon as the smoke cleared Exxon could have been initiating the coordination of communications and development of a strategy and plan with all pertinent groups.

A better understanding of how the media works in relation to delivering a prescribed message to different publics would also have been beneficial. As mentioned earlier, the public can and will sympathize with helpless animals. A good portion of media attention was given to oil-covered birds vividly depicted on television and in magazines. Even journalists said at the time that it would have been more sensible for Exxon to divert this attention by devising *proactive* programs the media could focus on. Since hard news sells, a program of hard-hitting environmental programs and principles could have been implemented. This strategy could have made the media a channel for communicating to the public that Exxon was aware of and cares about the environment and its inhabitants.

LESSONS LEARNED

Issue anticipation is the key to averting many crises. Some top management advisers insist that positive leadership is the only way to develop positive relationships. They believe that to think negatively would not be consistent with their goals or beneficial to the company. Exxon learned that even a very large company has a malleable reputation that can change in an instant.

Exxon was forced to realize that perceptions control reputation. In relation to other oil companies, Exxon's cleanup and spill control plan was reportedly top-of-the-line. However, by communicating specifics about the cleanup process, rather than the effects the spill would have on the environment, the company was not addressing the issues of concern. Displaying emotion and remorse for the outcome could have created a positive image of Exxon in the public's eye.

The hard lesson learned is that *anticipation,* while it may not prevent a crisis, certainly makes the road a little less bumpy. Ignoring possible situations that may occur, be they positive or negative, can lead to reputation and relationship disruptions that continue for years. An organization must be forward-thinking in order to survive in our volatile world. ∎

QUESTIONS FOR DISCUSSION

1. As evidenced by the Exxon case, perceptions speak louder than the actual facts. Can you think of anything more that Exxon could have done to avoid this public relations disaster and salvage its soiled reputation? Can you think of any proactive measures Exxon should take now to repair battered relationships with publics still disgruntled with the company?

2. Exxon received a blow to its reputation from the *Valdez* oil spill, but its profits really weren't hurt. Does its financial muscle and lack of real competition in the oil market move it beyond control of the court of public opinion? Why do you think this?

CASE STUDY 9-4   HOLDEN HEIGHTS HOSTAGE CRISIS

THE SITUATION LEADING UP TO THE HOSTAGE CRISIS

During the early morning hours of December 9, 1997, a man broke into a home in the Orlando suburb of Winter Park, Florida. Inside the house, he shot and killed a man and seriously wounded a woman. Then, he slipped into the pre-dawn darkness and disappeared.[1]

The Winter Park police suspected John Armstrong was the one responsible for this crime. Armstrong was a convicted felon and violent criminal offender, with crimes ranging from grand theft to attempted murder. He had served time in prison, but was released early.

Police spotted Armstrong, accompanied by his young daughter, driving on the freeway toward Orlando. Armstrong crashed his car into another vehicle and, leaving his daughter alone in the car, fled on foot into Holden Heights, a low-income neighborhood. Ignoring orders from the police to stop, he leaped through the front window of a nearby home occupied by Iris Vickson and Adrienne Phillips. At home with their two small children, 2-year old Tedi and 4-year old Malcolm, the women were surprised and frightened. Armstrong, with a gun in his hand, ordered the mothers out of the house and took the children as hostages, thus beginning a 3-day siege. The crisis participants were:

➤ **John E. Armstrong**—convicted felon and violent criminal released early from prison, and a suspect in a homicide in a suburb of Orlando

➤ **Tedi Priest**—2-year-old girl taken hostage in her Holden Heights home

➤ **Iris Vickson**—mother of Tedi Priest and resident of Holden Heights

➤ **Malcolm Phillips**—4-year-old boy taken hostage in his Holden Heights home

➤ **Adrienne Phillips**—mother of Malcolm Phillips and resident of Holden Heights

HOSTAGE CRISIS

Armstrong's actions created a crisis on two levels. The first crisis was a situation in which people's lives were in danger. The second was a public relations nightmare. Alone with the two young children, Armstrong started threatening to kill the children and making demands. The demands ranged from a get-away car to pizza.

The Orlando Police Department called a professional hostage negotiator to the scene. Inside the house, Armstrong was listening to the television news reports of the events at the scene while talking on the telephone with the police. At one point,

---

[1]This case was prepared by Jamie Karpinski, a senior at the University of Central Florida under the direction of visiting instructor, Frank R. Stansberry, APR, Fellow PRSA.

police got a listening device and were monitoring Armstrong's actions. The key resolution participants were:

➤ **Mayor Glenda Hood**—mayor of the City of Orlando

➤ **Jim DeSimone**—Communication Director, City of Orlando

➤ **Chief Bill Kennedy**—Orlando Chief of Police

➤ **Captain Frank Fink**—SWAT team commander

➤ **Lieutenant Bill Mulloy**—Public Information Officer for the City of Orlando

➤ **Captain Jerry Demings**—Commander of the Crisis Negotiations Team and Orlando Deputy Police Chief

After days of negotiating, Captain Jerry Demings and Chief Bill Kennedy decided the time was finally right to act. Armstrong had been awake for much of the 68-hour siege, taking only a few catnaps. The negotiations had ground to a halt. Armstrong kept promising to release the children but never did. He was a desperate man with nothing to lose.

Armstrong had finally fallen asleep. He was lying on a bed in the back bedroom with a gun at his side. The children were asleep inches away. The Orlando SWAT Team entered the house with orders by team commander Captain Frank Fink to keep the children safe at all costs. Once in the back bedroom, SWAT Officer Scott Perkins jumped onto Armstrong and shielded the children. Perkins' hand was shot during the rescue and Armstrong was killed. The children were returned safely to their frantic mothers.

PUBLIC RELATIONS CRISIS

One of the first things a public relations professional should know is that planning and preparation are invaluable. When disaster strikes, it is too late to prepare a crisis plan or build a legacy of trust. In this respect, the City of Orlando was right on target. Although city officials could not foresee this specific event, they were prepared for a crisis. The City of Orlando's mission statement calls for "Serving Orlando with innovation, responsiveness, knowledge, courtesy, and professionalism." This mission is the cornerstone of Orlando's legacy of trust with the community. The mission is held in high regard and followed by all city agencies. Because of the commitment to this mission, city officials began preparing a crisis plan in case of emergency. This plan was a large factor in the successful handling of the hostage crisis. For example, the Public Information Office (PIO) of the Orlando Police Department is usually run by one person—Lieutenant Bill Mulloy. However, as a part of the crisis plan, 12 new PIO officers were trained. This training had been completed a few months before the hostage crisis began. (All 12 officers were called to duty by the time the crisis ended.)

The media covered the story from the beginning. However, when Armstrong took the small children hostage, the media attention intensified. Not only were local media present, but national and international media in town on other business also covered the story. This international media presence made the handling of the information even more critical because Orlando and Central Florida are international tourist destinations. As a result, area leaders must continually emphasize the security and wholesomeness of the area to those whose travel plans might be influenced by any negative news reports.

However, because extra Public Information Officers were recently trained for crisis situations, the PIOs were able to satisfy all media requests for special interviews and give out timely information to meet news deadlines and the Orlando Police

Department (OPD) became the source of most of the information the media reported.

From the beginning, Orlando's media strategy was to meet the needs of the media without compromising the efforts to resolve the crisis. Included in this plan was the knowledge that the media can sometimes help with crisis resolution. For example, city and OPD officials made an early decision to let the electricity, phone, cable, and other external communication devices remain "on" inside the hostage site so negotiators could talk to Armstrong. This communication worked to the city's advantage in two ways.

First, without trustworthy information, people assume the worst. Rumors thrive in the vacuum of no information. Since the city was controlling the information flow, they kept control of the situation and what information was released. Second, if you have to say something, the truth is always best. The PIOs were honest with the media and told them of new developments as soon as they happened. This created a cooperative, positive atmosphere with the media. This cooperative atmosphere allowed hostage negotiators to communicate with Armstrong through the media—primarily television—throughout the ordeal.

Two messages were constant: appeal to the hostage-taker to release the children and surrender; and compliment Armstrong in an effort to keep him from harming the hostages. Complimenting Armstrong at first confused some of the media who knew the "outside" story—that OPD, given the opportunity, would use any means necessary to stop Armstrong. Background briefings cleared up this confusion and reinforced the policy of honesty with the media.

At the same time, the other target audiences were being addressed. This proves the wisdom of the strategy of speaking to niche audiences (as well as mass audiences) through the media. City residents, city offi-cials, and employees, and the population of Central Florida looked to the media for current information on the situation, but those viewing around the world were also important audiences.

Throughout dealings with the media, five basic message points were repeated. The media helped convey these messages to the public. These points were:

1. John Armstrong was responsible for his fate.
2. The children's safety came first.
3. The Orlando Police Department and its law enforcement partners did an excellent job.
4. This could have been prevented.
5. Expert testimony supports this view.

CONCLUSION

This crisis had both a successful hostage resolution and a successful public relations outcome. This can be attributed to several factors.

First, public relations must be involved from the beginning to have maximum impact. The cameras had been rolling ever since Armstrong was fleeing down the interstate. However, the City of Orlando was in control of the situation and helped the media get the information they needed and successfully solved the hostage crisis.

Next, public relations needs to always play its position and let other departments play theirs. It is highly unlikely that the PIOs would have been as successful at saving Tedi and Malcolm from their captor without the SWAT Team. It is also unlikely that the SWAT Team would have been successful at handling the media. The five key message points of the city were reinforced in every communication. This allowed a unified and constant message to reach the public.

Throughout the ordeal, Mayor Glenda Hood and the city's public relations officer,

Jim DeSimone, remained in constant contact with the SWAT team and the PIOs. The mayor knew that every aspect of the situation was being handled by experts and always knew the status of the rescue operation. However, the mayor's focus was to convey her whole-hearted support and encouragement for city employees. She also spent a lot of time behind the scenes visiting and encouraging the mothers of the hostages. The rescue was successful in part because Mayor Hood supported the plan.

The five message points the city used were addressed and accepted by both the media and the community. This crisis was successfully resolved because the city believed in its mission and the OPD had already established a legacy of trust with the citizens. The Mayor was behind the crisis plan. Departments worked together but managed their own specialties. The result was a coordinated effort that kept the various publics informed and satisfied throughout the 3-day ordeal. Armstrong was the only casualty. Good police work and good communication kept the situation under control. ■

QUESTIONS FOR DISCUSSION

1. Was this situation handled well from a public relations standpoint? Why or why not?
2. Five primary publics were identified by the OPD. List them and tell how successfully each was addressed.
3. Who was setting the agenda for the media coverage—the media or the city? How?
4. Why was it important that Mayor Hood supported the operation?
5. Did the city use One Clear Voice when addressing the media? How?
6. What could be done to improve the handling of the public relations aspect of this situation?
7. What was the outcome of each of the city's five message points at the end of the hostage crisis? Was the city successful in getting the message points out through the media?

CASE 9-5 A CLASSIC: ESTABLISHED RELATIONSHIPS SAVE A LANDMARK COMPANY

Of all the crises that can strike an organization, probably none is as threatening as a hostile takeover attempt. Sometimes one company wants to acquire a competitor or a firm that will add new markets or products. Often the raider has neither the intention nor the capability of operating the company. The objective is to obtain its asset value by selling off the company in pieces. In most takeovers, some dismembering, layoffs, or budget cutting must be done in order for the raider to pay off debt incurred to purchase the target company.

The final decision whether to allow a takeover rests with the stockholders. In an earlier time, they were largely individuals whose purpose in investing was to earn dividends and hope the stock would appreciate in value so they could sell it at a gain for their retirement. Such "little investors" in our era have been replaced by giant investment funds managed by shrewd professionals with sophisticated computer programs to guide their decisions. They work for mutual funds, pension funds, and other large-volume investors with billions of dollars that they must "keep working" for the benefit of their shareholders or members.

Under pressure to "grow" a pension fund's assets as large as possible, so that it will be able to meet commitments to retirees, investment managers "play the market," searing for maximum profits while guarding against any possible loss. As a result, their decisions can be ruthless. The slightest downturn in a company's fortunes may cause some investment managers to quickly sell large blocks of its stock.

On the other hand, when it appears that a stock may rise, they will buy large amounts and do what they can to keep the stock price going up. In recent times, one of the best ways to make a "killing" has been to accumulate the stock of a company targeted for takeover. Invariably, the price of acquiring the company is at a high premium over the normal trading value or actual worth of its stock. Price per share may rise 50 percent or even more during the bidding battle among rivals vying to take over the company, as each makes a tender offer to the stockholders at increasingly higher prices. It is really an auction, with each stockholder free to sell shares to the bidder of choice.

Faced with an unfriendly takeover, management and the board of directors must first decide whether it is in the present shareholders' best interests to sell. The best management teams and directors will also take into account the effect on stakeholders as well as stockholders, including employees and the community. If the raider is after asset value, planning to break up the company, they may conclude that operating the company will give better long-term value to shareholders, while selling it off piecemeal provides merely a one-time gain.

Then management must devise a defense to thwart the raider. By and large, such defenses are the *product of public relations*. In some cases, this means trying to convince the stockholders not to sell their shares to the raiders. In the case that follows, it meant persuading state legislators to pass new laws that make it difficult for raiders to accomplish their aims.

A PREMIER COMPANY

Dayton Hudson Corporation (DHC), headquartered in Minneapolis, *is one of the five largest retailers in America, with sales of over $18 billion annually.* It is also one of those rare companies that, almost from its inception, has been an innovator and leader. This is how James Shannon described DHC in the Minneapolis *Star and Tribune* at the time of its takeover troubles:

> In the 1880s and early 1890s, George Draper Dayton was a banker in Worthington, Minnesota. In that capacity he began to buy real estate in Minneapolis. In 1895 the original Westminster Presbyterian Church at the corner of 7th and Nicollet in Minneapolis burned to the ground. Because of the economic panic of 1893, the vacant lot (really an empty hole) at that site went unsold for more than a year. At the urging of his Minneapolis business conferees, Dayton in 1895 bought the land and constructed the store that today is the keystone of the Dayton Hudson retail chain.
>
> Known originally as the Dayton Co., and privately owned by the family of George Draper Dayton, the company went public in 1967. Now known as the Dayton Hudson Corp., its 1986 sales exceeded $9 billion. By 1993 Dayton Hudson Corporation had expanded to 33 states and operated 892 stores, including Target, Mervyn's, Dayton Hudson, Lechmere, and Marshall Field's, the famous Chicago-based department stores. It has 34,000 employees in Minnesota.

Ever since the company was privately owned by the Dayton family it has given 5 percent of its annual pretax profits to worthy causes in communities where it has significant presence. In 1986 it contributed $20,718,500 to the arts and to social-service programs nationwide, half of them in Minnesota.

In a community nationally known for its corporate support of the arts, social services, and education, the Dayton Hudson Corp. is the flagship for dozens of other publicly and privately held corporations committed to the proposition that a successful company has an obligation to be a good corporate citizen. In 1984 the University of California School of Business Administration named Dayton Hudson "the best managed company in America." As the first recipient of the Vanguard Award (for corporate social responsibility), Dayton Hudson was cited for its "unusual dynamism . . . entrepreneurial zeal . . . and its uncompromising ethical standards."

The company's 1983 Management Perspectives program, a participatory activity that attempted to identify and pass along for future use its corporate culture and values, determined that DHC's goal was to "be premier in all we do."

THE RAID BEGINS SUSPENSEFULLY

In mid-June 1987, after several weeks of unusually heavy trading in its stock, Dayton Hudson learned that it was the target of an unfriendly takeover. But who was the raider? Writers in the *Wall Street Journal* and other media speculated it was this one, then that one—but the company didn't know for sure. Rumors of a takeover attempt—and the escalating stock price that inevitably accompanies it—resulted in an extremely dangerous situation: Within a 3-week period, nearly 30 percent of DHC's stock changed hands, making the situation so fluid that someone could have taken control of the company at any time.

As a company statement issued via press release stated, "That means 30 percent of our stock is owned by people who have had it less than 15 days. They could care less about our customers, our employees or our communities. We have every reason to believe those shares moved from stable institutional investors to speculators, short-term investors and what are called arbitrageurs [a person working in a brokerage firm who trades in stock on speculation]."

Under Securities and Exchange Commission (SEC) regulations, whenever a stockholder accumulates 5 percent of any company's stock, it must report the fact. However, through various tactics, the purchaser may take as long as a year before making the report. Realizing the danger, management began taking steps to defend the company. In addition to usual activities, such as having investor relations staff scrutinize activity in the stock and media relations staff monitor news coverage, special steps were taken:

➤ CEO Kenneth Macke sent a memo to all corporate staff warning them not to speculate or comment on the situation, since that could fuel rumors (and the stock price); he also reminded them that the official spokesperson for the corporation was its vice president of public relations (VP-PR), Ann Barkelew.

➤ A task force was assembled to study what others had done in such situations, investigate all available data about the most likely raiders, and review new laws passed by some states to deal with hostile takeovers; included were representatives from public

relations, investor relations, public affairs, law, and outside consulting firms.

➤ On the morning of June 17, 1987, Macke set a meeting of the crisis team for 2:00 P.M. Its members were himself as CEO, the president and COO (chief operating officer), the CFO (chief financial officer), the general counsel, and the VP-PR. The objective was to determine action and timing "assuming I receive the 5 percent letter" today. Specific agenda items included: What actions are required? What actions are recommended? Will we have a press release and, if so, what will it say? Who will notify all concerned parties?

As speculation about a takeover and a possible raider swirled around the company, Barkelew fell back on established policy to handle the hundreds of media, stock market, and other inquiries. She reported to Macke: "I continue to stand on our corporate policy of no comments on rumors or speculation of this nature . . . and, except for the rumors, we know of no reason for the fluctuations in our stock price or trading volume."

SEVEN DAYS IN JUNE

The task force established the objective: "To build support for a special legislative session to enact tougher anti-takeover laws that would provide greater protection for all Minnesota-incorporated public companies." June 18, the day after the action and timing meeting, Macke requested and got a meeting with Governor Rudy Perpich. He briefed the governor at 3 P.M. on the situation—using a script and briefing paper prepared by public relations—and asked him to call a special legislative session to pass the new law.

Considering that the regular session of the legislature had ended only recently, and that special sessions are costly and unpopular, this was a bold move. It meant that the governor and legislative leaders had to be completely convinced of the severity of DHC's situation—and of the possibility that it could happen to other Minnesota concerns. This, in turn, meant that public relations and allied departments had to generate massive amounts of materials in an exceedingly short period.

When Macke went to meet Perpich, much of this material was already in his hands, thanks to late night and weekend work by public relations staff and its consulting firms.

At 8 P.M., Governor Perpich met with legislative leaders to rally support for the special session. He told the press afterward, "We will not act hastily but we will not hesitate to act to protect a good Minnesota company that provides about 34,000 jobs to Minnesotans." The news conference was held at 10:30 P.M., prompted by leaks about an imminent takeover bid, reported the *Star and Tribune.*

The next day, June 19, the raider communicated its intention to seek control of DHC. This action prompted two events: (1) June 20 news reports spread the fact widely and gave emphasis to another fact, that the suitor, Dart Group Corp. of Landover, Maryland, "had already attempted hostile takeovers of six other retailing firms," as the *St. Paul Pioneer Press* reported, and (2) DHC launched an intensive effort to win the public, other corporations, and legislators to its side. That day alone these events were staged:

➤ Macke met with editors in the morning, then appeared on a public affairs television show in the evening.

➤ In the afternoon he met with business and community leaders at DHC headquarters.

➤ A letter to the company's 34,000 employees in the state, over Macke's signature, asked for their active help "to support our state legislators in enacting tougher anti-takeover laws that will provide us and other Minnesota companies protection from stock market raids and other abusive tactics."

➤ Dayton Hudson Foundation called 200 community and arts organization leaders to a meeting at the Children's Theatre, where audience members urged the crowd to write or call their legislators and the governor, in order to protect the $9 million the company provided through its foundation that year to nonprofit groups in Minnesota.

➤ General Mills, Honeywell, and other prominent companies headquartered in the state issued supporting statements to the legislature and the media, as did the Minnesota Business Partnership, comprising chief executives of 75 of the state's largest companies.

➤ Backgrounders, question-and-answer pieces, in-depth discussions of the pros and cons of the legislation, data on Dart (including an unflattering *Fortune* article depicting it as a predatory outfit whose operating practices took advantage of suppliers and customers), and other material was widely distributed. The material brought forth substantial editorial support from state media in the days following.

Meanwhile, standby advertisements were prepared, ready to run if public opinion shifted against the special session. One pictured Dayton's Department Store's Christmas teddy bear, used for several years as a holiday premium and known as Santabear, with the caption "Who'll get custody?" A shopping bag stuffer was entitled, "A special session to keep Minnesota a special place." Even a glossary of terms used in takeovers was developed, explaining words and phrases such as *arbitrageur, white knight,* and similar jargon.

Survey research was undertaken both as a planning guide and, when results proved favorable, as a lobbying tool. Telephone interviews were conducted over the weekend in order to have information available when the decision about calling a special session was being made (See Figure 9-5).

THE PEOPLE AND THEIR ELECTED OFFICIALS DECIDE

As the week of June 22 began, DHC representatives visited cities and towns across the state seeking support. An employee rally was held, and massive media coverage continued. On Tuesday, key legislative committees met to hear testimony, including Macke's (See Figure 9-6). It appeared that sentiment was favorable toward the antitakeover law and the special session necessary to enact it. But for quick action, enough votes must be available to suspend the rules—rarely an easy proposition. Some committee members were not convinced, feeling that too much protection of current management could be as harmful in some cases as unfriendly takeovers.

As Governor Perpich considered whether to call the session, a freak occurrence brought yet more attention to Dayton Hudson's stock. A Cincinnati investment manager and member of a prominent family made a bid for DHC shares at a higher price than Dart was offering. After frantic trading, plus efforts to identify the validity of the offer, the New York Stock Exchange halted trading in DHC shares for 2 hours. In the end, the bid turned out to be bogus—another public relations challenge management had to contend with, and at the worst possible time.

Wednesday night, the governor called a 1-day special session for the next day. He had insisted that House and Senate leaders reach agreement. After the usual compromises and political posturing, plus adding some features of their own to the bill, they told Perpich they were ready to go into session.

When the vote came on Thursday, June 25, the House passed it 120 to 5, the Senate 57 to 0. The governor signed it into law that evening. The *Pioneer Press* lead next morning told the story:

> The prospect of a department store chain rallying a state government to save it from a corporate raider, doing it all over 7 days in June and with barely a whisper of opposition, would probably be seen as long odds by folks from other states.
>
> Dayton Hudson Corp. accomplished that in Minnesota Thursday with stunning swiftness by cashing in on customer goodwill built up over decades, the clout of 34,000 employees, a small army of top state lobbyists and the assistance of groups that have received millions of dollars in contributions.
>
> By any yardstick it was a boggling show of clout.

Thus ended one of the swiftest crisis responses ever witnessed. In spite of (or perhaps because of) the severity of the case, within a 7-day period Dayton Hudson was able to plan, execute, and succeed in a hostile takeover defense—thus becoming the only major takeover target to escape

Minnesota Resident Attitudes Toward a Special Session of the Legislature That Would Consider Changing Minnesota Law to Make Hostile Takeovers More Difficult

Question: "The Governor has announced that he may call a one day special session of the legislature that would consider changing Minnesota law to make hostile takeover of Minnesota companies more difficult. Which of the following statements best describes your feelings toward a special session to change the Minnesota law?"

	All Residents	Gender		Place of Residence		Political Affiliation		
		Male	Female	Seven County Metro	Out-of-state	Demo-crat	Repub-lican	Inde-pendent
I'm in favor of changing the law to protect Dayton Hudson from a hostile takeover.	7%	6%	7%	6%	8%	6%	6%	6%
I'm in favor of changing the law to make hostile takeovers more difficult as long as the law applies to all Minnesota corporations, not just Dayton Hudson.	78	76	81	82	72	85	77	79
I'm not in favor of a special session to consider changing the law.	12	15	9	10	15	6	15	12
Don't know	3	3	3	2	5	3	2	3
TOTAL	100%	100%	100%	100%	100%	100%	100%	100%
Number of Respondents	(772)	(384)	(388)	(515)	(257)	(222)	(158)	(346)

FIGURE 9-5   The results from the telephone interviews.

(Courtesy of Dayton Hudson Corporation.)

unscathed until that time. But the work wasn't over for public relations staff.

SAYING THANK YOU

Illustrating the attitude that built positive public relationships for the company over many years and enabled it to orchestrate such a rapid response to crisis, DHC put as much creativity and energy into expressing appreciation to its supporter as it had into the campaign. Some highlights:

➤ Life-size Santabears, wearing "There's no place like home. Thanks Minnesota" sandwich boards, greeted downtown visitors (See Figure 9-7).

➤ Employees signed a giant "Thanks Minnesota" banner, which was then placed in Minneapolis' major downtown center for others to add their names, before being sent to the governor (See Figure 9-7).

➤ "Thanks Minnesota" buttons were worn by employees, after Macke appeared at an employee ice cream social and thank-you party wearing one.

➤ All employees received a letter from the chairman thanking them,

FIGURE 9-6   Dayton Hudson Corp. leader Kenneth Macke, left, addresses special legislative hearing. Next to him is Representative Wayne Simoneau.

(Courtesy of *St. Paul Pioneer Press & Dispatch*, Mark Morson, photographer.)

urging them to pass their appreciation along to public officials and customers, then noting that only by redoubling efforts to make the company even better would they be truly free of raiders.

➤ Ads were placed, as well as publicity, and personal thank-you letters from Macke went to legislators.

➤ The next issue of the company's internal newsletter, *Courier*, reprinted Macke's remarks at the ice cream social, in which—by name—he thanked each headquarters employee who had taken part in the effort.

The takeover case generated 3,600 inches of newspaper coverage. *Corporate Exposure* newsletter, which tracks media coverage of companies, found Dayton Hudson in first place for the period—but also reported that the dominant tone of reportage was favorable to DHC.

After the legislation was passed, Dart Group quietly sold its holdings in Dayton Hudson. ■

QUESTIONS FOR DISCUSSION

1. In its various subsidiaries that operate stores across the country, Dayton Hudson has 168,000 employees. Why was it important to keep them informed of the Minnesota legislative effort? How would you have done it?

DHC FACES ANOTHER CRISIS

In 1991, DHC faced a new obstacle. A small group of employees at one of its Detroit-area stores voted to unionize, soliciting the United Auto Workers Union, since there was no union for retail employees. DHC contested the employees' vote to unionize and thus began the battle between the UAW and DHC. The UAW claimed DHC was antiunion. To protest the organization's refusal to unionize, the UAW organized a boycott and picketing of 17 DHC retail stores. It was set for the three biggest shopping days of the year, the three days after Thanksgiving.

Media coverage of the planned boycott was extensive. The UAW ran ads in many local newspapers entreating the public to shop "Anyplace But Hudson's." Yet, most all of the articles portrayed the company in a positive light, as willing to work with its employees, but not through the UAW. The UAW was portrayed as extreme in some newspaper articles. Often there were quotes from employees who had supported the union at the beginning and now just wanted the UAW to leave them alone. The UAW was portrayed as bullying and out to accomplish its own agenda, instead of looking after the needs of the DHC employees.

DEALING WITH THE BOYCOTT

Some measures that DHC public relations staff took to effectively combat the UAW boycott:

- Company spokespeople emphasized the negative effect a successful boycott would have on the employees, the very people the UAW was trying to represent.

- Supervisors and employees were positioned at the front door, apologizing to customers for the inconvenience, offering to throw away materials UAW protestors were distributing, and offering free refreshments to shoppers.

- Along with their usual holiday sales, DHC mailed out extra savings coupons to its charge card customers.

- Managers were prepared for inquiries from the media with a list of answers to questions that might be asked.

DHC officials were often the first quoted in response to the updates on the situation, giving an air of authority to what the company said. In addition, there were specific spokespersons who responded to media inquiries. DHC spoke with One Clear Voice before and after the boycott. This combination of public relations actions helped the stores have their most profitable Christmas season ever despite the boycott.

FIGURE 9-7   Santabears greet visitors to the IDS Center's Crystal Court at lunchtime with a message encouraging them to sign a huge thank-you banner to Minnesota from Dayton Hudson Corp. The *Minneapolis Star and Tribune* recorded the public response.

(News photo by Tom Sweeney, Staff Photographer.)

2. Dart Group Corporation had been the subject of unflattering news reports about its operations and reputation. Generally, the raider was depicted as profit-hungry and a haggler with its suppliers. How might this depiction have affected various publics in the DHC takeover attempt? How might it have affected other DHC stockholders? Legislators? Editors and reporters? Employees? Management? Communities in which the company operates? What motivations in each group would Dart's reputation have stimulated?

3. The new Minnesota law allowed corporate managements to take the effect on stakeholders as well as stockholders into account when deciding whether to accept a takeover bid. Without this provision, managements are apt to consider only whether the deal is good for shareholders. Is it fair and sound social policy for employees, customers, communities, local governments, and other stakeholders to be considered when they have purchased no stock? What investment do they have? Why should they be considered?

4. What influence on the case, if any, do you think the bogus offer had? Did it make matters better or worse for DHC?

CASE 9-6   SWISSAIR'S CRISIS MANAGEMENT: BEYOND THE CALL OF DUTY

INTRODUCTION

In the face of a tragedy or crisis, quick action is frequently the key to seizing the agenda and setting expectations. This is especially true when a major airplane crash occurs, one that attracts major media attention.

While mass media are useful when large numbers of diverse people must be informed, savvy communicators have found the Internet has value as well. Airline partners Swissair and Delta used this knowledge well in handling a crash where 229 people died.[1]

TRAGEDY STRIKES

Just 90 minutes after taking off from JFK International Airport on September 2, 1998, Urs Zimmerman, the pilot for Swissair Flight 111, reported smoke in the cockpit of the plane. Fifteen minutes later the airplane disappeared from the radar. Trying to reach Halifax International Airport (Nova Scotia) just 35 miles away, the plane plunged into the Atlantic Ocean.

Swissair employees were called immediately to implement its disaster emergency plan. The first priority was caring for the friends and relatives of the passengers on the ill-fated flight. The airline provided chartered flights to bring loved ones to the scene of the crash. Police provided protection to the mourners and shielded them from the crowds of people and reporters, who were required to stay 100 feet away and were allowed to speak only to family members who volunteered to be interviewed.

A DIFFERENT APPROACH

An article in *The Washington Post* reported that in the aftermath of the disaster, "Friends and relatives are full of praise for how the airlines (Swissair and its U.S. partner, Delta Air Lines) and investigators have accommodated their needs as best they could." Claire Mortimer, whose father and stepmother died in the crash, had these words for Swissair: "We are all so appreciative of the professionalism and dedication of the professional staff and volunteers."

Swissair made use of its Web site as a means of real-time communication on details of the crash. The airline's Internet team went into action as soon as news of the disaster was released. First, they replaced the airline's home page with text-only information on the disaster, because all-text pages download faster. Emergency phone numbers for Switzerland, Europe, and the United States were posted. The Web site contained links to the latest press releases on the rescue mission. Also available was a form to request information on specific passengers that could be submitted to Swissair. The information was posted in English, Swiss, French, and Italian. Interestingly, Delta's Web site contained only a short press release—which was posted four hours

---

[1]Delta Air Lines ended its partnership with Swissair in August 2000.

after the crash—containing contact numbers for family, friends, and the media.

FOCUS ON THE FAMILIES

The Aviation Disaster Family Assistance Act of 1996 requires the National Transportation Safety Board (NTSB) to ensure that airlines provide all families of crash victims with appropriate, caring assistance. The NTSB created the Office of Family Affairs, which works as the liaison between family members and the airline. Then, in December 1997, President Clinton signed into law the Foreign Air Carrier Family Support Act that required foreign carriers to file a family assistance plan with the NTSB by June 1998.

The two recent family assistance acts likely contributed to the handling of the post-crash period in the Swissair situation. Swissair and Delta clearly went beyond the call of duty in assisting the victims' loved ones: hundreds of Delta emergency employee crisis teams were critical to the response team at JFK Airport and in Halifax. The Delta employees had received training in media relations, contacting relatives, and grief counseling. Swissair assigned employee caregivers to each family, and immediately made available $20,000 to every family for travel and burial expenses.

Government officials and investigators also received praise for their handling of the aftermath of the Swissair crash. The Canadian military launched the largest search effort in its history. Local officials briefed families each day before releasing information to the public and press.

Swissair's swift and thorough response undoubtedly helped the public's perception that the airline was doing all it could to remedy what was a tragic situation for all involved. Relationships that are developed through successful resolution of problems frequently are stronger than any others.

Research consistently confirms that people have a larger trust and confidence in a company that has successfully overcome a problem than they do in those companies that have not experienced a problem.

It is too soon to be able to evaluate whether Swissair will continue to enjoy this "benefit of the doubt" with the flying public. But its care and concern immediately following the 1998 crash certainly won fans in the media and in the public arena. ∎

QUESTIONS FOR DISCUSSION

1. What can an airline spokesperson say to family and friends of those killed in a plane crash?
2. What is important to relatives and friends? What do they expect?
3. Did Swissair's actions meet those expectations? How?
4. Did the Internet improve communication with key publics for Swissair? How?
5. What is the proper role of the media in situations such as this?

PROBLEM 9-A When Associates Disagree in Handling an Emergency

Three months ago, you were hired to start a department at Reliable Steel Products Company. This is a young company with big ambitions. It is located in a medium-sized city in an area where industrial and residential building are predicted to boom. Reliable manufactures pipes, beams, rods, and other heavy parts for just about any kind of building.

After 3 months, your "department" consists of you and a secretary. Your outlook is bright, however. You report directly to the president, and she wants to be publicly known and highly regarded in the community and in the industry. To be of maximum help, you have done your homework by checking on the reputation of Reliable around town and in the industry. In the home community, Reliable and its president are not universally known, but employees, neighbors, and the people at the Chamber of Commerce feel that Reliable is well-managed, makes good products, and is a civic-minded neighbor. A few people did say that there have been a few accidents involving employees; it seems a rather dangerous place to work.

One morning, when the president is on her way to the state capital, you get a call from a reporter at the local daily newspaper. He says that an ambulance driver told him a Reliable employee had been killed a few minutes earlier, when some pipes rolled off a pile while a truck was being loaded in the shipping yard. The reporter asks for details.

You tell him you will check it out at once and get back to him. You call the safety supervisor. He blows up and insists that no details be released to any outsider until all the facts can be determined, the employee's family notified, the insurance company alerted, and the company lawyers informed. He says for you to hold off until the president returns the next morning. You agree on the priority of the employee's family, but explain that you cannot prevent the newspaper from publishing anything they have gotten elsewhere, whether it is accurate or not.

The safety supervisor says to take it up with the personnel director. You call her. She says they have someone out at the employee's home now, but she agrees with the safety supervisor that situations like this have all sorts of possible problems, with a chance of backlash. She thinks an unplanned response without the president's knowledge would be dangerous. She wants no part in it.

There are a number of alternatives open to you, but not much time to choose among them. What would be the best course to follow now? Everything considered, what immediate initiatives—if any—would you take?

What further issues can be anticipated as a result of the crisis? How would you recommend dealing with them?

PROBLEM 9-B What to Do When an Employee's Problems Affect the Company

You have been called in to offer public relations advice to an appliance service company involved in a crisis. ABC Appliance Repair, a local company with 10 employees, has become enmeshed in an employee's legal problems. One of the employees was accused of raping a young woman on the local college campus. The owner of ABC Appliance Repair is a boss who treats his employees like family. He didn't think twice about putting up bail to get his employee out of jail. Unfortunately the media got wind of the circumstances and it made the front page of the next morning's newspaper: "ABC Appliance Repair Pays to Free Alleged Rapist Employee."

The owner calls you, angry at the way the newspaper presented the case and afraid he will lose customers. He doesn't know what to do: Should he call the media and fight back? Take out an ad and plead his case? He believes in his employee and would pay the bail again if he had to. Maybe, though, he wouldn't have talked so freely with the reporter.

The case will be going to court in about a month. The employee, in the meantime, is coming to work. Already, however, the company is receiving calls from irate members of the community complaining about his actions. He's afraid of what this might do to his business. Two scheduled clients have called to cancel. It may get worse when his employee goes to court—especially if the media continues to follow the story.

To whom does he need to communicate? Prioritize his publics and identify how to reach each one. Then put together a plan (strategy and tactics) that will deal with the current crisis ABC Appliance Repair is facing.

What would you recommend the owner do about the media? Should he respond? If he does, what might happen? If he doesn't, how else can he communicate his message?

CHAPTER

10 STANDARDS, ETHICS, AND VALUES

Regulation of human conduct by standards rather than brute force or basic biological drive is the definition of civilization. Social conduct is regulated by five factors:

- Tradition: How has the situation been viewed or handled in the past?
- Public opinion: What is currently acceptable behavior to the majority of one's peers?
- Law: What is permissible and what is prohibited by legislation?
- Morality: Generally connotes a spiritual or religious prohibition; immorality is a charge usually leveled in issues on which religious teachings have concentrated.
- Ethics: Standards set by a profession, an organization, or oneself, based on conscience—what is right or fair to others as well as to oneself? (See box.)

Admittedly, these factors, as described, are attempts at pragmatic definitions. It would not be hard to get into an argument over the differences or the details. The point is that, however we use the words, there are forces that keep society functioning despite the strong pull of self-interest, ego, competitiveness, antisocial behavior, criminality, and other ills that could destroy it.

THE ROLE OF CONSCIENCE

Corporations and other formal organizations exist only on paper, and therefore have no conscience. Those who manage and decide for organizations may be guided by codes of ethics, but are also influenced by their personal ethics.

The difficulty in trying to pin down ethics in terms of standards or principles of conduct is that there is so little uniformity. Short of what is legal or illegal, determination of what kinds of conduct are acceptable, in various kinds of circumstances, comes down to the individual or the group conscience. And among individuals or groups having differing functional roles, the threshold of conscience can be high or low, near or far.

Consider the range of conscience or early warning sensations in a clergyman, prostitute, used-car dealer, illiterate, doctor of medicine, judge, or addicted derelict, to name but a few. Also, there are wide variations within each functional role, based on the personal makeup of the individual. The range varies from the person who feels that

ETHICS PROGRAMS ARE BIG BUSINESS

As evidenced by the cases you are about to read in this section, organizations today are finding it imperative to establish codes of ethics—and then to educate their members about them: two jobs for public relations.

Ethics training and education have become hot topics as centers such as the Josephson Institute of Ethics in California, the Ethics Resource Center in Washington D.C., and the Center for Business Ethics at Bentley College in Massachusetts, among many others, offer assistance to organizations to create ethics programs.

In 1991, the Center for Business Ethics established the Ethics Officer Association. An ethics officer is in charge of creating and maintaining an organization's ethics program. Currently the Association has 250 individual members representing more than 200 companies. Today 35 to 40 percent of major U.S. companies have an ethics officer, up from 15 to 20 percent 10 years ago.

The 2000 National Business Ethics Survey conducted by the Ethics Resource Center shows that companies today are doing more in terms of their ethics programs, compared to 1994. More companies have written ethics standards, ethics training programs, and means for employees to get ethics advice. A majority of employees are positive about ethics in their organizations. As a result, employees say they are more satisfied with their organizations overall. Concern for ethics is an important reason, they say, for continuing to work there.

What does this new emphasis on ethics mean for the practice of public relations? What many esteemed practitioners have been saying all along—without ethical behavior there is no credibility. And without credibility there is no business.

An already distrustful public is wary of the motives of business, government, and even nonprofit agencies, as scandal after scandal surfaces about improprieties and mismanagement. A solid commitment to an ethics program by management and employees can help to gain, regain, or hold public trust and credibility, both internally and externally.

Transparency and accountability are going to be matters of rising public concern around the world in the years ahead, according to Frank Vogl, a senior ethics advisor with Ethics Resource Center and a communication professional.

"anything in my own interest is right as long as I don't go to jail," to "anything that pricks my conscience is wrong, no matter what anyone else says or does."

Then, too, most people tend to prescribe for others ethical standards of conduct that they do not practice themselves.

Customs and changing times are significantly involved in ethics and standards. Gifts and favors of various kinds are accepted in many countries as part of the cost of doing, or expediting, business. U.S. businesses that are international in scope claim they must comply to compete. In this country, public attitude in general frowns on gifts and favors as thinly disguised forms of bribery or payoff.

As another example, the dogma and ways of groups committed to strict standards and stern discipline come under assault. Consider the pressure on the Amish people as they see the luxuries and laxity of their neighbors. Or the differing practices of orthodox and reform Jews. Or the Catholic dogma, or the "Protestant work ethic" opposing a wave of permissiveness, liberation of the young, and psychiatric forgiveness for lapses in self-discipline.

APPLICATION TO THE PRACTICE OF PUBLIC RELATIONS

Any effort to bring these considerations down to the practical world of public relations finds generalizations fraught with exceptions. The practice of public relations has been codified and disciplined for the 20,000 members of the Public Relations Society of American since 1950. In 2000, PRSA adopted a member code of ethics (See Figure 10-1). But there are more than 200,000 persons engaged in activities identifiable as public relations, most without equivalent standards or discipline.

That the public relations calling has been able to outgrow such labels as "flackery" and to rise above recurrent instances of news manipulation, cover-up, sugar coating, and some cases of deliberate deceit testifies eloquently to the potential power and promise of two-way communications and positive relationship building when the skills are turned to noble purposes.

For most practitioners, the Golden Rule is seen as an ethical guide—even as a definition of public relations. *If we do unto others as we would have them do unto us, harmonious public relationships will result.*

THE ASPIRATIONS AND CONCEPT ARE PURE

Consider the following concept. If people would communicate more—and better—in a spirit of compromise and reconciliation, most problems in human relations would be solved. There would be understanding and peace. Lifestyle would include self-discipline and acceptance of responsibility, affluence with charity, possession without greed or avarice, and personal integrity under rules of law and mutual respect.

It is in this area that the public relations function has sought to fulfill its aspirations by exerting an ethical and moral force as well as technical skill and, by doing so, developing an identity and a professional discipline of its own.

It has been a long road to travel, but the destination is getting closer: The body of knowledge has been codified; there is an accepted academic curriculum leading to a distinct, recognized public relations doctorate. Today, approximately 70 schools offer master's degrees or a graduate emphasis in public relation. Four universities offer doctoral programs specifically in public relations. There is still no *licensing* of practitioners but there is a Universal Accreditation Program formed in January 1998 by the Public Relations Society of America and nine other public relations organizations. Members with at least 5 years of full-time paid professional pr experience must pass a written and oral exam to be accredited APR.

MEMBER CODE OF ETHICS FOR THE PRACTICE OF PUBLIC RELATIONS

PUBLIC RELATIONS SOCIETY OF AMERICA

This Code was adopted by the PRSA Assembly in 2000. It replaces a Code of Ethics in force since 1950 and revised in 1954, 1959, 1963, 1977, 1983 and 1988.

STATEMENT OF PROFESSIONAL VALUES

These core values of PRSA members and, more broadly, of the public relations profession, provide the foundation for the Member Code of Ethics and set the industry standard for the professional practice of public relations. These values are the fundamental beliefs that guide our behaviors and decision-making process. We believe our professional values are vital to the integrity of the profession as a whole.

ADVOCACY:

- We serve the public interest by acting as responsible advocates for those we represent.
- We provide a voice in the marketplace of ideas, facts and viewpoints to aid informed public debate.

HONESTY:

- We adhere to the highest standards of accuracy and truth in advancing the interests of those we represent and in communicating with the public.

EXPERTISE:

- We acquire and responsibly use specialized knowledge and experience.
- We advance the profession through continued professional development, research and education.
- We build mutual understanding, credibility and relationships among a wide array of institutions and audiences.

INDEPENDENCE:

- We provide objective counsel to those we represent.
- We are accountable for our actions.

(continued)

FIGURE 10-1   Shown here is the Code of Professional Standards for the Practice of Public Relations, revised by PRSA in 2000. Each principle within the Code Provisions contains data on (a) Intent, (b) Guidelines, and (c) Examples of Improper Conduct. These will be continuously expanded by precedent-setting cases and experience in applying the Code. This Code applies to about 10 percent of public relations practitioners—those who are PRSA members. It was developed to serve as a foundation for discussion of an emerging *global* Code of Ethics and Conduct for the practice of public relations.

(continued)

LOYALTY:

- We are faithful to those we represent, while honoring our obligation to serve the public interest.

FAIRNESS:

- We deal fairly with clients, employers, competitors, peers, vendors, the media and the general public.
- We respect all opinions and support the right of free expression.

CODE PROVISIONS

Free Flow of Information
Core principle: Protecting and advancing the free flow of accurate and truthful information is essential to serving the public interest and contributing to informed decision making in a democratic society.

Competition
Core principle: Promoting healthy and fair competition among professionals preserves an ethical climate while fostering a robust business environment.

Disclosure of Information
Core principle: Open communication fosters informed decision making in a democratic society.

Safeguarding Confidences
Core principle: Client trust requires appropriate protection of confidential and private information.

Conflicts of Interest
Core principle: Avoiding real, potential or perceived conflicts of interest builds the trust of clients, employers and the publics.

Enhancing the Profession
Core principle: Public relations professionals work constantly to strengthen the public's trust in the profession.

FIGURE 10-1 *(continued)*

(Courtesy of PRSA.)

In the past, practitioners have functioned generally as skilled communicators and persuaders on behalf of the organizations that employ them. Ethical standards have tended to be the reflections of the employers and clients served. Putting it another way, the public relations voice has generally emerged publicly more as an echo of an employer's standards and interests than that of a professional discipline applied to the employer's problems.

The practitioner still may come on as narrowly organizational rather than broadly professional, but this situation is changing as both employers and the profession embrace a new wave of ethics. Today, public relations continues its struggle for broad recognition as advocates of understanding and public interest, qualified by academic discipline and professional accreditation.

WHAT IS ACCEPTABLE ETHICALLY?

- Is it acceptable for food companies, in the name of nutrition and education, to provide elementary schools with educational kits prominently featuring their labels, product photographs, slogans, and product recipes?
- Is it acceptable for a county agency supported by taxpayers to spend money for a public relations firm to put out its news and promote its work?
- Is it acceptable for a utility to include in the rates to customers the cost of donations it makes to charity, for which it gets credit as being generous?
- Is it acceptable for soft drink, cereal, and other product manufacturers to shower television and movie prop people with free merchandise so that their products appear to be "standard" on television and in motion pictures?
- Is it acceptable for big businesses to preach that their growth creates jobs, when many of them have doubled in sales over a 10-year period yet their employment total remains what it was 10 years ago?
- Is it acceptable for a corporation to hand out a news release at the outset of its annual meeting saying that its presentation was accorded a standing ovation?
- Is it acceptable for television networks to tie in a tire company blimp with their newscasts at sports events, giving the blimp owner free publicity?
- Is it acceptable for a public relations counselor to send a client a flattering clipping with a note, "I knew you'd like to see this as soon as we got it," as if the counselor had something to do with generating the publicity, though actually he or she had not?
- Is it acceptable for an incumbent member of Congress to use perks of office such as staff paid by taxpayers, free mailings, pork barrel (including $25 million for grasshopper control back home), and PAC money to clobber any opposition and perpetuate himself or herself in office?
- Is it acceptable for a public relations director to tell the public a lie on a matter of no real significance if the intent is to protect the privacy or reputation of his or her boss?
- Is it acceptable to use fear in advertising to raise funds for poor people flooded out of their homes? To help cut down on the sale of tobacco? To sell a fire detection device? Insurance?

- Is it acceptable for a congressperson to accept a box of oranges from a grateful fruit grower in his district? An envelope with $20 in it? Season tickets to the Washington Redskins games? A television set? A new automobile?
- Is it acceptable to announce publicly that an official has resigned "for personal reasons" when in fact he or she was fired for the good of the organization, or at the whim of a more powerful, jealous individual?

"So what" is often the reaction after reading these ethical situations. This comment comes from two different concepts: (1) I'd never do any of those, or (2) I'd have to wait until I saw what else was involved before I decided what I would do.[1]

With regard to the first concept, it would be the exceptional person who has a high standard and never goes against it. Lives are a mixture of doing exactly what we think should be done and being "flexible" where the area is more gray than black or white.

The second concept suggests situation ethics, where a person not only waits to make a decision but may make different decisions involving the same situation at different times. Ethics are often gray, but there are situations in which a person should be able to be counted on to do or not to do. Certainly your peers and employers want to believe this. The Public Relations Code of Ethics sets standards we are expected to follow.

References and Additional Readings

Baker, Lee. *The Credibility Factor.* Homewood, IL: Business One Irwin, 1992.

Bernays, Edward L., et al. *tips & tactics* (supplement of *pr reporter*, October 21, November 18, and December 2, 1985). Bernays and others express divergent views on the proposal that practitioners be licensed, like doctors and lawyers, in a three-part *tips & tactics* series.

Bovet, Susan Fry. "The Burning Question of Ethics: The Profession Fights for Better Business Practices." *Public Relations Journal* 49 (November 1993): 24-25, 29.

Brain, John. "Openness or Irrationality." *Public Relations Journal* 44 (December 1988). Editorial dealing with ethical questions in openness; cites cases involving Nestlé, Gerber, and Johnson & Johnson.

Center, Allen. "What About the State of the Art?" *Public Relations Journal* 32 (January 1976). A timeless discussion piece.

Center for Business Ethics at Bentley College, 175 Forest Street, Waltham, MA 02452-4705, 781/891-2981, http://ecampus.bentley.edu/dept/cbe. Established the Ethics Officer Association.

Cutlip, Scott, Allen Center, and Glen Broom. "Ethics and Professionalism." Chapter 5 in *Effective Public Relations.* 8th ed. Upper Saddle River, NJ: Prentice Hall, 1999.

Ethics Resource Center, 1747 Pennsylvania Ave. NW, Suite 400, Washington DC 20006, 202/737-2258, www.ethics.org. Conducts National Business Ethics Survey.

Ethikos (a bi-monthly publication, which joined forces with Rutgers University's *Corporate Conduct Quarterly* in 1998) takes a case study approach to corporate ethics and compliance programs. For sample articles go to www.singerpubs.com/ethikos.

Grunig, James, and Todd Hunt. *Managing Public Relations.* New York: Holt, Rinehart and Winston, 1984. See Chapters 3 and 4.

Hoffman, W. Michael. *The Corporation, Ethics & the Environment.* Westport, CT: Greenwood Publishing Group, 1990.

---

[1]For an interesting classroom exercise in professional ethics, see Lynne Masel-Walters, "Playing the Game: Ethics Situations for Public Relations Courses," *Public Relations Research and Education Journal* 1, Winter, 1984, pp. 47–54.

Jackson, Patrick, and John Paluszek. "Demonstrating Professionalism." *Public Relations Journal* 44 (October 1988). Discusses the options available for practitioners to demonstrate their value to society.

The Joseph & Edna Josephson Institute for Ethics provides a variety of materials and training tools to prepare business for ethical issues and scenarios. For more information contact, Joseph and Edna Josephson Institute of Ethics, 4640 Admiralty Way, Suite 1001, Marina del Rey, CA 90292-6610, 310/827-1864, www.josephsoninstitute.org.

Lesly, Phllip. *The People Factor: Managing the Human Climate.* Homewood, IL: Dow Jones Irwin, 1974.

McElreath, Mark. *Managing Systematic and Ethical Public Relations Campaigns.* New York: McGraw-Hill Higher Education, 1996.

Nevins, Allan, et al. *Public Relations Review* 4 (Fall 1978). A series of six scholarly lectures on the relationship of public relations to eras in U.S. history.

Newsom, Doug, Alan Scott, and Judy Van Slyke Turk. "PR Ethics and Social Responsibilities." Chapter 8 in *This Is PR: The Realities of Public Relations.* 6th ed. Belmont, CA: Wadsworth, 1996.

Olasky, Marvin. "The Aborted Debate Within Public Relations: An Approach Through Kuhn's Paradigm." Chapter 4 in *Public Relations Research Annual.* Volume 1. New York: Lawrence Erlbaum, 1989.

Pearson, Ron. "Beyond Ethical Relativism in Public Relations: Co-orientation, Rules and the Idea of Communication Symmetry." Chapter 3 in *Public Relations Research Annual.* Volume 1. New York: Lawrence Erlbaum, 1989.

Pearson, Ron. "Albert J. Sullivan's Theory of Public Relations Ethics." *Public Relations Review* 15 (Summer 1989): 52–61.

pr reporter Vol. 43 No. 11 (March 13, 2000). "Ethical Behavior Seen by Utility CEO as Essential Tool in New Competitive Electric Market—A Sample Program."

pr reporter Vol. 41 No. 35 (September 7, 1998). "Does Professionalism Translate to Ethical Practice?"

pr reporter Vol. 37 No. 19 (May 9, 1994). "False Fronts, Trying to Buy Relationships Demean Profession."

pr reporter Vol. 34 No. 43 (November 4, 1991). "Ethics Seen As (1) Competitive Advantage, (2) Way to Earn Trust, (3) Heart of Environmental & Social Responsibility Policies."

The Public Relations Body of Knowledge. New York: PRSA. See abstracts dealing with Ethical Issues.

tips & tactics—a supplement of *pr reporter*— Vol. 39 No. 5 (May 7, 2001). "Corporate Integrity & Globalization: The Dawning of a New Era of Accountability & Transparency" by Frank Vogl.

tips & tactics—a supplement of *pr reporter*— Vol. 38 No. 14 (October 30, 2000). "PRSA Changes Its Landmark Code of Ethics, Drops Enforcement Provision to Focus on Educating."

Walsh, Frank. *Public Relations and the Law.* Institute for Public Relations, University of Florida, P.O. Box 118400, Gainesville, FL 32611-8400, 1991. Summarizes laws and regulations that form the basis for the right of representation in the "court of public opinion" by all who seek to influence public and private decisions.

Walsh, Frank, and Philip Lesly. "Considerations of Law in Public Relations." Chapter 48 in *Lesly's Handbook of Public Relations and Communications.* 5th ed. Chicago, IL: NTC Business Books, 1998.

Ward, Gary. *Developing and Enforcing a Code of Business Ethics.* Babylon, New York: Pilot, 1989.

Wilcox, Dennis, Philip Ault, and Warren Agee. "Ethics and Professionalism." Chapter 3 in *Public Relations Strategies and Tactics.* 6th ed. New York: Longman, 2000.

CASES

CASE 10-1 FUND-RAISING—A QUESTION OF TRUST

Any organization, profit or nonprofit, must have credibility with its key publics. In the case of charity organizations, credibility and trust are perhaps more essential than in most. They inspire confidence from the public that their donations will be used for their intended purpose. Can this kind of credibility and trust be rebuilt once doubts about them have been raised?

BACKGROUND AND HISTORY

As a paragon in the field of charity work, the United Way provides support and important services to the community. These services include substance abuse counseling, crisis intervention, job training and placement, disaster relief, and literacy programs. Their multifaceted approach is reflected in their mission: To increase the organized capacity of people to care for one another.

Services are provided at a local level by independent, separately incorporated organizations administered by local boards of volunteers known as the United Way. The United Way of America (UWA) is the National Service and Training Center for community-based United Ways. The national branch does not raise or appropriate money. Rather, it furnishes the community-based United Ways with marketing support, national resources, administrative and personnel programs, and computer software, and it acts as a liaison with other charities,

national media and opinion leaders, and organized labor.

The first United Way (UW) was founded in 1887 in Denver, by religious leaders calling themselves "The Charity Organization Society." A year later the first "United Way" campaign raised $21,700. Regulations for charitable organizations were established within 30 years.

For a century the organization continued along a smooth road to success. In 1985, United Ways raised $2.33 billion, and the trend was toward an even greater increase in donations. By 1987, UWs numbered more than 2,300 across the country. In 1990, the United Way of America published the fifth annual environmental scan document—*What Lies Ahead: Countdown to the Twenty-first Century*—and for the first time, Americans gave over $3 billion to local United Way campaigns. The organization was certainly speeding on a lucrative yellow brick road. However, it was not prepared for the potholes and detours that lay ahead in 1992.

THE CRISIS

On February 16, 1992, the *Washington Post* and *Regardies Magazine* released a story about alleged misconduct by United Way of America's longtime president, William Aramony. After serving for 22 years, Aramony was publicly accused of wrongdoing and financial mismanagement.

The exposé examined such questionable issues as his:

➤ Management of the United Way of America

➤ Yearly salary of $463,000 including benefits

➤ Use of United Way money for travel and personal discretion (e.g., chauffeurs and expensive condominiums)

➤ Hiring practices: employing friends and family

➤ Installation of United Way "spin-off" companies such as Partnership Umbrella and United Way International, created both for profit and nonprofit

THE ENSUING EVENTS

The day the exposé appeared, Senior Vice President for Corporate Communications, Sunshine Overkamp, sent a memorandum to the chief officers and communications directors of all the local United Ways across the country. This memo included the article from the *Post*, and a number of *talking points* in an attempt to be responsive to the concerns of key audiences involved, including:

➤ Contributors

➤ Volunteers

➤ Staff

➤ The public

➤ The media

The memo also gave the numbers of telephone lines set up to handle questions. Another internal investigation was under way, at Aramony's recommendation, by outside counsel, Verner, Liipfert, Bernhard, McPherson, and Hand. The results were to be reported April 2, 1992.

In the weeks to follow, there were numerous follow-up articles in the *Washington Post*, as well as the *New York Times*, *USA Today*, *Time*, *Newsweek*, *U.S. News and World Report*, and many other publications. Overkamp distributed copies of these articles to the local United Ways across the country in an effort to keep them abreast of the situation.

The national office initially supported Aramony under the auspice of innocent until proven guilty. However, 11 days after the exposé was released, Aramony resigned as president of United Way. As Aramony announced his retirement, he apologized for his "lack of sensitivity to perceptions" about his management and spending techniques.[1]

The next day, a memo was sent to employees that Aramony's retirement took effect immediately and that no successor was chosen. The search for a new president and an investigation was announced by Chairman of the Board, John F. Akers, CEO of IBM. Kenneth W. Dam, another IBM executive, was named interim president and CEO of the United Way of America in a March 5 news release. One of the first tasks at hand was a thorough review of policies, practices, and procedures of UWA.

NATIONAL RESPONDS

On the national level, United Way of America took these actions to try to regain its credibility:

➤ Initiated its own investigation of Aramony's conduct.

➤ Updated local United Ways with breaks of new information and guides of how to respond.

---

[1]*Washington Post*, February 28, 1992, p. A10.

➤ Responded immediately to the affirmation of Aramony's misconduct by forcing him to resign and finding a reputable replacement.

➤ Fully disclosed events to the public and the media.

➤ Reformed ethics policy to prevent similar situations in the future.

The national organization responded to a negative reaction by locals over the question of Aramony's continued salary and opted to discontinue it, giving him only the same coverage as other retirees under UWA's group health plan. It was busy over the next few weeks putting policy into action and trying to reassure the local chapters. Here are some examples of what they did:

➤ Answered questions at a *3-day annual conference for volunteer leaders* and organized a series of *"listening forums"* organized to give local representatives a chance to give input.

➤ *Gave local UWs seats on the board.*

➤ *Financially cut off United Way International from UWA and put its chief operating officer on leave.*

➤ *Created a 15-person search committee for a new chief for UWA,* stating that the members were chosen with care "to represent a diverse balanced group of individuals dedicated to the United Way and the volunteer process."

➤ *Interim CEO Dam initiated face-to-face communication with local United Way leaders and volunteers by visiting Connecticut to meet with them on April 21, 1992.* He

answered questions and gave suggestions on how to restore credibility. Dam told them, "The public relations nightmare ultimately may serve as a springboard to redefine the organization's mission." He emphasized that the organization must be seen as more than just a fund-raising mechanism; it needed to be a builder of communities.[2]

Dam sent each UW a copy of the full report on the investigation and the work done to date on recommendations and closed his memo with this thought, "From this crisis, we can, working together, become stronger."

PICKING UP THE PIECES: THE LOCAL LEVEL

Once the scandal broke and Aramony resigned, the focus then turned to concentrating on regaining the public's trust in the United Way, so as not to damage the local chapters. The strategies developed in order to facilitate this difficult task differed among local United Ways. Many had their own strategies, which included:

➤ *Fact sheets* that positioned themselves as *not* associated with the national organization by emphasizing their autonomy (See Figure 10-2).

➤ *Refusing to pay national dues* until satisfied with investigations and resulting changes. (Some continue to refuse paying dues to this date, and there is evidence that this was the real reason the locals so quickly distanced themselves from national.)

---

[2]*The Danbury News-Times,* April 22, 1992, p. 1.

They Look Alike but They're *not* the Same

It's not just the *fine print...* Let's look at the facts.

FACTS:

- UNITED WAY of the NATIONAL CAPITAL AREA is your local United Way whose sole purpose is to serve *this* community. It is one of over 2,000 *local* and *autonomous* United Ways across the nation.

- Your local United Way sees that more than 90 cents out of every dollar collected goes directly to services.

FACTS:

- UNITED WAY OF AMERICA is the national trade association for local United Ways. It is not a headquarters and neither raises nor allocates any funds

- United Way of America sets no policy for local United Ways and is supported by dues of one percent from local United Ways.

Our suspended dues will go to local services.

We take our stewardship seriously. Our immediate response to this troubling controversy at the United Way of America was to suspend our payment of dues and call for a full and open investigation of the United Way of America and its spin-off operations.

In keeping with our dedication to serve this community, **the suspended dues payments will now be made available for increased programs and services needed in our community.**

| **Geoffrey Edwards**
Volunteer President
United Way of the
National Capital Area | **Ronald Townsend**
Chairman of
Trustees Assembly | **Burt K. Fischer**
1992 General
Campaign Chairman | **Sheldon W. Fantle**
Vice Chairman of Trustees
Assembly and Campaign
Advisory Chairman | **Delano E. Lewis**
1991 Campaign Chairman |

FIGURE 10-2 Many local United Ways used posters or fact sheets to demonstrate the difference between the local and the national organizations.

(Courtesy of United Way of the National Capital Area.)

➤ *Considered changing their name.*

➤ Many *circulated letters from the leaders of prominent organizations who encouraged their employees to continue supporting the local United Ways.*

➤ Organized *advisory panels* of key persons in the community to answer any questions and find the appropriate way to solicit them in the upcoming year.

LOCAL UNITED WAYS FILE FOR DIVORCE

A prevalent strategy was to *utilize the local media in order to distinguish between the local and national United Ways.* Here are two examples of the specific strategies some UWs implemented.

Making Lemonade Out of Lemons

The United Way of Massachusetts Bay used the Aramony scandal to educate the public of the autonomy existing between the local organization and the national. It released the amount of money that goes toward service projects, 91.4 cents of every dollar. In addition, it asked the press to be sensitive to its plight and use headlines using "United Way of America" or "National Charity" to help people differentiate between the local and the national organization. It convinced two major papers to run full-page ads for free that spread this information. The area's number one radio station ran a campaign two times a day saying, "Thanks to the employees at *x* company who last year contributed *y* dollars to the United Way campaign, 3,000 people were fed a hot meal at St. Francis House." This message helped

make "the connection between when they gave money and where it is going, how it is making an impact," explained Maureen Sullivan, director of public relations.

In addition to utilizing the local media, it maintained a policy of full disclosure and open communication by responding to every letter and call it received. It accepted invitations to meetings to further discuss the situation and urged CEOs to support the UW and to encourage their employees to do the same. Finally it planned a "Community Care Day" to gain community visibility, let donors know where the money goes, and have a positive impact on some lives.[3]

The United Way of Orange County (UWOC) response was to work with the local media to get a local perspective, with all the stories coming over the wire. It did a direct mailing of fact sheets to campaign coordinators of local companies, the local board of directors, and agencies that receive money from the Orange County United Way. This mailing included a position statement from UWOC. It planned attitudinal research at some organizations that conduct United Way campaigns to survey the damage and guide future tactics. It set up forums for the public attended by the local president and chairman of the board. It ran a pilot fund-raising campaign to find out what questions people might ask to help direct the fall campaign strategies.[4]

THE UNITED WAY RECOVERS

One year after the Aramony scandal rocked the United Way of America, the future looked difficult but not dismal. This comeback was partly attributed to the change in the structure and operation of the national organization.

---

[3]*pr reporter*, May 18, 1992.
[4]*New Milford Times*, June 4, 1992.

IT'S NOT JUST THE UNITED WAY

Until the United Way scandal occurred, charities often escaped public scrutiny because they tended to be judged on whether the cause they supported was worthwhile instead of that charity's actual performance, a reality that most for-profit organizations must contend with. Nonprofit organizations are not constrained by the marketplace pressures and electoral politics that regulate big business.

United Way is not the only nonprofit organization whose finances have been scrutinized. According to an article published in the *Wall Street Journal*, the financial expenditures of affiliates of the American Cancer Society create some difficult-to-answer questions. While many of these affiliates claimed spending 78 percent of their budgets on direct services to combat cancer, included in that amount was salaries and overhead, which is often up to 60 percent of the total budget.*

In addition, these charities often have huge cash reserves from which they are earning large amounts of interest. These cash reserves are often monies intended by donors to immediately be applied to combating cancer. Such asset holdings call into question both the fund-raising rhetoric and priorities of Cancer Society affiliates.

In the future, charities will not be given the free reign that they were given in the past. Americans now want positive proof that their money will be used for the purpose for which it was given.

The Wall Street Journal, March 13, 1992.

➤ *The Board was expanded to include members from local United Way chapters* who make up a third of the total; this board now meets four times a year instead of two times.

➤ *Created new volunteer oversight committees* in an effort to greater regulate the national organization.

➤ *Appointed Elaine Chao,* former director of the Peace Corps, as *president and CEO.*

➤ *Instituted a membership fee structure for local chapters that is lower* than the previous 1 percent of campaign requirement.

➤ Changed its objective to focus on *restoring confidence, instituting true accountability and quality management, and focusing on customer* (local United Way organizations) *satisfaction.*

➤ *Reduced salaries:* banned first-class travel for UWA officials.

The fund-raising results for United Way of America were not outstanding in 1992. Donations decreased 3.3 percent compared with those collected in 1991. However, according to evaluations completed by executives at the end of their corporation's UW fund drives, this decrease has largely been attributed to the recession and corporate downsizing, not to the Aramony shake-up.[5] In addition, other fund-raising organizations have been cashing in on the employee pledging progams, a trend that was prevalent even before the scandal. One dismal fact for UWA is that *almost one-third of local chapters still continued to refuse to pay dues,* which forced the UWA to cut its staff by one-third and its budget by millions.

ARAMONY CASE UPDATE

William Aramony was convicted in 1995 of defrauding the United Way of America of $600,000. He was found guilty of fraud, tax, and conspiracy charges and received a 7-year prison sentence. Shortly after his conviction, he sued the United Way for pension benefits and was awarded $4.4 million dollars. The United Way filed suit against him and a judge ruled that Aramony owed the United Way $2.02 million to cover salary and other funds he received while stealing from the organization. For a time, Aramony still stood to collect a balance of $2 million. In 2001, however, the U.S. Court of Appeals reversed a lower court ruling that Aramony was entitled to $2 million in pension benefits. This reversal cut his retirement award to just under $8,000.

A new level of awareness has been established among the public, regarding how and where charitable organizations spend their money. Because of the Aramony scandal, people will not let charitable institutions go about their business unchecked in the future. Potential donors now have an "excuse" not to give money unless charitable organizations can convince those people of their dedication to the cause for which they are raising money. ■

QUESTIONS FOR DISCUSSION

1. In the trend toward social responsibility in the 1990s, ethical considerations are often foremost in importance for operating an organization. Do you believe that an established ethical credo is more, less, or equally important for profit and nonprofit organizations? Why?

2. Was the UWA wrong to stand behind Aramony at the beginning of the scandal? Do you believe this stance caused further damage to the organization's credibility? Why or why not?

3. To keep a nonprofit organization running in the business world of today, managers often must adopt some of the standards of for-profit businesses. What limitations do you see for nonprofit organizations in adopting these standards and why? What advantages do you see?

4. Aside from the number of dollars campaigns bring in, what other ways can you think of to evaluate how successful local United Ways have been in distancing themselves from the national scandal?

---

[5]We thank Doris Burke, Director of Communications for United Way of Greater Manchester, New Hampshire, for the information provided for this case.

CASE 10-2   A CLASSIC: BABY FORMULA RAISES QUESTIONS

In capitalist theory, the law of supply and demand and the human virtues of honesty and fairness are determinants regulating competition in the marketplace. If and when these get out of kilter, appropriate restraints or regulations can be imposed by governmental authority.

However, laxity in self-imposed standards back in the 1960s led to a number of consumer protection laws and to the growing intervention of the consumer's advocate. The advocate came in the form of either a person or an organization, acting as investigator or quality control manager, on behalf of the consuming public. Over time, nongovernmental consumer protection and advocacy have come to involve the Better Business Bureaus, *Consumer Research* and *Consumer Reports* magazines, telephone hotlines, television programs, newspaper and magazine features, newsletters, and dozens of special interest groups with their networks for investigation and communication.

COMPETITION IS THE CULPRIT

Product producers who are in business for the long haul don't set out to deliver an unsafe, fragile, or overpriced product. Occurrences when consumers are harmed or abused by gutter-level tactics and ethics are the exceptions. More often, breaches of the buyer-seller relationship stem from competitive pressures resulting in use of substandard materials; inadequate research, testing, or quality control; improper packaging; overstated claims of product benefits or capabilities; or faulty instructions. When consumer complaints pile up and a protectionist group moves in or litigation threatens, product makers go on the *defensive*, sometimes to stonewall, and other times to recall, to replace, or to refund.

MOTHERS, BABIES, AND NUTRITION

To exemplify a breached buyer-seller relationship and a consumer group moving in, we have chosen powdered infant formula as the product, and two giant producers, Nestlé, the world food colossus based in Switzerland, and Bristol-Myers, a multibillion dollar U.S. company diversified in pharmaceuticals, household products, cosmetics, and may other products.

The problem arose when powdered infant formula was distributed by these two competitors in underdeveloped areas of the world. Medical studies conducted by world health organizations found that when the product was administered it was a contributing factor in malnutrition and the cause of diarrhea and a higher mortality rate in babies in underdeveloped countries (See Figure 10-3).

At the core of the problem was the reality that most infant formulas sold in underdeveloped countries come in powdered form, and these milk solids must be mixed with water before they are usable. According to the reports, babies frequently received contaminated milk because in many areas there is a general ignorance of hygiene, unclean water, or limited fuel for sterilizing bottles. These conditions prevented mothers from following formula preparations correctly.

FIGURE 10-3   Emotion-packed photo carried by *Mother Jones* magazine dramatically shows the impact of the use of powdered formula sold in underdeveloped nations.

HIGH COST OF POWDERED FORMULA

Moreover, according to the reports, the powdered formula was so expensive that mothers often diluted it to make it last longer. It was estimated that in Nigeria, where American-made formula was widely used, the cost of feeding a 3-month-old infant with formula was approximately 30 percent of the minimum urban wage. Making matters worse, there was a sweeping shift away from breast-feeding throughout developing countries. The shift was associated with the rapid urbanization of these countries.

Critics admitted that the infant formula manufacturers were not responsible for the trend away from breast-feeding. However, faced with stagnant or declining birthrates in the developed world, the critics maintained that these companies encouraged the abandonment of breast-feeding by stepping up their sales effort in the baby-booming areas of Latin America, the Far East, Africa, and the Middle East.

Profits from baby formula sales reached new highs for some of the companies. In 1975, Bristol-Myers enjoyed a 1-year record in profits largely because of formula sales. For another company, baby formula sales increased by more than 30 percent for 2 years in a row.[1]

ETHICAL MISCONDUCT, CLEVER MARKETING, OR SOCIAL IRRESPONSIBILITY?

Most of the criticism of the companies focused on how they achieved their sales. In underdeveloped countries, they relied heavily on "milk nurses" or "mother craft work-

[1]*New York Times*, September 11, 1975.

ers" who went into hospitals, clinics, and private homes to instruct new mothers on child care and on the advantages of using the company's formula. The "nurses" wore traditional nurses' uniforms, which, the critics charged, lent a spurious air of authority to their sales appeal, and in some cases they were paid on a commission or bonus basis, adding a conflict-of-interest charge to the matter of morality.[2]

As public awareness of the controversy grew, better-known organizations became involved. The Protein Calorie Group of the United Nations issued a statement that emphasized "the critical importance of breast feeding under the sociocultural and economic conditions that prevailed in many developing countries." Later, the Twenty-Seventh World Health Assembly passed resolutions strongly recommending the encouragement of breast-feeding as the "ideal feeding in order to promote harmonious physical and mental development of children." The resolutions called for countries to "review sales and promotional activities on baby foods and to introduce appropriate remedial measures, including advertisement codes and legislation where necessary."[3]

PUBLICITY CONTINUES FOR YEARS

The controversy continued at the publicity level 4 years before organizations within the United States adopted the role of consumer advocate. Perhaps the most influential advocate was the Interfaith Center on Corporate Responsibility (ICCR), a division of the National Council of Churches. The group represents 14 major Protestant denominations and more than 150 Catholic groups. In an annual report, ICCR stated that it "exists to assist its member boards, agencies and instrumentalities to express social responsibility with their investments. Members of ICCR agree that as investors in businesses, they are also part owners and therefore have the right and obligation to monitor the social responsibilities of corporations and act where necessary to help prevent or correct corporate policy that produces social injury."[4]

CONSUMER INTEREST STRATEGY

As an initial step, ICCR members filed shareholder resolutions with U.S. baby formula manufacturers, including Bristol-Myers. Management met with ICCR members and disclaimed any responsibility for formula misuse. Despite this disclaimer, other organizations supported the resolutions. The Ford Foundation joined the other shareholders in support of the resolution—calling for a report on sales and promotional activities. The president of the Rockefeller Foundation wrote to the chairman of Bristol-Myers requesting the "publication of all relevant information to the outer limits permitted by competitive considerations."

---

[2]Ibid.

[3]Other studies and reports were made both in the United States and in foreign countries. They told the same stories using different examples from different places in the world. While most of these reports went unchallenged by the producers of baby formula, one exception should be noted. An organization called Third World Action Group reprinted a report entitled *The Baby Killers*. The booklet was aimed at Nestlé and reported on infant malnutrition and the promotion of artificial feeding practices in the Third World. When the booklet was released in Switzerland, Nestlé sued for defamation. The suit made news throughout the world for 2 years before it was settled. In the end, Nestlé dropped three of the four defamation charges. On the fourth charge regarding the new title, *Nestlé Kills Babies*, the judge said that since it could not be shown that Nestlé directly kills infants—the mothers who prepare the formula are third-party intermediaries—the title must be defamatory. However, the judge imposed only minimal fines and asked Nestlé to "fundamentally rethink" its advertising policies.

[4]ICCR 1977 Annual Report.

TACTICS AND DEBATE

A short time later, Bristol-Myers published a 19-page report entitled *The Infant Formula Marketing Practices of Bristol-Myers Company in Countries Outside the United States.* ICCR called the report "an attempt to obfuscate the issue" and sought responses by experts in infant nutrition. Dr. Derrick Jelliffe, one of the early expert critics in the baby formula controversy, condemned the report as "inadequate and evasive." Within a couple of months, more than 20 ICCR members, joined by staff members of the Rockefeller and Ford foundations, met with Bristol-Myers management. The meetings changed little, and ICCR members filed another shareholder resolution with Bristol-Myers, requesting the correction of the company's report.

Four months after the ICCR resolution requesting a correction, Bristol-Myers issued a proxy statement stating that the company had been "totally responsive to the concerns [of ICCR members]" in the stockholders' resolutions. Feeling sure the proxy was inaccurate, the Sisters of the Precious Blood and ICCR members filed a lawsuit against Bristol-Myers. The suit charged Bristol-Myers with making a "misstatement" in its proxy and called for "a resolicitation of proxy votes, free from the taint of fraud." The Sisters of the Precious Blood submitted massive evidence in support of their claim, but the U.S. district judge dismissed the suit. The judge declined to rule on the accuracy of the proxy statement, saying the Sisters were not caused "irreparable harm" by the statement. The text of the decision implied that since a shareholder resolution is "precatory" or not binding on management, it is not relevant whether a company fails to tell the truth in responding to a shareholder proposal. Sometimes even the courts seem to condone or encourage ethical lapses.

SEC SUPPORTS SISTERS

The Sisters of the Precious Blood announced plans to appeal the dismissal on the grounds that the ruling "did not address the merits of the charge and makes a mockery of Securities and Echange Commission laws requiring truth in corporate proxy statements." The Securities and Exchange Com-mission added pressure to Bristol-Myers when it indicated a plan to file a brief in court in favor of the Sisters if the appeal went forward. In the end, the appeal did not have to be filed because Bristol-Myers agreed to send a report to stockholders that included evidence from Third World countries, details of sales of Bristol-Myers in poverty areas, and a description of the medical problems caused by these practices. Bristol-Myers also agreed to halt the use of all consumer-oriented advertising and to withdraw milk nurses.

About the same time as the Sisters of the Precious Blood filed their lawsuit against Bristol-Myers, members of Congress began to act on the controversy. The first step was a resolution co-sponsored by 29 members of Congress calling for an investigation of U.S. formula companies. A year later, an amendment to the International Develop-ment and Food Assistance Act urged the president to develop a strategy for programs of nutrition and health improvements for mothers and children, including breast-feeding. The report accompanying the House version of the amendment stated that "businesses involved in the manufacture, marketing, or sale of infant formula have a responsibility to conduct their overseas activities in ways which do not have adverse effects on the nutritional health of people of developing nations."

Legislative involvement continued the following year as the U.S. Senate subcommittee on Health and Scientific Research heard testimony on the infant formula controversy. Dr. James Post of Boston University stated that "for eight years, the industry's critics have borne the burden of proving that commercial marketing practices were actually contributing to infant malnutrition and morbidity. . . . From this time forward, the sellers of infant formula must bear the burden of proving that their products . . . actually serve a public purpose in the developing world." While no legislation came from the U.S. Senate, Senator Edward Kennedy did request that the World Health Organization sponsor a conference on infant formula promotion, marketing, and use.

Group action then fastened on Nestlé. However, when competition is international, what the U.S. Congress thinks or does is not always binding on foreign-based businesses. A responsive set of tactics came into play.

NESTLÉ FORMS COUNCIL

To disarm critics and defuse the issue, Nestlé led a number of large baby formula companies to form the International Council on Infant Food Industries (ICIFI). One of the major undertakings of ICIFI was the publication of a "Code of Ethics" for formula promotion. While the "Code" appeared to strengthen the position of baby formula manufacturers, it was criticized as being vague and meaningless. It was further weakened by the fact that two of the largest formula marketers, including Bristol-Myers, refused to join ICIFI.

While stockholder resolutions continued to put pressure on American companies, a new citizens' action group formed to bring pressure on Nestlé. INFACT (Infant Formula Action Coalition) began a national campaign. The Minnesota chapter initiated a boycott of Nestlé's products. The boycott became necessary, according to INFACT, because Nestlé did not change its policies on infant formula marketing techniques. INFACT made these demands of Nestlé:

1. Immediately stop all promotion of Nestlé artificial formula.
2. Stop mass media advertising of formula.
3. Stop distribution of free samples to hospitals, clinics, and homes of newborns.
4. Discontinue use of Nestlé milk nurses.
5. Stop promotion through the medical profession.
6. Prevent artificial formula from getting into the hands of people who do not have the means or facilities to use it safely.

Nestlé representatives made themselves available to groups across the United States. They met with representatives of various health advocate groups, medical professionals, and others. Nestlé's basic position stemmed from a history of manufacturing and selling formula in developing countries for more than 60 years. The root causes of infant malnutrition and mortality in the Third World, according to Nestlé, were poverty, lack of food, ignorance, and poor sanitation. Nestlé advocated breast-feeding, but stated that most Third World infants needed a supplement to mother's milk to sustain normal physical and mental growth for a period of months.

The national INFACT conference reacted to the meetings with Nestlé officials by deciding to continue the boycott. Boycott endorsements came from the Democratic Farmer-Labor Party of Minnesota and Ralph Nader. Nestlé representatives again met with action group representatives. Nothing was resolved, and the groups indicated that they would continue the boycott until Nestlé made substantial policy changes.

SPICING UP THE BOYCOTT TO BUILD A BIGGER CONSTITUENCY

To bring more attention to the boycott, action groups sponsored "Infant Formula Action Day" acros the United States. The activities included a Boston Nestea[5] Party, demonstrations, leafleting, letter writing, fasts, and other public events. Later the same year, INFACT sponsored a program called "Spook Nestlé." The program urged Halloweeners not to buy or accept Nestlé candies. Leafleting at grocery stores and film showings was also part of the program (See Figure 10-4).

The list of those endorsing the boycott continued to grow. At the top of the list was the governing board of the National Council of Churches, which had facilitated earlier meetings.

The stalemate continued for more than 5 years. Nestlé published a list of 19 excerpts from letters indicating support of Nestlé activities in Third World countries, but this action did not swing public opinion in its favor and end the boycott. The boycott cost Nestlé millions of dollars, yet these costs did little to actually hurt the giant corporation, which had profits in the billions during these years. What Nestlé wanted to get rid of was "the public relations nightmare." Church groups, labor unions, feminists, and other activists accused Nestlé of killing babies.

A CODE OF ETHICS IN PRACTICAL FORM

In the 1980s, the World Health Organization (WHO) tackled the problem by establishing the International Code of Marketing of Breastmilk Substitutes. The membership of WHO voted 118 to 1 to adopt the nonbinding code. The United States cast the one dissenting vote, claiming that the code's restrictions violated the constitutional guarantees of free speech and freedom of information.

The code restricted the promotion of infant formula, prohibited the widespread practice of free formula samples to new mothers and the use of "mothercraft" nurses, a long criticized marketing aspect. Advertisements and other promotions to the general public were forbidden, as were gifts to mothers given to promote the use of breastmilk substitutes. The code also required that manufacturers discontinue use of product labels that idealized the use of infant formula. All products were to be labeled explaining the health hazards of bottle feeding.

After the passage of the code in 1981 by individual governments, Nestlé changed several of its marketing practices, even in countries where the code had not formally been adopted. Despite these advances, the ICCR and the National Council of Churches found a long list of violations by Nestlé.

On its own, Nestlé released a revised set of policies designed to follow the code. The boycott continued, however, with focus on Nestlé's Tasters' Choice brand product. Several groups gathered and dumped 112,000 signatures onto the front steps of the company's headquarers in Switzerland.

A RESOLUTION OF SORTS

Just as it seemed as though the standoff would go on forever, Nestlé reached an accord with the protest groups in 1984. Bristol-Myers, Ross division of Abbot Laboratories, and Wyeth Laboratories, a unit

---

[5]Nestlé's brand of instant tea.

OF ALL THE PARTICIPANTS, WHO WON WHAT?

The news coverage of the accord between Nestlé and the health advocate organizations indicated that the health advocate organizations had won the long battle. For example, an article in *Newsweek* included a photo of a Nestlé ad with the subhead: "A Boycott That Hurt." The headline on the article stated, "Nestlé's Costly Accord." The lead in the story set the tone and clearly put the health advocate organizations in the winning position:

For the past 7 years, scores of religious, women's health and public-interest groups have waged a very rough and costly boycott against the Swiss-based Nestlé company. . . . Last week, after spending tens of millions of dollars resisting the boycott, Nestlé finallly reached the accord with the protesters.

Nestlé agreed to change four of its business practices as the basis of the accord.

1. Put information on labels.
2. Update and provide all information in literature.
3. Stop giving gifts to health officials.
4. Stop distributing samples and supplies.

WHAT YOU CAN DO ABOUT THE BOTTLE BABY SCANDAL

1. Boycott Nestlé. Nestlé is the largest infant-formula distributor in the Third World. A boycott of the company's products has been under way for some time in Western Europe; one in the U.S. began on July 4, 1977. Don't buy Taster's Choice/Nescafé/Nestlé Quik/Nestlé Crunch/Nestea/ Libby, McNeill & Libby products (Libby's tomato juice, canned vegetables, etc.)

2. Join the campaign. As we go to press, active groups in more than a dozen American cities are working to spread the Nestlé boycott, distributing articles and a documentary film called *Bottle Babies*, speaking about the problem in churches and on talk shows, and so on. To find out how to link up with the campaign where you live, write or call:

Interfaith Center on Corporate Responsibility 475 Riverside Drive New York, NY 10027 (212) 870-2294	Third World Institute of the Newman Center 1701 University Ave. Minneapolis, MN 55414 (612) 331-3437	Earthwork 1499 Potrero Ave. San Francisco, CA 94110

3. Sound Off. Clip or copy the coupon below and send it to:

Name of Your Representative
U.S. House of Representatives
Washington, DC 20515

Name of Your Senator
U.S. Senate Office Building
Washington, DC 20510

Send a copy of your letter to:

Bristol-Myers
345 Park Ave.
New York, NY 10022

Nestlé Co., Inc.
100 Bloomingdale Road
White Plains, NY 10605

Add a note to Nestlé saying that you are boycotting its products until it stops all promotion, advertising and free-sample distribution of infant formula in the Third World, and all distribution of formula anywhere where people do not have the money or the facilities to use it safely.

Dear_____:

The attached article details the growing problem of death and disease that results from aggressive infant-formula sales in the Third World. I am outraged by this practice. We need legislation that will bring it to a halt. Please inform me what you intend to do about this.

Sincerely,

FIGURE 10-4 Boycott Nestlé was promoted in a variety of ways, including advertisements such as this one appearing in *Mother Jones.*

of American Home Products, major baby formula manufacturers in the United States, also reached accords with the protestors.

Another incident with ethical overtones did not seem to rattle or deter Nestlé. In 1986, a suit hit Nestlé Beech-Nut Nutrition Corporation and its two top executives for selling formula apple juice that was not composed of the fruit juice. The company settled that for $2 million, legal costs, and some slump in sales, not an indigestible bite out of Nestlé billions in sales.[6] In 1988, two Beech-Nut executives, including the president, took the fall with a sentence of one year in jail and $100,000 in fines. Meantime, a *Wall Street Journal* article reported that an acquisitive-minded Nestlé, with plenty of cash, was back on the prowl paying $1.3 billion for some European food interests and bidding $4 billion for a British candy maker.[7]

AN UPDATE

In 1988, the International Baby Food Action Network (IBFAN) released a detailed and illustrated report on the international marketing practices of the infant food and feeding bottle industry prepared initially for the World Health Assembly. The report was titled "Still Breaking the Rules" and IBFAN continues to update this report (See Figure 10-5).[8]

The report indicated that the infant foods industry, in pushing its products around the world, continued to employ methods that "endanger infant health and undermine the efforts of national policy makers, primary health care workers, con-sumer protection organizations and international agencies which have worked for more than a decade to encourage mothers to implement inexpensive and simple measures, including breast-feeding, to protect their babies' health and lives."

In naming offenders, the report went beyond Nestlé and Bristol-Myers. The list was far-reaching, demonstrating that the international infant food market has attracted entries from many countries, making control or discipline extremely difficult. Success in competition comes first in business whether local or worldwide.

Also in 1988, *Action News,* a publication issued by an IBFAN member named "Action For Corporate Accountability," reported that despite the code, Nestlé continued to "dump supplies of formula on hospitals" and thus gave the impression of medical endorsement for artificial baby feeding. If Nestlé persisted, the planned responsive action would be a renewal of the boycott in the United States starting on October 4, 1988, the fourth anniversary of the date the first boycott was ended.

As promised, the boycott was initiated again that year and is still ongoing. Action for Corporate Accountability spearheaded the effort against Nestlé in the United States and has focused attention on another company in this most recent boycott, American Home Products. AHP and Nestlé control about 65 percent of the global infant formula market and refused to succumb to ACTION's demands to end the practice of supplying their formulas free to hospitals. It began circulating a petition and collected over 50,000 names that it has presented to

---

[6]"What Led Beech-Nut Down the Road to Disgrace," *Business Week*, February 22, 1988. pp. 124–128.
[7]John Marcom, Jr., "Acquisitive Nestlé, with Cash to Spare, Is Set to Continue Its Takeover Search," *The Wall Street Journal*, April 28, 1988.
[8]For a copy of the report, write to IBFAN USA, c/o ACTION, 129 Church Street, New Haven, CT 06510.

(Courtesy of IBFAN and Action for Corporate Accountability.)

Nestlé to pressure it with grassroots support. To emphasize its point, ACTION sent out frequent newsletters and fact sheets to update the violations Nestlé and AHP have recently committed in marketing and selling their baby formula worldwide. To follow up the U.S. effort, boycotts were initiated against AHP, Nestlé, and local formula companies in 12 other countries from 1988 to 1990.

In 1992, the "Baby-Friendly" Hospital Initiative was issued by UNICEF and WHO. It is a global campaign to foster support for breast-feeding and an effort to end the supply of free and low-cost formula to maternity institutions. Both AHP and Nestlé agreed to the initiative and to stop supplying hospitals with free samples of their formulas. However, ACTION remained unconvinced of the formula manufacturers commitment to the initiative, citing the company's behavior of "business as usual" as an indicator of how seriously the companies are taking the proposal. Enforcing the Baby-Friendly Hospital

Initiative also may be sticky, considering that "UNICEF and WHO have no power to implement this initiative globally," says ACTION's Executive Director, Dr. Idrian N. Resnick. "Only an intense campaign of consumer and media pressure will force these corporations to quit stalling and do what's right."[9]

And where is Nestlé in all this? Nestlé continued its efforts with the International Association of Infant Food Manufacturers (IFM) to prove its commitment to work with "international agencies, governments, non-governmental organizations, and all others concerned, to end all supplies of infant formula in developing countries except for the limited number of infants who need it." This statement, taken from a Nestlé policy update in December of 1990, suggests its continued commitment to ending free baby food supplies to hospitals of third world countries.

The battle continues and can be followed on the Internet. In 1999, Nestlé

---

[9]Taken from a press release issued by Action for Corporate Accountability on March 11, 1992.

released a publication titled "Nestlé Implementation of the WHO Code" in defense of its marketing practices. IBFAN declared it "a public relations offensive on the baby milk issue."

But once a company or organization behaves irresponsibly, it takes more than words to regain trust. Many are therefore undoubtedly asking, "Does Nestlé mean it this time?" ■

QUESTIONS FOR DISCUSSION

1. As between the open system and the closed system, which label fit the posture of Nestlé and of IBFAN, expressed in their policies and actions? How about proactive versus reactive?

2. To change people's opinions, there are several options in strategy and tactics such as persuasion, coercion, compensation, or compulsion. Which ones among these, or others, do you see employed by various opposing groups in this case study?

3. In 1988, when IBFAN announced a plan to renew the boycott of Nestlé products, would that clearly constitute a more effective or less effective threat as stated in a Chapter 1 maxim? Might the factor of mildness or harshness depend on Nestlé management's reaction based on its marketing strategy and practices? Whether it would or not,

what does that say to you about the practical application of maxims?

4. If you feel this was a matter on which the opponents could work out a reasonable resolution in the public interest, and both sides had professional counsel morally committed to reconciliation, what could have been done better or differently so that the matter wouldn't drag on for years? After you figure out your answer to this, try coming up with a resolution for the abortion issue. Are the intervening forces and stubborn issues the same?

5. Is it possible for Nestlé (and other baby formula manufacturers) to come to a definitive accord with these activist groups? What is the issue each is fighting for or against? Compare the underlying value systems of the two sides.

CASE 10-3 CORPORATE SOCIAL RESPONSIBILITY AND ETHICS: NIKE'S LABOR PRACTICES UNDER SCRUTINY

Corporations are no longer accountable to only their investors, nor can they base their success solely on high sales figures. A legacy of the social movements of the 1960s and a demand for political correctness now compels organizations to have practices in place that demonstrate their commitment to social responsibility.[1] Corporate social responsibility can include embracing the issues of environmentalism, animal testing, human rights, or other social or political concerns affected or perceived to be affected by an organization's policies. Corporations are now finding that stakeholders expect them to have an ethical, and not necessarily financial, interest in their policies and how those policies affect the rest of the world.

It has become important to organizations to cultivate their socially responsible image. Socially responsible corporate practices and ethical standards are a reflection of each organization. Corporations have learned that being socially responsible is good for business; that their beneficence also benefits the company.

While some companies are following through on their commitments, others only project the appearance of being socially responsible. This discrepancy between a company's environmental image and

actions has been referred to as "greenwashing." This term has earned an entry in the 10th edition of the Concise Oxford English Dictionary and is defined as "disinformation disseminated by an organization so as to present an environmentally responsible public image." Mark Twain must have experienced early versions of greenwashing in his time when he said, "The secret of success is honesty and fair dealing—if you can fake these, you've got it made."

If an organization is accused of social irresponsibility or demonstrating unethical practices, it may not necessarily be doing anything illegal. Violating an Environmental Protection Agency regulation or discriminating against an employee are illegal acts. Selling fur products or making a corporate donation to Planned Parenthood are not illegal but some may see these acts as unethical. Many companies have experienced boycotts based on their actions that are legal but perceived to be unethical.

The German philosopher Immanuel Kant (1724–1804), in his works on ethics, wrote, "Act only on that maxim through which you can at the same time will that it should become a universal law." Before a company advances a policy or produces a new product, it may want to address the

---

[1]Betsy Reed, "The Business of Social Responsibility," *Dollars and Sense*, May 1998; Jon Entine, "Corporate Ethics and Accountability," Corporate Governance Web site (www.corpgov.net).

issue of business ethics by asking the following questions:

➤ Will anyone be damaged or compromised by our actions?

➤ Will anyone gain an unfair advantage?

➤ Is there anything inherently wrong with these actions?

➤ If these practices reach the media, will we look bad?

➤ Are we able to feel good about utilizing these practices? Would we be happy applying the practices or policies to ourselves?

In other words, should the Golden Rule also apply to business practices? Does there have to be a trade-off between corporate social responsibility and making a profit?

NIKE'S PROBLEMS FORESHADOWED— NIKE FOREWARNED

Nike, Inc. is the world's number one shoe company and controls more than 40 percent of the U.S. athletic shoe market. It employs more than half a million people worldwide and contracts with factories throughout the world, many of which are located in Asia. Nike established its own Code of Conduct in 1992 to ensure that specific guidelines on wages and working conditions are followed at all of its facilities, including those under the supervision of subcontractors overseas.

Nike began to receive negative coverage concerning its labor practices in the early 1990s. In 1992, Jeff Ballinger, who had spent 4 years in Indonesia helping workers to organize unions, returned to the United States with information on abusive labor practices in Nike factories in Indonesia. In 1993, CBS flew Ballinger back to Indonesia to narrate a story on the workers' struggle for a living wage in those facilities.

After the CBS report, Nike received a flurry of negative media coverage from the press in both the United States and United Kingdom over the next 2 years. During this time, the company issued various press releases and statements asserting its commitment to the welfare of its workers and to improving factory conditions. Nike seemed to successfully endure the reactions to the bad press. After its stock price fell slightly at the end of 1993, it began a steady upswing starting in 1995.

SOMEONE BLOWS THE WHISTLE ON NIKE

In November 1997, a disgruntled Nike employee leaked a secret, internal report to The Transnational Resource and Action Center (TRAC), a San Francisco-based organization now known as Corporate Watch. Nike had hired the Ernst & Young accounting firm to audit the working conditions at one of its shoe manufacturing plants in Vietnam. The inspection report stated that workers were exposed to harmful levels of carcinogens because of poor air ventilation in the plant and that 77 percent of the employees had respiratory problems. The report also detailed that employees were forced to work 65 hours a week yet did not receive a living wage. This information seemed to contradict Nike's earlier statements of commitment to the welfare of its workers.

The Ernst & Young report was supplied to the *New York Times*, which then printed a story on it on November 8, 1997. Nike responded by pointing out that, soon after they had received the report, the problems were addressed and steps had been taken to improve the working conditions.

However, this time, with the release of the Ernst & Young report, the damage was done. The problem of Nike's apparent exploitation of its overseas employees, based on long hours and low pay, was now compounded by the issue of the unhealthy environmental condition of the factories. Six months later, Nike was presented with another hurdle.

In April 1998, a lawsuit was filed against Nike in a California Superior Court alleging that Nike's statements of protection of its workers amounted to false advertising under California's consumer-protection laws.[2] Under California's broad consumer-protection laws, a plaintiff is not required to prove he or she has suffered personal injury—only that there was a likelihood of deception.

The main question of the lawsuit is whether Nike's public statements are considered advertising for the company and therefore subject to truth-in-advertising laws, or if they are simply public statements that are protected by the First Amendment. As of early 2001, the case has been appealed to the California Supreme Court because an appellate court ruled that Nike's statements were protected free speech.

NIKE PUTS ITS BEST FOOT FORWARD

Nike was now experiencing some financial repercussions—drops in stock prices and sales—from the coverage of their labor practices that were viewed by many as exploitive and unethical. Nike was finally facing the fact that its policies *did* make it look bad in the press, were inherently wrong, and engendered a feeling of ill will. This time, the company took a more proactive approach.

In May 1998, at the National Press Club in Washington, D.C., Chairman and CEO Philip Knight announced Nike's New Labor Initiatives aimed at improving factory working conditions worldwide. The main elements of the Initiatives are:

➤ Increase the minimum age of new employees in the shoe factories to 18 years of age

➤ Improve the air quality by using the standards enforced by OSHA

➤ A commitment to a policy of open communications on corporate responsibility issues

➤ A pledge to allow independent monitoring of its factories by nongovernmental organizations (NGOs)

However, the Initiatives do not address the issues of forced overtime and increasing earnings to a living wage. In his speech, Philip Knight said, "These moves do more than just set industry standards. They reflect who we are as a company."

BOTH SIDES UTILIZE THE INTERNET

As the Internet has become an everyday resource for more and more people, companies of all sizes now use it as a worldwide marketing and public relations tool. If a company wants to let people know what it has to offer by promoting itself globally, the Internet provides that outlet.

The Internet is also an outlet for activism against corporations.[3] The online attacks can take place on specific Web sites, in chat rooms, or on Web bulletin boards. Negative postings on the Internet are considered a serious public relations problem by companies because millions of people could potentially see those messages. Controversial information about a company, whether factual or not, can result in a public

---

[2]Josh Richman, "Greenwashing on Trial," MoJo Wire (*Mother Jones Magazine* online), February 23, 2001.
[3]Jamie Carrington, "Answering to the Internet," *The World Paper*, October 2000.

relations nightmare that could take years to resolve.

Nike's Web site (www.nikebiz.com) became operational in 1996. The site contains a great range of information on the company, including a section entitled "Responsibility." Within that section, Nike addresses the issues of global community, the environment, and diversity. In the section on labor, the company provides information on factory monitoring results and updates on working conditions at various factory locations.

However, Nike also has to contend with "anti-Nike" Web sites such as Boycott Nike, Just Stop It, or Nikewages.org. These sites continue to provide information about the status of Nike's pledge to improve conditions for its workers. Judging by the names of these Web sites, it is clear that the operators of these sites do not think that Nike has fulfilled that pledge. (See Figure 10-6.)

2001—THE 3-YEAR ANNIVERSARY OF NIKE'S LABOR INITIATIVES

In May 2001, Nike, Inc., on the 3-year anniversary of the new labor initiatives, issued a press release that reviewed the successes and challenges of its corporate responsibility. It noted that Nike is "working collaboratively alongside human rights groups and various NGOs" and that it had "increased wages more than 100 percent over the past several years for entry-level Indonesian footwear factory workers." Despite these and other successes, the release also stated that "there is still progress to be made." As Dusty Kidd, Vice President of Corporate Responsibility put it, "As in every area of Nike's business, there is no finish line, and improving the lives and working conditions of the workers who make Nike products is no exception."

Within 24 hours of the release of Nike's statement, the *Wall Street Journal* reported on May 16, 2001 that Global Exchange, a human-rights organization, had accused Nike of failing to follow through on many of its 1998 initiatives. In addition to other criticisms, Global Exchange says that the living wage issue has still not been fully addressed and that Nike's factory monitoring resources are not truly independent of the company.

In recent years, Nike has continued to be a target of boycotts, media investigations, and international protest. A frequent complaint is that the company treats the labor problems as a public relations issue and not as a human rights issue in that it *presents* itself as a socially responsible corporation. Most any company would want to be viewed as doing the right thing but how much should good intentions alone be rewarded? And who determines if the socially responsible steps a corporation has taken is enough? ∎

QUESTIONS FOR DISCUSSION

1. Does Nike have a responsibility to monitor working conditions in plants owned and operated by contractors? Why?
2. Is a "low wage that is better than no wage" a sound public relations strategy for Nike? Why?
3. What role do falling stock prices and dwindling sales play in Nike's strategy and actions?
4. Is the working environment in a contract shoe plant an operational or a public relations problem?

FIGURE 10-6   A parody of Nike's advertisements created by the Adbusters Media Foundation which advocates "the new social activist movement of The Information Age."

(Adbusters Media Foundation Web site, http://adbusters.org/spoofads/fashion/Nike.)

CASE 10-4   DOW CORNING AND BREAST IMPLANTS: DEALING WITH THE PERCEPTION OF DECEPTION

One of the biggest headaches for manufacturers these days is the proliferation of product liability suits. Some companies are taking products off the market because of the risk of these suits, yet a number of the cases are filed with reason. What would be the responsible and ethical thing to do if a product has been implicated as defective or harmful, even if research may indicate the opposite? What can be done to make it up to those who may have been harmed or to allay the fears of those who *perceive* the product as harmful?

In the early 1990s, Dow Corning was faced with a great number of angry women when silicone-gel breast implants (manufactured by Dow Corning and several others) were indicated as a possible cause of health problems the women were experiencing. This case examines how public *perception* of Dow Corning's behavior evolved into a question of credibility for the organization.

The company *did* have an ethics policy in place since 1976 that was guiding decision making, but the public perceived that it was making business and legal decisions without addressing the ethical issues around the continued use of its breast implants.

HISTORY

The history of breast implantation in the United States is a long one. Since 1962, women have been paying to have doctors surgically enhance their breast size, for various reasons, through the use of silicone-gel

or saline solution implants encased in silicone envelopes. Many do it for self-esteem reasons (about 80 percent), and others want reconstructive surgery after having a mastectomy due to breast cancer (about 20 percent). Almost 2 million women have had breast implants to date.

Silicone-gel was the choice for many women because it seemed more "lifelike" after implantation. Saline solution implants (made of salt and water) are considered less risky for the body, but women chose them less often because they did not feel as natural and sometimes made "sloshing sounds."

Until 1991, the highest perceived risk from breast implantation was in the surgical procedure itself. (Like any device implanted into the body, it may have adverse effects in a small number of patients.) However, silicone's effects on the human body's autoimmune system were not known. An enormous amount of breast implant testing had been done beginning in the 1950s, but when the issue arose in the 1990s there was a perception that there was little, if any, product testing completed. Despite the amount of research that had been done, breast implants were alleged to be the possible cause of serious medical problems, including immunological disorders, arthritis, infections, reduced mammogram effectiveness, and cancer.

The possible risks of breast implants fall into two basic categories: those related directly to the breast (easy to observe) and those that may involve distant parts of the body (much harder to observe and difficult to measure).

Some of the possible breast-related risks are:

➤ Difficulty in detecting abnormalities in the breast when mammographic X-rays are taken

➤ Breast may harden—as a result of fibrous tissue growing around the implant—possibly causing discomfort and pain

➤ Breakage of the envelope, causing the gel filling to be released

Other risks are:

➤ Migration of the gel filling throughout the body (with possible unpleasant cosmetic effects)

➤ The perception that breast implants may cause autoimmune diseases

DOW CORNING'S ROLE

Dow Corning Corporation, jointly owned by The Dow Chemical Company and Corning, Incorporated, has been one of the most visible manufacturers of silicone-gel breast implants, although implants represented less than 1 percent of the company's sales. Dow Corning came under fire in 1991 when Marianne Hopkins, who had received silicone-gel breast implants in 1976, brought suit—claiming the product was responsible for damage to her immune system. The alleged cause was silicone leakage. With this case, many questions began to surface about implants.

One contributing factor to the uproar is that all medical devices were unregulated until 1976, 14 years after the procedure of breast implantation had begun. There was no standard of testing and regulation to follow. Devices in use before the regulations were considered "grandfathered," which meant the manufacturers of those products were not required to provide the Food and Drug Administration (FDA) with scientific evidence of safety and effectiveness. That stipulation in the law is based on the premise that more is known about the safety of a device that has been in use for some time than about one that is newly developed. However, if questions arise over time that cast any doubt about a grandfathered device's safety, the law gives the FDA the authority to go back and require that its manufacturer provide evidence to demonstrate it is safe and effective.[1]

In the 1980s, the FDA Devices Division did not have the budget or personnel to regulate adequately and had adopted a lax attitude in testing and regulating new medical devices put on the market. Finally, in April 1991, with intensified publicity and court cases, implant manufacturers were ordered to prove that their silicone implants were safe. This regulatory action had been recommended by an FDA advisory panel a decade earlier, although it had not been enforced—a damaging fact in forming public perceptions.

CREDIBILITY PROBLEMS

In June 1991, Dow Corning documents surfaced in a *Business Week* article that implied that the implant might have been rushed to market without proper medical testing. Top management was reassuring the general public of the relative safety of this product, but internal memos (created by those not aware of research taking place or past

---

[1]From "Background Information on the Possible Health Risks of Silicone Breast Implants," released by the FDA December 1990 and revised February 1991.

research that had been conducted) were being passed around that alleged there was awareness of animal studies that linked the implants to cancer and other illnesses. In addition, investigative reports dating back 25 years were brought to light indicating that implants could break or leak into patient's bodies. (Those reports had been a matter of public record, but now received attention with this new public scrutiny.) The company *appeared* as if it had been covering up the reports and hiding the true facts.

At first, Dow Corning attacked investigators. This action was interpreted as a lack of concern for the public interest and prompted many to criticize the company as lacking any code of corporate ethics, concerned only with covering itself legally. The irony behind this was that the company did have a code of ethics in place.[2] Some of the initial communications actions that it implemented to allay public misconceptions were:

➤ Developed a packet of information that physicians could share with their patients that was user-friendly and explained the research conducted by Dow Corning and others about the implants. It outlined the risks that could be possible with silicone breast implants. (See Figure 10-7.)

➤ Company physicians and scientists scheduled technical presentations at medical meetings to discuss the scientific implications of implants.

➤ Made public all proprietary information available to competitors in publicly releasing all the scientific studies used to support its Pre-Market Approval Application for the implant.

➤ Met directly with breast cancer support groups and representatives of other consumer groups, both for and against breast implants.

COMPANY IS DEALT PAINFUL LEGAL BLOW

Judgment in the Marianne Hopkins case has handed down in December 1991. She was awarded $7.3 million in compensatory and punitive damages, and Dow Corning was found to have committed fraud and malice by failing to disclose evidence from its research about the implants. With this damaging judgment, public scrutiny intensified and many questions were brought up in the media about the implants and what other information Dow Corning may have withheld.

The company was taking the hard line in dealing with this issue in the media. Dow Corning was finding it difficult to appear sympathetic to the women who did have problems without undermining its legal strategy and admitting fault. It appeared to be a classic case of legal versus public relations. And it was not helped by CEO Lawrence A. Reed, who unfortunately was not adept in media situations. This deficiency reduced his ability to take command of this crisis or to stay ahead of the critics. Reed's invisibility as a spokesperson confirmed the prevalent perception in the court of public opinion that the company was not concerned with the welfare of those who had received the implants.[3]

---

[2]Lee W. Baker, *The Credibility Factor*, Homewood, IL: Business One Irwin, 1992, p. 35. An informative book emphasizing the importance of ethics in the practice of public relations by examining the mistakes and successes of organizations in varying ethical situations.

[3]Kevin McCauley, "Dow Corning Fumbles PR in Breast Implant Crisis," *O'Dwyer's PR Services Report* 6 (March 1992), p. 1.

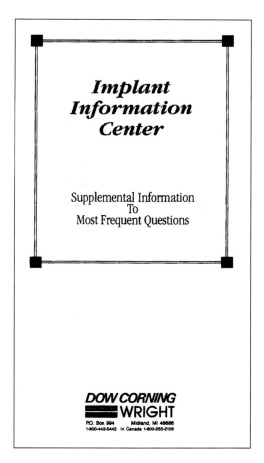

Implant Information Center

Supplemental Information
To
Most Frequent Questions

DOW CORNING
WRIGHT
P.O. Box 994   Midland, MI 48686
1-800-442-5442 In Canada 1-800-255-2156

FIGURE 10-7 This packet of information was distributed by Dow Corning to outline all the risks that could be possible with silicone breast implants.

The task of presenting the Dow Corning "voice" to the public was passed around to many people until it rested on the shoulders of the vice president in charge of health care, Robert T. Rylee, and others on his staff. There was no One Clear Voice responding to the public.

Reed's failure as a leader in the public eye was compared in the news media to the fumbling responses and lack of reaction from Exxon CEO Lawrence Rawl in handling the Valdez oil spill in 1989 (See Case 9-3). At Dow Corning, spokespeople were taking a reactive stance and focusing on the fact that there was little or no *scientific* evidence proving that the implants caused these health problems—ignoring the fact that women had gotten the implants for *emotional and cosmetic* reasons and would predictably respond on an emotional plane.

To deal with the barrage of questions from the public, Dow Corning set up an "Implant Information Hotline" in July 1991. By the end of the year that, too, was receiving criticism from the FDA and high-profile news media coverage. Callers to the hotline were being reassured by the operators about the safety of the implants, and Dow Corning was accused of overselling their safety. The company then agreed to send only printed information to callers. However, the operators of the hotlines were ultimately retrained to offer only factual information in order to allay any public misconceptions. More than 50,000 women called the hotline to obtain information.

THE FDA TAKES ACTION

On January 6, 1992, as public scrutiny intensified, FDA Commissioner David Kessler proposed a voluntary moratorium on the sale and use of silicone implants pending further investigation. Most all silicone-gel implant manufacturers complied.

Dow Corning complied with the request, still claiming that the implants did not have a damaging effect on the body. However, public and media scrutiny did not abate; instead it intensified. The *Wall Street Journal* and the *New York Times* ran articles giving Dow Corning failing marks for its handling of the crisis. The rising tide of lawsuits was threatening the corporation and further thinning its already waning credibility.

The *New York Times* stated that Dow Corning failed in the court of public opinion because it was ignoring how consumers respond to health threats:

1. Even a small number of people who feel they have been mistreated by a company or received a poor product can rally enough friends and allies to have a great impact against the company involved.
2. The number of defective or dangerous products often turns out to be higher than the company that manufactures them originally projects. With the publicity that the implants were receiving, many more complaints, both valid and invalid, were bound to surface.

3. Consumers who feel they have been deceived often become extremely upset. The information that leaked out over the years of litigation about the implants suggested that Dow Corning was trying to cover up information that may be damaging to its product without concern for the consumer.[4]

MEDIA COVERAGE INTENSIFIES PROBLEM

As the issue unfolded, Dow Corning began to track the media coverage of the controversy. While the news media were widely reporting the issue as it ensued, most of the coverage was incomplete and unbalanced (See Figure 10-8). Women were clamoring for information because of the intense media scrutiny. In order to respond to the need for information, Dow Corning took communications actions to reach out to those concerned:

➤ Became more responsive to the news media by distributing an 800-page book compiling memos, scientific studies, and related issues.

➤ Gave a grant to the American Society for Plastic and Reconstructive Surgical Nurses to distribute educational materials to patients.

➤ Proposed a national communications registry; a collaborative effort between the FDA, consumers, health professionals, and current and former breast-implant manufacturers to provide periodic newsletters to breast-implant recipients.[5]

---

[4]Barnaby J. Feder, "Dow Corning's Failure in Public Opinion Test," *New York Times*, January 29, 1992, pp. D1 & D2.
[5]Ralph C. Cook, Myron C. Harrison, and Robert R. LeVier, "The Breast Implant Controversy," *Arthritis and Rheumatism* 37, February 1994, pp. 1–14. A thoughtful article examining the medical issues and communication

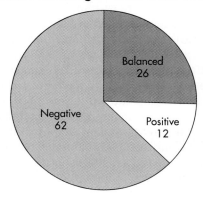

**Total Press Coverage
Slant Percentage – Year Total 1991**

Balanced
26

Negative
62

Positive
12

FIGURE 10-8   This graph illustrates the media tracking that showed an imbalance of coverage.

(Courtesy of Dow Corning.)

DOW CORNING RESPONDS

On February 10, 1992, Dow Corning began to take steps to repair its battered reputation. Lawrence Reed was replaced by Keith McKennon, a former Dow Chemical executive well known for his conciliatory abilities. McKennon had helped Dow steer itself out of potentially damaging public relations situations that involved the Agent Orange defoliant used in Vietnam. McKennon's attitude was much more take-charge and less defensive, and from the start of his appointment he was the company voice concerning the issue. In the spirit of this new openness, McKennon gave almost 100 interviews on the issue.

In keeping with this new attitude, Dow Corning announced in March 1992 its plans to get out of the breast-implant-manufacturing business. In addition, it promised to spend $10 million on research into the safety of the implants and would contribute up to $1,200 per patient (depend-ing on financial need) to remove the silicone-gel implants. While Dow Corning still maintained that the implants were safe, it was finally taking conciliatory actions that recognized the need for further research to satisfy the concerns of the FDA and those women possibly at risk.

Dow Corning succeeded in removing some of the damaging attention from the information that had suddenly been brought into public view. Now the company focused on the *positive* actions it would take in order to make restitution to those women who felt they had been wronged.

REBUILDING ITS CREDIBILITY

Dow Corning has succeeded in making small gains to win back public opinion. It is funding 30 laboratory and clinical safety tests and epidemiological studies on a global basis to establish the risks of the implants in the human body. Some women have been allowed to have the silicone implants if they

---

problems of the breast implant controversy, written by three Dow Corning scientists (available from the company, Midland, Michigan).

agree to become part of a long-term study on the implants' effects. Also, a national registry of those with implants has been proposed to help monitor their health.

In September 1993, the company announced that a global settlement had been proposed, a $4.75 billion fund for breast-implant recipients, funded by the manufacturers, suppliers, doctors, and insurance companies involved in the implant issue. It would give women the opportunity to recover money for their injuries over the course of 30 years. Dow Corning would contribute up to $2 billion to the fund over a period of 30 years. The fund would pay for checkups for women with implants, removal of the devices, and treatment of varied illnesses. Other terms of the agreement were:

➤ Recipients of any brand of breast implant would be included.

➤ Claimants would not be required to prove that their breast implants caused their injuries.

➤ Those who claimed the breast implants had caused damage to their health would be able to exclude themselves from the general settlement and then sue individually.

➤ A recipient of breast implants who had sued a financially unstable company would be able to submit a claim to the fund.[6]

CONTINUED CONTROVERSY

In the wake of this financial settlement, the effects of silicone implants continue to be greatly disputed. The FDA has engaged in heated debates with the American Medical Association (AMA) about the level of risk posed by silicone breast implants. To date, the AMA has supported allowing all women the right to have breast implants once they have been informed of the risks. Former FDA Commissioner Kessler disagreed because he felt physicians were not being responsible about informing women of risks, in spite of the fact the FDA panel that looked at the breast implant studies recommended the implants be kept on the market. He faulted physicians for using implants for 30 years without adequately discussing the risk.[7]

One irony is that, as the multibillion-dollar settlement was established by the other implant manufacturers, and Dow Corning filed for Chapter 11 to avoid the onslaught of more than 19,000 lawsuits, new evidence has emerged that shows no causal link between the implants and the autoimmune diseases allegedly caused by them. Since there is no link between the implants and the diseases they have been accused of causing, should Dow Corning still have to pay close to $5 billion to emerge from Chapter 11? Should women still be allowed to file lawsuits against Dow Corning? What would be the ethical thing for Dow Corning to do in the future? These questions pose some interesting public relations problems. ■

---

[6]"Dow Corning Nears Implant Settlement," Associated Press story, as it appeared in *Bangor Daily News*, September 10, 1993.

[7]Christopher Connell, "Doctors Protest Curb on Breast Implants," Associated Press story as it appeared in *Bangor Daily News*, December 1, 1993.

QUESTIONS FOR DISCUSSION

1. Dow Corning fumbled this crisis because it found it difficult to initially show concern for the recipients of breast implants while still maintaining a legal stance that endorsed the safety of the product. What could the company have done differently to keep this issue from rising to the epic proportions it did in the public arena? Could the entire issue have been avoided through appropriate communications?

2. Can a company act unethically and maintain credibility? Why or why not? Can you think of examples one way or the other? Is it unethical to withdraw a product from the public when there is no proof of a problem, thus denying the public access to the product?

3. Several companies manufacture implants. It is surgeons who suggest them to women and perform the operation. Yet only Dow Corning drew unfavorable public reaction. Why?

4. Whose responsibility is it to inform women who are interested in having breast implants of the risks of the procedure? Why do you believe this?

5. What are the ethical implications now that it has been found by scientific study that there is no known health effect of the implants? What are the implications for Dow Corning?

PROBLEM 10-A Whether to Blow the Whistle

You are nearing the end of your second year of employment as editor of the main publication for employees in one of the three largest nonprofit hospitals in the county. You have a good deal. Your boss, the director of public relations, a woman of about 35, listens to your ideas about the publication. You have converted it from a tabloid appearing once a month to a weekly illustrated newsletter. An audit shows that readers, including staff doctors and donors as well as employees, find it more dynamic. They like it. The only intervention you have had from your boss was near the end of your first year. At that time, she told you to follow the hospital's policy of getting three competitive printing bids annually and then to award the contract for the next year to a particular one of the three. You noted that this bid was not the lowest. Your boss explained that she preferred the quality of their work and added that the printing firm had made generous financial contributions to the hospital. At that time you followed the directions of your boss.

The future looks bright to you. And why not? You are aware that your boss has her eyes on the next job up, as director of development, a position now occupied by a woman scheduled to retire in a few years. You can see yourself succeeding your boss at that time.

Looking back, you consider your first 2 years to have been a period of learning the ropes and how the game goes in the hospital. During this period, the owner of the printing firm doing the newsletter has established a social relationship with you and your spouse, including taking you to dinner at their country club.

You have also noticed that the printer has a close personal relationship with your boss and the hospital's director of development. You know that they receive entertainment and gifts. When the director of development decided to buy a new car, the printer sent her to a dealer where she got a fantastic discount. As for the public relations director, your boss, she was sponsored for membership in the printer's "Executives Only" tennis club.

Here you are, finishing up your second year. A few days ago, quite by coincidence, you overheard some disconcerting comments during a cocktail party. The comments indicated that your boss's husband is the brother of the printer's wife—this you didn't know. Also, your boss apparently has had some sort of financial interest in the printing firm. Your director of development's daughter, you heard, has worked at the printing firm as a typist-receptionist. Someone at the party said that she earned more than other clerical employees, including those with greater skills and experience.

Naturally, this information is upsetting to you, and, to make matters worse, this is the week the three competitive printing bids for next year's contract have come in. You have looked at them. The present printer, whom you have again been told to favor, has submitted a bid 20 percent higher than the lowest of the three.

You have every right to be upset and in a quandary. If you grant the business for the coming year, amounting to $60,000, to the highest bidder, and someone in the treasurer's office questions it, you could be in big trouble. If you tell the present printer he has to submit a second bid at a figure 50 percent lower, you will be unethical in conduct and in contravention of the hospital's stated policy. Beyond that, what if one of the other bidders found out and turned in a complaint to the consumer advocate in the state's attorney general's office? If you take the matter to your boss, you may have to confront her with what you have heard about an apparent conflict of interest on her part.

Of course, an alternative would be to go over the boss's head to the director of development. She, too, has accepted favors from the printer on a social basis. Maybe she would just as soon not get involved. On the other hand, perhaps she has been involved in helping the printer get work from other departments in the hospital. If so, where would that leave you?

Then there is the hospital administrator. If you bypass both of your superiors in the structure, you will almost surely wind up with an unhappy working situation—or be out looking for a new position.

Finally, if you do nothing, are you committed to a standard of honesty or business ethics that you cannot live with?

Everything considered, what are you going to do—specifically, in what sequence, with what goals, and what personal strategy and tactics?

PROBLEM 10-B Write the Truth or "Make Us Look Good"?

You've just been hired by a prestigious philanthropic organization that donates a lot of money to help the poor and the undereducated. You are joining a well-oiled pr department where you report to the vice president. You are excited by the chance to "serve," to do something "meaningful" with your expertise.

At the first all-departments meeting you notice some derogatory comments being made about the people the organization serves. You overlook it as just people being people. But then as discussion comes up about where to focus the organization's money you notice the direction isn't where it's most needed but where the organization can get the most "bang for the buck" in terms of building its image.

You're beginning to have a dilemma. The organization does good deeds by giving out its money and helping others. But inside the culture stinks in the way it talks about its clients and where its goals are for the use of its money. No one else there seems to share your view—or at least no one acknowledges that they do.

Now your boss is asking you to write the news release announcing the organization's newest funding project and wants you to "make us look good. The folks getting the money won't mind if you make some of it up." You want to just write the truth and let that speak for itself, but you're afraid your boss might question your ability. You don't want to get fired. What will you do?

CHAPTER

11 | CAREER PREPARATION

The transition from graduating student to working professional can be one of the most profound changes in a young person's life. If a student has concentrated 100 percent on his or her studies and college life, the transition can be particularly difficult. Therefore, the savvy student will begin laying the groundwork for the inevitable job search early in his or her college career. As soon as a student completes the general education phase of his or her education, it is time to start considering the job situation. The job market in any area is a plastic thing—capable of changing at any time. The smart student will find ways to connect to the professional community as soon as possible and to develop some realistic expectations.

Among those expectations there needs to be the realization that, with a few exceptions, there is no one sitting "out there" awaiting your graduation—unless you have told them and shown them (a) you're worth waiting for and (b) you will be available the week after graduation. How you do that is the subject of this chapter.

A second beneficial realization is that the "career track" that your parents might have followed will not, in all likelihood, be there for you. Human resources forecasters estimate that the student graduating in the early 2000s will have as many as seven careers in his or her lifetime. That is not seven job changes—that is seven career changes.

Change is going to be the watchword of today's job seeking graduate and now is the time to prepare for it. Now is the time to be focused, dedicated, and committed to getting a good job, doing a good job, and preparing yourself for your next job—or career.

To be blunt, most first jobs are good for experience, for developing skills, and for getting your second job. Very few entry-level jobs today result in careers with that organization. Therefore, it is imperative that young professionals do all they can to make a profitable contribution to the first employer, while preparing to qualify for and find the next rung on the ladder to professional achievement.

Having said that, there is another important consideration of today's career realities. Today's entry-level candidates will probably be responsible for their own financial security. Most "baby boomers" will retire from their careers with a pension and some help from social security. Those benefits cannot be counted on for the future. In their place will be IRAs, 401(k) plans and personal investments. And the time to begin is with the first paycheck.

The time value of money is well known. A person committed to saving $2,000 a year for the first 10 years of his or her career can stop at that point and still have more money in a savings account than someone else who puts the same amount in the same bank for 40 years. That's the time value of money, and today's graduate must take charge of his or her future by investing in it early on. But, before one can save, one must earn. This chapter is devoted to helping students prepare for and succeed in the job search and career development.

RESOURCES ARE HANDY

College and university libraries and bookstores have selections of books and pamphlets providing career guidance information. In fact, some universities have offices that can provide you with information or set up interviews with practicing professionals.

It is not our purpose here to enlarge on those resources. You can focus on career options by researching those sources—and you should. It is as important to investigate before you start making calls, writing letters, or showing up for interviews as it has been to do your homework before showing up in class.

Some not-so-common informational resources about public relations job are listed at the end of this chapter.

We concentrate on straight talk about some of the unvarnished realities you will encounter as you launch yourself into a public relations career.

YOU ARE INVOLVED IN A MATCHING GAME

It has been said that many people working for a living spend their lives in jobs and in working environments in which they do not find much satisfaction. They feel constrained to stay in their job, or career track, simply because they need the paycheck to pay off student loans, a house mortgage, or maintain health insurance. These people put in 50 weeks of merely fulfilling the norm, take 2 weeks of vacation from it, and then do it over again.

Do not get caught in that trap. Unhappy employees generally share their unhappiness and their gripes with their associates, hurting morale and lowering productivity all around. But employers do not readily fire people in whom they have invested time and money to train, simply because they are not resident cheerleaders. So, as an employer, you may put up with less performance than you want; as an employee you become content with average expectations. It is, frankly, a bad deal for both employer and employee.

COMMITMENT COUNTS

Spend whatever time and effort it takes, including false starts, trial and error, to *match yourself to a career track on which you are so enthusiastic and deeply committed that other employers will try to hire you away.* Circumstances and your nature may dictate that you change employment on occasion, as a professional entrepreneur of your particular talents. You may prefer the route of choosing one company for the long haul and, step by step, climbing the ladder there. However, downsizing and reengineering offer no guarantees of employment security. You will discover early on whether fulfillment for you personally derives from growth within a single environment, or whether you have to respond to a 3-, 5-, or 7-year itch for totally new surroundings and challenges. Either way, your attitude going into any and every job should be one of commitment. That is contagious. It impresses your associates and bosses. It makes you attractive to other employers.

In seeking a match-up with an employer, particularly the first one, you will be ahead of the game if you set down in writing those values and characteristics that are critical to you. As a minimum:

- Culture and character of the workplace
- Opportunity for using skills, creativity, and professional growth
- Mission and social values of the organization
- Security and support systems versus risk taking and self-direction

SOME BASIC PRINCIPLES OF JOB HUNTING

For entry-level graduates who like things neat and orderly, we have tailored this list to reflect the working environment of today:[1]

1. Make your job search a full-time occupation: Be persistent in your efforts.
2. Use your personal and professional contact network for "hidden" jobs.
3. Be confident and enthusiastic but not immoderately so.
4. Know yourself: your strengths and weaknesses.
5. Be prepared. Do advance research about the company.
6. Get objective advice on how to prepare your résumé and cover letter.
7. Keep records of interviews: Never assume that a closed door will remain that way.

JOBS—THE WORK TO BE DONE

When an employer wants to hire a public relations practitioner, the job description will contain some or all of the following categories of skills, depending on whether a specialist or a generalist is sought. The more closely your skills and experience are related to the description, the better your chances (See Figure 11-1).

1. Writing
2. Editing
3. Submitting newsworthy material to appropriate outlets
4. Preparing speeches for others and giving speeches
5. Arranging for production of presentation materials such as PowerPoint slides and handouts

---

[1]Adapted from Leonard Corwen, "The 11 Rules of Job Hunting," *There's a Job for You*, Piscataway, NJ: New Century Publishers, 1983.

Editor/Writer/Photographer
We need a hard-working, quality-oriented, self-starter to write and edit a variety of publications, including Kieways (our four-color employee magazine), as well as marketing collateral materials, statements of qualifications, proposals and related documents.
Qualifications: Degreed applicants with 7-10 years of hands-on writing and editing experience, preferably in construction or a related technical field; excellent written communications and photographic skills; knowledge of publication design and production methods; and proficiency with Windows-based desktop publishing software. This Omaha, Nebraska-based position may involve significant travel or periodic assignments at other locations.
Kiewit is an Equal Opportunity employer. Applicants may respond as follows:
mail to:
Peter Kiewit Sons', Inc.

Experienced PR/Marketing Professional

The Scottsdale Center for the Arts & Scottsdale Museum of Contemporary Art are rapidly expanding. We need an energetic, experienced PR professional with people management experience to be our Assistant Director of Marketing. This position will manage the day-to-day activities and staff of the marketing office, the budget, and perform all promotional responsibilities. Two years minimum experience plus a bachelor's degree (B.A.) from a four-year college or university, related course work in non-profit management, arts administration, marketing or related experience and/or training, or equivalent combination of education and experience is required.

To apply for these positions, send your resume and cover letter to:
Scottsdale Cultural Council

Publicity Coordinator (Entry Level)

Conscientious, detail-oriented individual needed to assist fast-paced public relations department in the television industry. Must possess excellent verbal and written skills; think creatively and strategically; have a "creative eye" to work with photographers and artistic material; possess strong administrative skills and be able to handle several on-going projects simultaneously. Must be Internet savvy. Opportunity for growth. Req: College degree in related field. One year work experience and/or strong internships in entertainment industry. Word processing skills and knowledge of Adobe Photoshop.

Send resume and cover letter to:
Director, Human Resources
Procter & Gamble Productions

PR Professional
LifeLink Foundation, the non-profit organization dedicated to the recovery and transplantation of organs and tissues, is currently accepting applications for a public relations position based in Tampa. Applicants must possess excellent interpersonal, communication, and writing skills. Requirements include experience in coordination of events, public speaking, and working with volunteers. In addition, desktop publishing and healthcare experience are a plus. Minimum four-year college degree. Please send resume, salary requirements, and two writing samples to:
LifeLink Foundation
Public Relations Department

McKinney & McDowell, a boutique D.C. PR firm seeks acct. mngr. 5-10 yrs in PR w/grasp of public policy issues. Ability to strategize.
D.C. media contacts desired. Salary commensurate w/ experience.
Call C. Marshall

FIGURE 11-1 Ads from one publication give specifications. Entry-level openings are not frequently advertised, though one appears above. [Company addresses are deleted.]

(Reprinted with permission of PRSA's *Public Relations Tactics*.)

6. Programming campaigns and special events
7. Supervising institutional advertising programs
8. Preparing reports, position papers, and public statements
9. Monitoring meetings and interpreting conclusions
10. Training spokespersons; being one
11. Planning a budget, operating on it, and accounting for the outcome
12. Evaluating public opinion, program results, and competitive intelligence
13. Doing online research and database creation and manipulation

THE PUBLIC RELATIONS SKILL BASICS

In general, employers are looking for these basic traits or talents from a new employee:

1. Ability to write for publication or electronic media
2. Natural enthusiasm, easy to motivate
3. Mental maturity, a broad range of interests
4. Ability to express thoughts effectively
5. An attractive personality, with wit or humor and poise
6. Practical work experience gained while a student
7. A working knowledge of the graphic arts
8. Creativity in tying public relations to sales, promotion, and advertising
9. A good feel for community relationships
10. Computer skills: word processing, desktop publishing, graphics programs

The ability to write and speak persuasively is critical in public relations. If you do not possess those abilities you might be better off to choose another field of endeavor.

Of course, there are careers concentrated on opinion research, or lobbying legislators, or raising funds for charities, or staging public events. However, research findings have to be put on paper. Lobbyists present verbal statements of position, sometimes testify at hearings, or prepare testimony for clients to deliver. Fund-raising is done with written or oral appeals, whether direct mail or on a telethon. A public event, such as a postseason bowl game, never flies without dozens of written proposals, committee meetings, discussions, and the like, involving public relations or promotional people.

AUTHORITY AND ROLES

The level of authority and the assigned roles of practitioners vary from one organization to another. Roles have been categorized by research, on the basis of behavior and strategy reported by practitioners.[2] The roles are those of:

1. **Communications technician,** who prepares information for internal or external audiences.

---

[2]Scott Cutlip, Allen H. Center, and Glen M. Broom, "Practitioners of Public Relations," Chapter 2 in *Effective Public Relations*, 8th ed., Upper Saddle River, NJ: Prentice Hall, 1999. For a more complete description of roles, see Glen M. Broom and George D. Smith, "Testing the Practitioner's Impact on Clients," *Public Relations Review* 5, Fall 1979.

2. **Expert prescriber,** who defines problems, devises programs, and oversees implementation.
3. **Communication facilitator,** who provides liaison, interpretation, and mediation between an organization and its publics; increasingly practitioners have been designed as authorized spokespersons for the institutions that they represent.
4. **Problem-solving process facilitator,** who consults and collaborates on matters involving diagnosis, planning, implementation, and evaluation.

The ability to help an organization adjust to its total environment is the name of the game. At its highest levels, public relations is a *management function* that deals with strategic planning, issue anticipation, and stakeholder management internally and externally.

Professionals who excel in the art and science of communications are not born that way. *Most have struggled word by word, error by error, until they have mastered such things as spelling, syntax, and adverbs.* They have studiously gained a sophisticated understanding of the mission and the values of their employers, whether business, government, or private welfare, and the particular language, jargon, and symbolic gestures that prevail.

Effective communication is hard work. For those qualified and committed, the work is a labor of love.

JOB PROSPECTING

Your prospect list can be made up by types of employers you prefer, corporate versus nonprofit, in-house versus outside agency, and so on. Your list can be selected from potential employers in a city or a region where you prefer to locate. Or it can be made up on the basis of the kind of work atmosphere you prefer: small organization or large; heavy on news media relations, identity advertising, or community affairs. It can be based on the scope of an organization's activities, whether local, regional, or national. It can prioritize the kind of specialization or role you seek.

Most libraries have lists of employers and their headquarters, branches, or subsidiaries in any given community. Within public relations specifically, there are two mainstay resources. One is the Public Relations Society of America's directory. Each member of the society, including faculty, has a copy. The other consists of directories put out by the publisher of *Jack O'Dwyer's Newsletter.* One directory lists public relations firms, the other, corporations.

There are also directories at local chambers of commerce, membership rosters of local chapters of PRSA, the International Association of Business Communicators, and nonaffiliated local publicity and public relations clubs. If these are not available, try the Yellow Pages of the phone book.

Beyond just making a list, job prospecting or networking means meeting professionals through activities in PRSSA (Public Relations Student Society of America) and internships—going to their offices during breaks and introducing yourself, and keeping them up to date.

You should begin networking as soon as possible (yes, it can be done while you are in school), because you will need more than a short time; building contacts takes a year or more. Employment agencies may be helpful, particularly in metropolitan areas. But they usually do not deal with entry-level or graduate-level jobs. The best way to start creating a network is to successfully complete multiple internships and use those opportunities to not only learn professional skills but to build bridges to the professional community. The people with whom one works, the organization's or firm's customers, suppliers, and stakeholders can all become part of an assertive student's network.

RÉSUMÉ AND COLLATERAL MATERIAL

Your résumé should contain whatever a prospective employer needs to know about you. Of course, it needs to be presented in a logical sequence for quick digestion. The following should all be included in your résumé:

- Where can you be reached by mail or phone?
- What kind of job or career are you seeking? In a shrinking world and the global village coming, are you fluent in a foreign language? Will you relocate?
- What education and training have you had that are relevant? Are you proficient in computer-word processing, opinion research analysis, photography?
- What work experience, if any, have you had that was related to your job objectives? Have you been involved in an internship? Pro-Am Fellowship? School publication? Media? Agency?
- What work experience have you had (1) that shows that you are not afraid of work or (2) that helped you pay your way through school?
- What professional student associations did you belong to during school?

If possible, quantify the results of your internships and other related experiences. Most résumés list "output" without saying what resulted from these efforts. It is much better to say "wrote six news releases, five of which were picked up by local media, resulting in a 10 percent increased attendance at the special event" than to simply state that you wrote news releases. Outcomes are much more important to potential employers than mere output. It tells the employer that you are successful and can add value to the organization at once.

Your résumé might be helped by containing something unusual that catches the prospective employer's attention, that singles you out of the pack as an "interesting person," and provides a conversational gambit for an interview. In this last category, passive or general hobbies do not qualify. For example, the fact that you enjoy spectator sports, watching television or movies, walking, or traveling are commonplace. A specific, unusual hobby or activity does qualify. For example, "Teach piano privately." This says something interesting. So does "Speak three languages fluently," or "President of Student Association," or "Member air rescue squad," "Have sold five feature stories to national magazines," "Studied abroad for a year."

Describe your activities in terms of the skills an employer needs. Such information may be along the lines of "scheduling other employees in a summer job," "closing the store," "coordinating and updating a mailing list," or "answering complaint calls."

In dealing with references, the standard listing to put on your résumé is a phrase such as, "References are available on request." For convenience and legal reasons, most prospective employers will use the telephone in following up a reference. So be sure to have a phone number available if they request it.

A portfolio is an essential tool. "The degree is not enough. We need to know what skills you have," was the point made by one employer. A portfolio with examples of your communication skills in various media demonstrates that the prospective employee has passed the test of real-world experience.

To say "an employer wants experience, but won't give me a chance to get it" is no excuse for the student who wants to be prepared for a career upon graduation. There are any number of volunteer organizations who want volunteer public relations help, and a growing number of summer internships. A student needs to demonstrate initiative to gain some of this early experience. Be selfish—if a volunteer organization will not let you write for its newsletter, news releases, or public service announcements, do not volunteer for them—look for another organization.

A portfolio should have in it a résumé and any other information about you—awards and the like—near the front. Next, samples of your published writing in school papers, commercial newspapers, magazines, and so on. The next section should contain some material on graphics, photography, and video. All of this material helps the prospective employer understand that you have good, sharp skills that you can put to work *now.*

Obviously, material for a portfolio cannot be produced overnight. Most students work 1 or 2 years collecting their work from a variety of organizations for a portfolio. Do not wait until next quarter or semester; begin now to gather material for your portfolio.

A **cover letter** can be the deciding factor in getting you an interview. It should be short and should not duplicate the résumé. It should, in the first sentence, express your interest in, or admiration for, the specific organization's mission, or products or services, or whatever else attracted you to it. Put another way, your letter should tell *why you are applying to them,* not why you are casting bait on the ocean, or why you desperately need a job. In your cover letters, the pronouns *you* and *your* are preferable to *I* and *my* in starting sentences. Practice using them. In order to be specific about the organization, you will need to do some research on the company. This research also helps in the next step—the interview.

THE MOMENT OF TRUTH

People are hired for all sorts of reasons, not all of them objective or based on merit. There is nepotism. The boss's nephew gets the job. There is the supplier-customer relationship. The daughter of a customer joins the public relations department of a major supplier. The son of the president of a cosmetic manufacturer joins the firm that serves that manufacturer. The owner of a firm hires a son or daughter and pays three times what the offspring is worth to skim off some profit and reduce taxes in the process.

An employer may be in need of a particular skill, such as that involved in the production phase of printed literature. Specialization, over general capability, will be the deciding factor in that situation.

An applicant may bring to an employer some experience in working for news media, or a broad range of media contacts. Similarly, an applicant may have connections with legislators, a political orientation, experience with a Political Action Committee (PAC), or a citizen group important to the employer. Such special considerations can weigh heavily. These are only a few of the many realities.

EVERYTHING ELSE BEING EQUAL

You should assume, in trying for public relations jobs, that you will not be the only applicant. Each applicant will probably have résumé, portfolio, and available references and will get a shot at the job. Each will probably be almost as intelligent, ambitious, well-trained academically, and available as you are.

The single most prevalent deciding factor is the interview (See Figure 11-2). The interview is where it all comes together and a choice is made.

At the interview, "first impression," personal appearance, poise, compatibility, personality, attitudes, and articulation come into play. The interviewer wonders, "Would this person fit into our scheme of things? Would this person bring us something we need? Would this person wear well, be more than worth the time and money we invest? Would this person add value to our organization? Would this person grow, if we want that, or would this person be content in what we have to offer, if we want that?"

For your part, while projecting yourself against what you perceive the employer to need and want, putting your best foot forward, you will be getting some answers to your own questions. Would I like it here? Could I get excited about what these people say is important to them? Is there room to advance, if that is what I want? Or, considering my personal situation, is there security and safety here, if it is what I want most?

WHAT TO TALK ABOUT

Many topics, expected and unexpected, can come up in exploratory interviews. You would be ahead of the game to make notes after your first couple of interviews and to be prepared. One student reported the following questions asked by most interviewers:

- Tell me about yourself.
- Why do you think this would be a good place to work?
- What do you consider your strengths?
- Your weaknesses?
- What do you hope to be doing five years from now?
- Have you any questions you'd like to ask?
- What did you have in mind for a starting salary?
- If you got the job when could you start?

There were other questions related to the résumé and comments by the interviewers about their "employee program," what salary they generally started a "trainee" at, and some plugs for the organization's "promotion from within" policy.

FIGURE 11-2 Projecting a positive first impression at an interview.

(Art by Gaston Lokvig. Courtesy of Women in Communications Inc.)

AN OVERALL APPROACH

On the theory that practice makes perfect, do not go for your first interview at the place you would most like to work. Practice on a couple of places not so high on your list. If one of them offers you a job, you can take it, or ask for time to think it over, and check out your preferred choice in a hurry. There is nothing unethical about doing this. If an employer has three likely candidates, the choice is often delayed. You have the same option, carefully used.

Be honest. There are some questions an employer cannot ask by law. At the same time the interviewer may assume that the status of personal relationships may affect job performance. If the interviewer "guesses" that you will get married and move, you might lose a job opportunity. Volunteer enough information to let the interviewer know how long you expect to be in the area, or discuss professional goals that will help put your personal life in some perspective.

There is a lot to be gained by using any informal contact you may have at an organization to find out in advance about expected standards of behavior and dress for a formal interview. You can learn much about the customs and standards prevailing simply by looking around at the people and the workplace on your first visit.

In the interview, you are not expected to volunteer information that would hurt your chances. But **do not deliberately conceal something that can come back to haunt you later on.** If you are asked whether you can type, and you do it by hunt-and-peck, you are better off to say that you are not a touch typist, rather than be asked to flip off a news release or a letter for the boss late one afternoon and not get it done. If an employer asks if you can handle photography, the question is not whether you own an instamatic.

More and more employers of public relations professionals are assuming word-processing, desktop publishing, and video experience. A writing test may also be required. Again find out in advance whether a company has any special interview procedures. One type of test provides you with a one-sentence statement of fact and indicates that the person administering the test will answer questions you need answered to write the story. In fact, the person has a long list of questions and answers. Once you have finished your questions, you are provided with a word processor and given a set time to write the story.

Another writing exam lets you take the material home. Still other interviewers have wanted to know what you know about local media and placement of a particular story.

Some organizations are also requiring a personality profile of prospective employees. These provide the employer with general personality characteristics and some indication of how this kind of person would fit into the organization. Some of these personality inventories indicate level of initiative, follow-through, and detail work. Such indicators may be important to the office makeup. Regardless of what you may think of these inventories, do not try to "outguess" them. If you do not answer openly, the results may look significantly different from the way you want to be perceived.

Most interviews are open-ended. **Make sure you know what is supposed to happen next, or is not going to happen at all, before the interview ends, or you leave.** There should be a stated conclusion by the interviewer. "We'll call you," or "We're talking to some more people, and we'll get back to you." Or "There is somebody else here we'd like you to meet," or "Could you come back again next week?" or . . . "We appreciate your interest, but we are looking for someone who has a little different experience." If you do not hear a conclusion, ask for one. "Is there anything else I can supply to help you reach a decision?" or "When do you plan to make your decision?" or "Should I check back with you later?" Do not let yourself be left hanging out on the line. **If you are out of the running for the job, it is better to know that and get on to the next opportunity, rather than waste time until a long period of silence on the employer's part and worry on yours answer the question.**

Regardless of how you come out, write a note of thanks for the time and consideration given by the person who interviewed you. Doing so is good manners, but there can be more to it. Suppose that you were runner-up, and the first choice did not take the job. You're in. Also, every friend has a friend. If you made a favorable impression, the interviewer may tell a colleague at another organization that you "ran a close second." And you might get a call.

You will know that you have entered career heaven when the hours, the days, weeks, and months on a job go by so fast that you sometimes lose track of them. That is an infallible test.

References and Additional Readings

Almy, Robert E., and Vivian Harris. "Piloting Your Career Through Turbulent Economic Seas." *Communication World* 8 (December 1991): 24–26.

Bovet, Susan L. "Firms Use Internships to Test Entry-Level Job Seekers." *Public Relations Journal* 48 (September 1992): 26–28.

Brett-Elspas, Janis. "Self-Marketing for Career Success." *Public Relations Journal* 46 (March 1990): 10–11, 39.

Careers in Public Relations. Pamphlet from Public Relations Society of America. Available from PRSA, Professional Resource Center, 33 Irving Place, New York, NY 10003. Also available online at www.prsa.org/career/careeroverview.html.

"Lessons Learned: What Winners Would Study Today." *Public Relations Journal*. (October/November 1994): 40. An excerpt from the "Pursuing Professional Excellence" issue in which Gold Anvil Winners were asked what they would do if given the opportunity to re-do their formal education.

Maister, David. "Why Employees and Their Needs Will Get the Emphasis in PR Departments and Firms Themselves," *pr reporter* Vol. 32, No. 16 (April 18, 1988). Analysis of talk to Counselors Academy.

PRSA offers a career overview reading room online for people new to the profession. The site contains many helpful articles: www.prsa.org/career/readingroom.html.

PRSA/IABC Salary Survey 2000. Online at www.prsa.org. Free to members; $50 for nonmembers.

Workinpr.com is a Web site where you can post your résumé and find job listings as well as internships and entry-level positions.

Index